Using PROCOMM PLUS® for Windows™

ALAN C. ELLIOT
ALAN G. RAY

Screen reproductions in this book were created using Collage Plus from Inner Media, Inc., Hollis, NH.

This book is based on PROCOMM PLUS for Windows, Version 1.0.

Publisher: Lloyd J. Short

Associate Publisher: Rick Ranucci

Product Development Manager: Thomas H. Bennett

Book Designer: Scott Cook

Production Team: Claudia Bell, Brad Chinn, Michelle Cleary, Brook Farling, Bob LaRoche, Jay Lesandrini, Caroline Roop, Linda Seifert, Susan M. Shepard, Tina Trettin, Lisa Wilson, Phil Worthington

CREDITS

Product Director
Walter R. Bruce III

Acquisitions Editor
Chris Katsaropoulos

Production Editor
Lori A. Lyons

Editors
Sara Allaei
Kelly Currie
Diana R. Moore

Technical Editors
David Rasmussen

Gary L. Litwiller
Quality Assurance Technician
DATASTORM TECHNOLOGIES, INC.

Composed in *Cheltenham* and *MCPdigital* by Que Corporation

DEDICATION

To my ever-supportive wife, Annette

—A.C.E.

ALAN C. ELLIOTT

Alan C. Elliott is an assistant director of Academic Computing Services at the University of Texas Southwestern Medical Center in Dallas. He holds a master's degree (M.A.S.) in statistics from Southern Methodist University and an M.B.A. degree from the University of Texas at Arlington. He is the author of several books, including *Introduction to Microcomputing with Applications*, *A Daily Dose of the American Dream*, and *PC Programming Techniques*. He is also the author of Que's *Using Norton Utilities 6* and revision author of Que's *Using PROCOMM PLUS for Windows*, 2nd Edition, and is a coauthor of the 1985 and 1988 editions of the *Directory of Statistical Microcomputing Software*. He is author of the software packages Kwikstat (Data Analysis), PC-CAI (Computer Assisted Instruction), and Information Please (Free-Form database), published by TexaSoft. His articles have appeared in professional and popular periodicals, including *PC Week*, *Collegiate Microcomputer Journal*, *Communications in Statistics*, and *American Statistician*.

ALAN G. RAY

Alan G. Ray is the vice president of SYNAPPSYS Inc., a company specializing in Windows application development. He has been involved in microprocessor software and hardware design since the Intel 4004 microprocessor became available. Alan has developed microprocessor-based products using serial data communications ranging from environmental data acquisition to oil and gas well logging. He has written instructional materials and held technical seminars on these as well as other PC products at locations throughout the world. He was instrumental in the design and development of WinComm, a Windows communications program developed by SYNAPPSYS and was a part of the development team for PROCOMM PLUS for Windows.

TRADEMARK ACKNOWLEDGMENTS

The conventions used in this book have been established to help you learn to use the program quickly and easily. As much as possible, the conventions correspond to those used in the PROCOMM PLUS for Windows documentation.

The names of screens, menus, and options appear in headline-style uppercase letters. For example,

Choose the Scrollback Buffer To option from the Edit menu.

Hot-key letters you can press in combination with the Alt key to access commands and menu options are underlined. For example, to access the File menu, you press Alt-F.

File names and directory names are written with all uppercase letters (GOLF1.DRW).

Material you are to type appears in *italic* type or is set on a line by itself. Messages that appear on-screen are in a special typeface.

CONTENTS AT A GLANCE

TABLE OF CONTENTS

I Introducing PROCOMM PLUS For Windows

III Becoming a PROCOMM PLUS For Windows Expert

Introduction

Welcome to *Using PROCOMM PLUS for Windows*. With PROCOMM PLUS for Windows as your magic carpet and with this book as your companion and guide, you are about to explore the exciting world of computer-to-computer communications.

PROCOMM PLUS for Windows is a communications program that is fun to use and full of impressive features. Its Windows interface makes learning easy, particularly if you have experience with any other Windows-based program. If you have used a DOS-based version of PROCOMM PLUS, you will find that all of your favorite features are still intact and accessed easily with pull-down menus, Action icons, and shortcut keyboard commands.

In large measure because of its upbeat personality, PROCOMM PLUS for Windows is one of the easiest communications programs to learn to use. PROCOMM PLUS for Windows can often transform dull and highly technical procedures into a few easy keystrokes or mouse clicks. If you don't remember exactly how to perform a task, PROCOMM PLUS for Windows provides an ever-present help facility, never more than a click or a keystroke away.

Because PROCOMM PLUS for Windows is so easy to use, you may wonder whether you need a book to help you. Ease of use is a relative concept, and many people find PC communications in general a difficult area to understand. Although PROCOMM PLUS for Windows makes communicating fun, it cannot fully insulate you from the many technical terms and concepts that seem to pop up at every turn. As your companion and guide, this book teaches you how to navigate through these terms and concepts. With this book at your side, you are about to take an enjoyable and rewarding journey into the world of electronic bulletin boards, online information services, and electronic mail.

What Is PROCOMM PLUS for Windows?

PROCOMM PLUS for Windows is a full-featured communications program complete with terminal emulation, automated dialing directory, error-correcting protocols, and a powerful script language. Published by DATASTORM TECHNOLOGIES, INC., Columbia, Missouri, PROCOMM PLUS for Windows is a commercially marketed descendent of the popular user-supported communications program ProComm, first released in 1985. This book covers PROCOMM PLUS for Windows, with some references to the current DOS version, PROCOMM PLUS Version 2.01.

PROCOMM PLUS for Windows is designed to enable you to connect your modem-equipped computer with other computers through standard telephone lines. Using PROCOMM PLUS for Windows, you can transfer and receive computer files, access an on-line information service, sign on to a powerful mainframe computer, or simply chat with another computer operator by typing messages on your computer's keyboard. PROCOMM PLUS for Windows provides these capabilities in a way that seems natural and familiar, and easy to comprehend. Indeed, one of the advertising slogans and trademarks used by DATASTORM is the phrase "intuitive communications." After you use PROCOMM PLUS for Windows for a short while, you will agree that this slogan accurately describes this program and its features.

Even though the program is designed to be easy and intuitive to use, PROCOMM PLUS for Windows doesn't scrimp on powerful features. The program has 10 built-in file-transfer protocols, can emulate 34 types of computer terminals, contains a dialing directory facility that can store and speed-dial 250 entries per dialing directory with an unlimited number of directories, and includes a bulletin-board-like Host mode—complete with electronic mail. PROCOMM PLUS for Windows even enables you to record your keystrokes so that you can play them back later— to sign on to an information service, for example. For the power user, PROCOMM PLUS for Windows also is completely programmable through the script command language, Windows ASPECT. In short, PROCOMM PLUS for Windows is all the communications program you will ever need.

What's New in PROCOMM PLUS for Windows?

Since the introduction of the user-supported program ProComm in 1985, DATASTORM has progressively enhanced the program while remaining true to its original design concepts. Although this is the first Windows version of PROCOMM PLUS, a current DOS version of PROCOMM PLUS, Version 2.01, is available. If you have used PROCOMM PLUS 2.01, you may be interested in some of the differences between the two versions. The following list shows some of the new or different features of PROCOMM PLUS for Windows:

- Use of the Windows Interface

- Use of the Windows Notepad editor instead of PCEDIT

- New Windows extensions to the ASPECT language

- Meta key buttons on the Terminal Display screen

- Action bar icon commands on the Terminal Display screen

- More extensive context-sensitive Graphical Help Facility

- Display of GIF files as they are downloaded

- ASPECT run-time debugger

To run PROCOMM PLUS for Windows, you must be using an IBM-compatible computer running Microsoft Windows Version 3.0 or higher. You also usually must have a modem installed in your computer (referred to as an internal modem) or connected to one of your system's serial ports (usually called an external modem). If you have a choice, the modem should recognize the Hayes AT command set (usually referred to as a Hayes-compatible modem), but you can use virtually any modem with PROCOMM PLUS for Windows. (A modem is not an absolute necessity. Many people use PROCOMM PLUS for Windows to connect directly to a mainframe or another PC. In this case, you need a special cable called a null-modem cable. Refer to Appendix B for more information about null-modem cables.)

Who Should Read This Book?

Using PROCOMM PLUS for Windows is for you if you are a new PROCOMM PLUS for Windows user who wants to get the most from this fantastic product. Experienced ProComm and PROCOMM PLUS users also will find this book helpful in gaining a clear understanding of the Windows interface used in PROCOMM PLUS for Windows.

This book assumes that you are using PROCOMM PLUS for Windows. The approach of this book reflects the software it describes. You don't have to be a computer expert to learn to use PROCOMM PLUS for Windows. This book makes no assumptions about your background in computers or communications. If you are a new user of communications software, start at the beginning of the book and move through it at a comfortable pace. More experienced users can skim Part I and study the text more closely beginning in Part II. Power PROCOMM users may want to breeze through Parts I and II and concentrate on Part III.

What Is Covered in This Book?

This book is divided into three major parts: Part I, "Introducing PROCOMM PLUS for Windows"; Part II, "Getting Acquainted with PROCOMM PLUS for Windows"; and Part III, "Becoming a PROCOMM PLUS for Windows Expert."

Each part is written with you, the user, in mind. This book is not a substitute for the PROCOMM PLUS for Windows manuals; it takes a different approach. This book covers subjects in a tutorial manner—it is not just a reference to program features. This book covers the finer points of making this program work for you, expanding beyond the basic descriptions in the program's manual.

The divisions of the material enable you to "jump in" at any point of your expertise. If you are a beginner to PROCOMM PLUS for Windows or communication, you will want to begin with the introductory chapters in Part I. If you already are a PROCOMM PLUS user, you may want to skim the introductory material and begin with Part II. To go beyond the knowledge required for a casual user, you will want to cover the material in Part III. The following sections describe in more detail what is covered in the three parts of the book.

Part I: Introducing PROCOMM PLUS for Windows

Part I is intended to help you quickly develop a basic understanding of communications concepts and terminology and the fundamentals of PROCOMM PLUS for Windows.

Chapter 1, "A Communications Primer," is a basic introduction to communications, with an emphasis on how it relates to PROCOMM PLUS for Windows. You learn what it means to use PROCOMM PLUS for Windows to "communicate" with another computer and how to recognize the various hardware components necessary to use PROCOMM PLUS for Windows. This chapter also presents a few simple rules for selecting the right modem for your needs.

Chapter 2, "Getting Around in PROCOMM PLUS for Windows," gives you a quick tour of PROCOMM PLUS for Windows' most fundamental features. You learn how to start the program, understand the basic PROCOMM PLUS for Windows Terminal Display window, use PROCOMM PLUS for Windows menus, and access the context-sensitive help system.

Part II: Getting Acquainted with PROCOMM PLUS for Windows

The largest amount of information in this book is presented in Part II. Here you learn how to use the major features of the program—those that you will use daily as you become a proficient PROCOMM PLUS for Windows user.

Chapter 3, "Building Your Dialing Directory," explains how to use the many features of the PROCOMM PLUS for Windows dialing directory, including how to manage multiple directories.

Chapter 4, "A Session with PROCOMM PLUS for Windows," introduces you to the most commonly used features of the PROCOMM PLUS for Windows Terminal Display mode—the commands you need to know when you are on-line.

Chapter 5, "Transferring Files," explains how to use PROCOMM PLUS for Windows to send and receive electronic files to and from another computer. The chapter includes explanations of how to use the file-transfer protocols available in PROCOMM PLUS for Windows.

Chapter 6, "Using the Windows Notepad Editor," describes how to use the Windows Notepad editor, the quick but simple editor supplied with Microsoft Windows and used in PROCOMM PLUS for Windows. This chapter also explains how you can attach another text editor so that you can activate it from within PROCOMM PLUS for Windows.

Chapter 7, "Automating PROCOMM PLUS for Windows with Meta Keys and Script Files," explains how you can "teach" PROCOMM PLUS for Windows to perform many tasks automatically by using the Record mode. This chapter also introduces you to some of the basic concepts relating to the creation and use of PROCOMM PLUS for Windows scripts.

Part III: Becoming a PROCOMM PLUS for Windows Expert

Part III covers the most technical features of the program. After you are comfortable with the topics presented in Parts I and II of the book, Part III shows you how to fine-tune the program and take advantage of some of its most powerful capabilities.

Chapter 8, "Tailoring PROCOMM PLUS for Windows," discusses how to change COM port and line settings, as well as the many options in the PROCOMM PLUS for Windows Setup facility. The Setup facility enables you to make adjustments to more than 100 characteristics of PROCOMM PLUS for Windows.

Chapter 9, "Using Host Mode," explains how to use the bulletin-board-like Host mode. The chapter discusses how to prepare and manage a simple company electronic bulletin board, including how to assign and manage user privileges, and how to administer the electronic mail facility.

Chapter 10, "Terminal Emulation," offers a description of the terminal emulation capabilities of PROCOMM PLUS for Windows. The chapter includes an explanation of how you can customize the translation table and keyboard mapping of your terminal.

Chapter 11, "An Overview of the Windows ASPECT Script Language," provides an overview of the programming capabilities of the powerful script command language, Windows ASPECT. An in-depth discussion of all the commands and capabilities of the Windows ASPECT script language is beyond the scope of this book.

Chapter 12, "Examining Some Advanced Features of Windows ASPECT," discusses the general script writing process and the major components of a Windows ASPECT script. This chapter also covers several of the advanced features of Windows ASPECT using sample scripts. Two of the sample scripts described also include a tutorial covering the operation of the Dialog Box editor and the User Window Builder programs.

Using the Appendixes

For those of you who have not yet installed PROCOMM PLUS for Windows, Appendix A, "Installing and Starting PROCOMM PLUS for Windows," describes the steps necessary to install and start PROCOMM PLUS for Windows. Specific instructions are included for installing PROCOMM PLUS for Windows. This appendix also explains how to use several special start-up parameters.

Appendix B, "Installing a Modem," explains the basics of installing a modem for use with PROCOMM PLUS for Windows. This appendix includes a discussion of connecting internal modems and external modems, as well as connecting two computers with a null-modem cable. A special section covers using PROCOMM PLUS for Windows with the new error-control and data-compression modems.

Appendix C, "ASCII Codes," contains a list of ASCII characters and their decimal and hexadecimal codes, which can be used in scripts and Meta commands.

Now that you know what to expect, you're ready to get started with PROCOMM PLUS for Windows.

Introducing PROCOMM PLUS for Windows

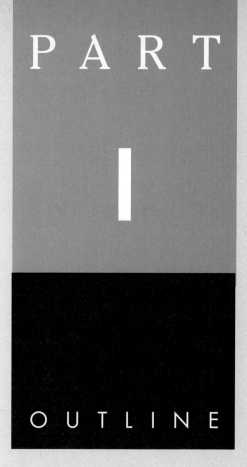

A Communications Primer

This book focuses on using your PC and the PROCOMM PLUS for Windows program to communicate with other computers over telephone lines. If PROCOMM PLUS for Windows is your first communications program, you may feel as if you're in a foreign country with an unfamiliar language. Use this chapter as a brief travel brochure and a minitutorial to help you learn the native dialect of PROCOMM PLUS for Windows.

This chapter first describes the most common uses of communications programs and then introduces you to many of the terms and concepts fundamental to understanding communications. Take a few moments to go through this chapter. Discover what you can do with PROCOMM PLUS for Windows. Become comfortable with terms like *modem* and *bits per second*. You then will be ready to move on to Chapter 2, "Getting Around in PROCOMM PLUS for Windows."

Using Your Computer To Communicate

Using PROCOMM PLUS for Windows divides your potential uses for communications programs into three major categories: PC to PC, electronic bulletin board systems, and on-line services. Communications programs do have other uses, and some overlap may exist in these categories. This division is useful, however, for the purposes of this book and to help you think about ways you can use PROCOMM PLUS for Windows. The following paragraphs give you a brief synopsis of each usage category.

Communicating PC-to-PC

PROCOMM PLUS for Windows enables you to communicate from one PC to another PC over telephone lines. The purpose of this communication usually is to transfer computer files—such as word processing, spreadsheet, and database files—between computers. Transferring files between PCs is covered in Chapter 5.

Host mode, a special mode of PROCOMM PLUS for Windows, enables you to authorize other PC operators to connect by telephone line to your PC to transfer files, even when no one is at your PC's keyboard. Host mode is described in Chapter 9.

Suppose that you are the plaintiff's attorney in a multimillion-dollar product liability lawsuit. You have just flown 1,500 miles to interview the chief executive officer of the defendant company. When you arrive, you find that you forgot to pack the 30-page list of questions you worked on all week. Because you had the foresight to leave your office PC turned on with PROCOMM PLUS for Windows running in Host mode, you're in luck. Using the laptop PC you brought on the trip and PROCOMM PLUS for Windows, you call and connect to the PC in your office. In just a few minutes, you retrieve the list of questions, which is filed on your desktop PC's hard disk.

Many companies that routinely have to send computer files across town or across the country dedicate a computer to file transfer. With PROCOMM PLUS for Windows, each district sales manager in a large sales force can send the monthly sales report spreadsheet to a PC at the regional headquarters. After consolidating the district figures into a regional report, each regional manager can transfer the report to the PC at corporate headquarters. This method is faster and cheaper than express mail or even facsimile (FAX). This method also provides live data in a working spreadsheet at every level without the need for someone to enter the same numbers several times.

Accessing Electronic Bulletin Boards

The most popular use of communicating with a PC probably is to connect to electronic bulletin board systems (BBSs). As the name implies, bulletin board systems provide a medium through which computer users can obtain and share information.

Nearly all BBSs provide traditional-style bulletins—announcements or information posted by the operator of the bulletin board to be read by the various BBS users. BBSs also provide an important medium for computer users who want to share information.

BBSs usually have areas, often called conferences, where users can leave public messages—similar to tacking three-by-five cards on a cork bulletin board. The message areas typically are divided by topic or subject matter. When you find an area that interests you, you can read the messages others have left, and you can participate in the discussion by leaving messages of your own.

You can find BBS conferences on nearly any topic you can think of—astronomy, ham radio, finance, gun-control legislation, computer programming, engineering, science, mathematics, travel, and many others. Sometimes entire bulletin boards are devoted to the exchange of ideas in a particular area of common interest.

Electronic bulletin boards most often are run on PCs or other microcomputers, usually by a computer hobbyist entirely at his or her own expense. Some bulletin boards, however, charge subscription fees or ask for donations to defray the costs of buying and maintaining the sophisticated computer systems.

Many BBSs are run on PCs with a huge storage capacity—often over several hundred megabytes. These boards enable you to send and receive complete files, including program files. These bulletin boards often are your best source for useful tips and practical software, especially when you are just learning to use the PC. BBSs frequently have hundreds and sometimes thousands of application programs, utility programs, games, and text files that can make your PC easier and more fun to use. Figure 1.1 shows the menu of a typical bulletin board file system.

Some software on bulletin boards has been released to the public domain by the software authors, and anyone is free to use the software at no charge. Most of the more powerful programs, however, are referred to as shareware, freeware, or user-supported software. You can use shareware—including ProComm 2.4.3 (the DOS-based shareware version of ProComm)—at no charge, but on a trial basis only. If you decide to continue using a program, you are obligated to pay a registration fee to the program's author in order to license your copy.

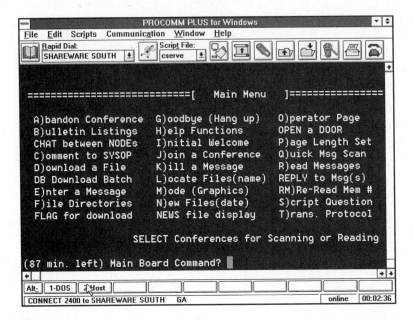

FIG. 1.1

A typical PC bulletin board menu.

> **NOTE**
>
> Because of recent publicity concerning the spread of computer viruses, you may mistakenly conclude that viruses usually come from the use of bulletin boards. Many viruses, in fact, have been found recently in shrink-wrapped software and in new machines. All legitimate bulletin board systems test every uploaded file for the presence of virus programs, giving you good protection against downloading a virus. When you use a bulletin board service that is a member of a professional organization, such as the Association of Shareware Professionals (ASP), you can be confident that the board is taking precautions against the spread of virus activity.

The PROCOMM PLUS for Windows Host mode has several features found in typical bulletin board software, including a file-transfer system and a message system. The Host mode may be all you need to set up a small bulletin board for your personal or office use. Host mode is not, however, adequate for use as a full-fledged public BBS. This facet of PROCOMM PLUS for Windows is covered extensively in Chapter 9, "Using Host Mode."

Using On-Line Services

On-line services generally are run on large computer systems that can handle simultaneous use by multiple computers connected over multiple phone lines. Often you connect to an on-line service through a public data network (PDN), a special type of long-distance network for communication by computers. Figure 1.2 shows a menu from the popular on-line service CompuServe.

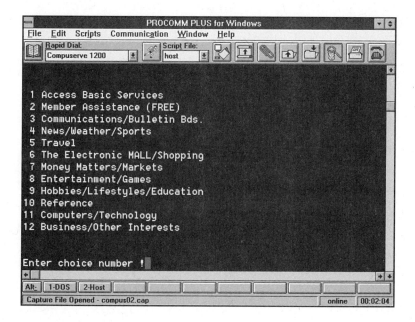

FIG. 1.2

A menu from CompuServe, an on-line service.

The primary business of most on-line services is to sell information—news, stock quotes, airline schedules, and so on. Some on-line services, such as medical journals or law reporters, have specialized information. Many others make available information on a wide variety of subjects.

The most popular services offer several additional features. Electronic shopping malls enable you to order merchandise right from your keyboard. CB-simulators enable you to converse through your computer with many people at once. Figure 1.3 shows a current weather map downloaded from CompuServe. This is one example of current information available from on-line services.

Some on-line services specialize in electronic mail—an electronic substitute for paper or voice communication through which you send private correspondence to another subscriber. Instead of sorting through a stack of mail in your "in" box, you log on to the electronic mail system to check your electronic mailbox. The system greets you with the message You have mail. You read your mail on-screen, saving to disk the important correspondence and tossing everything else into the bit-bucket (that is, deleting it).

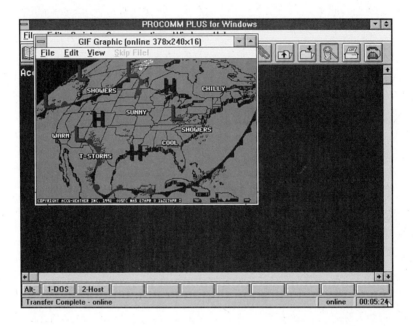

FIG. 1.3

A weather map from CompuServe.

The most popular on-line services are similar to bulletin boards, but on a larger scale. These services provide dozens of electronic forums for the exchange of ideas among individuals and groups. Many computer hardware and software manufacturers, including DATASTORM TECHNOLOGIES, INC., the publisher of PROCOMM PLUS for Windows, host one or more of these on-line forums. These vendor-hosted forums make the manufacturers more accessible to users and help distribute information about patches and upgrades. These forums also provide valuable feedback to the manufacturer and enable users to share tips and techniques on using the vendor's products. Many vendors consider user input gathered from on-line forums an important factor in future product-development decisions.

Countless other reasons exist for communicating with your PC over telephone lines—from electronic banking to playing interactive games.

Learning the Lingo

Your first step in learning how to use PROCOMM PLUS for Windows is to become familiar with a few new words and phrases.

Communications terminology has developed over the short history of computing in a way not unlike that of a spoken language. Some terms have been coined by communications experts when necessary to describe a new apparatus or a new communications concept, but other terms seem to have sprung up on their own and are kept alive by continual usage. Like the words of any language, the definitions of many communications terms are accepted universally. Meanings of some other terms, however, seem to have changed over time or location. The rest of this chapter introduces you to a number of communications-related terms and concepts you need to understand to get the most from PROCOMM PLUS for Windows.

Understanding Modems

You probably already know how to use your PC for word processing, spreadsheets, and information management. Certainly, you are familiar with telephones. Learning to use a PC to communicate over telephone lines should be an easy next step. The problem, however, is that telephones are designed to transmit voice, but computers need to send a different type of signal. Most of the complexity of communications boils down to this rather subtle distinction.

Analog and Digital Signals

Understanding a little bit about how telephones transmit voice signals can help you comprehend more easily how computer data is sent. When you make a sound with your voice, your vocal chords cause the air to vibrate in a wavelike motion. The vibrating air, called a *sound wave*, causes a listener's eardrum to vibrate, enabling the listener to hear the sound you make. The *frequency* of the sound wave (the number of wave cycles in a given period of time) is heard as pitch. The *amplitude* (size) of the wave is heard as volume.

When you speak into your telephone, the telephone electronically converts the sound wave of your voice into an *electromagnetic wave* that can be transmitted over telephone lines. The frequency and amplitude of this electromagnetic wave correlate directly to the frequency and amplitude of the sound wave. As the sound wave's frequency varies up or down, the electromagnetic wave's frequency varies up or down in the same proportion. As the sound wave's amplitude varies, so does the electromagnetic wave's amplitude. In other words, the electromagnetic wave is an *analog* of the sound wave. The signal your telephone sends over the telephone lines often is referred to as an *analog signal* (see fig. 1.4). When this signal reaches the other end of the line, the phone at that end converts the signal back into a sound wave.

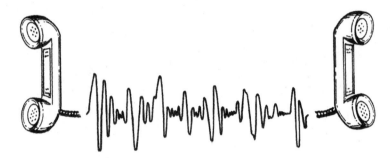

FIG. 1.4

The analog signal transmitted by telephones.

Computers can communicate directly with one another by sending data over a cable. Computers do not, however, communicate by sound waves. They understand only discrete electrical pulses that represent numbers. All data is encoded as a stream of 1s and 0s called *bits*. A bit (short for *binary digit*) is the most basic form in which a PC stores information. To transmit a bit with a value of 1, for example, the computer may set the line voltage to –12 volts (direct current) for a set length of time. This set length of time determines the transmission speed. The computer may transmit a bit with a value of 0 by setting the voltage to +12 volts for a set length of time. A typical transmission speed is 1,200 bits per second. At that speed, each voltage pulse is 1/1200th of a second in duration. Some PCs and compatibles can send as many as 115,200 bits per second, with each pulse lasting only 1/115200th of a second.

When one of the communicating computers needs to send the code 01001011, for example, the computer sets the voltage to +12 volts for one unit of time, –12 volts for one unit of time, +12 volts for two units of time, and so on. (The unit of time can be any set length of time agreed on by the two computers—2,400 units of time per second is typical.)

The square-shaped waves shown in figure 1.5 illustrate the voltage pulses that the computer uses to transmit this code. Because a signal of this sort is transmitting bits (binary digits), it usually is called a *digital signal*.

Within the next five years, Integrated Services Digital Networks (ISDNs) will be able to carry simultaneous voice, data, and image transmissions. This capability already is available in some areas of the country. Until

ISDNs are more widely available, however, your PC's digital signal has to be converted (*modulated*) to an analog signal in order to be sent over the phone lines. The analog signal then must be converted (*demodulated*) back to a digital signal before your PC can communicate with another computer at the other end. The piece of hardware that accomplishes both modulation and demodulation is the aptly named *modem*, short for *mo*dulator-*dem*odulator (see fig. 1.6). Without a modem at each end of the phone line, the two computers cannot communicate.

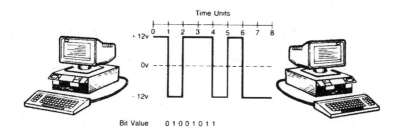

FIG. 1.5

The digital signal 01001011 transmitted directly between two computers, without using modems or a phone line.

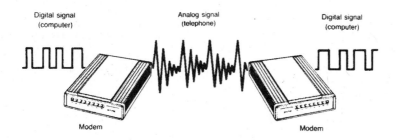

FIG. 1.6

Two modems transmitting computer data over telephone lines.

Modem Speed

Although all modems modulate and demodulate transmitted signals, all modems are not equal. The most important difference among the various types of modems available for use with your PC is the maximum speed at which they can transmit data.

Only a few years ago, communications programs used modems that sent data at a maximum rate of 300 bits per second (*bps*). To put this transmission rate into perspective, consider the number of bits required to represent meaningful information. All information stored and used in your PC is represented by combining eight bits at a time, called a *byte*.

When you are transmitting text or typing at your keyboard on-line (connected to another computer), each character sent to the other computer is represented in ASCII (American Standard Code for Information Interchange). The IBM version of ASCII uses one byte, or eight bits, to represent each character.

At 8 bits per character and 300 bits per second, you would think that the modem could transfer 37.5 characters per second, or 375 five-letter words per minute. PCs, however, normally add to each byte two extra bits, called *start* and *stop bits* (see "Understanding Serial Ports" later in this chapter). Consequently, a speed of 300 bps results in a data-transmission speed of approximately 30 characters per second, or about 300 five-letter words per minute. In comparison, a fast typist usually averages less than 80 words per minute.

This rate is fast enough when you simply want to type an instruction to a remote computer or chat (type messages back and forth) with another user on-line. This rate is not exactly speedy, however, when you are sending a long document that you already have typed. At about 1,000 words per page, sending a 10-page document could take nearly half an hour. If you send the document over long-distance lines, use of a 300-bps modem can translate into expensive telephone bills.

In recent years, modem speeds have increased and prices have decreased. Soon after IBM introduced the PC in August 1981, the Smartmodem 300 and Smartmodem 1200 by Hayes Microcomputer Products became the standard modems for business use. Since 1987, the entry-level standard for PC modems seems to have become the 2400-bps modem. More recently, a growing number of users are using 9600 baud modems. Technological advances in the manufacture of integrated circuits and fierce competition have brought the prices of this category of modems down so far that you have little, if any, reason to buy a less capable modem.

You sometimes may hear the term *baud* used synonymously with bits per second, but they do not mean the same. Although 300-bps modems also are referred to as 300-baud modems, 1200-bps modems do not operate at 1200 baud; they usually operate at 600 baud.

Baud is a technical term that means the number of symbols per second sent over a communication line. (The term is named after J.M.E. Baudot, a French telegraphy expert.) Each symbol may be represented by a certain voltage, a certain combination of frequencies (*tones*), or a certain wave phase (*angle*). Each symbol may be able to represent more than one bit. In 2400-bps modems, for example, each symbol represents 4 bits. Although the modem transmits only 600 symbols per second (600 baud), data is transmitted at 2400 bits per second (4×600).

The term baud has been misused so often that its technical meaning largely is ignored. You therefore can assume that the salesperson who wants to sell you a 1200-*baud* modem means a 1200-bps modem. Similarly, when PROCOMM PLUS for Windows uses the term baud, read it to mean *bits per second*.

Smartmodems are not the only modems available, but they have several built-in features that, if properly driven by communications software, can substantially automate many communications functions. With the Hayes Smartmodems, for example, you can store a list of telephone numbers in your computer and then have the modem dial the number to call a particular computer. This feature usually is called *auto-dial* capability. With older, less "smart" modems, you had to dial the number manually each time (using a telephone hand set) and then push a button to activate the modem. Hayes Smartmodems also can be programmed to answer the phone and automatically connect to an incoming call from another modem—an *auto-answer* capability. Many earlier modems required you to answer the phone yourself and then press a button after you heard the carrier tone (a high-pitched tone generated by the calling modem).

Hayes-Compatible Modems

The series of software commands that activate the Hayes Smartmodem's smart features usually begin with the letters *AT* (short for attention). This command set therefore has come to be known as the *AT command set.* To dial a telephone number by using touch-tone, for example, PROCOMM PLUS for Windows sends to the modem (through a serial port) the command ATDT followed by the telephone number.

Because of the early lead in sales of Hayes modems, most communications software assumes that your modem understands the AT software command set. Consequently, almost every modem manufacturer has adopted the AT command set as the de facto standard command language for modems intended for use with PCs. Modems that recognize this command set often are called *Hayes-compatible* modems. Not all so-called Hayes-compatible modems, however, implement the entire command set. In that sense, some modems are more compatible than others.

When Hayes introduced the Smartmodem 2400, the company also introduced new commands to the AT command set. Other manufacturers have implemented this *extended AT* command set to varying degrees. You can use PROCOMM PLUS for Windows effectively, regardless of whether your modem supports the extended AT command set. Using a modem that supports the AT command set is the most convenient, however.

New Standards

The majority of 2400-bps modems available today can communicate with each other, and most are so similar in basic function that they practically constitute a commodity. Technology, however, marches on. Just as 2400-bps modems gradually have replaced the 1200-bps versions in general business usage, 2400-bps modems with error-control and data-compression capabilities are becoming the next low-end standard.

Hayes and other modem manufacturers also have introduced even faster modems—some capable of speeds of up to 19,200 bps. The CCITT (Consultative Committee on International Telephone and Telegraph), an international communications standards organization and an agency of the United Nations, has adopted a standard for 9600-bps modems, called *V.32*. The CCITT recently has adopted another standard, named *V.32bis*, which provides for up to 14,400 bps. Prices for these modems are substantially higher than for 2400-bps modems, but the use of V.32 and V.32bis modems is increasing among PC users who do a large amount of data transfer over telephone lines.

Error-Control

To be effective, transmission of computer data must be error-free. The detection and elimination of errors in computer data transmissions usually is called *error-checking*, or *error-control*. Although a telephone line doesn't have to be perfectly clear of static or interference for effective voice transmission, a slight variation or interruption of a computer signal can change completely the meaning of the data the signal carries.

All communications programs such as PROCOMM PLUS for Windows can run checks on incoming data to determine whether any errors were introduced into the data during transmission. The techniques used to perform this error-checking are called *error-checking protocols*. (A *protocol* is a set of agreed-on rules.) Chapter 5, "Transferring Files," discusses the various protocols available in PROCOMM PLUS for Windows and how best to use them.

Instead of requiring that the communications software perform error-control, several manufacturers now produce modems that do this chore. When compared to the results of software error-checking, error-detection and the overall speed of transmission improve when the modem handles error-control. For this feature to work, however, the modems on both ends of the connection must be using the same error-control protocol.

Two types of error-control protocols have developed a significant following. Fortunately, an industry standard has emerged that incorporates the two competing error-control schemes.

■ Hayes Microcomputer Products produces a line of modems called the Hayes V-series modems. At the low end of this line is a 2400-bps modem that performs error-control by using a method called Link-Access Procedure for Modems (*LAPM*).

■ Nearly all other PC modem manufacturers, however, produce modems that support a different set of error-control protocols—the Microcom Networking Protocol (*MNP*) Classes 1 through 4, developed by Microcom, Inc. The MNP protocols are progressive. A modem can support Class 1, Classes 1 and 2, Classes 1 through 3, or Classes 1 through 4. The higher the class, the faster the transmission. These protocols are not compatible, however, with LAPM.

Two 2400-bps modems using the two different standards can communicate, but only as 2400-bps modems without modem-based error-control. (Your software must take care of error detection to ensure that line impairment during transmission doesn't corrupt the transmitted data.)

In 1989, the CCITT established an error-control standard called *V.42*. This standard includes the protocol used by Hayes V-series (LAPM) as well as MNP Classes 1 through 4 error-control protocols, with a bias toward LAPM. When connected to another modem, a V.42-compliant modem attempts to use the LAPM protocol. If this approach fails, the V.42 modem then attempts to use the MNP protocols. If the other modem supports neither of these error-control protocols, the V.42 modem acts like a standard 2400-bps modem without error control.

Data Compression

Many modems that provide built-in error-control also *compress* the data as it is sent. A compatible modem on the other end decompresses the data. Compressing data is similar to sitting on a loaf of bread, squeezing out the air, but leaving the nourishment.

A modem compresses data by matching long strings (sequential patterns) of characters in the data with entries in a "dictionary" of known strings. Each entry in the dictionary has an *index value* or code. The sending modem finds a code for each string of characters in the data and transmits only the codes. The receiving modem in turn converts these codes back into the original data.

By reducing the number of characters the modem has to send, this process often can more than double the effective transmission speed. In other words, a 2400-bps modem using data compression sometimes can send as much information in the same length of time as a 4800-bps modem not using data compression.

As with error-control methods, two data-compression standards have developed in the PC modem market. This time, however, a CCITT standard replaces them both. Hayes Microcomputer Products V-series modems perform data compression by using a proprietary algorithm. Many other PC-modem manufacturers follow Microcom's lead and use the MNP Class 5 data-compression algorithm. Again, these two competing data-compression methods are not compatible.

In September 1989, the CCITT ratified the *V.42bis* standard, which adds data compression to the existing V.42 error-control standard. The data-compression scheme included in this new standard is neither the Hayes algorithm nor the MNP algorithm. The CCITT V.42bis proposes, instead, the use of an algorithm known as the British Telecom Lempel-Ziv (*BTLZ*) compression algorithm.

The V.42bis standard does not include MNP data compression (MNP Class 5). Many manufacturers, however, produce modems that support V.42bis data compression as well as MNP data compression. Hayes has upgraded its V-series modems to include V.42bis and MNP Class 5.

Appendix B includes an explanation of how to use PROCOMM PLUS for Windows to take full advantage of the advanced capabilities of Hayes V-series, V.42-compliant, and MNP modems.

External versus Internal Modems

In addition to modems capable of transmitting data at different speeds, manufacturers often produce modems in external and internal versions. Each type offers several advantages.

An *external modem* typically is a metal or plastic box about 10 inches by 6 inches by 2 inches, with a panel of LED (light emitting diodes) on the front. The modem is connected to your PC by a serial cable and powered by an AC adapter. The external modem has at least one telephone jack for connecting the modem to the telephone line and often a second jack for connecting a telephone. Figure 1.7 shows a drawing of a Hayes V-series Smartmodem 9600.

Minimodems, a relatively new subset of external modems, are small enough to fit in your pocket and can run on batteries. These minimodems typically plug directly into a serial port on your computer (see fig. 1.8) and are particularly handy for laptop computer users.

The external modem has the following advantages:

- ■ You can move it easily from one computer to another.

- ■ You can use an external modem with nearly any type or brand of computer that has an asynchronous serial port (see "Understanding Serial Ports," later in this chapter).

- ■ An external modem can be shared by several computers through a serial switch box; only one computer uses the modem at a time.

- ■ Although an external modem takes up some space on your desk, you often can stash it under your desk telephone or on top of your PC.

■ Pocket-sized modems usually can plug directly into a serial port, taking up no room on your desk.

■ External modems usually have a panel of LEDs (lights) that enable you to monitor continuously the state of certain modem parameters.

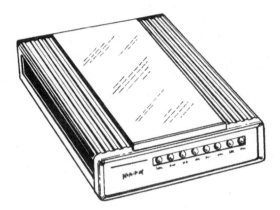

FIG. 1.7

An external Hayes V-series Smartmodem 9600.

FIG. 1.8

A pocket-size modem.

Table 1.1 lists the meanings of the LEDs on the front panel of external Hayes modems and most external Hayes-compatible modems.

Table 1.1. Hayes Smartmodem LEDs

LED	Meaning
HS	High Speed
AA	Auto-Answer
CD	Carrier Detect
OH	On Hook
RD	Receive Data

continues

Table 1.1. Continued

LED	Meaning
SD	Send Data
TR	Terminal Ready
MR	Modem Ready

On the negative side, an external modem usually is a little more expensive than an internal modem with otherwise identical features from the same manufacturer. An external modem also requires your computer to have an available serial port and a serial cable.

Each *internal modem* is built on a circuit board that plugs into an empty expansion slot inside your PC, thus taking up no room on your desk. Some internal modems are long enough to fill up a long expansion slot; others need only a half-size slot.

Because an internal modem is designed to work only with a PC (or PS/2—the same internal modem does not work in both), internal modems usually are bundled and sold with PC communications software. This setup is an advantage, unless you don't like the software.

The major disadvantage of an internal modem is that it is inconvenient to use with several different computers. If you need to move a modem among several computers or want to share a modem, an external modem is the better choice. Also, because most IBM PS/2s do not accept expansion boards designed for PCs (PCs, XTs, ATs, or compatibles), you cannot move an internal modem from a PC into a PS/2. For some users, the lack of status LEDs also is an annoyance.

Understanding Serial Ports

Before data can be transmitted by your modem, your PC must send the data from your keyboard or disk to the modem. The computer sends data to the modem through a serial port in your PC. A *serial port*, or *COM port*, is an outlet through which your computer can send data as a stream of bits, one bit at a time (that is, *in serial*). Data normally moves around the computer eight bits at a time—referred to as *in parallel*.

You can think of the internal modem as having its serial port built in. When you use an internal modem, you don't connect the modem to a serial port. A special chip on the modem, called the *UART* (universal asynchronous receiver/transmitter), performs the same function as a serial port; it converts the parallel signal into a serial signal. When you install the modem, you must configure it as one of your computer's COM ports (see Appendix B, "Installing a Modem").

On IBM PC, PC/XT, and PS/2 computers, as well as most compatibles, each serial port is a D-shaped connector that has 25 protruding metal pins and is located on the back of the computer. This type of connector is called a *DB-25 M* (*male*) connector. The connector on the serial cable that attaches the modem to this serial port has 25 holes to match the male connector's 25 pins. This connector is called a *DB-25 F* (*female*) connector.

The serial ports on IBM PC AT computers and most compatibles use D-shaped connectors with 9 protruding pins, called *DB-9 M* connectors. To connect a serial cable to such a port, the cable must end in a *DB-9 F* connector.

Depending on the brand of computer, each port is marked, if at all, with the label *COM*, *Serial*, or *RS-232*. (RS-232 is a published communications hardware standard with which PC serial ports comply.)

DOS 3.3 and higher can support as many as four serial ports. Earlier versions of DOS support only two serial ports. DOS refers to the serial ports as COM1, COM2, COM3, and so on. Even if your version of DOS does not support more than two ports, PROCOMM PLUS for Windows still enables you to use up to COM4. In other words, PROCOMM PLUS for Windows gets around the DOS limitation.

Appendix A explains how to inform PROCOMM PLUS for Windows in the initial setup which COM port is connected to the modem. Chapter 8, "Tailoring PROCOMM PLUS for Windows," also describes how to change this setting later.

Asynchronous versus Synchronous Transmission

Data sent through a serial port comes out as a stream of bits in single file, but each bit means nothing by itself. Because a PC stores information in eight-bit bytes, the receiving computer must be able to reconstruct the bytes of data from the stream of bits. Computers use two ways to identify clearly each byte of data sent through a serial port: *asynchronous transmission* and *synchronous transmission*.

PCs use the *asynchronous* method to send data through a serial port. The sending PC marks with a start bit the beginning of each byte that is to be transmitted. This start bit informs the receiving computer that a byte of data follows. To mark the end of the byte, the PC sends one or two stop bits (the number of stop bits is a user option). The stop bits inform the receiving computer that it has just received the entire byte. Timing is not critical with this procedure.

When you set up PC communications software to communicate with another computer, you need to specify whether to use one or two stop bits. The number of stop bits used on your end must match the number used by the computer on the other end. In PROCOMM PLUS for Windows, you select the number of stop bits when you set up a list of phone numbers you want to call with your modem. This list, called the *dialing directory*, is described in Chapter 3.

When in doubt, use one stop bit. This choice is the default in PROCOMM PLUS for Windows (the setting PROCOMM PLUS for Windows uses if you don't specify another setting). You will seldom, if ever, find two stop bits used by another computer.

When computers use the *synchronous* method of transmitting data, bytes of data are sent at precise intervals. Both the sending and receiving modems must be synchronized perfectly for this method to work properly.

Because a PC uses the asynchronous method to send data through its serial port, a *protocol converter* is required for a PC to communicate with a computer using the synchronous method. The protocol converter converts the signal from asynchronous to synchronous. Many mainframe computers communicate only in synchronous mode, but they often have an asynchronous dial-in port with a built-in protocol converter. This design enables PCs and other computers to connect by using an asynchronous signal.

Synchronous transmission can achieve higher transmission rates, but it requires higher-quality telephone lines. Telephone lines used for synchronous transmission often are specially prepared and used exclusively for that purpose. These lines usually must be leased from the telephone company, making synchronous transmission extremely expensive for use in everyday PC communications.

Data Bits

As mentioned previously, the PC uses eight bits at a time to represent a byte of data. Because exactly 256 ways are available to arrange eight 1s and 0s (2 to the 8th power), eight bits are needed to represent each of the 256 characters in IBM's extended ASCII character set. Many other types of computers—including mainframes used by on-line services—use only seven data bits per byte. The ASCII character set used by these computers includes only the first 128 characters of the IBM extended ASCII character set (2 to the 7th power equals 128). These 128 characters include all the numbers and letters (upper- and lowercase), punctuation marks, and some extra control characters. Special characters, such as foreign letters and box-drawing characters, require all eight bits.

When you create the PROCOMM PLUS for Windows dialing directory, you specify for each computer you plan to call whether data occupies the first seven bits or all eight bits of each byte. PROCOMM PLUS for Windows calls this specification the *number of data bits*. Other programs may use the term *word length* or *character length* for the same specification. You sometimes may use your PC to communicate with another PC that needs eight data bits per byte. At other times, you may communicate with a type of computer that can use only seven data bits per byte. The only way to know for sure which setting you need is to ask the operator of the other computer.

A simple rule of thumb is to use eight data bits for PC-to-PC or PC-to-bulletin-board connections. All PCs need eight-bit bytes to represent the full IBM character set and to transmit program files. When calling an on-line service, such as CompuServe, or another mainframe-based system, use seven data bits. Most such systems are run on computers that can handle only seven data bits per byte.

Parity Checking

An error in transmission of even a single bit can change completely the meaning of the byte that includes that bit. To help detect these errors as they occur, some computers use the eighth bit of each byte as a *parity bit*. The parity of an integer (whole number) is whether it is odd or even. You can use a parity bit in two ways. Both methods add the other seven digits in each byte and check whether the sum is an even or odd number.

When using the *even parity method*, the computer sets the value of the parity bit (either 1 or 0) so that the total of all eight bits is even. If the sum of the first seven bits is odd, such as 0000001, the parity bit becomes a 1. The eight-bit byte transmitted is therefore 00000011. If the sum of the first seven bits is even, such as 0010001, the parity bit becomes 0, and the eight-bit transmitted byte is 00100010. In both cases, adding all eight bits results in an even number—2 in both of the examples. The receiving computer then adds the digits of each byte as it is received. If the sum is odd, an error must have been introduced during transmission, so the computer software asks that the byte be sent again.

Similarly, the *odd parity method* assigns the value of the parity bit so that the sum of all digits in each byte always is an odd number.

One parity bit method, known as *mark parity*, always sets the parity bit to the value 1. Another method, known as *space parity*, always sets the parity bit to the value 0.

Parity-checking provides rather minimal error-checking when compared to the many other more sophisticated error-checking methods now available in software (see Chapter 5, "Transferring Files") and hardware (see "New Standards," earlier in this chapter).

The parity-check method is not available if the eighth bit in each byte is needed to represent data (such as when transmitting the full IBM extended ASCII character set) or to transmit non-ASCII files (such as all programs that run on your PC and most data files used with word processing, spreadsheet, and database programs). As with the number of stop bits and the number of data bits, you specify parity in PROCOMM PLUS for Windows in the Dialing Directory window.

For PC-to-PC communication, including transmission to bulletin boards, use the None (no parity) setting. When connecting to an on-line service, you usually have to use Even parity. If you are connected to an on-line service and are receiving nothing but strange-looking characters, you probably have parity set to None. Try changing the parity to Even. (Changing the parity setting after you are connected is explained in Chapter 8.)

Understanding Telephone Line Requirements

Both external and internal modems must be connected to a working telephone line. The modems, however, do not require a special type of telephone line; a voice-quality line is sufficient. You can use touch-tone or pulse dial service because nearly all auto-dial modems can dial either type of signal. Refer to Appendix B for information on installing your modem and connecting it to your telephone line.

CAUTION: One relatively new telephone service can cause problems for modem transmission. The feature, usually known as *call waiting*, is available from an ever-increasing number of telephone companies. Call waiting uses an audible click or beep to alert you to an incoming call while you are talking on the line. If your modem is on the line, this call-waiting signal may disrupt and even disconnect your transmission.

If you have this type of service and plan to use your modem during periods when you may receive incoming calls, you should consider having the service removed. In some areas, you can disable the feature temporarily by typing a special code on your telephone keypad or by transmitting the code in a PROCOMM PLUS for Windows dial command. (For more information, see Chapter 8 on setup.) Check with your local telephone company to determine whether such a code is available and, if so, how to use it.

Summary

This chapter briefly described the most common uses of communications programs. It also introduced you to many of the terms and concepts fundamental to understanding communications. As you use this book to help you learn to use PROCOMM PLUS for Windows, you probably will run across several other new communications concepts and terms. You now have a solid foundation on which to build.

Turn now to Chapter 2 to begin learning how to get around in PROCOMM PLUS for Windows.

Getting Around in PROCOMM PLUS for Windows

Now that you have read Chapter 1 and you have a fundamental understanding of communications, you are ready to explore PROCOMM PLUS for Windows. This chapter helps you get started by giving you an idea of how PROCOMM PLUS for Windows looks on-screen and by explaining how the program makes requests and responds to your actions. This chapter introduces you to the Terminal window, the pull-down menus, keyboard commands, and the Action bar menu. You also learn how to use the PROCOMM PLUS for Windows help system and how to exit from PROCOMM PLUS for Windows.

Before you can use PROCOMM PLUS for Windows, of course, you must install it on your computer and activate the program. Appendix A discusses installation and start-up. If you need help installing PROCOMM PLUS on your hard disk or getting the program up and running, turn to Appendix A before you read any farther in this chapter.

Because PROCOMM PLUS for Windows runs under the Windows environment, the descriptions in this chapter assume that you have some experience using Windows and are familiar with using a mouse. If you need more information about using Windows, you can refer to Que's *Using Windows 3.1*, Special Edition.

After you start the program, PROCOMM PLUS for Windows briefly displays its logo screen. After a few seconds, the Terminal window appears, as shown in figure 2.1.

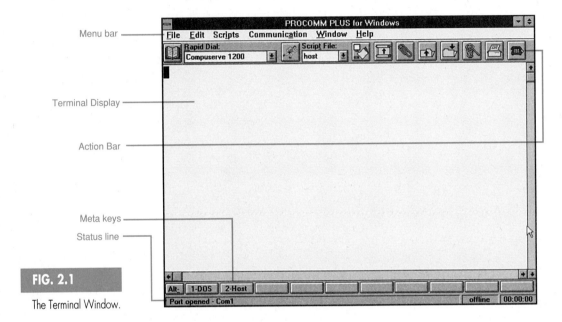

Menu bar

Terminal Display

Action Bar

Meta keys

Status line

FIG. 2.1

The Terminal Window.

Understanding the Terminal Window

The Terminal window is the program's main screen. The Terminal window displays text transmitted by the computer with which you are communicating. The Terminal workspace includes the Terminal Display, the Action bar, and the scroll bars at the right and bottom of the Terminal Display. These are described as follows:

- The Terminal Display is the main rectangular portion of the screen. Communication from another computer is displayed here.

- The Action bar is the bar just above the Terminal Display, which contains several icons representing various options. These icons are described in detail later in the section "Using the Action Bar."

- The scroll bars at the right and bottom of the Terminal Display enable you to scroll vertically or horizontally to see information that may have scrolled off the screen. To use the scroll bars, use the mouse to point to the arrows at the top or bottom (or left and right) ends of the scroll bar, and click. This causes the screen to scroll in the direction of the arrow. You also can point to the location button on the scroll bar, click, and drag the button in the direction where you want to scroll.

With some terminal emulations, the font being used is small enough to allow the entire screen to appear in the display area. In this case, no scroll bars are needed.

When you enter the Terminal window, you see a cursor—a small rectangle—at the top left of the Terminal Display, right under the open book icon. At the bottom of the screen are the Terminal window's meta keys and status line.

The meta keys are "button" commands. These meta keys can be programmed to execute commands that you specify. Meta keys are discussed in more detail in Chapter 7, "Automating PROCOMM PLUS for Windows with Meta Keys and Script Files."

The status line, below the meta keys line, contains information about the current communications session. In figure 2.1, for example, the message at the far left of the status line displays the message Port opened Com1. This means that PROCOMM PLUS for Windows is communicating through the computer's number 1 communications port. Other messages may appear in this area during a communications session.

The right portion of the status line contains the message offline, which means that you are not currently connected to another computer. When you connect to another computer, this message changes to online. The message 00:00:00 is a clock that displays the connect time after you connect to another computer. This time information is helpful particularly if you are connected to a service that bills by the amount of time connected.

NOTE If the last message on the status line incorrectly displays online, even when you first start PROCOMM PLUS for Windows and before you have called another computer, see Appendix B, "Installing a Modem." The Carrier Detect (CD) setting on your modem probably is set so that PROCOMM PLUS for Windows thinks that a carrier signal (the signal generated by another modem) is always present. Change this setting so that the modem monitors the existence of a carrier and raises the CD signal high (tells PROCOMM PLUS that a carrier exists) when a carrier from another modem is detected.

Although the largest portion of the Terminal window is blank, this window comes alive after you connect to another computer.

Using the Keyboard and Mouse

PROCOMM PLUS for Windows works with any PC-, AT-, or PS/2-style or equivalent keyboard (see fig. 2.2). Because the program contains commands that use the keyboard, you need to be familiar with your keyboard. As in all Windows programs, using a mouse for some processes is highly recommended. Many times, however, you may want to use keystrokes instead of the mouse. This book uses the labels found on an IBM Enhanced keyboard to describe keys you should press.

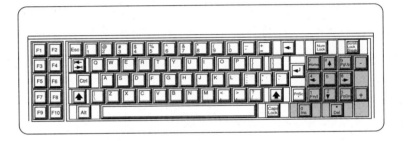

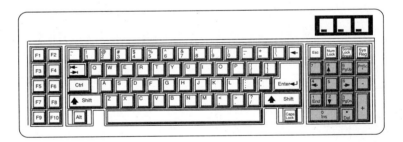

FIG. 2.2

The IBM PC keyboard (top), the IBM Personal Computer AT keyboard (center), and the IBM Enhanced keyboard (bottom).

When PROCOMM PLUS for Windows is emulating a particular type of terminal, it translates some keys in special ways. Chapter 10 describes the PROCOMM PLUS for Windows terminal emulation. Chapter 10 also includes tables that show how PROCOMM PLUS for Windows translates the programmable keys, such as cursor-movement keys and function keys, for each type of terminal.

Using the Action Bar

The PROCOMM PLUS for Windows Action Bar menu is the graphical control center for PROCOMM PLUS for Windows. This menu contains a selection of commonly used commands. Action commands are the same as commands available through the pull-down menu interface, but the action commands usually are quicker and easier to access than the menu command. The menu versions of these commands are covered later in the section "Using the Pull-Down Menus."

To choose a command on the action bar, point to the Action Bar icon with the mouse pointer and click. This section briefly describes the commands on the action bar and will refer you to other sections in the book if more detailed information on the command is available.

Using the Dialing Directory Action Command

The Dialing Directory icon is an open book, like a phone directory. This command enables you to store, edit, and specify which phone numbers can be used to initiate communication sessions with other computers. When you click on the Dialing Directory icon, the Dialing Directory Window appears. Chapter 3, "Building Your Dialing Directory," provides a complete description on how to use the Dialing Directory.

Using the Rapid Dial Drop-Down List Box

The Rapid Dial drop-down list box displays the name of an entry in your active dialing directory. In figure 2.1, for example, the displayed entry is Compuserve 1200. To dial the displayed entry quickly, point to the entry and click twice or, using the keyboard, press Alt-R, and then press Enter. This initiates a call to that entry.

Notice the down arrow at the right end of the Rapid Dial box. This tells you that a drop-down list box is available. When you point to the down arrow and click once, a list of the available entries in the active dialing directory appears. You then can point to one of the entries and click to initiate a call.

Using the Start Script Action Command

 The Start Script icon looks like a person running. Next to the Start Script icon is a drop-down list box labeled Script File. In figure 2.1, an ASPECT script named host appears in this box. When you click the Start Script icon, the ASPECT script currently selected in the Script File list box is started. An ASPECT script is a program that causes PROCOMM PLUS for Windows to run automatically through a series of commands (such as logging on to a system).

To select a script file from the drop-down box, follow these steps:

1. Point to the down arrow at the right of the box and click once.

2. The drop-down box containing a list of available script files appears.

3. Point to the script you want to select and click.

More information about using Script files is given in Chapter 7, "Automating PROCOMM PLUS for Windows with Meta Keys and Script Files," and in Chapter 11, "An Overview of the Windows ASPECT Script Language."

Using the Setup Action Command

 The Setup icon contains a picture of a terminal, a folder, and a color bar. When you click this icon, the Current Setup window appears. You use this window to specify information about your modem, terminal emulation, colors, and mode. Detailed information on using the Setup window is given in Chapter 8, "Tailoring PROCOMM PLUS for Windows."

Using the Scrollback/Pause Action Command

 The Scrollback/Pause icon looks like a scroll with an up arrow. Click this icon to pause the display of characters to the Terminal Display area. Use this icon when your information is scrolling too quickly for you to read. When you click the icon again, the display of characters to the screen resumes.

Using the File Clipboard Action Command

The File Clipboard icon looks like a paper clip. Use this option to cut the names of download files from the display screen and paste them to the host system. This process is described in Chapter 4, "A Session with PROCOMM PLUS for Windows."

Using the Send File Action Command

The Send File icon looks like a file folder with the arrow pointing up. During a communication session with another computer, you may want to *upload* (send) a file from your computer to the host computer. When the host computer is prepared to receive a file, click this icon to send the file or files from your computer. This process is described in detail in Chapter 5, "Transferring Files."

Using the Receive File Action Command

The Receive File icon looks like a file folder with an arrow pointing down. During a communication session with another computer, you may want to *download* (receive) a file from the host computer to your computer. When the host computer is prepared to send your computer a file, click this icon to receive the file. This process is described in detail in Chapter 5, "Transferring Files."

Using the Capture Action Command

The Capture icon looks like a butterfly net. Use this icon to begin or end the capture of text as it is displayed on the Terminal Display. When you click this icon, you are asked to enter the name of the capture file (where the information that is captured is stored). While capture is in progress, you can end the process and close the capture file by clicking the Capture icon again. This process is described more in Chapter 4, "A Session with PROCOMM PLUS for Windows," in the section titled "Capturing a Session to Disk."

Using the Printer Action Command

The Printer icon looks like a printer. When you click this icon, the information displayed on the terminal screen is echoed to the printer. This enables you to capture a hard copy of the information while it is being displayed to the screen. If the printer is printing the information being displayed, clicking the printer icon terminates printing.

Using the Hangup Action Command

The Hangup icon looks like a telephone. When a communication session is in progress, the telephone handset is off the hook. When you click this icon, the telephone connection is broken (disconnected). The icon then displays a telephone with the handset on the hook.

Using the Clear Screen Action Command

The Clear Screen icon looks like a monitor with a windshield wiper. This icon is displayed only on computer monitors using a Windows video driver with a resolution of 800×600 or higher. When you click this icon, the screen is cleared and reset to its default colors.

Using the Start Record Action Command

The Start Record icon looks like a cassette tape. This icon is displayed only on monitors using a Windows video driver with a resolution of 800×600 or higher. Use this icon to begin a recording session, in which your keystrokes and the host computer's prompts are recorded to a file. This file then can be used in preparing a script. Recording and using a script are covered in Chapter 7, "Automating PROCOMM PLUS for Windows with Meta Keys and Script Files."

Using the Playback File Action Command

The Playback File icon looks like a record player. This icon is displayed only on monitors using a Windows video driver with a resolution of 800×600 or higher. Use this icon to display the contents of a captured file to the Terminal Display. This file then can be used in preparing a script.

Using the Compile/Edit Action Command

The Compile/Edit icon looks like a hammer, screwdriver, and a piece of paper. This icon is displayed only on monitors using a Windows video driver with a resolution of 800×600 or higher. Click this icon to enter the Compile/Edit dialog, which is used to create, edit, and compile ASPECT scripts. This is described in Chapter 7, "Automating PROCOMM PLUS for Windows with Meta Keys and Script Files," and in Chapter 11, "An Overview of the Windows ASPECT Script Language."

Using the Pull-Down Menus

In addition to the commands provided in the Action bar, you can invoke more PROCOMM PLUS for Windows features by selecting options from the pull-down menus. This menu system is a standard feature of all windows applications and operates like any other Windows program.

To extend a pull-down menu, select the menu item (such as File) by using the mouse or the keyboard. To select a menu item with the mouse, point the mouse pointer at the menu item and click. To select a menu item using the keyboard, hold down the Alt key and simultaneously press the underlined letter of the menu item. To extend the File menu, for example, press Alt-F (see fig. 2.3).

After the menu is extended, you can choose an item from the menu by pointing to the item with the mouse pointer and clicking or by pressing the key associated with the underlined letter of the option—the *hot key*. In figure 2.3, for example, the O in Open Dialing Directory is underlined. This means that, with the File menu extended, you can press O to choose that option.

Some options also have short-cut commands that you can use without first extending the menu. To the right of the Kermit Command option, for example, is the short-cut command Alt-K. This means that you can choose the Kermit Command option by pressing Alt-K without first extending the File menu. To close an extended menu, press the Esc key, or click on another area of the screen.

The triangles at the right of some options (see the Kermit Command option) mean that when you choose that option, a submenu appears, enabling you to specify other options. Notice the small a icons next to some items in the menu. This mark tells you that an action command equivalent to this command is available.

This section describes each pull-down menu and tells you where in the book you can get additional information about the menu items.

Understanding the File Menu

The File menu contains options for using several kinds of files with the PROCOMM PLUS for Windows program. To extend the File menu, select File by clicking it with the mouse, or by pressing Alt-F. Figure 2.3 illustrates the extended File menu.

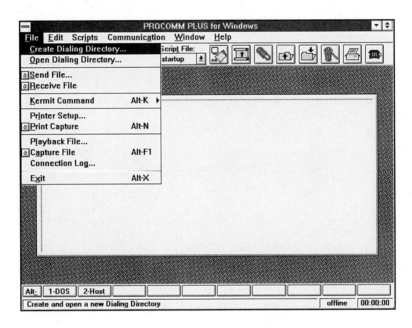

FIG. 2.3

The extended File menu.

The first two entries in the File menu deal with dialing directories. These options enable you to store, edit, and specify which phone numbers can be used to initiate communication sessions with other computers (see also "Using the Directory Action Command," earlier in this chapter). A complete description on how to use the Dialing Directory is contained in Chapter 3, "Building Your Dialing Directory."

The Send File and Receive File options are related to the Send (Upload) and Receive (Download) Action bar icon options. During a communication session with another computer, you may want to upload (send) a file from your computer to the host computer or download (receive) a file from the host computer to your computer. When the host computer is prepared for you to send it a file, choose the Send File option. When the host computer is ready for you to receive a file, choose the Receive File option. This process is described in detail in Chapter 5, "Transferring Files."

The Kermit Command option (Alt-K) is related to the Send File and Receive File commands and is a particular process of transferring files from one machine to another. Kermit also is described in Chapter 5, "Transferring Files."

The Printer Setup option is used to describe to your computer what kind of printer you have and how it is installed. Setting up the printer and other features of the program are described in Chapter 8, "Tailoring PROCOMM PLUS for Windows."

The Print Capture option (Alt-N) enables you to capture the information displayed to the Terminal Display on your printer. Use this option to begin or end the printing of text as it is displayed on the Terminal Display. When you choose this option the first time, you turn the print option on. While printing is on, you can end print capture by selecting the option again.

The Playback File option is the same as the Playback Action command (record player). Use this option to display the contents of a captured file to the Terminal Display. This file then can be used in preparing a script.

The Capture File option (Alt-F1) is the same as the Capture Action command (butterfly net). Use this option to begin or end the capture of text as it is displayed on the Terminal Display. When you choose this option, you are asked to enter the name of the capture file (where the information that is captured is stored). While capture is in progress, you can end the capture and close the capture file by choosing this option again. This option is described more in Chapter 4, "A Session with PROCOMM PLUS for Windows," in the section titled, "Capturing a Session to Disk."

The Connection Log option enables you to tell the program to record information about each connection (when you connect to another computer). This option also is controlled in the setup options, as described in Chapter 8, "Tailoring PROCOMM PLUS for Windows."

The Exit option (Alt-X) enables you to exit the PROCOMM PLUS for Windows program. If you attempt to exit the program while you are still in communication with another computer, you are asked if you want to disconnect before exiting the program. The message You are still online. Continue with disconnect? appears, and you must respond with a Yes or No.

Understanding the Edit Menu

The Edit menu contains options that enable you to manipulate information on-screen. Figure 2.4 shows the extended Edit menu.

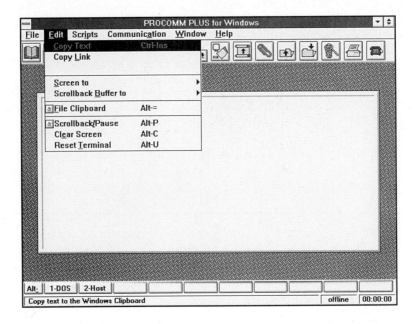

FIG. 2.4

The Edit menu extended.

The Copy Text command enables you to copy text on the Terminal Display and place it into the Windows Clipboard, where it then can be inserted into other Windows applications. The Copy Text command works only when the Terminal Display has been paused (Alt-P). When the Copy Text command is not available for use, it is grayed, or dimmed, on the Edit menu. To copy text to the Windows Clipboard, follow these steps:

1. Pause the display by pressing Alt-P.

2. Click on the first character of the text to copy and drag the mouse to the last character of the text you want to copy. The selected text is highlighted.

3. Choose the Copy Text option.

4. Press Alt-P to resume scrolling.

The copied information is now in the Windows Clipboard and can be inserted into another Windows application. You can use the Copy Text command, for example, to capture information that you want to move into a word processor, such as Word for Windows.

The Copy Link option is used to send information from the PROCOMM PLUS for Windows program to a linked program. The use of this information is covered in Chapter 11, "An Overview of the Windows ASPECT Script Language."

The Paste Text option is used to send information currently in the Windows Clipboard directory to the COM port (your communication port), and then to the linked (remote) computer. Therefore, if you use the Copy Text command to capture some information into the Windows Clipboard, you can send that information back (perhaps to another computer) by pasting it from the Clipboard to the communications port. When you paste information from the Windows Clipboard, the information in the Clipboard is not erased, so you can paste the information multiple times.

The Paste Text option is effective only for standard ASCII text. If the information in the Clipboard contains extended ASCII characters, the result of pasting may not be predictable.

The Screen To option enables you to capture the contents of the current Terminal Display screen to the Windows Clipboard, a capture file, a disk file, or to your printer. When you select the Screen To option, you are asked to choose one of these four destinations. The shortcut key for sending the screen to the Windows Clipboard is Alt-V, the shortcut key to send the screen to a file is Alt-G, and the shortcut key to send the screen to the printer is Alt-L.

The Scrollback Buffer To option is similar to the Screen To option, except that it sends the contents of the entire buffer, which contains several pages of information from the current session. The size of this buffer is set in the Terminal settings procedure (see Chapter 8, "Tailoring PROCOMM PLUS for Windows"). When you choose the Scrollback Buffer To option, you are asked to choose to capture the information to the Windows Clipboard, the capture file, a disk file, or to the printer.

The File Clipboard option (Alt-=) enables you to capture file names from the display window and to then later access and copy the names back to the screen when needed. This is helpful when you are searching for names of files to download from a host computer. You can capture these names into the File Clipboard. When you are ready to download the files, you can access these names from the Clipboard. This process is explained in detail in Chapter 5, "Transferring Files," in the section "Working with Files."

The Scrollback / Pause option (Alt-P) is the same as the Pause Action command described earlier. When you choose this option, it pauses the display of characters to the Terminal Display area. Use this option if you want to read information that is scrolling too quickly. When you choose the option again, the display of characters to the screen resumes.

The Clear Screen option (Alt-C) clears the display screen and resets colors to the default colors. It does not erase information in the scrollback buffer.

Like the Clear Screen option, the Reset Terminal option (Alt-U) clears the screen. Reset Terminal also clears the scrollback buffer and resets the Terminal window.

Understanding the Scripts Menu

The Scripts menu contains options concerning scripts. Figure 2.5 shows the extended Scripts menu.

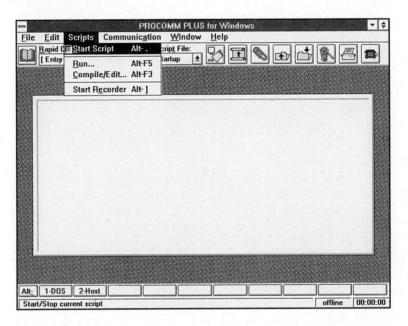

FIG. 2.5

The extended Scripts menu.

The Start Script option (Alt-.) begins execution of a script you have chosen previously in the Start Script Action command (see "Using the Start Script Action Command" section earlier in this chapter). More information about creating, compiling, and using script files is given in Chapter 7, "Automating PROCOMM PLUS for Windows with Meta Keys and Script Files," and Chapter 11, "An Overview of the Windows ASPECT Script Language."

The Run option (Alt-F5) enables you to choose a script file and then run it. PROCOMM PLUS for Windows compiles the script file if it has not been compiled already.

The Compile/Edit option (Alt-F3) enables you to create, edit, and compile script files.

The Start Recorder option (Alt-]) is the same as the Start Record Action command described earlier in the section "Using the Start Record Action Command." Use this option to begin a recording session, in which your keystrokes and the host computer's prompts are recorded to a file. This file then can be used in preparing a script. Recording and using a script are covered in Chapter 7, "Automating PROCOMM PLUS with Meta Keys and Script Files."

Understanding the Communication Menu

The Communication menu contains options concerning communicating between your computer and another computer. Figure 2.6 shows the extended Communication menu.

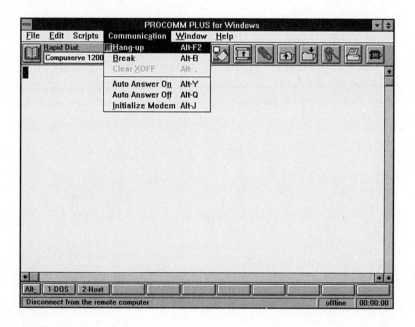

FIG. 2.6

The extended
Communication menu.

The Hang-up option (Alt-F2) is the same as the Hang-up Action option. When you choose this option, the phone line connection is terminated. The hang-up method is specified in the Current Setup options. This option is described in Chapter 8, "Tailoring PROCOMM PLUS for Windows."

The Break option (Alt-B) causes the program to send a time-delay signal, called a break, to the attached computer. Use this command to tell the other computer than you want to interrupt a current process.

The Clear XOFF option is used when the flow of data has been stopped by an XOFF character. To resume the flow, choose this option. If Clear XOFF is not available, it will appear grayed in the menu.

The Auto Answer On option (Alt-Y) sets up your modem to answer the phone and initiate communications with the calling computer. When auto answer is on, the modem automatically answers any incoming calls. Auto Answer is discussed more in Chapter 9, "Using Host Mode."

The Auto Answer Off option (Alt-Q) turns auto answer on your modem to off, enabling you to answer the phone by voice and preventing the modem from answering calls.

The Initialize Modem option (Alt-J) tells PROCOMM PLUS for Windows to send the modem initialization command to your modem. You may need to initialize your modem to clear your COM port before running another program that also uses your COM port. The initialization command sent as a result of the Initialize Modem option is defined in the Modem Setup window, as described in Chapter 8, "Tailoring PROCOMM PLUS for Windows."

Understanding the Window Menu

The Window menu contains options specifying what windows will be shown on the Terminal window. Figure 2.7 shows the extended Window menu.

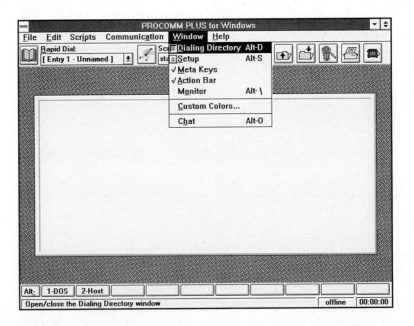

FIG. 2.7

The extended Window menu.

The Dialing Directory option (Alt-D) is the same as the Dialing Directory Action command. This command enables you to store, edit, and specify which phone numbers can be used to initiate communication sessions with other computers. When you choose the Dialing Directory option, the Dialing Directory window appears. A complete description on how to use the Dialing Directory is provided in Chapter 3, "Building Your Dialing Directory."

The Setup option (Alt-S) is the same as the Setup Action command. When you choose this option, the Setup window appears. Use this option to specify information about your modem, terminal emulation, colors, and mode. Detailed information on using the Setup window is given in Chapter 8, "Tailoring PROCOMM PLUS for Windows."

The Meta Keys option enables you to toggle between showing the Meta Keys options at the bottom of the screen and not showing them. The advantage of not showing them is that you gain an extra line for text to be printed on-screen. When the Meta Keys option is on, a check mark appears to the side of the option. When the option is off, no check mark appears.

The Action Bar option enables you to toggle between showing and not showing the Action Bar option. When the Action Bar option is on, a check mark appears to the side of the option. When the option is off, no check mark appears.

The Monitor option (Alt-\) enables you to open a window that displays unformatted information coming through the serial port. When no check mark appears beside the Monitor option, the monitor option is off. When you choose this option, a check mark appears, and information in a Windows Monitor screen is displayed in a split-screen fashion. Characters are displayed in hexadecimal codes on the left and in normal ASCII characters on the right of the split screen. This mode is useful for programmers who need to observe communications as they happen in order to debug a communication process. Figure 2.8 illustrates a monitor in the split-screen mode.

The Custom Colors option enables you to choose colors for the setup and operation of the program. This is covered in detail in Chapter 8.

The Chat option (Alt-O) enables you to switch to a communication mode where you can have a *real-time* conversation with a person using the other computer. Sometimes this is the computer operator for a large computer, or it may be another PC user. Chat mode is discussed more in Chapter 4, "A Session with PROCOMM PLUS for Windows."

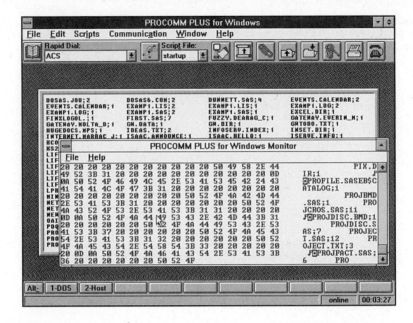

FIG. 2.8

An example of a
Windows Monitor
screen.

Getting Help

PROCOMM PLUS for Windows contains an extensive help system. From
virtually any window in the system, you can access the Help system by
pressing F1, Alt-Z, or Alt-H, or by choosing Help from the menu bar. Because so many help possibilities exist, this section covers a sampling of
ways to access the Help system.

From the Terminal Display menu bar, select the Help pull-down menu.
The extended Help menu is shown in figure 2.9.

When you choose the Contents option (Alt-Z) from the Help menu, a
window like the one illustrated in figure 2.10 appears. This window contains several icons, each representing a "chapter" in the help system.
The help system chapters are as follows:

Basics	Modem
Menus	Mouse
Terminal	Fonts
Directory	Colors
Setup	Keyboard

To open one of these chapters, point to the appropriate icon with the
mouse pointer and click. If you point to the Basics icon and click, for
example, the window illustrated in figure 2.11 appears.

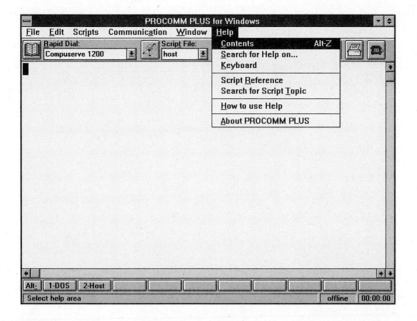

FIG. 2.9

The Help menu
extended.

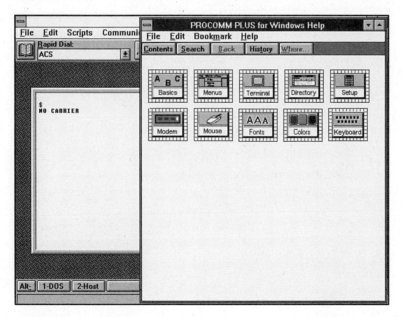

FIG. 2.10

The Help Contents
Window.

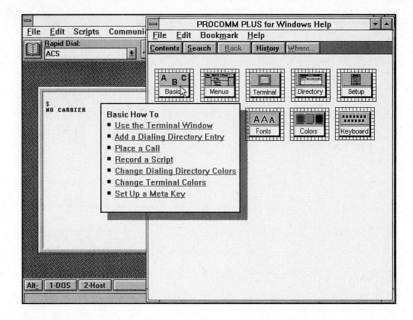

FIG. 2.11

The Help Basics
Window.

Each Help window contains a menu bar with options like the ones displayed on the Help, Contents window—File, Edit, Bookmark, and Help. The items on these menu bars are accessed the same as any Windows menu. To open the File menu, for example, press Alt-F or click File using the mouse. The following list describes options on the Help window menu bar:

■ *File*. Enables you to choose which help file to access and to print the information in the window

■ *Edit*. Enables you to copy help information into the Windows Clipboard

■ *Bookmark*. Enables you to mark a help item so that you can return to it easily using the History option

■ *Help*. Provides information on how to use the Help Window

The button bar under the Help menu bar contains the options Contents, Search, Back, History, and Where. To choose one of these options, point to the button with the mouse pointer and click, or press Alt plus the underlined character. The following list describes these buttons:

■ *Contents*. Displays a contents screen for the Help information in the Window

■ *Search*. Enables you to search for a topic by name

■ *Back*. Displays the last Help Window you viewed

■ *History*. Displays a list of each screen you have viewed. You can choose to return a screen by choosing that item in the list box.

■ *Where*. Tells you where an option is found within the program. If you are displaying help about the Edit command and choose <u>W</u>here, for example, the program informs you that the <u>E</u>dit menu is extended by pressing Alt-E or by pointing to the <u>E</u>dit option on the Menu bar and clicking.

Notice the underlined information in figure 2.11. Underlined words or phrases on a help screen tell you that you can get more information about that topic by clicking on the word or phrase. If you point to the phrase Use the Terminal Window and click, for example, a new help window appears (see fig. 2.12). This window contains more information about the Terminal window.

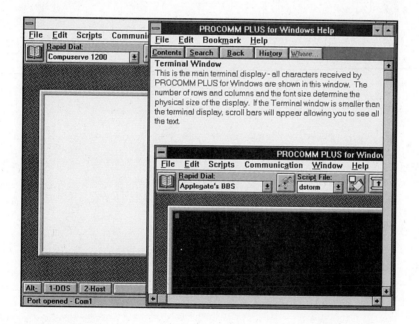

FIG. 2.12

The Terminal Window
Help Screen.

When a Help Window such as the Terminal window appears, you can often point to items on-screen and get additional information. If you click the <u>F</u>ile option on the Terminal window help screen illustration, for example, another Help window appears (see fig. 2.13). This Help window gives you more information about the <u>F</u>ile option. As you can see, you have an almost unlimited number of ways you can browse through the help system.

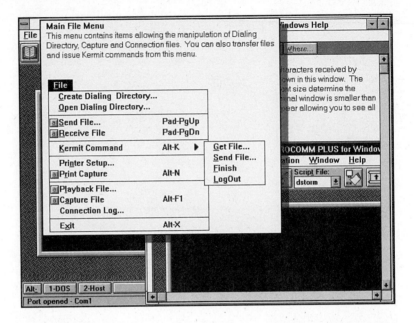

FIG. 2.13

The Main File Menu.

The Search For Help On option from the Help pull-down menu displays the Search screen shown in figure 2.14. This screen enables you to search for help by entering a word. In figure 2.14, for example, po has been typed into the entry area. As you enter a word, the menu locates the available topics in the help system. Thus, the words *Port, Port Connection*, and so on, currently are shown in the list box. When the word defining the topic of interest appears, you can press Enter or click the topic name. A help window similar to the one illustrated previously in figure 2.12 then appears.

When you choose the Keyboard option from the Help pull-down menu, a screen like figure 2.15 appears. This screen contains additional topics available on the subject of the keyboard. To select a topic, point to the underlined topic with the mouse pointer and click. A help window similar to the one shown previously in figure 2.12 then appears.

The Script Reference option from the Help pull-down menu displays a screen like figure 2.16. This screen contains additional topics available on subject of Script Reference. To select a topic, click the underlined topic. A help window similar to the one shown previously in figure 2.12 then appears.

When you choose the Search For Script Topic option from the Help pull-down menu, a search screen shown in figure 2.17 appears. This is similar to the search screen shown in figure 2.14. To search for a script command, begin entering the command name. When the command name appears, press Enter to display more information about the command.

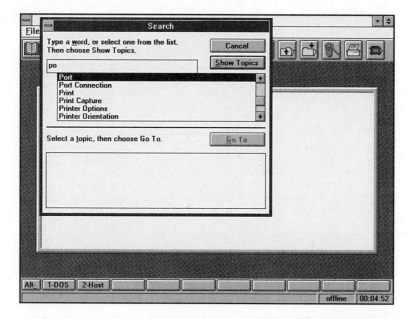

FIG. 2.14

The Search for Help
Window.

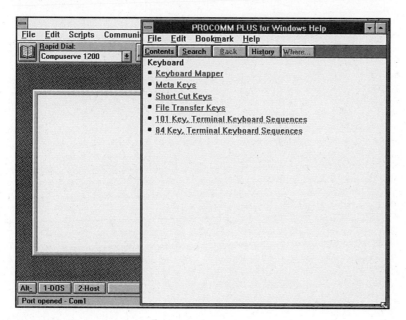

FIG. 2.15

The Keyboard Help
Window.

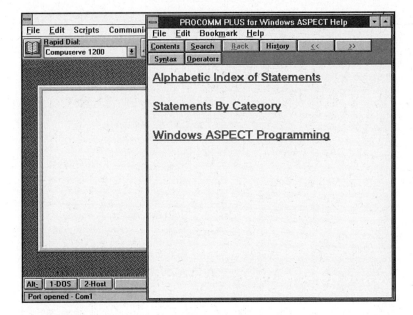

FIG. 2.16

The Script References
Help Window.

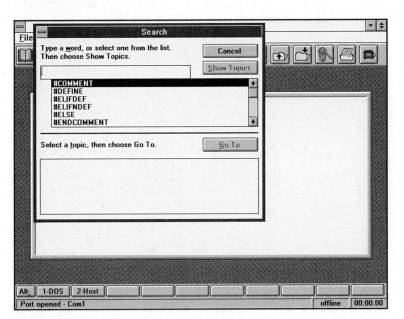

FIG. 2.17

The Search For Script
Topic Help Window.

The How To Use Help option from the Help pull-down menu displays a screen like figure 2.18. This screen contains an index to the Help system. As you can see, several topics on this screen are underlined. To display more information about an underlined topic, click that topic.

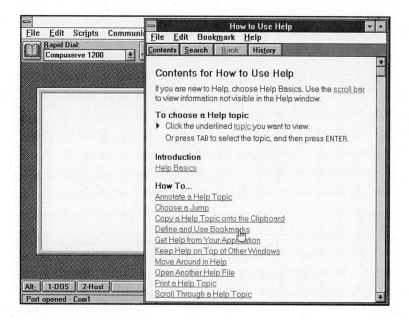

FIG. 2.18

The Contents of How To Use Help Window.

When you choose the About PROCOMM PLUS option from the Help pull-down menu, the opening screen containing the copyright information and your registration number appears.

Exiting PROCOMM PLUS for Windows

Before you turn off PROCOMM PLUS for Windows, you should sign off or disconnect from any active communications session. When the status line at the bottom of the screen indicates that PROCOMM PLUS for Windows is OFF-LINE, you can quit the program. From the Terminal Display, press Alt-X (Exit) or choose Exit from the File pull-down menu. PROCOMM PLUS for Windows exits and returns you to Microsoft Windows.

If you forget to disconnect from an active communications session before exiting PROCOMM PLUS for Windows, the program reminds you with the prompt You are still online. Continue with disconnect? and you must respond with Yes or No.

Summary

This chapter continued your introduction to PROCOMM PLUS for Windows, giving you a look at the Terminal window, the menu bar, the Action commands and the PROCOMM PLUS for Windows help system. You also learned how to exit PROCOMM PLUS for Windows.

Now that you have completed Part I of this book, move to Part II, "Getting Acquainted with PROCOMM PLUS for Windows."

Getting Acquainted with PROCOMM PLUS for Windows

Building Your Dialing Directory

As explained in Chapter 1, most PC communication is accomplished over telephone lines. Consequently, the first step toward communicating with another computer—whether next door, across town, or across the country—usually is to dial a telephone number. PROCOMM PLUS for Windows enables you to store commonly used phone numbers in its dialing directory. The dialing directory is your computer's automated telephone book—you can easily access numbers on-screen, letting the computer do the work.

Phone dialing, however, is not the only purpose of the Dialing Directory window. This window helps you do several other chores necessary for successful PC communications. Through the Dialing Directory window, you establish your computer's communications settings—such as transmission speed, parity, data bits, and so on.

In this chapter, you learn how to do the following:

- Use the Dialing Directory window to control the process of dialing and connecting to remote computers.

- Build dialing directories.

- Add, edit, and delete directory entries and dialing codes.

- Dial another computer by using a single dialing directory entry, a dialing queue, and the Manual Dial feature.

- Manage one or more dialing directory files more easily.

■ Print a dialing directory.

■ Switch between multiple dialing directories.

■ Sort dialing directory entries.

Appendix A contains instructions for converting a DOS PROCOMM PLUS dialing directory to a directory you can use with PROCOMM PLUS for Windows.

Examining the Dialing Directory Window

PROCOMM PLUS for Windows gives you four ways to display the Dialing Directory window from the Terminal Display screen:

■ Press Alt-D from the Terminal display screen.

■ Click the Directory Action icon.

■ Press Alt-W (Windows menu) and then press D.

■ Click the Window menu item and then click Directory.

You also can have the directory displayed at start-up via the Setup option.

To close the Dialing Directory window, select Exit from the File menu. As you can see in figure 3.1, the dialing directory contains no entries after you install PROCOMM PLUS for Windows.

Notice that the Dialing Directory window appears at the center of the Terminal Display screen. You can Maximize the window so that it covers the entire screen by pointing to the small up arrow at the upper right of the Dialing Directory window. Figure 3.2 and subsequent figures show the Dialing Directory in Maximized mode.

The Dialing Directory window contains three major parts. For convenience and clarity, this chapter calls these sections, from top to bottom, the Dialing Directory menu, the entry section, and the command section.

Using the Dialing Directory Menu

The Dialing Directory menu consists of four items: File, Edit, Dial, and Help. These menu items operate the same as other Windows menus. You can use the keyboard or the mouse to select or extend a menu item:

- With the keyboard, press and hold Alt as you press the underlined letter of the menu item.

- With the mouse, point to the menu item and click.

The following sections describe the options in the Dialing Directory menu and how to use them to manage your dialing directory.

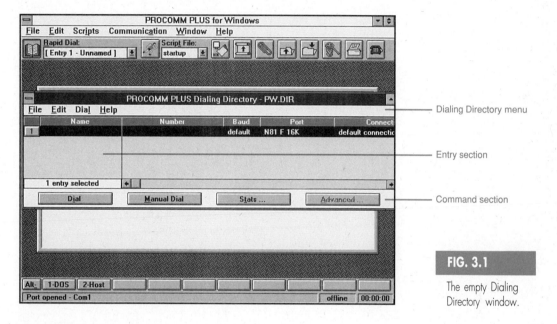

Dialing Directory menu

Entry section

Command section

FIG. 3.1

The empty Dialing Directory window.

Using the File Menu

You use the File menu in the Dialing Directory window to manage directory files. Figure 3.2 shows the File menu extended.

To choose an option from the File menu, press the underlined letter of the option name or click the option name. The Ctrl commands next to the Open and Print options tell you that you do not have to extend the File menu to access these options. To select Open, for example, you can press Ctrl-X without having to first extend the File menu.

The following list describes the options on the File menu:

- *Open (Ctrl-X).* Enables you to open a Dialing directory.

- *Save Directory.* Enables you to save the information in the directory. This should be done if you change information in the dialing directory.

■ *Save As*. Enables you to save the directory under a different name. When you choose this option, you are asked to enter the name for the directory.

■ *Print (Ctrl-L)*. Enables you to print the contents of a directory to a line printer.

■ *Exit*. Closes the Dialing Directory window and returns you to the Terminal Display.

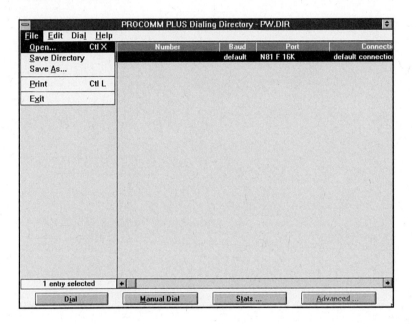

FIG. 3.2

The Dialing Directory File menu extended.

After you choose the Open option on the File menu, the Open Dialing Directory window appears (see fig. 3.3). You can see that the File Name list box contains three file names:

PCPLUS.DIR, a converted directory from the DOS version of PROCOMM PLUS. (See installation instructions for conversion information.)

PW.DIR, the default directory, which initially contains no entries.

TOPBBS.DIR, which contains the phone numbers of the top Bulletin Board Systems (BBS) around the country.

Your dialing directory may contain additional directory file names.

To choose a directory to open, double-click the directory name in the File Name box, or click the directory name once and then click OK.

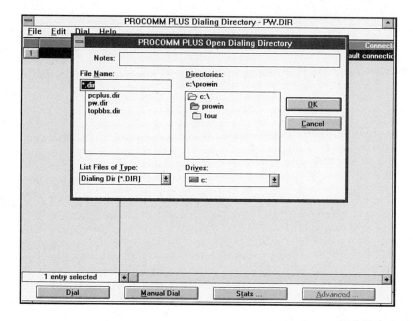

PROCOMM PLUS Dialing Directory - PW.DIR
File   Edit   Dial   Help

FIG. 3.3

The Open Dialing
Directory window.

To open the TOPBBS.DIR directory, for example, double-click
`topbbs.dir`. The Open window closes, and the Dialing Directory window
then contains directory entries as shown in figure 3.4.

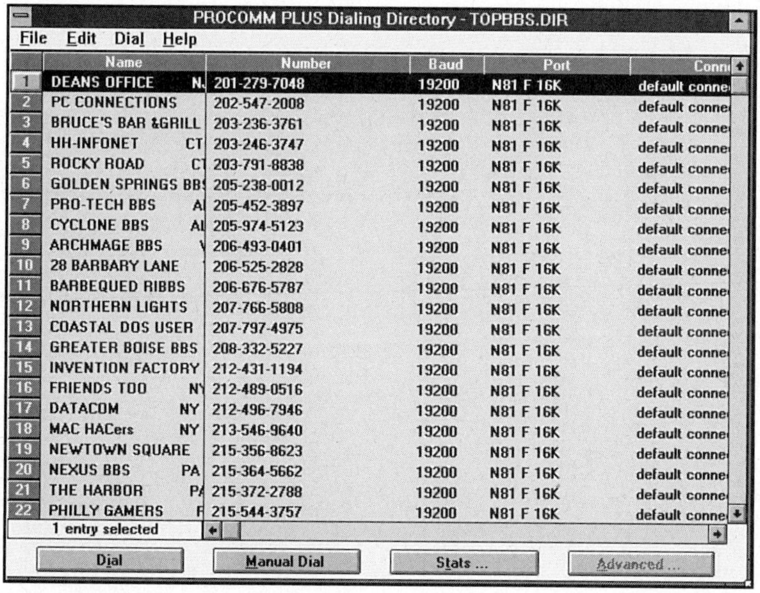

FIG. 3.4

Dialing Directory
showing TOPBBS.DIR
entries.

You can use the Directories box in the Open Dialing Directory window to look for PROCOMM PLUS DIR files in other disk directories (refer to fig. 3.3). To look at another disk directory, double-click the c:\ entry. A disk directory tree appears, and you can choose a directory from the tree. The DIR files from that directory then become listed in the File Name box.

Use the List Files of Type list box to open files without the standard DIR extension. The Drives list box enables you to look for files on another disk directory.

The Notes option associated with a Dialing Directory entry is an ASCII text file that contains information about that directory. For example, you can place a description of the entry, information about how to use the remote computer that the entry will call, or anything else of interest. The information in the Notes file does not interact with the called computer, but is simply a place to enter notes to yourself.

Editing Entries in the Dialing Directory

The main portion of the Dialing Directory window is the entry section. This part of the screen contains the list of phone numbers that you want PROCOMM PLUS for Windows to dial. The maximized Dialing Directory window normally displays only 22 entries at a time, but you can scroll this portion of the screen to display any of the other entries in the directory. Each directory can contain up to 250 entries.

When you first display the Dialing Directory window, PROCOMM PLUS for Windows highlights (displays in inverse video) the first entry, as shown in figure 3.4. You move the highlight to another entry in order to select it. Several dialing directory commands require that you first highlight (select) the entry to which the command should apply. To highlight an entry, click the entry number button at the far left of the screen, or press the up- and down-arrow keys to move the highlight to the entry you want and press the space bar.

This section first describes how to edit an existing entry, and then explains how to use the options on the Edit menu to undo changes, cut, copy and paste, add a new entry, insert, delete, sort, and find entries.

Editing Information in Existing Directory Entries

Each entry in the directory stores the following information:

Name   Capture File
Phone Number   Meta File

Baud (transmission speed)   KBD File
Port   XLATE File
Connection type   Notes File
Script file name   Password
Terminal type   User ID
Protocol   Miscellaneous Information
User Settings

For successful communication, some of these settings must match those of the computer at the other end of the telephone line. The following paragraphs describe the purpose of each entry and how to edit it.

Editing the Name Field

The Name field contains a name for the entry. A name can be up to 24 characters long. To edit an existing name entry, follow these steps:

1. Double-click the name to edit.

   The entry now is in Edit mode.

2. Enter and edit the information in the field.

3. Press Enter or press Tab or Shift-Tab to lock the changes into place.

Editing the Number Field

The Phone Number field contains the telephone numbers of the computers that you want to call. Each phone number must include any dialing codes needed to successfully call the number. In your office, for example, you might need to dial 9 to get an outside line. If so, you would specify 9 as a phone number prefix during the installation procedure. You also can specify this phone code in the Current Setup window, as described in Chapter 8, "Tailoring PROCOMM PLUS for Windows."

The section "Setting Dialing Directory Options," later in this chapter, covers a method of defining dialing codes. These codes enable you to summarize long access codes (such as with MCI or Sprint long distance) to one or two letter codes.

Editing the Baud Field

Like Name and Number, most directory fields can be edited by double-clicking the entry. Some fields, however, open list boxes or dialog boxes when you double-click the entry.

If you double-click a Baud entry, for example, a list box appears (see fig. 3.5). This box lists the available options for baud settings. If the setting you want is not shown in the list, click the up or down arrows on the scroll bar to move the list up and down until your option is visible. Click the option you want. You often will just use the default baud and will not have to change the value of this entry. The list box closes and the entry contains your new selection.

	PROCOMM PLUS Dialing Directory - TOPBBS.DIR				
File	Edit	Dial	Help		
	Name	Number	Baud	Port	Conne
1	DEANS OFFICE N.	201-279-7048	19200	N81 F 16K	default connec
2	PC CONNECTIONS	202-547-2008	9600	N81 F 16K	default connec
3	BRUCE'S BAR &GRILL	203-236-3761	19200	N81 F 16K	default connec
4	HH-INFONET CT	203-246-3747	38400 / 57600	N81 F 16K	default connec
5	ROCKY ROAD CT	203-791-8838	115200	N81 F 16K	default connec
6	GOLDEN SPRINGS BB	205-238-0012	19200	N81 F 16K	default connec
7	PRO-TECH BBS Al	205-452-3897	19200	N81 F 16K	default connec
8	CYCLONE BBS Al	205-974-5123	19200	N81 F 16K	default connec
9	ARCHMAGE BBS V	206-493-0401	19200	N81 F 16K	default connec
10	28 BARBARY LANE	206-525-2828	19200	N81 F 16K	default connec
11	BARBEQUED RIBBS	206-G7G 5707	19200	N81 F 16K	default connec
12	NORTHERN LIGHTS	207-766-5808	19200	N81 F 16K	default connec
13	COASTAL DOS USER	207-797-4975	19200	N81 F 16K	default connec
14	GREATER BOISE BBS	208-332-5227	19200	N81 F 16K	default connec
15	INVENTION FACTORY	212-431-1194	19200	N81 F 16K	default connec
16	FRIENDS TOO NY	212-489-0516	19200	N81 F 16K	default connec
17	DATACOM NY	212-496-7946	19200	N81 F 16K	default connec
18	MAC HACers NY	213-546-9640	19200	N81 F 16K	default connec
19	NEWTOWN SQUARE	215-356-8623	19200	N81 F 16K	default connec
20	NEXUS BBS PA	215-364-5662	19200	N81 F 16K	default connec
21	THE HARBOR PA	215-372-2788	19200	N81 F 16K	default connec
22	PHILLY GAMERS F	215-544-3757	19200	N81 F 16K	default connec

1 entry selected

Dial	Manual Dial	Stats ...	Advanced ...

FIG. 3.5

The Baud list box.

Editing the Port Field

When you click a Port field, the Port Settings dialog box appears (see fig. 3.6). This box contains several settings you can choose to describe the communication port. Detailed descriptions of these options are covered in Chapter 8, "Tailoring PROCOMM PLUS for Windows."

The Parity, Data, Stop, Duplex, and Com Buffer boxes contain radio button options. This means that, like a radio button, when you select one of the options, all others are deselected.

The check boxes in Flow Control and Drop DTR To Hangup are selection boxes. Each box can be selected (filled with an X) or not selected (empty) independently.

The Break Length, Start, and Stop options contain numbers. To change the number in one of these boxes, click the box once and then type the number you want. Press Tab to move to the next field.

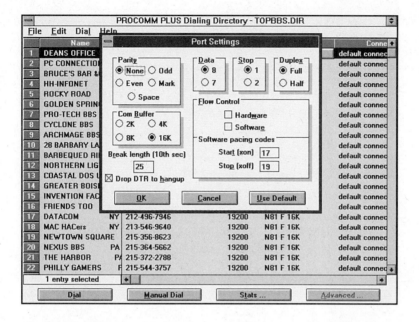

FIG. 3.6

The Port Settings
dialog box.

If you change information in the Port Settings dialog box and really mess
things up, don't worry. Just click the Use Default option. All items will be
returned to their default state.

To exit this dialog box and use your changes, select OK. To cancel all
changes you have made in this box and return to the entry, select
Cancel.

Editing the Connection Field

The Connection settings enable you to choose from a list of modems you
specified at installation or you added later. You choose selections from a
drop-down box that you access by pressing the space bar or by double-
clicking.

Editing the Script Field

In its most basic form, a *script* is a series of keystrokes recorded in a file
to be "played back" later. More complex scripts are programs that can
control the entire PC communications process. You can create a script
to sign on to an electronic mail system, check your mail, download and
save to disk any mail in your electronic mailbox, and then sign off. Chapter 7 shows you how to automate PROCOMM PLUS for Windows by using
scripts, and Chapter 11 gives you an overview of the powerful script
programming language, Windows ASPECT.

If you create a script and want PROCOMM PLUS for Windows to run it as soon as the program connects to a particular computer, type the name of the script in the Script field for that computer's dialing directory entry. This option enables you to choose a selection from a drop-down box that you access by pressing the space bar or by double-clicking.

Editing the Terminal Field

The Terminal entry field already contains the default Terminal type you selected during installation. This entry field contains a drop-down box from which you can choose a number of different terminal types. You choose the terminal type according to what computer you will be calling. If you are connecting to a mainframe computer through an on-line service or some other gateway or protocol converter, you need to know which type of terminal your PC should emulate. The VT102 emulation probably is the most popular. If you are connecting to another PC—particularly when you want to access a PC bulletin board—try ANSI-BBS first. This option enables you to choose a selection from a drop-down box that you access by pressing the space bar or by double-clicking.

Editing the Protocol Field

The Protocol entry field already contains the default file-transfer protocol you indicated when you installed the program. This setting is of interest only if you intend to send or receive files to or from the other computer. The Protocol field contains a drop-down box that enables you to choose from the list of available protocols. The most commonly used protocols for transferring files between PCs are YMODEM and ZMODEM. For more information on transferring files, refer to Chapter 5.

Editing the User Settings Field

The User Settings field enables you to choose a file that contains a group of setup options you use to customize PROCOMM PLUS for Windows. For more information on the Current Setup command, refer to Chapter 8, "Tailoring PROCOMM PLUS for Windows."

Editing the Capture File Field

The Capture File is used to capture information as it is displayed on the Terminal display. When you double-click a Capture File, the Capture File Options dialog box appears (see fig. 3.7). You use this dialog box to choose the options in this box. You can select one of three recording options and three control options.

When you click Capture File, a drop-down list appears, enabling you to specify an existing capture file to create a new one.

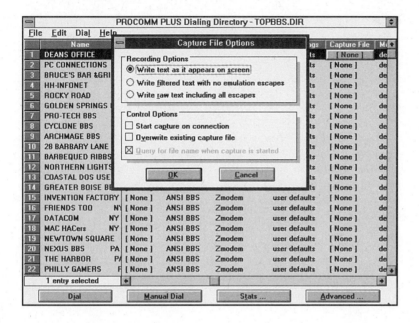

FIG. 3.7

The Capture File Options dialog box.

Editing the Meta File Field

The Meta File field is used to store names of Meta key files, which contain information to send text strings and to run external programs or ASPECT scripts. You usually leave this field set to the default. Meta keys are described in Chapter 7, "Automating PROCOMM PLUS for Windows with Meta Keys and Script Files."

Editing the KBD File Field

In the KBD File field, you can enter the name of a keyboard remapping file, which enables you to define keyboard mapping associated with a terminal emulation. Usually, you leave this option set to the default so that you can use PROCOMM PLUS for Windows' default key mappings. Keyboard mapping is discussed in Chapter 10, "Terminal Emulation."

Editing the XLATE File Field

The XLATE File is the name of a translate table used to modify incoming and/or outgoing characters.

Editing the Notes File Field

In the Notes field, you can enter a brief text description of the dialing directory entry, such as information about the remote system to be called. For more information on using this field, see the "Using a Notes File," later in this chapter.

Editing the Password Field

The Password entry field enables you to specify a password associated with the entry. The ASPECT language can use this password to automate logging on to a computer. Be aware, however, that this password is not encrypted and can be read easily. For this reason, you should be careful not to use a password in this field for a secure system. Usually, you should leave this field blank.

Editing the USER ID Field

The user ID field is provided to enable you to place a user name that might be needed when you log onto another system. Like the Password field described in the preceding section, the user ID can be used from an ASPECT script to automate your logon sequence.

Editing the Miscellaneous Field

The Miscellaneous field enables you to place in the dialing record any other information that may be needed in an ASPECT script or that can be used when searching for a record.

Using the Dialing Directory Edit Menu Options

Besides editing an entry directly on-screen, the Edit menu gives you several other ways of manipulating the directory entries. The extended Edit menu is shown in figure 3.8. The next few paragraphs describe how to use the options in this menu.

Using Undo

The Undo option on the Edit menu enables you to undo changes you have made in an entry line. If you change the name in an entry and then decide you made a mistake, for example, you can select the Undo option to return the entry to its previous value. Undo affects only the last change you made.

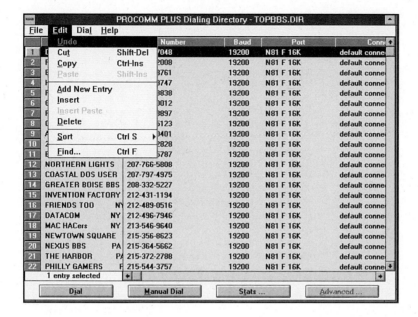

FIG. 3.8

The Edit menu
extended.

Cutting, Copying, and Pasting

The Cut and Copy options usually are used to move or copy entries from one area in the directory to another. You use the Cut (Shift-Del) option to remove an entry or an item in an entry (such as baud rate) from the directory list. The cut information is placed into the Windows Clipboard. You then can paste the information from the Clipboard to another area in the dialing directory.

To cut one or more entries, first select the entry or entries to cut. Selecting entries is used not only for the Cut option, but also for Copy and Dial.

You can use four different methods to select entries from the Dialing Directory:

1. Point to the entry number of the first entry to select with the mouse pointer, then click and drag the mouse down the list until all the entries you want are highlighted.

2. Hold down the Ctrl button, then point to an entry with the mouse pointer and click. Continue holding down the Ctrl button until you have clicked on (highlighted) all entries you want to select.

3. To highlight a series of entries using the keyboard, use the up- and down-arrow keys to place your cursor on the first entry to select. Then, while holding down the Shift key, press the up- or down-arrow key to highlight entries.

4. To use the keyboard to select (or deselect) individual entries, use the up- and down-arrow keys to point to the entry, then press the space bar. If the entry is not selected, this selects it. If the entry is selected, this deselects it.

Figure 3.9 shows a dialing directory with several entries selected (highlighted). To cut these entries, choose Cut from the Edit menu or press Shift-Del. The entries will vanish from the directory, and the information will be placed in the Windows Clipboard. After you have placed one or more entries in the Clipboard, you then can paste them elsewhere. You can place only one "cut" in the Clipboard at a time. When you perform another cut, previous information in the Clipboard is deleted.

A Copy (Ctrl-Ins) is performed the same as a Cut. The difference is that Cut removes the entries from the directory, and Copy does not.

	Name	Number	Baud	Port	Conn
1	DEANS OFFICE N.	A201-279-7048B	1200	N81 F 16K	default conne
2	PC CONNECTIONS	A202-547-2008B	1200	N81 F 16K	default conne
3	BRUCE'S BAR &GRILL	203-236-3761	19200	N81 F 16K	default conne
4	HH-INFONET CT	203-246-3747	19200	N81 F 16K	default conne
5	ROCKY ROAD C	203-791-8838	19200	N81 F 16K	default conne
6	GOLDEN SPRINGS BB	205-238-0012	19200	N81 F 16K	default conne
7	PRO-TECH BBS A	205-452-3897	19200	N81 F 16K	default conne
8	CYCLONE BBS A	205-974-5123	19200	N81 F 16K	default conne
9	ARCHMAGE BBS V	206-493-0401	19200	N81 F 16K	default conne
10	28 BARBARY LANE	206-525-2828	19200	N81 F 16K	default conne
11	BARBEQUED RIBBS	206-676-5787	19200	N81 F 16K	default conne
12	NORTHERN LIGHTS	207-766-5808	19200	N81 F 16K	default conne
13	COASTAL DOS USER	207-797-4975	19200	N81 F 16K	default conne
14	GREATER BOISE BBS	208-332-5227	19200	N81 F 16K	default conne
15	INVENTION FACTORY	212-431-1194	19200	N81 F 16K	default conne
16	FRIENDS TOO NY	212-489-0516	19200	N81 F 16K	default conne
17	DATACOM NY	212-496-7946	19200	N81 F 16K	default conne
18	MAC HACers NY	213-546-9640	19200	N81 F 16K	default conne
19	NEWTOWN SQUARE	215-356-8623	19200	N81 F 16K	default conne
20	NEXUS BBS PA	215-364-5662	19200	N81 F 16K	default conne
21	THE HARBOR PA	215-372-2788	19200	N81 F 16K	default conne
22	PHILLY GAMERS F	215-544-3757	19200	N81 F 16K	default conne

FIG. 3.9

Dialing Directory entries selected.

After you perform a cut or copy, the Paste option becomes available (no longer grayed in the menu). To paste the entries that have been cut or marked for copy, first highlight the entries where you want the pasted information to be placed. Next, choose Paste from the Edit menu, or press Shift-Ins. This paste overwrites any information that may be in the highlighted entries before the paste. To paste and insert, see the discussion of Insert Paste later in this section.

> **CAUTION:** When you paste information from the Clipboard, remember that you are covering up (pasting over) the information in the highlighted area—thus replacing entries. Use this option only if you want to replace information. Use Insert Paste to add information without deleting anything.

The Copy command is useful in copying an individual entry field from one entry to one or more other entries. The default TOPBBS directory, for example, has all baud fields set to default. To change the baud fields to 19200 baud, use the following procedure:

1. Change an entry to 19200.

2. Place your cursor on the entry field to copy. Click to highlight the field, or press the space bar once.

3. Select the Copy option from the Edit menu, or press Ctrl-Ins. This places a copy of the field contents into the Windows Clipboard.

4. Highlight the entries where you want to copy the information.

5. Choose the Paste option from the Edit menu, or press Shift-Ins. The information from the Windows Clipboard is pasted into the highlighted entries.

The Insert Paste option is like pasting, except that it moves down existing entries in the list to allow for those you have cut or marked for copy. To perform an Insert Paste, select an entry and then choose Insert Paste. The information currently in the Windows Clipboard is inserted below the highlighted entry. Insert Paste should be used only when moving entire entries.

Adding and Inserting Information

When you choose the Add New Entry option from the Edit menu, the cursor is placed at the bottom of the directory list at a blank entry. You then can enter information into the entry fields (Name, Number, and so on) that you need to specify in order to define the information for a connection to another computer. To enter information using the keyboard, follow these steps:

1. Press Tab to move the cursor to the field where you want to enter information. The entry field is highlighted.

2. Press the space bar to place the field into entry mode, and then enter the information you want.

3. Repeat these steps to enter the next entry field information.

4. After you finish entering information, press Enter to dial the number.

To use the mouse to enter information, point to the entry field with the mouse pointer and double-click. Enter the information in the field and press Tab or double-click the next entry field. Enter information in this way until you have defined all information needed for this entry.

The Insert Entry option is like the Add New Entry option, except that the new entry is placed at the highlighted location, pushing other entries down the list.

Deleting Dialing Entries

You use the Delete option to delete one or more dialing entries. To delete a single entry, highlight the entry and choose Delete from the Edit menu. To delete several entries, highlight (select) entries as described earlier in "Cutting, Copying, and Pasting," and then choose Delete from the Edit menu.

Sorting the Dialing Directory

When you choose the Sort (Ctrl-S) option, a submenu like the one shown in figure 3.10 appears. When you select a Sort option, the entries in the directory list are displayed in the sorted order chosen.

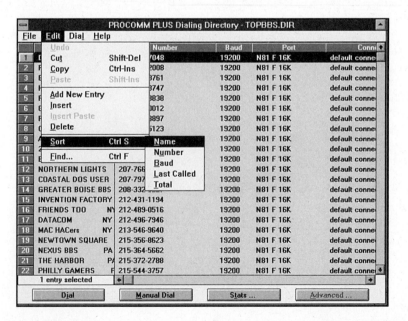

FIG. 3.10

The Sort submenu.

You use the Find (Ctrl-F) option to search the entries for a particular string of characters. The Find entry box is shown in figure 3.11. To find an entry containing the word *shareware*, for example, enter that word in the Find What box and press Enter. A search begins and if a match is found, the entry containing the search word is highlighted.

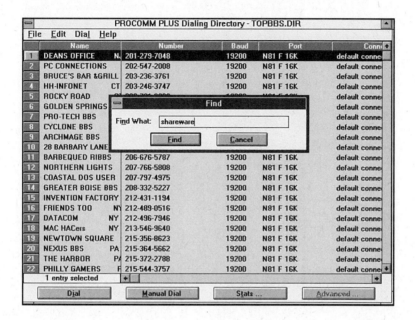

FIG. 3.11

Entering information in the Find box.

More often than not, you don't know the entry number (the number to the far left of the entry name). PROCOMM PLUS for Windows provides a quick and easy way to search for the entry by name, using the following steps:

1. From the Dialing Directory window, press Ctrl-F to select Find.

2. At the Find What prompt, type the search criterion—any portion of the entry's name. You can use upper- or lowercase letters.

3. Press Enter.

4. PROCOMM PLUS for Windows searches the directory for the first match—an entry in which the name contains the characters specified in the search criterion.

5. When searching, the program starts at the currently selected entry and searches entries numerically toward the end of the directory.

If PROCOMM PLUS for Windows does not find a match by the time it reaches the end of the directory, the program starts at entry number 1 and searches down toward the current entry. If no match is found, PROCOMM PLUS for Windows displays the message TEXT NOT FOUND and then removes the Find window from the screen.

Suppose that you want to call the SHAREWARE SOUTH bulletin board, which is listed in your dialing directory. From the Dialing Directory window, follow these steps:

1. Press Ctrl-F to select Find.

2. PROCOMM PLUS for Windows displays the Find box with the Find What prompt.

3. Type *shareware* and press Enter (refer back to fig. 3.11).

4. PROCOMM PLUS for Windows finds the first entry that contains the letters you typed (see fig. 3.12).

   Notice that the program finds the first entry that contains SHAREWARE, even though you typed *shareware* (all lowercase).

Using the Dial Menu

The ultimate purpose of each entry in a PROCOMM PLUS for Windows dialing directory is to set up your computer for communication with another computer and then to instruct your modem to dial that computer's telephone number. In this section on using the Dial menu, you learn the following:

- How to dial a number by using a single directory entry

- How to manually dial a number

- How to create a *dialing queue*—a series of entries for PROCOMM PLUS for Windows to use in sequence

When you use one of the methods described in this chapter to initiate a call, PROCOMM PLUS for Windows sets the transmission speed, line settings (parity, data bits, and stop bits), duplex setting, error-checking protocol, terminal emulation, and other settings according to the values stored in the entry's fields. The program then instructs the modem to dial the telephone number stored in the entry's Number field.

The Dial menu, as shown in figure 3.12, contains options for making calls. To initiate a dial from the directory, first highlight the entry you want to dial, and then select Dial from the Dial menu, choose the Dial button from the bottom of the Dialing Directory window, or double-click and entry.

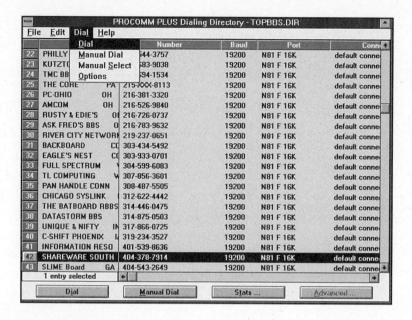

FIG. 3.12

The Dial menu
extended.

Using Manual Dial

If you want to call a number that is not in your dialing directory, you can perform a manual call by choosing Manual Dial from the Dial menu. After you choose this option, the Manual Dial window appears (see fig. 3.13). Enter in this window the number you want to call and press Enter to initiate the call.

Using Manual Select

The Manual Select option enables you to specify more than one number to dial. Figure 3.14 shows the entry box for Dial Selections. When you enter several numbers, in which each number refers to an entry in the directory, you are placing these numbers in a dialing queue. Figure 3.15 shows a dialing queue with four entries.

Another way to place several numbers in the dialing queue is to select entries as described in the earlier section "Cutting, Copying, and Pasting," and then choose Dial from the Dial menu. The next section describes how to use the Dialing Queue.

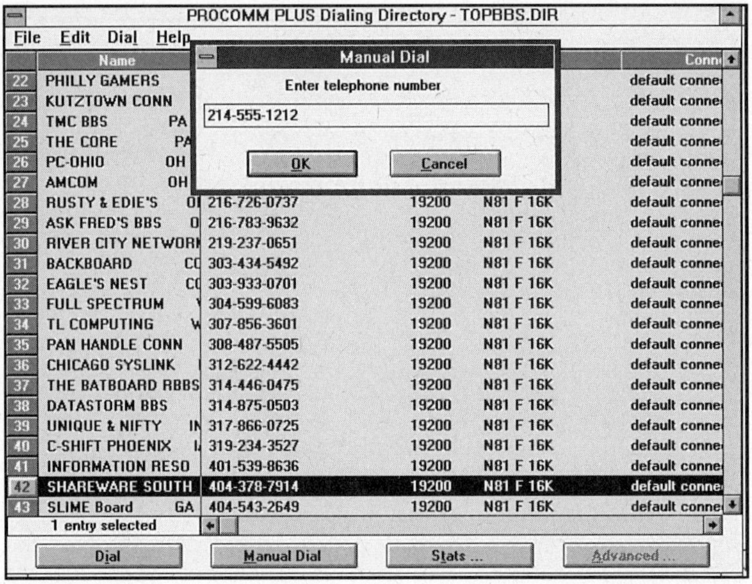

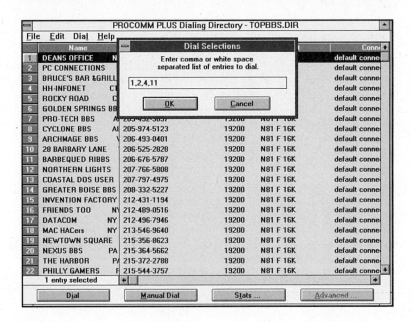

FIG. 3.13

Dialing a number
manually.

FIG. 3.14

Entering multiple dial
selections.

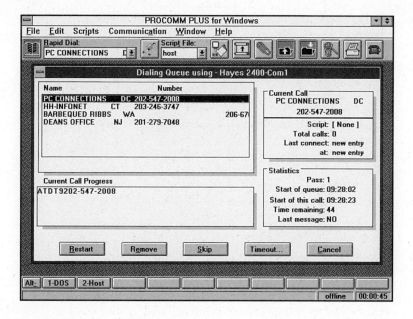

FIG. 3.15

The Dialing Queue.

Using a Dialing Queue

PC communications is a popular hobby. As you become familiar with PROCOMM PLUS for Windows and start using it, you may find that many bulletin boards are next to impossible to connect with because of their popularity.

Trying to connect to one of these busy bulletin boards can be very frustrating. Even when using PROCOMM PLUS for Windows' automatic redial capability, you may wait for hours before connecting to a single bulletin board. Or, if you try to call several boards in succession, you are tied to the keyboard, searching for a number that doesn't ring busy.

PROCOMM PLUS for Windows' *dialing queue* can free you from this tedium by enabling you to create a list of entries you want PROCOMM PLUS for Windows to dial in succession. If the first entry is busy or doesn't answer, PROCOMM PLUS for Windows tries the second. If the second is busy or doesn't answer, the program tries the third, and so on.

PROCOMM PLUS for Windows gives you two ways to create a dialing queue:

■ You can use the Manual Select option on the Dial menu. You must know the entry numbers of the entries you want PROCOMM PLUS for Windows to use. From the Dialing Directory window, select Dial. PROCOMM PLUS for Windows displays a dialog box similar to the one shown earlier in figure 3.12. In the entry box, type a list of numbers, separating the entry numbers with spaces or commas. Press Enter after you type the last entry number.

■ You can highlight entries by using the method described in the earlier section "Cutting, Copying, and Pasting," and then select Dial from the Dial menu, or click the Dial button.

After you create your list of entries, PROCOMM PLUS for Windows then displays the Dialing Queue window and begins to dial the first entry's telephone number (refer to fig. 3.15). PROCOMM PLUS for Windows adjusts the transmission speed and line settings and instructs the modem to begin dialing the number. After the program successfully connects to the other computer, the Terminal mode screen appears.

If the number dialed is busy or doesn't answer within the time specified in the Statistics box in the Dialing Queue window, PROCOMM PLUS for Windows automatically hangs up. The program then displays the message PAUSING... in the Statistics box and begins a countdown counter. When the number of seconds specified for Pause Between Calls in the program setup reaches zero, PROCOMM PLUS for Windows moves to the next entry listed in the queue and begins to dial that entry's telephone number.

If a connection is successful, PROCOMM PLUS for Windows removes that entry from the queue. When you finish communicating with the computer, you can easily restart the dialing queue. Open the Dialing directory by clicking the Directory Action icon. The Dialing Directory will be displayed with the previous connection deselected and all remaining entries in the dialing queue still selected. Select Dial from the Dial menu to re-enter the Dialing queue. PROCOMM PLUS for Windows starts again with the first number in the dialing queue. This process continues until a connection is made or until you choose Cancel or press Esc.

A busy signal or no answer causes PROCOMM PLUS for Windows to pause the dialing for the specified period of time and then move to the next entry in the queue. When a connection is made, the program returns to the Terminal display. When your communication with the remote computer is finished, you can restart the dialing queue.

The Dialing Queue window contains several information boxes and button options.

■ The top left box contains a list of the entries in the queue. The highlighted entry in the box is the one currently being dialed.

■ The Current Call box gives the name, number, and script name (if any) being used.

■ Total Calls tells you how many times you've connected to this entry.

- Last Connect tells you the date of the last connection and the time of that call.

- The Current Call Progress box shows the telephone number as it is being dialed. If there are other messages from the modem, such as CONNECT 2400, they also will be reported in this box.

- The Statistics box tells you how many attempts have been made at dialing this number.

- Start of Queue time is the time you first entered the queue.

- Start of This Call is the time the computer began dialing.

- Time Remaining tells you how many seconds the queue allows for the connection to be made before going to the next entry.

- Last Message reports any messages to you about the calling sequence.

PROCOMM PLUS for Windows takes advantage of another handy call-progress reporting feature available on many modems. Your modem may be able to detect when someone or something other than a modem answers your call. If so, your modem refrains from sending a carrier signal. Instead, the modem hangs up and sends a signal to PROCOMM PLUS for Windows that a voice was encountered. PROCOMM PLUS for Windows then displays the message VOICE in the Last Call field of the Dialing box.

After your modem successfully connects to the modem of the computer with which you want to communicate, your modem sends a message to PROCOMM PLUS for Windows. Older Hayes-compatible modems send only the message CONNECT, regardless of the speed at which they connect. Most newer Hayes-compatible modems, however, are more specific. After these modems connect at 300 bps, they send the message CONNECT. If they connect at 1200 bps, the message is CONNECT 1200. Connecting at 2400 bps results in the message CONNECT 2400.

PROCOMM PLUS for Windows displays the message in the Last Message field of the Statistics box. In addition to this visual connect signal, PROCOMM PLUS for Windows also sounds several beeps on your computer to alert you. This feature enables you to leave the room while you wait for your modem to connect to the remote computer. Just don't forget to listen for the beep.

For any of these modem-generated call-progress monitoring features to work properly, your modem must send progress reports, or *result codes*, that PROCOMM PLUS for Windows can understand. Most Hayes-compatible modems can send messages back to PROCOMM PLUS for

Windows as words, such as CONNECT, NO DIAL TONE, or BUSY. These messages are what PROCOMM PLUS for Windows expects. These modems also can send numeric result codes, such as 1, 6, or 7.

If the call-progress features don't seem to work on your system, check your modem setup, as described in Chapter 8, "Tailoring PROCOMM PLUS for Windows."

The following option buttons at the bottom of the Dialing Queue box enable you to control the dialing process.

- ■ *Restart*. Causes the queue to return to the top entry and begin dialing that entry again.

- ■ *Remove*. Removes the highlighted entry from the queue.

- ■ *Skip*. Causes the dialing queue to skip the highlighted entry and move to the next entry.

- ■ *Timeout*. Enables you to reset the timeout length for the queue. When you choose this option, you are prompted to enter a time amount in seconds. The default time is 45 seconds.

- ■ *Cancel*. Enables you to cancel the dialing queue and return to the Dialing Directory window.

Setting Dialing Directory Options

The Options selection on the Dial menu enables you to choose directory settings and dialing codes for the Dialing Directory. After you choose Options, the Dialing Directory Options window appears (see fig. 3.16).

Changing the Directory Settings

At times, you may want to increase or decrease the time the program waits for a connection from the default 45 seconds. You can change this setting with the Wait For Connection setting in the Dialing Directory Options box. To change this setting, select the Wait box and enter a new number in seconds. You also can change the Make Attempts and Wait Between Attempts settings.

The Drop DTR between calls option is set by default to On (the selection box contains an X.) DTR stands for Data Terminal Ready and is one of the circuits on your serial line (see Chapter 8 for more information on DTR). After you drop (cut off) the DTR signal with most modems, this causes the telephone to hang up, which is normally what you want to happen between calls. Certain PBX systems and other specialized equipment (including most pocket modems), however, do not function properly if DTR is dropped and require that you unselect this option.

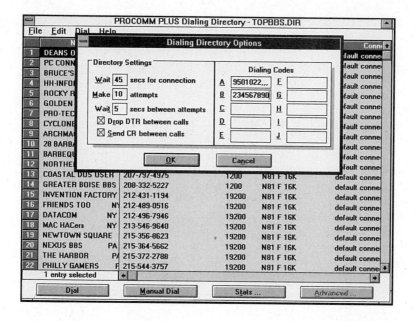

FIG. 3.16

The Dialing Directory
Options window.

The Send CR Between Calls option is by default set to On. Modems usually expect a CR (Carriage Return) to be sent between calls. Some PBX
systems, however, may respond to the CR by entering a menu system. In
this case, you would deselect the Send CR option.

Using Dialing Codes

As you build your PROCOMM PLUS for Windows dialing directory, you
may find that you are entering a certain string of numbers over and over
again.

Some long-distance carriers require that you dial a special sequence of
numbers before dialing the regular telephone number. You can include
that access sequence with every directory entry's telephone number.
With PROCOMM PLUS for Windows' special shorthand dialing codes,
you can incorporate a string of numbers by reference without typing the
entire string. You can establish up to 10 dialing codes in each Dialing
Directory Option dialog box.

This box contains 10 entry boxes, each labeled with a letter from A
through J. Each entry can hold one dialing code. To enter information in
a box, select the box and then type the number you want to establish as
a dialing code. Each code can contain up to 24 characters, which can be
any displayable character but must be recognizable by your modem in
order to be of any value. (Consult your modem's manual for available

dialing codes.) Most typically, you type numbers, hyphens, and paren-theses in dialing codes. The numbers instruct your modem to dial the telephone, and the hyphens and parentheses make the phone number easier for you to read but have no effect on the dialing.

Sometimes you may want the modem to pause during the dialing proce-dure. If you want the dialing code to dial a long-distance telephone car-rier, for example, you may need the modem to pause after dialing the long-distance access code.

If you have a Hayes-compatible modem, you can add commas to the dialing code to tell the modem to pause. (If you don't have a Hayes-compatible modem, check your modem manual for a pause code.) Each comma usually pauses the modem for two seconds. You add three com-mas if you want your modem to pause the dialing for six seconds—be-tween the dialing of a phone number and a five-digit extension, for example.

Figure 3.16 shows numbers assigned to dialing codes A and B. When you use this code in a dialing directory telephone number, the modem dials the telephone number 9501022, pauses for six seconds (the three com-mas), and then continues with the dial.

Many office telephone systems require that you dial 9 or some other digit to get an outside line. You then must wait for a second dial tone before you continue to dial. For this reason, most Hayes-compatible modems recognize the letter W as a command to pause and wait for a second dial tone before continuing to dial the telephone number. (Check your modem documentation to make sure that your modem recognizes this command.) Suppose that you create the following dialing code:

    9W111-2222,,,33333

When used in a directory entry telephone number, this code tells the modem to take the following action:

9	Dial 9.
W	Wait for a second dial tone.
111-2222	Dial the rest of the number as soon as the modem detects the dial tone.
,,,	Pause for six seconds.
33333	Dial the five-digit extension.

After you add the dialing codes you want, choose OK to close the win-dow and return to the Dialing Directory window. To modify a dialing code, just return to the Dialing Directory Options window to redisplay the Dialing Codes box.

You can use a dialing code in any entry in the dialing directory, or when performing a manual dial. You typically use dialing codes in many entries, or you probably would not have gone to the trouble of creating the codes in the first place.

Suppose that you decide to create a directory entry to call FRIENDS TOO, which requires the long-distance access codes shown in dialing codes A and B in figure 3.16. Rather than retype the access code, you can use dialing code A in your directory entry. From the Dialing Directory Options window, double-click the telephone number for this entry, or press the space bar, to add dialing information to the entry. The A code dials the initial access code. You then dial the phone number, and you enter another code, represented by B. In the entry, therefore, you would type the following code:

A212-431-1194B

When you use this entry to dial FRIENDS TOO, PROCOMM PLUS for Windows first sends the number stored in dialing code A to the modem, then sends the telephone number, and finally sends the second access code.

> **T I P**
>
> If you have the call-waiting feature on your telephone, a communications session may be interrupted when an incoming call causes a beep on the line. In many phone exchanges, you can cancel this call-waiting feature for the current call by entering the code *1170* before dialing the number. If this feature is available in your area, you may want to assign the prefix 1170 to one of your dialing codes or add it to the dial prefix (for example, ATDT1170). Then you can use that dialing code with all entries so that your communications calls are not interrupted or terminated unexpectedly by incoming calls.

Getting Help

To enter the Help Window, select Help from the Dialing Directory menu. This brings up the Help window as described in Chapter 2.

Monitoring Progress

The result of setting up your Dialing Directory is the ability to make calls. When you dial the phone through the program, the modem takes over and does the work. When a dial is in progress, the Rapid Dial window is displayed on-screen. Some modems have a built-in speaker so that you can monitor each call audibly. If your modem has a speaker, and if everything goes as planned, you hear the dial tone, the number being dialed, and then the ringing. When the modem on the other end answers the line, you hear a high-pitched tone, called the carrier tone, then a hissing sound, and finally nothing. The hissing sound is the sound made by the modems as they "shake hands" and begin communicating. Your modem turns off the speaker because the sounds generated by the modems as they send data back and forth would have no meaning to you.

As you may expect, however, things don't always go exactly as expected. If you do not hear a dial tone, you hear a busy signal, or you hear a voice answering the call, you can terminate the call quickly by pressing Esc or by choosing Cancel. PROCOMM PLUS for Windows sends an instruction to the modem to stop dialing and hang up the phone.

Figure 3.17 shows a call in progress in the Rapid Dial window display.

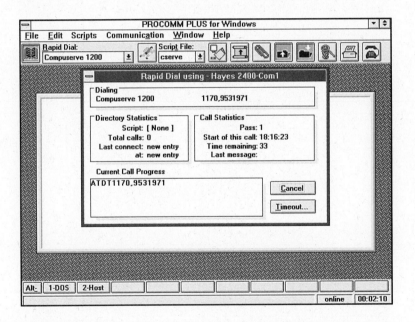

FIG. 3.17

The Rapid Dial window.

Many modems also take care of several monitoring chores for you and send status reports to your computer. These modems can do the following:

■ Recognize and inform PROCOMM PLUS for Windows of the absence of a dial tone and the presence of a busy signal

- Inform PROCOMM PLUS for Windows when a connection to another modem is successful

- Give the transmission speed at which the modems are communicating

PROCOMM PLUS for Windows monitors these status reports and informs you of the call's progress in the Rapid Dial window's Dialing box, which appears immediately after you specify the entry to dial.

The Dialing box helps you visually monitor the status of the call. In this window, PROCOMM PLUS for Windows lists the name and telephone number of the system your modem is dialing and keeps you informed about several other parameters.

If your modem detects no dial tone after it begins to dial the telephone, the modem stops dialing and sends the code NO DIAL TONE. PROCOMM PLUS for Windows in turn displays this message in the Last Message field of the Call Statistics box. Similarly, the call may proceed to the point at which the modem detects a busy signal, in which case the modem sends the message BUSY.

When the modem sends either of these messages, it also stops dialing the number and hangs up the phone line (often referred to in modem documentation as going *on hook*). PROCOMM PLUS for Windows then counts down the pause time in the Time Remaining field.

NOTE In some special circumstances, you don't want your modem to wait for a dial tone before trying to complete the call. This dialing method is often called *blind dialing*. If your phone system generates a dial tone that your modem cannot detect, you need the modem to dial blindly. For instructions on how to modify the initialization command to enable you to use blind dialing, refer to "Setting Modem Options" in Chapter 8 and to your modem's manual.

While pausing the dialing procedure, PROCOMM PLUS for Windows counts the number of seconds that have elapsed since the last attempted call, displaying the count in the Time Remaining field. PROCOMM PLUS for Windows waits the number of seconds indicated in the Wait Between Attempts field in the Dialing Directory Options window (refer to figure 3.16), increments the Pass field by 1, and sends an instruction to the modem to dial the number again. The Wait Between Attempts setting is necessary to let the modem get ready to redial.

The length of time PROCOMM PLUS for Windows pauses between calls is set by default to five seconds. You can increase or decrease this time by adjusting the amount in the Dialing Directory Options dialog box or in the Current Setup window (refer to Chapter 8 for more details).

Figure 3.18, for example, shows PROCOMM PLUS for Windows beginning pass number 2 because the time for connection had expired on the first try. (Note that the Last Message field displays the message NO CARRIER.) The Wait Between Attempts field is set at 5, so the modem waits five seconds, as indicated in the Time Remaining field, and dials again. PROCOMM PLUS for Windows continues this procedure until it successfully connects to the other modem or until you stop the dialing by pressing Esc or by choosing Cancel, or until the value in the Make Attempts field is reached.

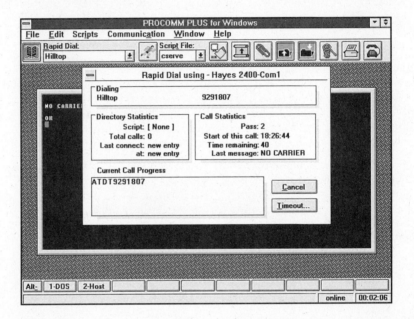

Even if your modem does not recognize a busy signal, PROCOMM PLUS for Windows has another feature that can help you. After sending the instruction to the modem to dial the telephone number, PROCOMM PLUS for Windows waits the length of time set in the Wait for Connection field of the Dialing Directory Options box (refer to fig. 3.16). If the modem does not complete a connection in that length of time—because the line is busy or because the other end does not answer—PROCOMM PLUS for Windows automatically hangs up and pauses the dialing. After the time span indicated in the Wait Between Attempts field, PROCOMM PLUS for Windows tries the call again. The program repeatedly attempts to connect to the modem on the other end of the line until the connection is successful, until the value in the Make Attempts field is exceeded, or until you cancel the call—whichever comes first.

Managing Your Dialing Directory

A PROCOMM PLUS for Windows dialing directory is a small database—a collection of information arranged in fields (columns) and records (rows). Each dialing directory entry is a record in the database, and each column (Name, Number, Baud, and so on) is a field.

Up to this point, this chapter has concentrated on how to create, edit, delete, and use directory entries—one at a time, or in groups (as a dialing queue). Like any database program, PROCOMM PLUS for Windows enables you to perform certain functions on the entire database—the entire dialing directory. The remainder of the chapter describes how to use these directory-wide functions to manage your dialing directory database.

Printing the Directory

Although finding and displaying an entry in the dialing directory is easy, having a hard copy to look at sometimes is more convenient. You can print a copy of the directory on paper, using your printer. You also can print to File—send a copy of the directory to a disk file so that you can print it later.

To print your dialing directory, press Ctrl-L (Print Directory) from the Dialing Directory window or select Print from the File menu. The Print dialog box appears (see fig. 3.19). To print the entire directory to the printer, press Enter or click OK.

The directory will be suitable for printing on 80-column paper and will include the information you normally see on-screen under the column headings Name, Number, Baud, and Terminal.

The Print dialog box has the following options:

- *Print to File*. Sends output to a file instead of the printer. You then can print this information using the Windows or DOS print options or merge this information into a word processing file.

- *Selection*. Prints only those entries highlighted (selected) as described in the section "Cutting, Copying, and Pasting" earlier in this chapter.

- *Pages*. Enables you to specify the beginning and ending page to print. If your directory is shorter than one page in length, this option is gray—not available.

■ *Print Quality*. Contains a drop-down box from which you select the desired print quality. The following options are available:

High
Medium
Low
Draft

These options mean different things for different printers. Check your printer documentation or do a sample print with each option to see how each option affects the printout on your printer.

■ *Copies*. Enables you to choose the number of copies to print.

■ *Collate Copies*. Enables you to cause the pages to be printed from last to first, making them come out in the right order on some printers.

■ *Setup*. Enables you to change the printer from the default printer chosen at installation.

■ *Cancel*. Exits the Print dialog box without printing.

Before printing, make sure that your printer is turned on, properly connected, and loaded with paper; then press Enter or select OK to begin printing.

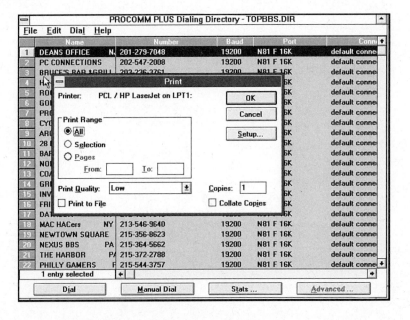

FIG. 3.19

The Print dialog box.

Building and Using Other Dialing Directories

Although PROCOMM PLUS for Windows limits you to 250 entries per dialing directory, the program does not limit the number of directories you can build. In effect, then, you can manage as many directory entries as you want. PROCOMM PLUS for Windows, however, can work with only one directory file at a time.

You may need to create a new directory to hold all your entries. Suppose that you live in the Washington, D.C. metropolitan area, which encompasses parts of two states and the District of Columbia. You easily could compile a list of area bulletin boards that is longer than 200 entries.

One convenient way to divide the entries into groups is by state or district. You can create one directory named VA.DIR for Virginia bulletin boards, another named MD.DIR for Maryland, and a third named WASHDC.DIR for Washington, D.C. You may want to give the directory for bulletin boards in your home state the name PW.DIR so that PROCOMM PLUS for Windows uses it by default every time you start the program.

To create a new dialing directory, select the Create Dialing Directory option from the Terminal Display window File menu. Enter information in the entries. Select the Save As option from the Dialing Directory menu. You are prompted to enter a file name, as shown in figure 3.20. The new directory then will be saved under that name.

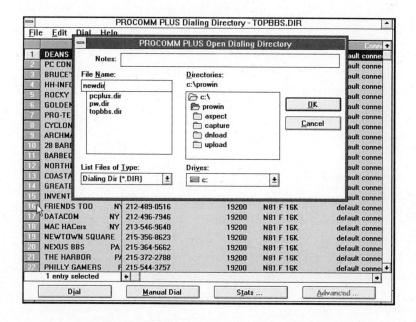

FIG. 3.20

The Open Dialing Directory dialog box.

> **NOTE** A valid DOS file name can contain one to eight characters, including the letters A through Z, the numbers 0 through 9, and the following symbols:
>
> !@#$%^&()-_}'~{
>
> Spaces are not permitted.

You can create an unlimited number of dialing directories in this manner, each with the capacity to hold up to 250 entries.

DATASTORM TECHNOLOGIES, INC., distributes a supplemental directory with PROCOMM PLUS for Windows named TOPBBS.DIR. This directory contains the top bulletin boards around the country.

To use this directory, press Ctrl-X or choose Open from the File menu in the Dialing Directory window, then choose TOPBBS from the list of files displayed.

Using a Notes File

The Notes field in the Dialing Directory window enables you to access a text file in which you can enter information associated with the highlighted dialing entry. When you double-click the Notes field, a drop list appears. One of the entries in the list is Create. After you choose Create, the Create New Notes File dialog box appears (see fig. 3.21). In this box, enter the name of the notes file in the File Name field to be used for this entry and press Enter. The Notepad editor appears, in which you can enter information about the directory entry. A sample note file is shown in figure 3.22.

If you already have defined the name of a note file for the entry, the editor displays the contents of that file. You can enter new information,or change the current information in the file. For more information on this editor, see Chapter 6, "Using the Windows Notepad Editor."

Using the Dialing Directory Command Buttons

At the bottom of the Dialing Directory window are four button options— Dial, Manual Dial, Stats, and Advanced.

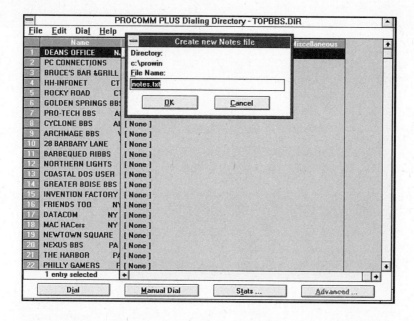

FIG. 3.21

The Notes File dialog box.

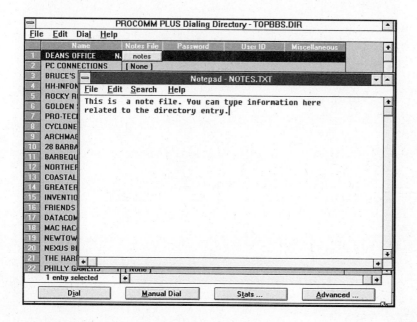

FIG. 3.22

A sample Notes file.

You can use the Dial button to initiate a Dial for the highlighted directory entry. This is similar to choosing Dial from the Dial menu.

You can use the Manual Dial option to dial a phone number that is not in the current dialing directory. This option is similar to the Manual Dial option in the Dial menu.

The Stats option displays a screen that gives you information about the currently selected entry. A sample Stats screen is shown in figure 3.23.

You cannot use the Advanced option on most entry fields. This option usually is grayed, which means it cannot be chosen. Advanced shows in normal colors on some entry fields, such as the Capture File dialog box, meaning that you can choose it. Choosing Advanced is the same as double-clicking the entry or pressing the space bar.

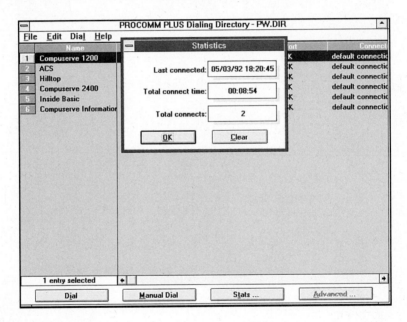

FIG. 3.23

The Stats Window.

Summary

This chapter described how to use the Dialing Directory window to control dialing and connecting to remote computers. You learned how to build dialing directories and how to add, edit, and delete directory entries and dialing codes. You learned how to dial another computer by using a single dialing directory entry, a dialing queue, and the Manual Dial feature. You also learned how to print a dialing directory, how to choose among multiple dialing directories, and how to sort dialing directory entries.

A Session with PROCOMM PLUS for Windows

This chapter focuses on the primary commands you use during a PROCOMM PLUS for Windows communications session. You first learn the steps you must take in order to connect with another computer—as a *calling computer* or an *answering computer*. You then learn how to use PROCOMM PLUS for Windows to converse with a person or another computer program. Next, the chapter discusses how to manage the information that flows to and from the other computer, including several ways to capture some or all of this information for later viewing. Finally, you learn how to disconnect from the other computer.

Most of the commands explained in this chapter are commands that you execute from the Terminal Display window (see fig. 4.1). These commands were introduced in Chapter 2. Although you can invoke many of the features through the PROCOMM PLUS for Windows menu bar, this chapter emphasizes the quicker shortcut keyboard commands and Action commands.

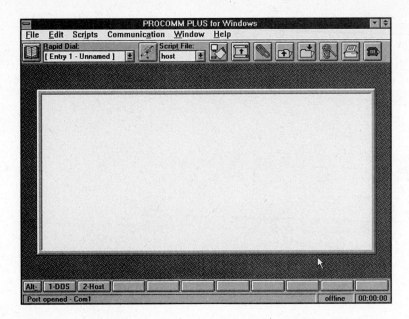

Connecting

The first phase of each PROCOMM PLUS for Windows communications
session is the connection phase, usually done through modems and telephone lines. One modem is set to Auto Answer mode so that it answers
the telephone line after the phone rings. The other modem is instructed
to dial the appropriate number and listen for a modem's answer. Although this scenario is typical, it is not the only way to use PROCOMM
PLUS for Windows to connect PCs for communication. This chapter discusses the normal connection method of using modems to place and
answer telephone calls. It also describes how to connect computers using a telephone line already in use for voice communication as well as
how to connect PCs to communicate without a modem.

Initiating a Call

When you use PROCOMM PLUS for Windows to connect to another computer, your computer usually does the calling. After the computer you
intend to call places its modem in Auto Answer mode (Alt-Y), you instruct your modem to place the call. (See the following section, "Receiving a Call," for more information.) Host systems, such as bulletin boards
and on-line services, always set their modems to Auto Answer. If you

want to connect to a PC that is not a host system, you may have to place a voice call to the other PC's operator to request that the system modem be set to Answer mode.

To call another computer, click the Directory Action icon or press Alt-F, D to display the Dialing Directory screen (see fig. 4.2). If the current default dialing directory is not the one you want, select Open from the File menu to select the desired directory. Select a directory entry and press Enter to dial the number associated with that entry. (See Chapter 3 for more information on dialing directory entries.) PROCOMM PLUS for Windows instructs the modem to dial the appropriate telephone number. When the modem on the other end answers, the modems begin to communicate.

	Name	Number	Baud	Port	Conn
1	DEANS OFFICE N.	201-279-7048	1200	N81 F 16K	default conne
2	PC CONNECTIONS	202-547-2008	1200	N81 F 16K	default conne
3	BRUCE'S BAR &GRILL	203-236-3761	1200	N81 F 16K	default conne
4	HH-INFONET CT	203-246-3747	1200	N81 F 16K	default conne
5	ROCKY ROAD C	203-791-8838	1200	N81 F 16K	default conne
6	GOLDEN SPRINGS BB	205-238-0012	1200	N81 F 16K	default conne
7	PRO-TECH BBS A	205-452-3897	1200	N81 F 16K	default conne
8	CYCLONE BBS A	205-974-5123	1200	N81 F 16K	default conne
9	ARCHMAGE BBS	206-493-0401	1200	N81 F 16K	default conne
10	28 BARBARY LANE	206-525-2828	1200	N81 F 16K	default conne
11	BARBEQUED RIBBS	206-676-5787	1200	N81 F 16K	default conne
12	NORTHERN LIGHTS	207-766-5808	1200	N81 F 16K	default conne
13	COASTAL DOS USER	207-797-4975	1200	N81 F 16K	default conne
14	GREATER BOISE BBS	208-332-5227	1200	N81 F 16K	default conne
15	INVENTION FACTORY	212-431-1194	19200	N81 F 16K	default conne
16	FRIENDS TOO NY	212-489-0516	19200	N81 F 16K	default conne
17	DATACOM NY	212-496-7946	19200	N81 F 16K	default conne
18	MAC HACers NY	213-546-9640	19200	N81 F 16K	default conne
19	NEWTOWN SQUARE	215-356-8623	19200	N81 F 16K	default conne
20	NEXUS BBS PA	215-364-5662	19200	N81 F 16K	default conne
21	THE HARBOR P	215-372-2788	19200	N81 F 16K	default conne
22	PHILLY GAMERS F	215-544-3757	19200	N81 F 16K	default conne

FIG. 4.2

The Dialing Directory window.

Remember that the communications parameters—transmission speed and line settings (parity, data bits, and stop bits)—must be the same for the calling computer and the answering computer. Otherwise, transmitted data is unintelligible when received. If your modem connects with the modem of the other computer but gibberish (a stream of characters that doesn't mean anything) comes across your screen, check the communications parameters.

Even if the communications parameters are set properly, you may still receive unintelligible information. This problem can occur because of "noisy" telephone lines that cause a loss of synchronization between the sending and receiving modems. If you suspect poor line quality, terminate the communications session and try again. Sometimes the transmission quality of telephone lines improves significantly when you use the lines during off-peak hours, when fewer people are using the lines to place calls.

Receiving a Call

As explained in Chapter 1, one of the four types of PC communication is PC-to-PC communication. Because you may at some time be on the receiving end of a PC-to-PC connection, you need to know how to set up PROCOMM PLUS for Windows and your modem for receiving.

When someone calls you on the telephone for the purpose of voice communication, you don't do anything until you hear the phone ring. You then pick up the phone and say "Hello" to begin the conversation; you have learned that you are supposed to answer the ringing telephone. Similarly, when another computer's modem is calling, you want your modem to answer the phone and connect with the calling modem. Before this sequence of events can happen, you must set your modem to Auto Answer mode so that it can pick up a ringing line and "say hello" with its carrier signal to start the "conversation."

If you can dedicate a telephone line for your computer's use, you can set up PROCOMM PLUS for Windows so that each time you use the program it places your modem in Auto Answer mode. (Chapter 8 explains how to set the initialization command to send the Auto Answer command to the modem.) Then, when the phone rings, your modem always answers with the carrier signal.

If the calling modem and your modem are compatible, the two modems "shake hands" and begin a communications session. When shaking hands, the two connected modems send signals until the signals are synchronized for successful communication. You then can use PROCOMM PLUS for Windows to send and receive information to and from the remote computer.

If you sometimes use your modem's telephone line for voice communication, you cannot always leave the modem in Auto Answer mode. With your modem in Auto Answer mode, anyone who calls—a modem or a person—gets the modem's carrier signal. You therefore should place your computer's modem in Auto Answer mode only when you expect another modem to call your number. You usually need the operator of the calling computer to inform you so that you can place your computer's modem in Auto Answer mode. Thus, two telephone calls are often required: one voice call, followed by a modem call. See "Connecting During a Voice Call" later in this chapter for more information.

Although you can use the initialization command to set up your modem so that it is always in Auto Answer mode, PROCOMM PLUS for Windows provides two ways to place your modem temporarily in Auto Answer mode. You can invoke the Host mode (described in Chapter 9, "Using Host Mode") or use the Alt-Y (Auto Answer) command.

When you enter Host mode, remote users can use their computers to call your computer, using the PROCOMM PLUS for Windows Host mode as a small computer bulletin board. PROCOMM PLUS for Windows Host mode provides file uploading and downloading as well as a rudimentary electronic mail system (see Chapter 9 for more information).

If you expect a call from another computer but you don't want to use Host mode, place your modem in Auto Answer mode by pressing Alt-Y (Auto Answer), or select the Auto Answer On option from the Communication menu. PROCOMM PLUS for Windows sends the appropriate command to your modem and displays the command on-screen. The following Auto Answer command is used by PROCOMM PLUS for Windows for Hayes-compatible modems:

    +++ATS0=1

The three plus signs (+++) instruct the modem to go into Command mode in order to read the command that follows. The command ATS0=1 then instructs the modem to go into Answer mode and answer the telephone after the first ring. You can tell that your modem has received and executed the command when the modem displays OK on-screen beneath the Auto Answer command (see fig. 4.3). Refer to Chapter 8 to learn how to instruct the modem to wait for more than one ring before answering the line.

To turn off Auto Answer mode, choose the Auto Answer Off (Alt-Q) option from the Communication menu, or type the following command, starting at the left margin of the Terminal Display window, and press Enter:

    ATS0=0

The modem displays the response OK on-screen, indicating that it understands the command and has turned off Auto Answer. The modem no longer answers the phone. Alternatively, you can use the Alt-J command to reinitialize the modem, with the same effect.

When two modems are communicating, one is in Originate mode and the other is in Answer mode. These modes refer to the way in which the modems send and receive data at the same time. (Auto Answer mode refers to the capability of the modem to answer an incoming telephone call automatically. When a modem is in Auto Answer mode, the modem is ready to answer a call but is not yet in Answer mode.) After the modem answers a call from another modem, the answering modem communicates with the calling modem in Answer mode, and the calling modem communicates in Originate mode. The next section explains how to switch your modem to Answer mode without first using Auto Answer mode.

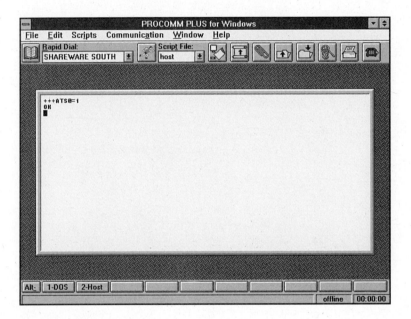

FIG. 4.3

Instructing the modem to answer the next call on the first ring.

Connecting during a Voice Call

Occasionally, you may be in the middle of a telephone conversation with an associate when you decide that you want to connect your computers. You may, for example, want to send your associate a copy of the spreadsheet file you were just discussing. Ideally, each of you has a second, separate telephone line, and you can use the procedures described in "Initiating a Call" and "Receiving a Call" earlier in this chapter to make the connection.

Most users, however, have their modem connected to the same line as their telephone. You can, of course, hang up and use the modems to place and answer the call again. Making the connection without hanging up, however, is more convenient (and more economical if the call is a toll call).

To connect computers over the same phone line as your voice call (with Hayes-compatible modems), both operators start PROCOMM PLUS for Windows and display the Terminal Display window. The line settings (transmission speed, parity, and so on) must be the same at both ends. (To check settings, click the Setup Action icon to view your current system setup, or choose Setup from the Windows menu.) Decide which computer is to act as the originate computer; the other will act as the answer computer (it doesn't matter which one you choose). The operator of the answer computer then types the following command, starting at the left side of the Terminal Display window, and presses Enter:

ATA

This command places the modem in Answer mode and causes the modem to begin transmitting the carrier signal.

In the meantime, the operator of the originate computer should type the following command, starting at the left side of the Terminal Display window, and then press Enter:

ATD

This command places the modem in Originate mode. The modem then "listens" for a carrier signal from an Answer mode modem.

Using a Direct Connection

When two computers are close enough to be connected by a cable (within 50 feet), you don't have to use a modem. Instead, connect the computers by a null modem cable. (Refer to Appendix B for information on building a null modem cable.) Null modem cables or adapters are readily available from most computer and office supply stores and generally cost less than five dollars. Connect the cable to the serial port you designated when you installed PROCOMM PLUS for Windows. If you need to use a different serial port, refer to Chapter 8.

With a null modem cable, the communications connection is established as soon as you start PROCOMM PLUS for Windows. You can tell that the two computers are connected properly if you can type in the Terminal Display window of one computer and see the results in the other. If you see nothing or you see characters different from what you are typing, make sure that all the communications parameters are properly set.

Conversing

After you are connected to another computer, you can send and receive information in several ways. At some point in nearly every communications session, you send information by typing it at the keyboard, and you receive information on your screen that is typed by the operator or program at the other end. In essence, you are carrying on the computer equivalent of a conversation.

When you use PROCOMM PLUS for Windows to "converse" in this manner, you need to understand three PROCOMM PLUS for Windows features: Duplex mode, carriage return/line feed, and Chat mode. The discussions that follow describe these features.

Understanding Duplex

Through continual usage, *duplex* has acquired a meaning that is a bit different from its original definition. When used most accurately, duplex refers to the capability of a modem to send and receive information at the same time. A modem that can send and receive data simultaneously is referred to as a *full-duplex* modem. *Half-duplex* modems, on the other hand, operate like a one-lane bridge; they cannot send and receive data at the same time. The modem continually switches from Send mode to Receive mode and vice versa in order to communicate with another modem—much as a CB radio does.

When your computer is connected to a host computer (such as an on-line service or bulletin board) through a full-duplex modem, the computer at the other end typically echoes back to your screen any character you type on your keyboard. This echo provides a crude but effective way to confirm that the other computer received the character you typed. Consequently, when the host computer echoes characters to your screen, PROCOMM PLUS for Windows refers to the mode as Full-duplex mode.

Sometimes the computer on the other end does not echo characters to your screen. PROCOMM PLUS for Windows refers to this mode as Half-duplex mode. When your computer is connected to another computer using Half-duplex mode, PROCOMM PLUS for Windows must provide the echo in order for you to see what you are typing.

To find out what duplex mode you currently are using, click the Setup Action icon or select Setup from the Window menu; then choose Port Settings from the Current Setup menu. As figure 4.4 shows, the current setting for this computer is Full duplex, as the Full radio button is filled in the Duplex box. This Port Setting box also contains the settings for other communications parameters, such as Parity, Data bits, Stop bits, and so on. When you connect two computers, all the settings in this box should be the same for both computers. Figure 4.4 shows the most common settings for these parameters.

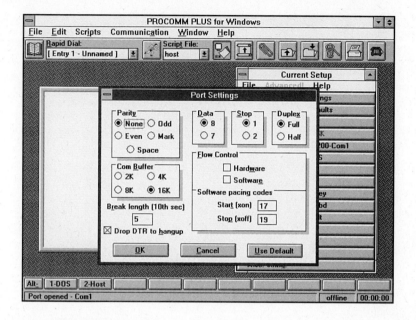

FIG. 4.4

The Port Settings window.

The default settings for these parameters are established during installation. For more detailed information on the meaning of these parameters and how to change them, refer to Chapter 8, "Tailoring PROCOMM PLUS for Windows." The default settings are overridden by different settings in a dialing directory entry (see Chapter 3).

Just as other communications settings must match at both ends of the PC communications line, the duplex mode of your computer's modem must match the mode of the computer on the other end. Otherwise, one of two problems occurs:

- *Double Characters.* This condition occurs when the computer on the other end echoes the characters you send back to your screen, but you have set PROCOMM PLUS for Windows to Half-duplex mode. You may type *Hello*, for example, but see HHeelllloo on-screen. To solve this problem, switch PROCOMM PLUS for Windows to Full-duplex mode.

- *No Characters.* This condition occurs when the other computer does not echo characters you transmit back to your screen, and you have set PROCOMM PLUS for Windows to Full-duplex mode. You may type *Hello*, for example, but not see any characters on-screen. Again, switch your modem to Half-duplex mode to correct the problem.

Toggling Carriage Return/Line Feed

You probably are familiar with the way an electric typewriter works. After you type a line of text, you press the Return key to advance the paper one line and move the typing element to the beginning of the new line. Although you press a single key, the results are two distinct operations. Advancing the paper by one line often is referred to as a *line feed*, and repositioning the typing element to the beginning of the line is called a *carriage return* (a term carried over from manual typewriters).

For you to be able to read more than one line of text on your computer's screen, something analogous to the typewriter's line feed and carriage return must occur at the end of each line. Indeed, the same terms describe these operations in the context of your computer's screen.

If PROCOMM PLUS for Windows receives characters in a continuous stream—with no carriage returns from you or the remote computer—the program automatically inserts line feeds and carriage returns. If you type a line of characters at the Terminal Display window or receive a line of characters transmitted by another computer, PROCOMM PLUS for Windows displays the characters one by one across the screen, starting in the uppermost line of the Terminal Display window. When PROCOMM PLUS for Windows receives the 80th character or space, filling up the line, the program moves the cursor down one line (a line feed) and returns the cursor to the left side of the screen (a carriage return) before placing the next character or space on-screen. If you are using 132-column mode, the cursor moves down one line (line feed) after the 132nd character in a line.

Figure 4.5 shows the Terminal Display window after a remote user typed a message without pressing Enter. The word *wonderful* is split over two lines, but PROCOMM PLUS for Windows does insert a line feed and carriage return.

The other user usually presses Enter after typing each line of text, as if using an electric typewriter. Although this method prevents words from being broken, it raises another issue: when PROCOMM PLUS for Windows receives a carriage-return character (from the keyboard or from a remote computer), should the program translate the character as a carriage return only (CR) or as a carriage return and line feed (CR/LF)?

Your answer to this question depends on how the computer on the other end is operating. The discussions that follow can help you decide whether PROCOMM PLUS for Windows should add a line feed and how to add that line feed.

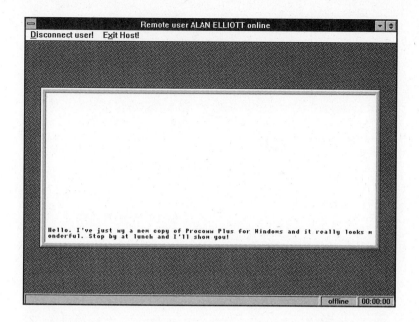

```
─        Remote user ALAN ELLIOTT online          ▼ ◆
Disconnect user!   Exit Host!
```

Hello. I've just my a new copy of Procomm Plus for Windows and it really looks w
onderful. Stop by at lunch and I'll show you!

```
                                        offline  00:00:00
```

FIG. 4.5

Sending a message
without pressing Enter.

Most host computers, such as on-line services and bulletin boards (including PROCOMM PLUS for Windows Host mode), add a line feed to each carriage return. If PROCOMM PLUS for Windows also adds a line feed, everything on-screen will be double-spaced. For this reason, when you install PROCOMM PLUS for Windows, the Incoming CR to CR/LF option in the Terminal Settings window (from the Current Setup menu) is turned off (the block does not contain an X), as shown in figure 4.6. To check this setting on your computer, click the Setup Action icon or choose Setup from the Window menu. Then select the Terminal Settings option from the Current Setup menu. This causes the Terminal Settings window to be displayed. The Incoming CR to CR/LF option is in the right-hand box labeled Other Options. This settings box contains a number of other options, discussed later in detail in Chapter 8, "Tailoring PROCOMM PLUS for Windows."

If you plan to connect to a PC that is not operating as a bulletin board, select Incoming CR to CR/LF (the box should contain an X). Because you probably connect to on-line services and bulletin boards more often than to a PC, however, you may want to leave the default Incoming CR to CR/LF option deselected (no X in box).

You can easily tell whether you need to change the setting. If all lines of characters you type or receive from another computer overwrite the preceding lines, you need to select Incoming CR to CR/LF (X in box). If you notice that all text on-screen is double-spaced, deselect Incoming CR to CR/LF.

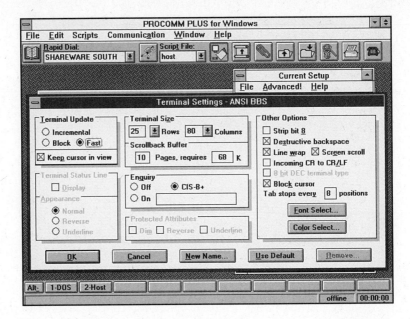

When you use the PROCOMM PLUS for Windows Chat mode, it doesn't matter what you choose for the CR Translation setting. PROCOMM PLUS for Windows displays incoming information and text you type without extra lines and without overwriting lines.

Using Chat Mode

When you carry on a two-way conversation with the operator of another computer, you may have difficulty separating what you are typing from what the person at the other end is typing. If you both type at the same time, the letters all run together on your screen, resulting in unintelligible alphabet soup. To help you solve this problem, PROCOMM PLUS for Windows provides Chat mode.

To start Chat mode, press Alt-O (Chat Mode) from the Terminal Display window or select Chat from the Window menu. PROCOMM PLUS for Windows opens a small Chat Window (see fig. 4.7). The major part of the screen contains incoming messages (remote), and the Chat screen contains messages you enter to send to the other computer (local).

The remote section of the Chat mode screen contains information received from the computer at the other end of the line (the remote computer). You see only the remote user's side of the conversation in this portion of the screen.

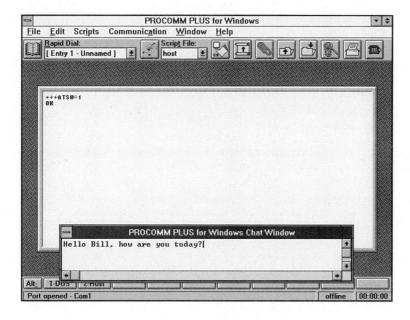

FIG. 4.7

The Chat window.

If incoming text scrolls off the screen, you can use the scrollback feature to review it again. (See "Displaying the Scrollback Buffer" later in this chapter for an explanation of how to review information after it scrolls off the screen.)

Your side of the conversation appears in the local Chat Window section of the Chat mode screen.

In addition to enabling you to distinguish easily between your input and the remote user's input, the Chat mode has two other advantages:

■ You do not have to worry about whether PROCOMM PLUS for Windows is in Full-duplex or Half-duplex mode. The CR Translation setting doesn't matter either. PROCOMM PLUS for Windows always displays exactly what you type.

■ In Chat mode, PROCOMM PLUS for Windows does not send a line of text until you press Enter. Before you press Enter, you can read and edit the line before the remote user sees it. This feature eliminates the embarrassment of having an audience for your typing errors. You can review each line before sending it to the remote computer. You also can change this option in the Current Setup window so that PROCOMM PLUS for Windows sends each character as you type it on-screen (see Chapter 8).

To edit a line in the local section of the Chat mode screen (before you press Enter), use the Backspace key to erase characters. Each time you press Backspace, PROCOMM PLUS for Windows erases the character to the left of the cursor. After you erase the incorrect characters, type the correct information and press Enter to send the line. You also can use the cursor keys to edit a line before pressing Enter.

To exit Chat mode, press Alt-O or Alt-F4, or click the window command box and choose Close.

You may at first be tempted to use Chat mode all the time, but you quickly will find that few of the commands available from the Terminal Display window have any effect from the Chat mode screen. Only Alt-P (Scrollback/Pause), the Print and Capture commands, and the meta keys (Alt-0 to Alt-9) operate in Chat mode. You probably will want to use the Chat mode screen when you are conversing directly with someone who is typing messages to you on the other end of the line. Several on-line services, for example, offer the capability of chatting with other users who are connected to the system. These on-line service features are sometimes called CB simulators, referring to the types of communications popular on CB radios.

Managing Incoming Information

When you use PROCOMM PLUS for Windows and PC communications to gather information, you need to be aware of three basic properties of the Terminal Display window:

- Depending on your hardware and terminal emulation, you have a limited number of lines and columns to deal with. The most common mode is 24 lines by 80 columns. If you are using an EGA or VGA monitor, you can set up your window to hold as many as 132 columns. When in 132-column mode, you can scroll through the 132 columns by clicking the horizontal scroll bar or by pressing Alt-right arrow and Alt-left arrow (see Chapter 8).

- Information scrolls by quickly. If you are using a modem that operates at a transmission speed of 1200 bps, information can flow in at a rate of approximately 1,000 six-character words per minute. Only speed readers can read that fast. A 2400-bps modem can receive twice as many words per minute. At 9600 bps, the information really flies by. Obviously, at this rate you can never read all the information as it scrolls across your screen.

- Information is not saved automatically. PROCOMM PLUS for Windows does not automatically save information that another computer sends to your Terminal Display window. After the text flows off the top of your screen, the information is gone unless you take some affirmative step to save it. (You usually can capture some scrolled information by using the scrollback feature, as discussed later.)

These three properties are true of any PC communications program. PROCOMM PLUS for Windows, however, provides several features that enable you to overcome these limitations easily. The discussions that follow explain how best to use these features to manage incoming information. You can capture and save the information by using the scrollback feature, described in "Displaying the Scrollback Buffer" later in this chapter.

Pausing the Screen

Most bulletin boards and on-line services pause at the end of each screenful of information; you must press Enter or some other key to indicate that you are ready to see the next screen. You may encounter a lengthy bulletin or file, however, that scrolls up your screen so fast that you cannot read it; and the system displaying the file does not automatically pause after each screenful of information. In this situation, you can use the PROCOMM PLUS for Windows Screen Pause feature to stop the scrolling long enough to read the pertinent information.

In the Terminal Display window, the best way to stop the scrolling of information temporarily is to press Ctrl-S. Many remote systems, including most on-line services and bulletin boards, support a flow-control method known as XON/XOFF. These systems stop transmitting information when they receive an ASCII (American Standard Code for Information Interchange) character referred to as XOFF. This character is the same one that you generate by pressing Ctrl-S on your keyboard. The remote system continues its transmission after receiving another ASCII character known as XON. The XON character is the same character generated when you press Ctrl-Q.

Displaying the Scrollback Buffer

The preceding section explains how to pause the screen to read information that is being displayed on-screen. You can use PROCOMM PLUS for Windows' scrollback feature, however, to review data even after it scrolls off the screen.

PROCOMM PLUS for Windows continually saves the information that scrolls across your screen. The data is saved to a portion of memory called the *scrollback buffer*. This buffer is a temporary storage area that is emptied every time you exit PROCOMM PLUS for Windows and return to Windows. The scrollback buffer usually can hold more than 19 pages. You can set the buffer size in the Current Setup window's Terminal Advanced Options (see Chapter 8). When the scrollback buffer fills, PROCOMM PLUS for Windows discards the oldest data first to make room for the new data on-screen.

To see the data stored in the scrollback buffer, press Alt-P or choose Scrollback/Pause from the Edit menu. PROCOMM PLUS for Windows displays the last few lines (the number of lines on the screen depends on your font size, video mode, and window size) that scrolled off the Terminal Display (or Chat mode) window. Figure 4.8 shows an example of information stored in the scrollback buffer.

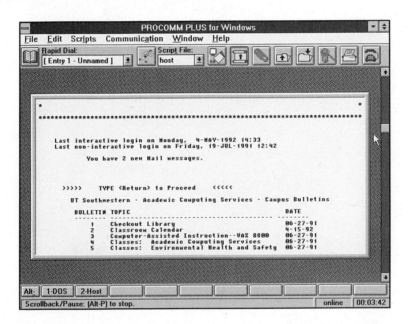

FIG. 4.8

The Scrollback Buffer screen.

Notice the scroll bar at the right side of the Scrollback Buffer screen. This bar enables you to scroll through the information in the buffer. Obviously, you cannot view all the lines stored in the scrollback buffer at once. Because many lines may contain only a few characters, the scrollback buffer often holds many screens that scrolled off the top of the Terminal Display screen. To scroll through the buffer, point to the up- or down-arrow key on the scroll bar and click. The buffer moves in the direction of the arrow. You also can point to the locator button on the scroll bar, click, and hold while dragging the button up or down. This causes the buffer to scroll up or down.

If you prefer to use keyboard commands, pressing Page Up and Page Down as well as the up- and down-arrow keys enables you to scroll through the buffer. To exit the scrollback buffer, press Alt-P or select Scrollback/Pause from the Edit menu.

Saving and Printing the Scrollback Buffer

Occasionally you may want to keep a copy of the scrollback buffer. The buffer may contain a list of telephone numbers you want to keep, for example. To save the scrollback buffer to disk, select Scrollback Buffer To from the Edit menu. PROCOMM PLUS for Windows displays a submenu with four options (see fig. 4.9).

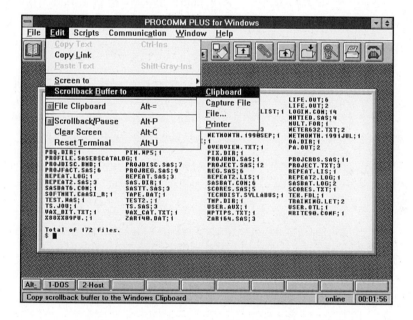

FIG. 4.9

The Scrollback Buffer To submenu.

These options enable you to choose where to send the contents of the scrollback buffer. If you want to send a copy to the Windows Clipboard so that you can paste it elsewhere in the program or into another Windows program (such as your word processing program), select the Clipboard option from the submenu.

Similarly, you can choose to save the contents of the buffer to the currently defined capture file, to a file (you will be prompted to enter the name of the file), or to the printer.

If you want to save or print only a portion of the buffer, highlight the portion of the buffer you want to save. With the selected text highlighted, select the Scrollback Buffer To option from the Edit menu; then choose the destination from the submenu.

If you decide to save the buffer to a file, the result is a plain ASCII file that you can read and edit with any editor or word processing program that can handle ASCII files. You also can choose to play back the file (display it on-screen) directly from the Terminal Display window by choosing the Playback option from the File menu. This option causes the contents of the file to be displayed and recaptured into the scrollback buffer.

To return to the Terminal Display window (or to the Chat mode window if you were in Chat mode when you pressed Alt-P), press Alt-P again, or select Scrollback/Pause from the Edit menu.

Using the File Clipboard To Capture File Names

At times, you may be logged onto a remote computer in order to download files. As you search for files that you want to download, you write down their names so that you can remember them when you want to download them. PROCOMM PLUS for Windows has a better way. The File Clipboard command enables you to capture file names from the screen and place them in a list that you can reference later.

To store file names in the File Clipboard while you are logged onto a remote computer, first press Alt-=, select File Clipboard from the Edit menu, or click the Clipboard Action icon (the paper clip). You are placed in the scrollback buffer as described previously. You then can use the scroll bar or cursor commands to locate the place in the buffer that contains one or more file names you want to capture. You may need to move the File Clipboard window to view sections of the scrollback buffer.

As figure 4.10 shows, the File Clipboard file list box contains the files currently in the Clipboard. You can type file names in the Clipboard by using the keyboard, or you can capture the file names from the buffer. To enter names manually, click the top box in the file list box, or press Tab until this box is highlighted. Then type in a file name. The File Clipboard holds a maximum of 1,000 file names.

To capture files from the screen, make sure that the Clipboard can identify a file name. The number in the Separator Character box tells the Clipboard what ASCII character separates the file names. Common separators are a space (ASCII character 32) or a carriage return (ASCII 13). In this particular display, the file names are followed by a semicolon (;),

ASCII Character 59. Highlight the Separator box, and then enter *59*. Currently, the Clipboard is pointing to the file LIFE.OUT, which is highlighted at the left of the screen and which appears in the top box of the file list box. (Refer to the ASCII code table in Appendix C.)

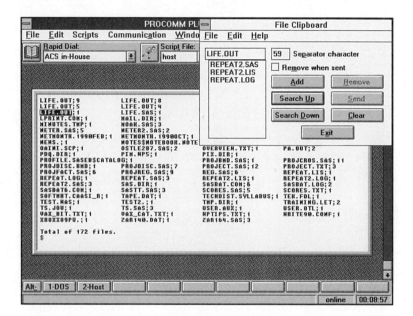

FIG. 4.10

Capturing file names from the Scrollback Buffer screen.

When a file name is listed in the top box of the file list, choosing Add places the file name in the actual list (below the box), or double-clicking on a file name automatically adds it to the Clipboard. To search up or down in the buffer for file names, choose Search Up or Search Down.

To remove a file name from the file list, press Tab to highlight the file name or click the file name, and then choose Remove.

The Send option sends a file name to the other computer. For example, when the Terminal Display window contains a prompt asking for a file name, you can open the File Clipboard, select a file name, and choose Send. The selected file name is pasted onto the Terminal Display window as if you had typed it from the keyboard.

The Remove When Sent option box enables you to tell the program to remove a file name from the list after it has been sent. This option is selected when an X fills the box and deselected when the box is empty.

To clear the file list, choose the Clear button. Choose Exit to close the File Clipboard.

The Clipboard window also contains three pull-down menu options: File, Edit, and Help. The File command contains the options Open, Save As, and Exit. The Save As option enables you to save the Clipboard in a file and then open it later. The Exit option closes the Clipboard window. The Edit command contains the options Copy and Paste. Copy places selected file names in the Windows Clipboard. The Paste option pastes the contents of the Windows Clipboard to the file list, enabling you to move information from the Windows Clipboard to another application or to move information currently in the Windows Clipboard into the File Clipboard. The Help option brings up the PROCOMM PLUS for Windows Help window.

The file names you have captured in the File Clipboard can be sent to the screen later at a download prompt, enabling you to use this captured list of file names to specify a list of files to download. Chapter 5 includes more information on using the Clipboard file list, including editing and deleting file names in the Clipboard.

Taking a Snapshot of a Screen

Periodically during a communications session, you may decide that you want a copy of a single screen. As described in "Saving the Buffer to a File" earlier in this chapter, and "Capturing the Session to Disk" later in this chapter, PROCOMM PLUS for Windows offers several ways to save much more than one screen. Many times, however, one screen is all you need. You can use the Edit menu's Screen To feature to save a single screen at a time.

To save to disk the data displayed on the Terminal Display window, select the Screen To option from the Edit menu. A submenu displays, as shown in figure 4.11. From this submenu, you can choose to save the screen to the Windows Clipboard, to the currently defined capture file, to a file you specify, or to the printer. Shortcut-keys are available to capture the screen to the Clipboard (Alt-V), to capture it to a file (Alt-G), or to print it to the printer (Alt-L).

If you choose to capture the screen to a file, the Copy Screen To File dialog box appears (see fig. 4.12). This standard Windows file entry dialog box enables you to enter the name of the file in which the screen information will be stored. In this case, the file name PW.TXT has been entered in the file box. Like any other Windows file box, you can change drives and directories to define where the file is to be saved. When you have specified the file name, click OK or press Alt-O.

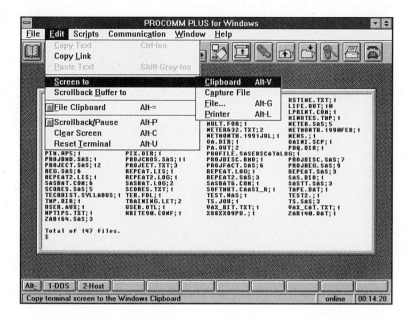

FIG. 4.11

The Screen To submenu.

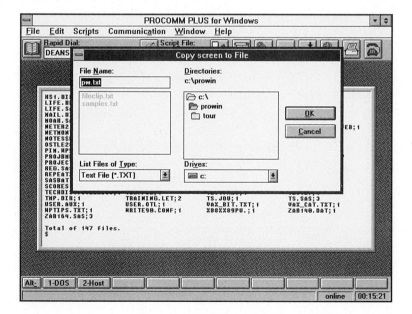

FIG. 4.12

The Copy Screen to File dialog box.

Capturing the Session to Disk

As discussed previously, by pressing Alt-G (save screen to a File), you can save a screenful of information. By pressing Alt-P (Scrollback/ Pause), you can save up to the size of the scrollback buffer. PROCOMM PLUS for Windows also provides the Capture File feature, which enables you to capture part or all of a session directly to disk without using the Screen To or Scrollback/Pause command.

To capture information that scrolls off the Terminal Display window to disk, click the Capture Action icon (which looks like a butterfly net) or choose Capture File from the File menu (press Alt-F1). PROCOMM PLUS for Windows opens a dialog box prompting you for a capture file name.

Specify a disk file to receive the captured data by typing a valid DOS file name and pressing Enter. Usually, you use a CAP file extension for capture files. When you install PROCOMM PLUS for Windows, the default log file name is DEFAULT.CAP.

After you define the capture file, PROCOMM PLUS for Windows begins capturing to the specified disk all file characters that subsequently are displayed to your Terminal Display window. If the capture file in use already contains data, PROCOMM PLUS for Windows adds the new data to the end of the file. To remind you that PROCOMM PLUS for Windows is capturing the session to disk, the program displays the message `Capture file open` in the status line at the bottom of the Terminal Display screen.

The Capture File feature does not capture information already on-screen when you press Alt-F1 (Capture File). If you want to save the current screen to disk, press Alt-G (Screen Snapshot).

Using the Capture File feature is much like turning on your VCR to record a ball game or movie for viewing later. Even if you miss something the first time through, you can look at it again as often as you want.

When using the Capture File feature, you can skip information that you don't want to save to the log file. Perhaps, for example, you have been reading your electronic mail and saving a copy to disk, but you are about to read a particularly sensitive piece of correspondence that you don't want to save.

To suspend the Capture File feature temporarily, press Alt-F1 (Capture File). PROCOMM PLUS for Windows already has logged to disk any information on-screen, but the program does not save additional information on the Terminal Display window until you reactivate the capture file. PROCOMM PLUS for Windows displays the message `Capture File Closed` in the status line to remind you that the Capture File feature is suspended. To resume saving the session to disk, press Alt-F1 and press

Enter at the file name prompt. PROCOMM PLUS for Windows displays the message Capture File Open in the status line, indicating that all incoming and outgoing data is being saved to the log file.

During Chat mode, you also can activate the Capture File feature to capture the incoming messages, but not what you type in the Chat window.

Viewing a File with Playback

With PROCOMM PLUS for Windows' Playback File feature, you can display the information that you have saved to a disk file with the Scrollback feature, the Screen Snapshot feature, or the Capture File feature. You also can play back (display) any file that contains only ASCII characters.

To display the contents of a file created by PROCOMM PLUS for Windows or to display any other ASCII file on the disk, select File, Playback File from the Terminal Display window. PROCOMM PLUS for Windows opens a file entry dialog box similar to figure 4.12.

Type or select the name of the disk file you want to view and press Enter. Unless you specify a directory, PROCOMM PLUS for Windows looks for the file in the current DOS directory.

After PROCOMM PLUS for Windows finds the file you specify, the file appears in the Terminal Display window (see fig. 4.13).

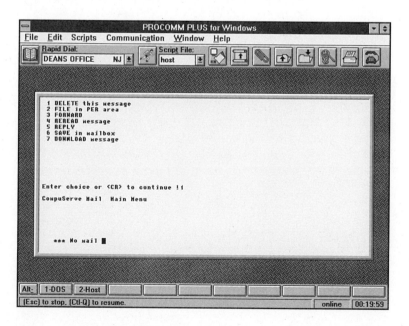

FIG. 4.13

Playing back a capture file.

When PROCOMM PLUS for Windows displays a file in the Scrollback window, you can scroll the screen by using the scroll bar.

With the Playback File feature, you can read ASCII files, but you cannot edit them. PROCOMM PLUS for Windows does, however, enable you to access a text editor whenever you want to edit an ASCII file. You may want to edit a short ASCII message that you intend to send through an electronic mail service, for example. Refer to Chapter 6 for an explanation of how to use the Windows Notepad editor.

Sending Information to Your Printer

In addition to saving to disk any information displayed on-screen during a communications session, you can send the information to your printer. Press Alt-N or click the Printer Action command icon (Printer On/Off) to toggle on this feature. PROCOMM PLUS for Windows indicates that it is sending incoming and outgoing characters to the printer by displaying the message Starting Print Logging in the status line of the Terminal Display window. PROCOMM PLUS for Windows then sends all characters that appear on-screen to your printer.

To turn off printing, press Alt-N or click the Printer icon (Printer On/Off) again. PROCOMM PLUS for Windows changes the message in the status line to Printer Closed and stops sending information to the printer.

PROCOMM PLUS for Windows' capability to print a communications session is limited by the fact that no handshaking or flow control occurs between PROCOMM PLUS for Windows and the printer. PROCOMM PLUS for Windows sends data to the Windows printer driver regardless of whether the printer is functioning or is ready to receive data.

Another method of printing your session is to use the PROCOMM PLUS for Windows Capture File feature to save the session to disk. Then use the DOS COPY command to send the file to your printer. If you save your on-line session to the default log file DEFAULT.CAP, for example, use the following DOS command to print the file:

    COPY *capture.cap* PRN

You also can use the Windows File Manager Print option to print the file.

Clearing the Screen

During a communications session, you may want to clear the screen completely. Perhaps you are about to receive important information from a remote computer and you want to remove extraneous data from the screen; or you may have completed a session with one remote computer and want to clear the screen before calling the next computer. To clear the Terminal Display window, select Clear Screen from the Edit menu.

Although pressing Alt-C (Clear Screen) erases all information from the screen, the command does not erase the screen contents from the scrollback buffer. Refer to "Displaying the Scrollback Buffer" earlier in this chapter for a description of how to review information that no longer is displayed on-screen.

When you press Alt-C (Clear Screen), PROCOMM PLUS for Windows also resets screen colors to those established in the Terminal Color Options screen of the setup utility (see Chapter 8). Some remote computers may send codes to your computer that have the effect of temporarily changing screen colors. If you encounter this problem, you can use the Alt-C (Clear Screen) command to return the colors to normal.

Viewing Elapsed Time

Whether your computer is connected to an on-line service or over a toll telephone line, or both, you undoubtedly want to keep close tabs on the connection time. Most on-line information services—as well as the telephone company—charge you by the minute, so you need to be aware of just how long you have been connected. You can get this information by using PROCOMM PLUS for Windows' Elapsed Time feature.

To determine the amount of time elapsed since you have begun a communications session, look at the clock at the bottom right of the Terminal Display window. This clock begins counting when a connection begins, indicating how long you have been communicating.

Ending a Call

The last step in any communications session is to hang up the line. When you are connected to an on-line service or a bulletin board, you issue the sign-off command that is appropriate for that system. The host computer usually drops the line first, and you see a few meaningless characters on-screen followed by the message NO CARRIER. This message indicates that the modem at the other end has stopped transmitting and that your modem is going to hang up the telephone line.

Sometimes, however, you must disconnect the line from your end. You may have connected to an on-line service such as CompuServe, through a public data network such as Telenet. After you log off the on-line service, you still are connected to the network. From the Terminal Display window, click the Telephone Action icon (Hang Up), press Alt-F2, or select Hangup from the Communication menu. PROCOMM PLUS for Windows changes the icon from a phone off the hook to a phone on the hook and sends the signal to your modem to hang up the telephone line.

Make sure that the modem did drop the telephone connection. Pick up a telephone connected to the same line as the modem and listen for a dial tone, or look at the offline/online indicator at the bottom right of the Terminal Display window. If the line is still open, the modem didn't hang up the line. See Appendix B for an explanation of how to install and set up a modem properly for use with PROCOMM PLUS for Windows to ensure that the modem hangs up the telephone line when instructed to do so.

Summary

This chapter discussed the major PROCOMM PLUS for Windows commands used during a communications session. You learned how to connect to another computer, how to converse with a person or computer program on the other end, and how to manage incoming and outgoing information. Finally, the chapter explained what you need to do to end the communications session.

Turn to Chapter 5 for a discussion of how to use PROCOMM PLUS for Windows' capabilities for transferring files.

Transferring Files

This chapter explains how to use PROCOMM PLUS for Windows to send and receive electronic files to and from another computer—an operation referred to as a *file transfer*. In concept, transferring a file from one computer to another is nearly the same as copying a file from one disk drive to another. You are making an electronic duplicate, or copy, of the original file and then placing the copy in a different location. From the user's perspective, however, file transfer between computers is significantly more complicated than file transfer between disk drives. This chapter shows you how to perform this operation easily by using PROCOMM PLUS for Windows.

First, you learn the basic steps to take when sending a file from your computer to a remote computer (the computer on the other end of the telephone line). You then learn what to do to receive a file that is transmitted by a remote computer. Next, the chapter discusses when and how to use the file-transfer protocols available in PROCOMM PLUS for Windows. Finally, you learn some commands for handling these files you send and receive, including listing file directories, using the File Clipboard window, accessing DOS from within PROCOMM PLUS for Windows, and downloading a special type of file—GIF files.

Sending Files

File transfer is a two-way street. PROCOMM PLUS for Windows enables you to send and receive computer files to and from the remote computer. The steps you take to send a file are similar to but not exactly the same as the steps necessary to receive a file. This section describes how to send one or more files to a remote computer.

In PROCOMM PLUS for Windows, the phrases *send a file*, *upload a file*, and *transmit a file* mean the same thing. They refer to the act of transferring a computer file from your computer to a remote computer. Sometimes new users are confused by the term *upload*. You may think, for example, that it refers to uploading a file to your computer—which would be receiving a file. When used in PROCOMM PLUS for Windows, however, the phrase *upload a file* means to send a file to another computer. This usage is easiest to understand in the context of sending files to a host computer, such as a bulletin board. When you send a file to the bulletin board, you are uploading the file to the host. Receiving a file from the host is called downloading a file.

Before you can use PROCOMM PLUS for Windows to send a file, you must be connected to the remote computer and you must be at the Terminal Display window. If the remote computer is a PC that is not operating a bulletin board or running PROCOMM PLUS for Windows Host mode, you must inform the remote computer's operator that you are about to upload a file. For file transfer to occur, the remote operator must begin the appropriate download procedure soon after you execute your upload procedure.

When you are connected to a host system (an on-line service, such as CompuServe, or a PC bulletin board, for example), you inform the host program, by selecting an appropriate menu option or command, that you intend to upload (send) a file. (The exact command depends on the host program with which you are communicating.) You usually have to type the name of the file (or select a file name from a file list) you are going to upload to the host and indicate a file-transfer protocol.

A *protocol* is a mutually agreed-on set of rules. A *file-transfer protocol* is an agreed-on set of rules that control the flow of data between two computers. An *upload protocol* is a file-transfer protocol that is available for you to use when uploading files to another computer. The agreed-on rules often screen transmitted data for errors introduced by the transmission process. This error-screening process usually is referred to as *error checking* or *error control*. Because not all telephone systems have been optimized for sending computer data, you cannot assume that the signal between your modem and the receiving modem will remain clear enough to achieve an error-free transmission. Even one lost bit can change critically the content of the information you are sending. Using a file-transfer protocol that performs error checking ensures that the data received by the remote computer is the same as the data your computer sends. Refer to "Examining File-Transfer Protocols" later in this chapter for more information on each of the protocols available and for details on how to decide which one to use. Like most other communication parameters, the file-transfer protocol you choose must match that used by the remote computer.

When the host (remote computer) instructs you to begin your transfer, you begin the upload procedure by clicking the Send File Action icon (the file folder with the up arrow) or choosing the Send File option from the File menu. (Some protocols, such as CIS-B, automatically determine that you are uploading, and you do not have to click the Send File icon.)

PROCOMM PLUS for Windows then displays the Send File window. Figure 5.1, for example, shows the Send File window that appears when you're using the XMODEM protocol. To move from box to box in this window, press Tab, point to the box with the mouse pointer and click, or press Alt plus the underlined letter of the option.

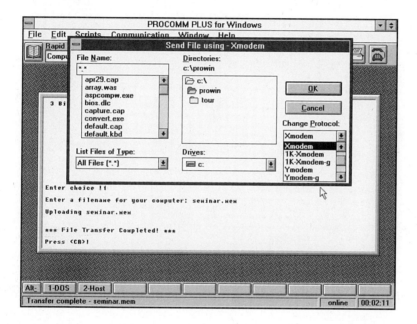

FIG. 5.1

The Send File window for a transfer with the XMODEM protocol.

Notice in the lower right corner of the window the Change Protocol drop box (currently extended) that contains a list of upload protocols available for you to use when you upload a file. If the currently selected protocol is okay, you do not need to change protocols. But, you do need to enter the name of the file to upload in the File Name box in the top left corner of the window.

To enter a file name manually, select the File Name box and type the file name, or you can choose a file name from the file list below this box. If you want to look at file names in other directories, point to C:\ in the Directories box and double-click to bring up a directory tree. You then can change directories by just clicking the directory.

The List Files of Type option in the Send File window enables you to specify what kinds of files to list in the file list. You also can type *.txt* in the File Name field, for example, to list only files that have a TXT extension. The Drives option enables you to look for files in other disk drives.

After you have indicated the file name to upload, click OK or press Alt-O to exit this box. The upload then begins.

When you initiate an upload, PROCOMM PLUS for Windows displays an upload progress window containing a progress bar, as shown in figure 5.2. This window tells you the file-transfer protocol in use and the name of the file being sent and also gives you the following information:

- *Percent Complete*. The progress of the upload

- *Byte Count.* The number of bytes uploaded so far

- *Corrections*. The number of errors in transmission that are corrected

   When XMODEM detects an error, for example, the protocol requests that the block be resent. If XMODEM detects an error in the same blocks 15 times, the protocol aborts the transfer. Otherwise, if the block arrives without an error, XMODEM acknowledges that it has received the block correctly, and the next block is sent. The occurrence of many errors usually means that the modems are not communicating clearly—probably as a result of poor telephone line quality.

- *Transfer Status*. Any messages about the upload

- *Bytes/Second*. The speed of transmission

- *Time Remaining*. The approximate time remaining for the upload

- *File Length*. The total size of the file being uploaded

If you decide to cancel the upload as it is taking place, click the Cancel button in the dialog box, or press Alt-C.

When you start PROCOMM PLUS for Windows, the current default protocol is the one you defined during installation. After you call a remote system by using the dialing directory, the dialing directory entry establishes the current protocol as the one you placed in the dialing record. (Refer to Chapter 3, "Building Your Dialing Directory.") If you want to use a protocol other than the current default, you can change protocols by clicking the Setup Action icon and then the Protocol option. Alternatively, choose Setup (Alt-S) from the Windows menu and then select Protocol from the Current Setup menu. The Current Setup menu with the Protocol option selected (extended) is shown in figure 5.3. To select a protocol, click the name or use the up- and down-arrow keys to highlight the protocol name and press Enter. Close the Current Setup menu by clicking File and then Exit, or by pressing Alt-F, then X.

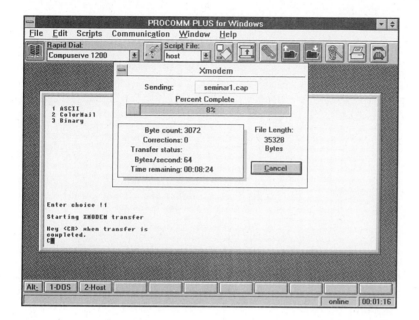

FIG. 5.2

The upload progress window.

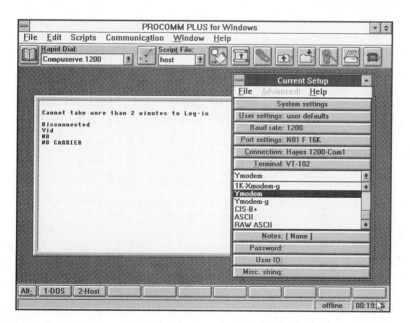

FIG. 5.3

Selecting a protocol from the Current Setup menu.

NOTE   Several file-transfer protocols available in PROCOMM PLUS for Windows enable you to specify multiple files for uploading. Refer to the discussions later in this chapter on the protocols KERMIT, YMODEM BATCH, YMODEM-G BATCH, and ZMODEM for more information on transmitting multiple files.

When you are connected to another PC that is using PROCOMM PLUS for Windows (or a DOS version of PROCOMM PLUS), file transfer is easiest if your computer or the other PC uses the Host mode. Refer to Chapter 9, "Using Host Mode," for details on how Host mode handles file transfer.

When you have a lengthy file to send, you typically want to use the fastest transmission method possible. Because of the need for error checking, however, information sent as a file is transmitted more slowly than the same amount of information transferred as straight ASCII characters without error checking. Some file-transfer methods are faster than others. The pros and cons of the various protocols are covered in "Examining File-Transfer Protocols" later in this chapter.

Since 1987, many modem manufacturers have offered relatively expensive modems that perform error checking in hardware. These hardware-based error-checking, or error-control, modems not only do a better job of detecting errors caused by telephone line problems but also are much faster than the error-checking methods used by software-based file-transfer protocols. The *de facto* standard as of 1989 was a series of protocols developed by Microcom, Inc., and known as MNP (Microcom Networking Protocol) Classes 1 through 4. An internationally recognized standard known as CCITT V.42 (refer to "New Standards" in Chapter 1), however, has become the official industry standard. To maintain compatibility with existing modems, V.42 incorporates MNP Classes 1 through 4 as a fall-back standard. When a V.42 connects with a modem that doesn't support the V.42 error-control method but does support MNP Classes 1 through 4, for example, the V.42 modem uses MNP.

In addition to the file-transfer protocol, a few other factors affect just how fast you can send a file to a remote computer. Not surprisingly, transmission speed of the modems at each end of the connection most directly affects the speed at which you can transmit files. Modems that have a maximum transmission speed of 2400 bps potentially can transmit files at twice the speed of a 1200-bps modem, and these faster modems are widely available at reasonable prices.

Another way you can dramatically increase effective file-transfer speed is through either of the two related techniques known as *file compression* and *data compression*. File compression is analogous to sitting on a loaf of bread. A file-compression program squeezes the "air" from a file so that it takes up less space. The significant information—the "bread"—is still there, but in a compressed form. After you transmit the compressed file, someone at the other end runs a program that decompresses the file, putting it back in the form that is expected by the word processing program or other type of program that created the file. File-compression programs can compress some files more than others. The most popular programs of this type often can shrink a file by more than half and sometimes by as much as 75 percent or more.

You can obtain excellent file-compression software from most PC user groups and PC bulletin boards. These shareware programs not only compress files but also can create a library (or archive) file from multiple normal DOS files. You can use one of these archiving programs, for example, to bundle four spreadsheet files and three word processing files into a single archive file. This archive file is compressed so that its size in bytes is perhaps half the total size of the seven files that comprise the archive file. You then can transmit one file to a colleague rather than send seven separate files.

File compression and file archiving are useful particularly when you want to upload or download software that requires a number of different files in order to operate. The user-supported (often referred to as shareware) program Procomm 2.4.3, for example, normally is found archived into two or three large files on PC bulletin boards. After you download the files, you use an archiving program to decompress and unarchive the many files needed to run Procomm. Be aware, however, that at least two competing programs of this type are used widely to compress and archive files stored on bulletin boards. You have to use the correct program to be able to unarchive and decompress a file you download. You usually can tell by the file-name extension of the bulletin board file which program was used to compress and archive the file (for example, ARC versus ZIP).

Data-compression schemes (as opposed to file-compression programs) do not require that you run a program to compress the file before you send it. Instead, the data is compressed by the modem as you send the file and decompressed at the other end by the receiving modem. The net effect is that the file is sent faster. Many modem manufacturers produce modems that support a data-compression scheme known as MNP Class 5, developed by Microcom, Inc. When this data-compression scheme is used with the MNP Classes 1 through 4 error-control protocols, a 2400-bps modem can achieve an effective transmission rate of more than 4800 bps. Hayes V-series modems achieve similar results by using a different (incompatible) data-compression scheme. The CCITT V.42bis standard includes a third data-compression scheme for modems, which achieves even faster transmission speed results. CCITT V.42bis was ratified in September 1989 and is becoming the industry standard.

Receiving Files

PROCOMM PLUS for Windows enables you to send and receive computer files to and from a remote computer. The steps you take to receive a file are similar to but not exactly the same as the steps necessary to send a file. This section describes how to receive a file.

In PROCOMM PLUS for Windows, the phrases *receive a file* and *download a file* mean the same thing. They refer to the act of receiving a computer file sent to your computer by a remote computer. The term *download* is easiest to understand when used in the context of obtaining a file from a host computer, such as a bulletin board. Receiving a file from the host is called downloading a file from the host. Conversely, when you send a file to the bulletin board, you are uploading a file to the host.

Before you can receive a file from a remote computer, you should be at the Terminal Display window. If the remote computer is a PC that is not operating a bulletin board or running PROCOMM PLUS for Windows Host mode, you must inform the remote computer's operator that you are about to start downloading a file. The operator should begin the upload procedure first, and then you should immediately begin your download procedure. Most protocols are receiver-driven; that is, the sender does not begin uploading data until receiving a signal to start from the receiver. The only exception is the ASCII file-transfer protocol. The receiver should begin the download procedure before the sender begins uploading. Otherwise, the first few characters of the file are lost.

When you are connected to a host system, you usually inform the host program that you intend to download a file by selecting an appropriate menu option or command. You usually have to type the name of the file you are going to download from the host and select a file-transfer protocol.

A *download protocol* is a file-transfer protocol that you can use when you are downloading files from another computer. The file-transfer protocol you choose must match that used by the remote computer (the computer from which you are downloading the file). Refer to "Examining File-Transfer Protocols" later in this chapter for more information on each of the protocols.

When the host instructs you to begin your transfer procedure, you begin the download procedure. To download a file, click the Receive File Action icon (looks like a file folder with a down arrow) or choose Receive File from the File menu. PROCOMM PLUS for Windows displays the Receive File dialog box, which is essentially the same as the Send File dialog box in figure 5.1.

Some protocols automatically "tell" PROCOMM PLUS for Windows that you are beginning a download. ZMODEM, for example, automatically initiates the download, so you do not have to click the Receive File Action icon or choose <u>R</u>eceive File from the <u>F</u>ile menu. Instead, you see the Receive File Action icon automatically reverse its colors, telling you that it is being selected. This autodownload feature is one of the reasons that ZMODEM is becoming increasingly popular.

NOTE PROCOMM PLUS for Windows enables you to specify multiple files for downloading. Refer to later sections in this chapter on the protocols KERMIT, YMODEM (Batch), YMODEM-G (Batch), and ZMODEM for more information on downloading multiple files.

After you enter the name of the file to download in the File <u>N</u>ame field in the Receive File dialog box, PROCOMM PLUS for Windows searches the download directory for a file with the same name (refer to "Setting File and Path Options" in Chapter 8 for an explanation on how to assign a download directory). If you are using a version of XMODEM or YMODEM and a file already exists with the name you specified, a dialog box appears with this message:

```
The file already exists
replace existing file?
```

Select Yes to continue or No to cancel the transfer.

When you download a file with XMODEM, you must tell the host computer the file to send and also tell your local computer what to name the received file. When you are using COMPUSERVE B+, KERMIT, YMODEM (Batch), or YMODEM-G (Batch), you don't have to respecify a file name for the local computer. PROCOMM PLUS for Windows uses the file name you or the operator of the other computer specified to the remote computer. If the file already exists on your computer, the new file is given the same name, but with the first character replaced by a dollar sign ($). If you are downloading a file named REPORT.TXT, for example, but it already exists on your computer, the downloaded file is named $EPORT.TXT.

After you start the download procedure and the remote computer begins its upload procedure, PROCOMM PLUS for Windows displays the download progress window, which is essentially the same as figure 5.2.

As soon as your computer receives the entire file, the computer beeps, and this message appears at the bottom of the screen:

```
Transfer completed - filename
```

PROCOMM PLUS for Windows then removes the progress window from the screen and returns to the normal Terminal Display window.

Examining File-Transfer Protocols

When you type a message in the Terminal mode or Chat mode, PROCOMM PLUS for Windows sends ASCII characters to the screen of the remote computer. The operator of the remote computer can detect transmission errors simply by reading the characters on-screen. If a character looks like hieroglyphics, it reflects a transmission error. Most computer files, however, are not stored entirely as ASCII characters. Computer programs, most word processing files, spreadsheet files, database files, and other types of computer files contain data that cannot be displayed on-screen as it is transmitted. These non-ASCII files typically are referred to as *binary files* (although ASCII is technically a binary—base 2—code). To send binary files, you must use a file-transfer protocol that can send data without displaying it to the screen, and you must take steps through software or hardware to detect data errors that may be caused by degradation of the telephone signal.

Each time you begin uploading or downloading files by using PROCOMM PLUS for Windows, you can choose among several file-transfer protocols. The following guidelines can help you decide which protocol to use:

- *Use matching file-transfer protocols.* The same file-transfer protocol must be used on the sending and receiving ends of the file-transfer process. This requirement limits the number of protocols available to you during any particular communication session to the protocols that PROCOMM PLUS for Windows and the remote program have in common.

- *Use the ASCII or RAW ASCII protocol only for ASCII files.* When sending or receiving a file that contains only printable ASCII characters, you have the option of choosing the ASCII or RAW ASCII protocol. These protocols send data character by character, just as when you type a message at the keyboard. You can display the data to the screen during transmission by checking the Display Text option in the Setup Utility ASCII Transfer Options screen. The ASCII protocols, however, do not perform error checking. You cannot use the ASCII protocol for binary files. You can use RAW ASCII for binary files, because no characters are stripped (including null and EOF), but no error checking is done. You usually use RAW ASCII in situations in which a stream of exact bytes must be sent to a host or a device (such as process-control equipment that has no binary protocol).

- *Send and receive the largest blocks.* For maximum transmission speed when sending binary files, use the file-transfer protocol that sends blocks of the largest size. In PROCOMM PLUS for Windows, the 1K-XMODEM, 1K-XMODEM-G, COMPUSERVE B+ (when used with CompuServe Quick B), YMODEM, YMODEM (Batch), YMODEM-G (Batch), and ZMODEM protocols can send blocks of 1,024 bytes. KERMIT also can send large blocks, although it defaults to small blocks.

■ *Send and receive multiple files.* Some PROCOMM PLUS for Windows file-transfer protocols enable you to send or receive multiple files with one command. This type of transfer often is called a *batch transfer.* You can send the files SALES892.WK1 and SALES992.WK1, for example, in one upload procedure. When asked for the file name, type *.wk1*. By using the global character (the asterisk), you tell PROCOMM PLUS for Windows to list all file names with the extension WK1. You then select from the list the files you want to send.

PROCOMM PLUS for Windows then sends these files one at a time. The PROCOMM PLUS for Windows protocols that can send or receive multiple files are COMPUSERVE B+, KERMIT, YMODEM (Batch), YMODEM-G (Batch), and ZMODEM.

■ *Send and receive file characteristics.* Several file-transfer protocols available in PROCOMM PLUS for Windows also send with the file such file characteristics as file name, file size, and the date and time the file was last changed. When you are downloading a file, this information enables PROCOMM PLUS for Windows to make full use of the progress window. The protocols that transmit at least one of these file characteristics include 1K-XMODEM, 1K-XMODEM-G, COMPUSERVE B+, IMODEM, KERMIT, YMODEM (Batch), YMODEM G (Batch), and ZMODEM.

■ *Use sliding windows on PDNs and over long-distance lines.* When you connect to a host computer over a public data network (PDN), such as Tymnet and Telenet (or any other packet-switching network), or over long-distance telephone lines that may go through satellite relays, most file-transfer protocols can be slowed significantly. PDNs and satellite relays often cause an appreciable increase in the time needed for the receiving computer to reply to each block sent. The sending computer can spend a great deal of time just waiting. The KERMIT and ZMODEM protocols, however, take advantage of the full-duplex nature of your modem (refer to "Understanding Duplex" in Chapter 4 for a discussion of duplex and related concepts). Instead of waiting for a reply before sending another block, the protocols send blocks and watch for the reply to previous blocks simultaneously. These protocols send several blocks before requiring any reply. ZMODEM probably is the best choice for use on public data networks.

■ *Use appropriate protocols with error-control modems.* If you are using a modem that performs error control in hardware, such as a modem that supports MNP Classes 1 through 4 or CCITT V.42, use a PROCOMM PLUS for Windows protocol that sends data without doing any error checking in software. The protocols in this group are 1K-XMODEM-G and YMODEM-G (Batch).

File-transfer protocols used in PC communications programs and on host computers are not always named in the same way they are named in PROCOMM PLUS for Windows. The protocol called XMODEM in PROCOMM PLUS for Windows, for example, sometimes is called XMODEM/CRC by other communications programs. Previous versions of PROCOMM contained a protocol called YMODEM, which now is referred to as 1K-XMODEM. The current YMODEM used in PROCOMM PLUS for Windows is essentially the same as 1K-XMODEM, but YMODEM allows multiple files to be transferred. Purists may argue for hours about the "correct" names for these protocols, but just familiarizing yourself with the protocols implemented in PROCOMM PLUS for Windows is more practical. Then you can recognize the protocol you need at any particular time. Table 5.1 lists the most important properties of the available protocols so that you can compare them at a glance. Each protocol is discussed in more detail in the sections that follow.

Table 5.1. PROCOMM PLUS for Windows File-Transfer Protocols

Protocol	Error-checking	Block size	Mult. files	Name	Size	Date	Sliding windows
1K-XMODEM	CRC	128/1024	No	No	No	No	No
1K-XMODEM-G	None	128/1024	No	No	No	No	No
ASCII	None		No	No	No	No	No
COMPUSERVE B+	CRC	512/1024	No	Yes	No	No	Yes
KERMIT	CRC/Checksum	1024 max	Yes	Yes	Yes	Yes	Yes
RAW ASCII	None		No	No	No	No	No
XMODEM	CRC/Checksum	128	No	No	No	No	No
YMODEM (Batch)	CRC	128/1024	Yes	Yes	Yes	No	No
YMODEM-G (Batch)	None	128/1024	Yes	Yes	Yes	No	No
ZMODEM	CRC	128/1024	Yes	Yes	Yes	Yes	Yes

As you read the remainder of this chapter, you may wonder why so many file-transfer protocols are available, yet so few differences exist among them. The reason lies in the fact that the majority of the communications software written for PCs has been developed by hobbyists for hobbyists. Commercial success has not been a significant factor in determining the viability of these public-domain or user-supported programs. Many different programs have flourished, and no one program has dominated. Everyone seems to have a favorite bulletin board program and terminal program (such as PROCOMM PLUS for Windows and its other siblings, PROCOMM PLUS for DOS and the Shareware version of ProComm). Although the XMODEM file-transfer protocol is a common thread among virtually all of the popular PC communications programs, its built-in limitations have led to the development of many enhanced versions of XMODEM.

In an effort to provide you with the capability to communicate with almost anyone's favorite bulletin board or terminal program, PROCOMM PLUS for Windows gives you a list of choices. Table 5.1 and the discussions that follow can help you sort through these protocols and decide which one will become your favorite.

ASCII and RAW ASCII

ASCII (American Standard Code for Information Interchange) forms the lowest common denominator among the countless programs that run on a PC and the many different types of computers that proliferate in our high-tech society. Virtually every word processing, spreadsheet, and database program that runs on a PC can create an ASCII file. Most likely, every computer with which you will ever need to communicate can handle ASCII characters. The primary reason that you need to know how to use the ASCII file-transfer protocol, however, is that most electronic mail systems can display only ASCII characters.

Most PC programs are character-based (with the notable exception of programs that run under such graphics-based programs as Microsoft Windows and OS/2 Presentation Manager). Each character or symbol you see displayed on-screen is represented in memory by one of the codes referred to collectively as the *ASCII character set*. This chapter calls this group of codes the *IBM character set*.

If you are communicating with another computer using PROCOMM PLUS for Windows Host mode (or other versions of ProComm), you can choose to download an ASCII file and enter the file name, and the Host mode begins downloading the file from the host machine to your local machine. If you are connected to a machine using another kind of communications program, you must cause the remote computer to begin its ASCII send procedure before you begin receiving the file.

Alternatively, if you are uploading an ASCII file, you must make sure that the host machine is in receive mode. On an electronic mail system, this point occurs when the system expects you to type your message. Issue the proper command to the host or bulletin board so that it is waiting for ASCII text to be sent. Because a variety of hosts and bulletin boards exist, the proper command depends on the host's software. Usually, you initiate a "receive" by choosing that option from a menu on the host system.

NOTE   PROCOMM PLUS for Windows transfer options contain two versions of ASCII: Standard and RAW ASCII (sometimes referred to as RASCII). RASCII does not perform translation, filtering, or flow control of the information being transferred. Whereas you normally would use ASCII on text files, you can use RASCII on binary files because no characters are stripped (including null and EOF).

When the remote system is ready for you to begin transmitting a file, follow the procedure described in "Sending Files" earlier in this chapter, selecting ASCII or RAW ASCII as the file-transfer protocol. The remote computer cannot distinguish whether PROCOMM PLUS for Windows is sending the ASCII characters from a file or whether you are typing them at the keyboard.

After PROCOMM PLUS for Windows finishes sending the entire file, the computer beeps. To complete the transfer, you must remember to inform the remote computer that you no longer are sending ASCII characters and that you want to save the file. If you are sending a message to an electronic mail system, for example, you issue the command that means to save and send the message.

Although the ASCII and RAW ASCII file-transfer protocols perform no error checking, PROCOMM PLUS for Windows does enable you to control several aspects of an ASCII upload through the Current Setup menu's ASCII Transfer Options screen shown in figure 5.4. To get to this screen, click the Setup Action icon or choose Setup from the Window menu. From the Current Setup menu, choose ASCII as the Protocol option, and choose to edit the advanced option by clicking Advanced! or by pressing Alt-A. The ASCII Transfer Options screen enables you to select how to handle the carriage return and line feeds (CR/LF) and set other upload and download options. Refer to Chapter 8 for discussions of these features.

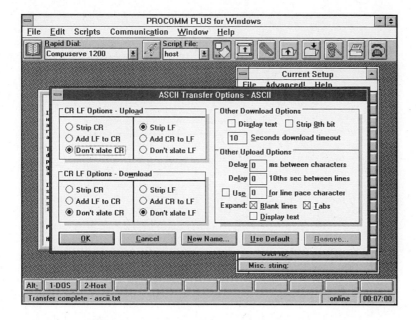

FIG. 5.4

The ASCII Transfer
Options screen.

Some of the options used with plain ASCII transfers do not apply to RAW ASCII. The RAW ASCII Transfer Options screen is illustrated in figure 5.5. To get to this screen, click the Setup Action icon or choose Setup from the Window menu. Then choose RAW ASCII as the Protocol option, and choose to edit the advanced option by selecting Advanced!. The Download options that you can choose for RAW ASCII are Display Text, which indicates whether the text should display or not, and Seconds Download Timeout, where you specify the seconds needed without transmission to signal timeout. The Upload Options enable you to choose how many milliseconds (ms) to delay between characters uploaded, how many tenths of a second to pause between lines, and what character to use as the pace character—usually 13, which is a line feed. You also can choose whether to display text that is being uploaded. For more information on the translation table, refer to Chapter 8.

After a file is received, the transfer ends when the ASCII download timeout is reached or when a ^Z is received. The timeout setting usually is 10 seconds; remember that you can change this setting in the RAW ASCII Transfer Options screen. Optionally, you can end the transfer at any time by choosing Cancel. As an alternative to the ASCII download protocol, you can use the log-file feature to save incoming information to disk. Refer to "Capturing the Session to Disk" in Chapter 4 for an explanation of the log-file feature.

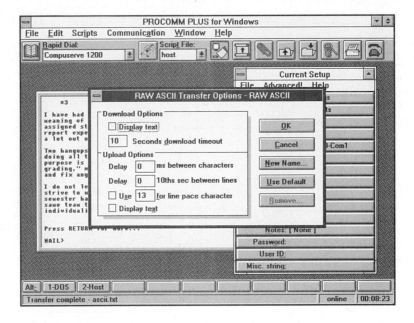

FIG. 5.5

The RAW ASCII
Transfer Options
screen.

COMPUSERVE B+

Use the COMPUSERVE B+ file-transfer protocol with the CompuServe B, Compuserve B+, or CompuServe Quick B protocols when uploading and downloading files on the CompuServe on-line service.

The primary difference between the CompuServe B+ and CompuServe Quick B protocols is that Quick B has sliding windows. As implied by the name, CompuServe Quick B transfers files faster than CompuServe B. The B+ protocol introduces some new enhancements to the Quick B protocol, which gives COMPUSERVE B+ some of the advantages of the ZMODEM protocol. Currently, the B+ protocol is the one you should select for use on CompuServe.

Never use XMODEM to transfer files to or from CompuServe. The delays caused by packet switching result in excessive timeout errors, aborted transfers, and generally slow transmissions.

To take best advantage of the COMPUSERVE B+ protocol, select the CIS-B+ option in the Enquiry box in the Current Setup menu's Terminal Settings screen, as shown in figure 5.6 (refer to "Setting Terminal Enquiry" in Chapter 8 for more information). To get to this screen, click the Setup Action icon or choose Setup from the Window menu. Then choose the Terminal (here it is a VT-102) and select Advanced!

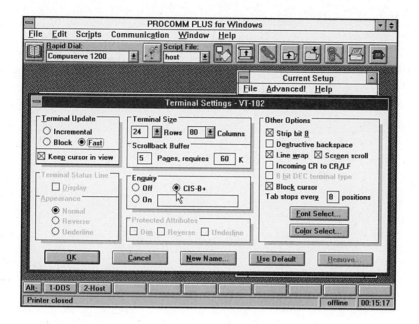

FIG. 5.6

The Terminal Settings
screen with CIS-B+ for
Enquiry selected.

Alternatively, you can add the following line to your CompuServe log-on script file:

SET ENQ CISB

Add the preceding line somewhere in the script after the log-on ID and password have been transmitted.

By selecting CIS-B+ in the Terminal Settings screen or placing the SET command in your log-on script, you enable PROCOMM PLUS for Windows to recognize an Enquiry (ENQ) signal from CompuServe, and you instruct PROCOMM PLUS for Windows to begin its upload or download procedure when it encounters the ENQ signal. Refer to Chapters 7 and 11 for more information about script files.

Suppose that you want to download the file DTP11B.ARC from the DATASTORM library on CompuServe. You first select the name of the file you want to download—DTP11B.ARC, in this case. Then issue the appropriate CompuServe command to begin a download and choose the CompuServe QB protocol from the CompuServe Download menu.

CompuServe prompts you to type the file name for your computer. Type the name you want to use for the file on your computer. After you press Enter, CompuServe sends the ENQ signal to PROCOMM PLUS for Windows, and PROCOMM PLUS for Windows begins the download. You never have to click the Receive Files Action icon to begin the download.

KERMIT

KERMIT is the name of a program, a file-transfer protocol, and a famous frog. In fact, the program and protocol are named after the Jim Henson muppet, Kermit the Frog. Unless specifically noted otherwise, this section discusses the file-transfer protocol KERMIT rather than the Kermit program.

KERMIT was developed in 1981 at Columbia University by Frank da Cruz and Bill Catchings and released into the public domain. In contrast to XMODEM, which requires eight data bits to operate, KERMIT can be used on computers that can handle only seven data bits (many mainframe computers, for example) and still can manage to transmit files that contain bytes made up of eight bits per byte. Since 1981, KERMIT has been implemented on countless brands and models of computers, from mainframes to microcomputers. Consequently, PROCOMM PLUS for Windows also provides this protocol for you to use.

Since its introduction, KERMIT has enjoyed numerous enhancements. The PROCOMM PLUS for Windows version of the KERMIT file-transfer protocol has all the properties listed in table 5.1, including multiple-file transfer and transmission of file name, size, date, and time. KERMIT's data blocks have a maximum length of 1,024 bytes. KERMIT also uses the sliding windows technique to increase transmission speed over satellite-relayed lines and packet-switching networks. As icing on the cake, the version of KERMIT implemented in PROCOMM PLUS for Windows also includes data compression to increase transmission speed even further.

With KERMIT, you can send several files during one transfer. To specify several files at a time in a Send File screen, such as figure 5.7, first specify what files to list in the File Name list box. If you want to list only TXT files, for example, enter the file specification *.txt in the text box at the top of the file list. Usually, the default is *.*, which means that all files in the selected directory are listed. You can place any file specification here, using DOS wild-card characters * and ?. Also, the List Files of Type option enables you to filter what files will appear. Press Ctrl-T or click this box. Click the down arrow once to extend the selection box so that you can choose a filter option. Usually, the setting for this option is All Files (*.*).

After you have entered a file specification, you can choose one or more files from those listed in the File Name box. Hold down the Ctrl key and click a file name in the file list. The file appears highlighted. Continue holding down the Ctrl key and click a second file to highlight it. Continue this procedure until all files you want to send are highlighted. Figure 5.8 shows a File Name box with several files selected.

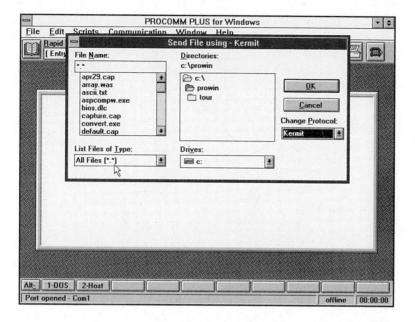

FIG. 5.7

The Send File window for KERMIT.

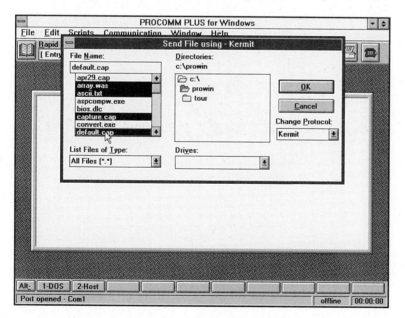

FIG. 5.8

Selecting several files to send.

After you specify what files to send, choose OK to begin the file transfer. PROCOMM PLUS for Windows displays a KERMIT progress window, in which you see the progress of one file at a time (see fig. 5.9).

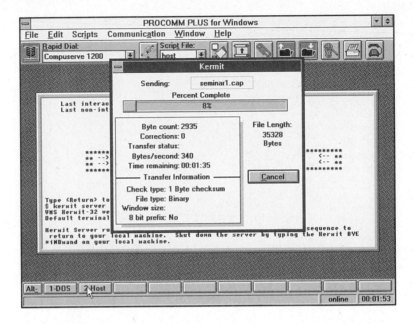

FIG. 5.9

The KERMIT progress window.

Because KERMIT is evolving continually and is implemented on so many different computer systems, not all versions have exactly the same features. To maintain complete compatibility among all KERMIT implementations, the protocol performs a unique "handshake" at the beginning of the transmission. This handshake can be described as *feature negotiation*.

Each computer sends the other a block (packet) that contains a list of features implemented in that computer's version of KERMIT. The transmission then proceeds, using the features that the two KERMITs have in common. Options for the KERMIT transfer are controlled from the Kermit Transfer Options dialog box, as shown in figure 5.10. To get to this window, click the Setup Action icon, or choose Setup from the Window menu; then select Kermit as the Protocol from the Current Setup menu and select Advanced!.

The Kermit Transfer Options window enables you to choose the default characters and other options related to the KERMIT protocol. Figure 5.10 shows the default settings. Usually, you should not have to change these options unless the computer you are communicating with cannot recognize your KERMIT transfer.

Downloading files with KERMIT is similar to uploading. First, inform the remote computer that you want it to use KERMIT to send files to your computer. Also, specify the names of the files to the remote computer.

When the remote computer is ready to send a KERMIT transfer, click the Receive File Action icon or select Receive File from the File menu. PROCOMM PLUS for Windows displays the progress window and executes the file transfer.

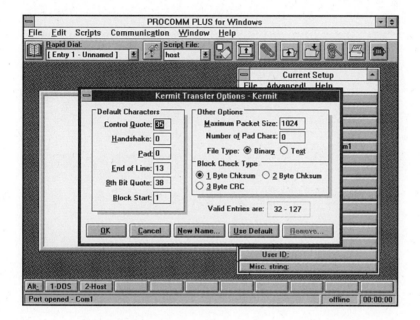

FIG. 5.10

Setting KERMIT transfer options.

Remember, when you are uploading or downloading files, using any PROCOMM PLUS for Windows file-transfer protocol, you can abort the entire transfer in midstream by choosing Cancel.

When you are communicating with a system that is running the Kermit Server program (as opposed to using just the KERMIT file-transfer protocol), you execute uploads and downloads in a manner different from the method described in the preceding paragraphs. First, you must switch to the Kermit Server mode on the other system. Issue the appropriate command for the KERMIT program that system is using (for example, on many VAX computers the command is KERMIT SERVER) and press Enter.

When the remote computer is running the Kermit Server mode, press Alt-K or select Kermit Command from the File menu. Figure 5.11 shows the Kermit Command submenu that appears. These commands have an effect only when you are using PROCOMM PLUS for Windows to communicate with the KERMIT program in Kermit Server mode.

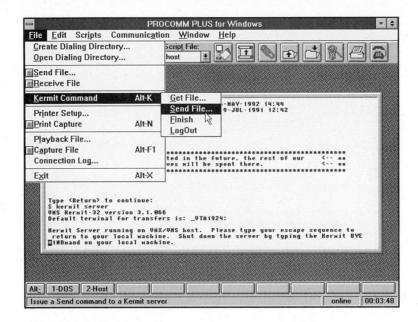

FIG. 5.11

The Kermit Command
submenu.

The Kermit Command submenu includes the following commands:

■ *Get File...* Select this command when you want to receive (download) one or more files from the remote computer. PROCOMM PLUS for Windows removes the KERMIT menu from the screen and displays a dialog box requesting one or more file names. (This dialog box is similar to fig. 5.8.)

Enter the name of the file you want to download and choose OK. The remote KERMIT Server program may enable you to use wildcard characters to specify the files to be received. After you specify one or more file names and press Enter, PROCOMM PLUS for Windows displays the KERMIT progress window and works with the server to execute the transfer.

■ *Send File...* Select this command to send one or more files to the remote computer. PROCOMM PLUS for Windows displays a dialog box requesting the name of a file or a selection of files.

■ *Finish.* Select this command to quit the Kermit Server mode without leaving the KERMIT program. The server issues a message, such as Good-bye, and you return to the KERMIT program's normal prompt.

■ *LogOut.* Select this command to quit the KERMIT Server mode and to log out of the KERMIT program altogether. (Depending on how you are connected to KERMIT, this command also may disconnect you from the remote computer.)

XMODEM, 1K-XMODEM, and 1K-XMODEM-G

The most widely available PC-based file-transfer protocol is XMODEM. Like so many other communications terms, XMODEM can mean different things to different people, so you need to understand a little about the background of this protocol, as well as how PROCOMM PLUS for Windows uses the term.

As most broadly used, the term XMODEM refers to a file-transfer protocol included in the program MODEM2, written by Ward Christensen and introduced in 1979. This file-transfer protocol originally was called the MODEM protocol and was intended to transfer files between computers running the CP/M operating system. Over the years since 1979, however, the MODEM file-transfer protocol has become known as XMODEM and has been implemented in countless communications programs for use in transferring files between computers running many different operating systems. Virtually all popular communications programs for IBM PC-type computers include an implementation of XMODEM. Since its introduction, several "new and improved" versions of the protocol have appeared under various names. PROCOMM PLUS for Windows has included two variants of XMODEM called 1K-XMODEM and 1K-XMODEM-G.

The original XMODEM used the checksum error-checking scheme. This method of detecting errors is adequate for low-speed data transmission (300 bps or less) but can miss errors that are more likely to occur when you're sending data at higher transmission speeds (or over noisy phone lines). One popular variation of XMODEM adds the CCITT CRC-16 error-checking scheme, which is much more reliable than the checksum method at the higher transmission rates.

The CRC-16 version of XMODEM often is called XMODEM/CRC, for obvious reasons, but PROCOMM PLUS for Windows refers to the protocol simply as XMODEM. PROCOMM PLUS for Windows' use of the name in this manner leads to no problems, however, because the CRC-16 version of XMODEM is "backward compatible" with the checksum version. In other words, you can use PROCOMM PLUS for Windows's XMODEM to send or receive a file to or from a computer that is using the original checksum version of XMODEM or the newer CRC-16 version.

Several other modified versions of XMODEM seem to have overtaken XMODEM in popularity. To varying degrees, these other protocols over-come XMODEM's recognized weaknesses: 128-byte blocks, no multiple file transfers, no file characteristics transferred, and no sliding windows. The 1K-XMODEM version of XMODEM is a CRC XMODEM with a 1,024-byte (1K) packet rather than the 128-byte packet. The 1K-XMODEM-G version of XMODEM is the same as the 1K-XMODEM but provides no software error detection and relies on the modem error-correction hardware to provide that function.

Other protocols that have evolved directly or indirectly from the original XMODEM protocol are SEALINK, TELINK, WXMODEM, YMODEM (Batch)—often called YMODEM or YMODEM-G (Batch), and ZMODEM.

Never use XMODEM to transfer files to or from the on-line service CompuServe. The delays caused by packet switching result in excessive timeout errors, aborted transfers, and slow transmissions. Use the COMPUSERVE B+ protocol instead (see "COMPUSERVE B+" earlier in this chapter).

YMODEM (Batch) and YMODEM-G (Batch)

The YMODEM protocol was introduced in 1985 by Chuck Forsberg, of Omen Technology Inc., as an extension of Ward Christensen's XMODEM protocol. As implemented originally, Forsberg's YMODEM protocol includes CRC-16 error checking; 1,024-byte blocks; multiple file transfer; and transmission of file name, file size, and the date and time each file was last modified. Forsberg's YMODEM also includes an option called the G option, which enables you to take full advantage of modems that perform error control.

The developers of PROCOMM PLUS for Windows chose to provide YMODEM in two varieties:

- *YMODEM (Batch).* This version uses 1K blocks, enables you to perform multiple file transfers, and includes a header block with the file name and size.

- *YMODEM-G (Batch).* This version is the same as the YMODEM protocol but does not provide software error detection during transmission. For error checking, this protocol relies on an error-control modem like a Hayes V-series modem, a modem that uses MNP Classes 1 through 4, or a CCITT V.42-compliant modem.

To send or receive single or multiple files, you can use any one of the two YMODEM protocols available in PROCOMM PLUS for Windows. When receiving files with YMODEM or YMODEM-G, you don't specify the transfer file names because the protocol sends the file names with the file.

You can use the YMODEM (Batch) protocol to send the files SALES892.WK1 and SALES992.WK1, for example, by using a single upload command. First, inform the remote computer operator or host program (the bulletin board or on-line service, for example) that you are about to upload files, using the YMODEM (Batch) protocol. Then, from the Terminal Display window, click the Send File Action icon or choose <u>S</u>end

File from the File menu. PROCOMM PLUS for Windows prompts you to enter the file specification on a Send Files window similar to figures 5.7 and 5.8.

To select several files in the File Name list box, hold down the Ctrl key and click a file name (such as SALES892.WK1) in the file list. The file appears highlighted. Continue holding down the Ctrl key and click a second file (such as SALES992.WK1) to highlight it. Continue this procedure until all files you want to send are highlighted. After you specify what files to send, choose OK to begin the file transfer. PROCOMM PLUS for Windows displays a progress window and begins transmitting the first file (SALES892.WK1 in this example). After sending the first file, PROCOMM PLUS for Windows transmits the second file (SALES992.WK1 in this example). When no more files remain to be sent, PROCOMM PLUS for Windows sounds a beep and removes the progress window from the screen.

To download multiple files with YMODEM (Batch) or YMODEM-G (Batch), you must specify the file names to the remote computer. When the remote computer is ready to transmit, click the Receive File Action icon or choose Receive File from the File menu. The first file transfer begins, and PROCOMM PLUS for Windows displays the progress window. Because YMODEM (Batch) and YMODEM-G (Batch) send the file name of each file transmitted, you don't have to provide the file names to PROCOMM PLUS for Windows. Also, because the sending computer transmits the size of each file, PROCOMM PLUS for Windows can make full use of the progress window.

Some bulletin boards enable you to indicate multiple file names to transfer that cannot be specified with the * and ? file-specification wild cards. PROCOMM PLUS for Windows's File Clipboard feature enables you to collect file names to download and then paste them as a list in response to a prompt for multiple file names. See "Using the File Clipboard Window" later in this chapter for more information.

ZMODEM

The ZMODEM protocol was developed by Chuck Forsberg of Omen Technology for the public domain under a Telenet contract in 1986. This protocol has rapidly become a favorite among many users and its implementation into PROCOMM PLUS 2.01 for DOS, and now PROCOMM PLUS for Windows is an important upgrade from the previous versions.

ZMODEM was designed to eliminate many of the problems or limitations associated with older protocols such as XMODEM and YMODEM while taking advantage of new technologies in modem hardware. Forsberg says "The ZMODEM file-transfer protocol provides reliable file and command transfers with complete end-to-end data integrity between application programs. ZMODEM's 32-bit CRC catches errors that continue to sneak into even the most advanced networks." PROCOMM PLUS for Windows' ZMODEM implementation supports 16- and 32-bit CRC error-checking options, which you can specify in the ZMODEM Options Setup Utility screen (see Chapter 8). The 32-bit option, which is the default, provides high data-integrity checking and is slightly slower than the 16-bit option.

Because ZMODEM has buffering and windowing modes, it can work efficiently on a number of data networks. ZMODEM provides faster transfers than other protocols—particularly with error-correcting modems—on timesharing systems (such as CompuServe), satellite relays, and any other kinds of packet-switched networks. The sophisticated error-correction capabilities make ZMODEM useful if you are transferring information over noisy telephone lines.

ZMODEM's benefits are not just limited to its technological advances. ZMODEM also is easy to use. Its Auto Download feature enables you to skip some of the steps necessary with other protocols. After you specify a download, for example, the ZMODEM transfer begins without you having to initiate the protocol (by clicking the Receive File Action icon) or having to type the file name again. Unlike many other protocols, ZMODEM can preserve a file's date and time stamp as well as the file's exact size during transmission, which eliminates the annoying problem of having unneeded characters at the end of a file—a common problem with some other protocols.

The Crash Recovery feature in ZMODEM is also impressive. If a download is interrupted before completion and is restarted, ZMODEM can pick up where the download left off, saving you valuable connect time. ZMODEM also has multiple-file capability, which means that you can specify file transfers by using global characters (such as *.WK1).

Of the file-transfer protocols available in PROCOMM PLUS for Windows, ZMODEM probably is the best to use when transferring files to and from PC bulletin boards or on public data networks. The protocol's 1,024-byte block size, coupled with multiple-file-transfer capability, automatic transfer, and sliding windows, makes ZMODEM a fast protocol that also is easy to use. In all, ZMODEM currently is the best general-purpose file-transfer protocol available in PROCOMM PLUS for Windows.

Working with Disk Files You Send and Receive

The upload and download capabilities of PROCOMM PLUS for Windows operate on DOS files that reside on your computer's disk. This section describes several PROCOMM PLUS for Windows features that make managing these disk files an easier task. The material explains how to list the files on the current working directory, how to collect file names in the File Clipboard window, and how to access DOS commands from within PROCOMM PLUS for Windows.

Listing a Directory's Files

As you upload and download files, you frequently need to review the names of the files on your disk. Perhaps you cannot remember the name of the file you want to send to the other computer. Maybe you are not sure which file names you have used already.

To see a list of files in any directory, switch from the PROCOMM PLUS for Windows window to the File Manager window. You can minimize the PROCOMM PLUS for Windows window by clicking the down arrow in the top right corner of the window. Then, using the File Manager, you can view a directory of file names. For more about using the File Manager, see Que's book *Using Windows 3.1*, Special Edition.

Briefly, to see a list of file names, follow these steps:

1. Minimize the PROCOMM PLUS for Windows window.

2. Double-click the File Manager icon in the Main window. A directory tree appears.

3. Double-click the directory tree to view file names in that directory.

If you do not want to use the File Manager to examine a directory of files, you can choose the DOS Prompt icon from the File Manager window, which takes you back to the DOS prompt. You then can use DOS commands to list directories. To get back to Windows, type *exit* at the DOS prompt and press Enter. (For more information on using DOS from within PROCOMM PLUS for Windows, see the later section, "Accessing DOS Commands from PROCOMM PLUS for Windows.")

Using the File Clipboard Window

You can use the PROCOMM PLUS for Windows File Clipboard window to collect, store, and edit file names to be used for transfer. As you are browsing through information on a host system, you often may run across the name of a file that you want to download. If you don't write down the name of the file, you may forget it when you want it. PROCOMM PLUS for Windows enables you to capture the file name from the screen and copy the name into the File Clipboard window. Then, when you need to type the file name in response to your host's request for a file name to download, you can get the name (or names) from the clipboard.

To access the File Clipboard window, click the Clipboard Action icon (looks like a paper clip) or choose File Clipboard (Alt-=) from the Edit menu. The File Clipboard window appears (see fig. 5.12).

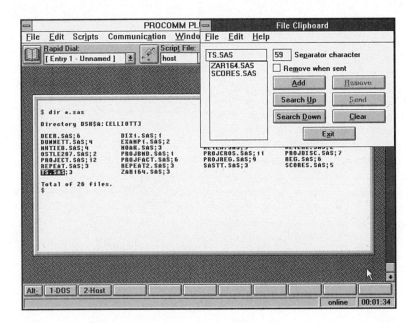

FIG. 5.12

The File Clipboard window.

The File Clipboard window contains a file list on the left side and several option buttons on the right. Initially, the file list is empty. You can enter a name into the file list manually by pressing Tab until the text box at the top of the list is highlighted—or by pointing to the box and clicking—and then typing a name. Figure 5.12 shows the name TS.SAS entered into this box.

You can select the Search Up or Search Down button. When you choose to search, PROCOMM PLUS for Windows finds a file name from the screen and places the name in the box at the top of the file list. To add that file name to the list, choose the Add button. If you do not want to capture that file name, search again for another. You can continue with this procedure and store up to a thousand names in the file list.

If you want to clear all files from the list, choose the Clear button. If you want to remove one or more files from the list, highlight one or more file names and then choose Remove.

After you have file names listed in the File Clipboard window, they stay there as long as you are in PROCOMM PLUS for Windows. You can save them permanently by selecting Save from the File menu in the File Clipboard window. You save a list under a file name so that you can have as many different lists as you like. During another session, you can get saved file names back by selecting Open from the File menu.

When you are connected to another computer, and it is ready to receive a file name for downloading or for some other command, you can access the File Clipboard window and paste file names at the prompt. In figure 5.13, for example, several file names have been selected from the file list. (Remember, you have two options for selecting names from the list. You can point to each name with the mouse pointer, hold down the Ctrl key, and click; or you can press Tab to get to the file box, hold down the Shift key, and press the up- and down-arrow keys to highlight the file names.) Choose the Send button or press Alt-S to paste the highlighted file names to the Terminal Display screen.

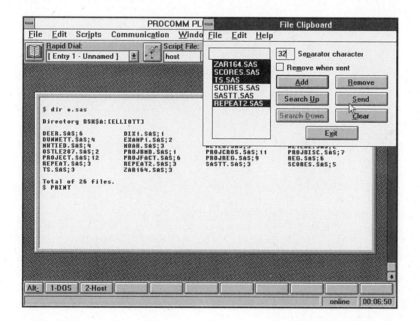

FIG. 5.13

Several files selected in the File Clipboard window.

If you select the Remove When Sent option so that an X appears in the box, any file name you send to the Terminal Display screen is then removed from the file list box.

Accessing DOS Commands from PROCOMM PLUS for Windows

If you do much transferring of files with PROCOMM PLUS for Windows, you may want to perform such DOS functions as copying files, renaming files, deleting files, making directories, and so on without using the Windows File Manager. Leaving PROCOMM PLUS for Windows every time you need to accomplish one of these DOS tasks can be inconvenient, especially if you are on-line to another computer. Consequently, Windows provides a way for you to access the DOS prompt from within Windows without disconnecting from an ongoing communications session.

To access the operating system (DOS) from the Terminal Display window, press Alt-1 (the number 1) or click the 1-DOS meta key at the bottom of the Terminal display screen. Windows loads another copy of the operating system (PC DOS or MS-DOS) into memory (RAM). This action does not disconnect you from an open modem connection.

After PROCOMM PLUS for Windows loads the second copy of the operating system, DOS usually displays the following prompt:

```
C:\cur-dir>
```

where cur-dir is the name of your current working directory. This prompt is the DOS prompt. In other words, you can execute any DOS commands from this prompt.

You may, for example, want to copy several files from a floppy disk to the current working directory on your hard disk. Use the DOS COPY command from the DOS prompt for this purpose.

While working at the DOS prompt, you can use the DOS CD (or CHDIR) command to switch to a different DOS directory. Then type *exit* and press Enter. The Windows Program Manager returns to the screen. You also should see the PROCOMM PLUS for Windows icon on-screen. Double-click this icon to return to PROCOMM PLUS for Windows.

Downloading GIF Files

PROCOMM PLUS for Windows contains a special feature for GIF (Graphics Interchange Format) files. These files contain graphic images and commonly are found on bulletin boards. GIF files are designed so that they are transportable among computer systems such as DOS, AMIGA, MACINTOSH, and others, which makes GIF a popular format for distributing picture files. The Smithsonian Institution, for example, distributes a number of pictures through bulletin board systems by using GIF files.

When you use PROCOMM PLUS for Windows to download a GIF file, instead of the normal progress window, a GIF window opens, and you see the picture take shape as the transfer is occurring.

CompuServe, for example, contains a weather information forum (GO WEATHER). This forum contains current weather maps that you can download to your system. Figure 5.14 shows a downloaded map that indicates the current weather conditions for the United States. To get this screen, request a download of a weather map from the Weather Forum on CompuServe. PROCOMM PLUS for Windows detects the file being downloaded, so you do not have to choose the Receive File Action icon. First a blank window appears, and then the picture is filled in as the transfer progresses.

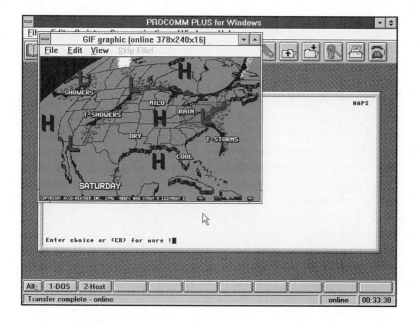

FIG. 5.14

An example of a downloaded GIF file.

When the transfer is complete, you can use the menu bar in the GIF window to save the image to a file.

Summary

This chapter explained how to use PROCOMM PLUS for Windows to send and receive electronic files. You first learned the basic steps to send a file from your computer to a remote computer and then learned how to receive a file that is transmitted by a remote computer. Next, you explored when and how to use the file-transfer protocols available in PROCOMM PLUS for Windows. Finally, you learned how to view files in a directory, collect file names in a File Clipboard window, use a Windows Gateway feature to access the DOS operating system, and download a GIF file.

Now that you are familiar with how to transfer files, you need some files to send. Turn to Chapter 6, "Using the Windows Notepad Editor," to find out how to create text files by using the PROCOMM PLUS for Windows text editor.

Using the Windows Notepad Editor

Notepad is a simple Windows text editor intended to help you create and edit files made up entirely of characters from the ASCII character set. Using Notepad, you can create ASCII files that contain up to 50,000 characters per file. Notepad has some of the characteristics of a typical Windows word processor, such as block copy and block move, word wrap, and adjustable margins. Notepad is intended to function as a simple word processor/text editor, enabling you to create and modify scripts and edit note files and the connection log.

This chapter discusses how to start Notepad from PROCOMM PLUS for Windows and explains how to perform the following operations with Notepad:

- Enter text

- Move around in a file

- Change text in an existing file

- Copy, move, or delete portions of text

- Search for character strings

- Save ASCII text to a disk file

The Notepad program probably is all the editor you will need to create and edit notes and scripts within PROCOMM PLUS for Windows. You may already have a text editor, however, that you prefer to use.

PROCOMM PLUS for Windows enables you to substitute your text editor for Notepad so that you can activate your text editor from PROCOMM PLUS for Windows. The last part of this chapter discusses how to add a different text editor to PROCOMM PLUS for Windows and how to start the text editor directly from Windows.

Starting Notepad from PROCOMM PLUS for Windows

To give you quick access to a text editor, PROCOMM PLUS for Windows enables you to activate Notepad from three areas in the program:

- As the editor for compiling and editing scripts

- As the editor for notes in the dialing directory

- As the editor for the connection log

You also can activate the Notepad editor from the Windows Program Manager. Later in this chapter, in the section "Starting Notepad from Windows," you see how you can also access Notepad from the Windows menu. The next several sections show you how to begin Notepad within each of these areas of PROCOMM PLUS for Windows.

Using Notepad To Compile and Edit Scripts

You use scripts to automate repetitive steps you might take when using PROCOMM PLUS for Windows. The ASPECT language is used to create the script programs. As with most other programming languages, you must use some kind of editor to enter the program commands. PROCOMM PLUS for Windows uses the Windows Notepad Editor, which is the editor packaged with Microsoft Windows.

To use Notepad to compile or edit a script, select the Compile/Edit option from the Scripts menu, or press Alt-F3 (see fig. 6.1).

A file selection dialog box similar to figure 6.2 appears on-screen. You use this screen to select the file to edit or compile. Compilation of a script is covered in Chapters 7 and 11. This discussion is concerned primarily with editing a script.

Notice in the List Files Of Type box in the bottom left corner of the screen that *.WAS files are selected to be listed. The WAS extension stands for Windows ASpect file. This is an ASCII-type file containing the lines of programming for a script.

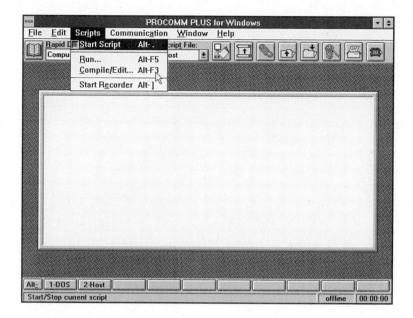

FIG. 6.1

Selecting Compile/
Edit from the Scripts
menu.

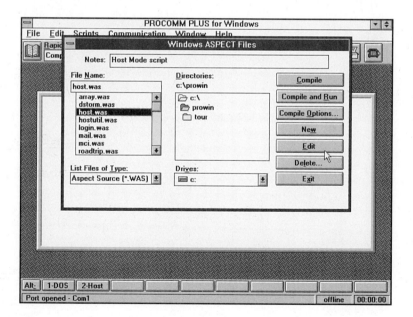

FIG. 6.2

The Compile/Edit file
selection dialog box.

To select the script to edit, click the file name in the File Name list box. If you prefer the keyboard, press Tab until the File Name list box is highlighted; then press the up- and down-arrow keys to highlight the file you want to edit and press Enter. You can use the Directories and Drives options to locate files on other drives or in other directories.

The option buttons on the right side of the dialog box contain compilation and edit options. The options that will be discussed in this chapter are New, Edit, Delete, and Exit. The New option enables you to enter Notepad under a new name, one not found in the list box. This action creates a new file. You choose this button if you are entering a new script. The Edit option enables you to edit the currently highlighted file. The Delete option enables you to delete the highlighted file or files in the File Name list box. If you want to exit the dialog box without performing any more of these tasks, choose Exit. You are then returned to the Terminal Display window.

When you select Edit, the Notepad window containing the contents of the selected script file appears. The Notepad window shown in figure 6.3, for example, contains the HOST.WAS file provided on your PROCOMM PLUS for Windows disk.

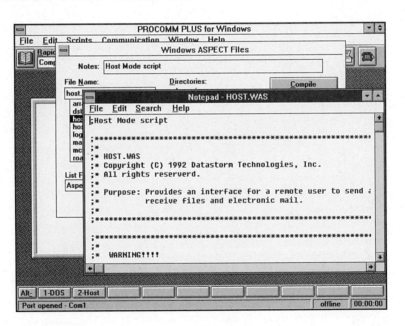

FIG. 6.3

Displaying a script file in the Notepad window.

> **WARNING:** Do not change the script files provided to you on the PROCOMM PLUS for Windows disk unless you are sure of your changes. Making a backup copy of the original file before making changes to it is a good idea.

Information on the individual Notepad commands is covered in a later section of this chapter, "Using the Notepad Editor Commands."

Using Notepad To Edit Note Files

One of the options in each dialing directory entry (see Chapter 3, "Building Your Dialing Directory") is Notes. This option enables you to enter information about the dialing directory entry. When you are editing or entering a new dialing directory entry, double-clicking the file name listed in the Notes field (or pressing Alt-A with the file name in the Notes field highlighted) begins Notepad. An example of Notepad used to edit a note file is shown in figure 6.4.

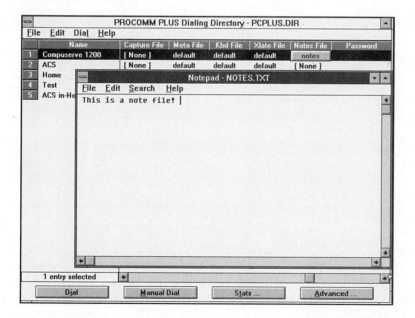

FIG. 6.4

Using Notepad to edit a note file.

Information on the individual Notepad commands is covered in a later section of this chapter, "Using the Notepad Editor Commands."

Using Notepad To Edit the Connection Log

Each time you use PROCOMM PLUS for Windows to connect (or attempt to connect) to another computer, the information about the connection is collected in a file called PW.CLG. This file is the *connection log*. The value of this log is that it helps you keep track of your activity. This log can be particularly helpful if you must record long-distance telephone numbers you call.

To edit or view the connection log, select the Connection Log option from the File menu in the Terminal Display window (see fig. 6.5).

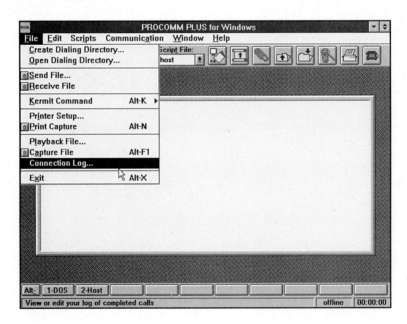

FIG. 6.5

Choosing Connection Log from the File menu.

When you choose Connection Log, the Connection Log dialog box appears (see fig. 6.6). The Include Status Line Information in Log option is a selection box. When you select this box, and an X appears inside the box, you tell the connection log to collect any messages that appear in the Terminal Display screen's status line, including messages about uploads, downloads, printer status, and so on. With this option selected, you get much more detail about the session in your log, but if you always have the option on, it eventually makes the connection log very big. To select or deselect the option, click the box, or press Tab until your cursor is on the box and then press the space bar to change the setting.

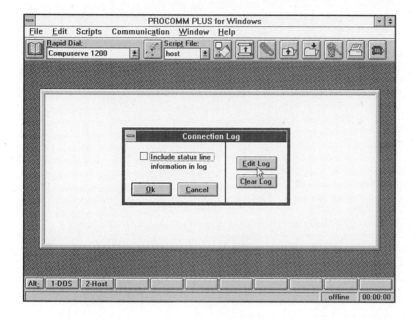

FIG. 6.6

The Connection Log dialog box.

The Edit Log button enables you to edit the contents of the connection log by using Notepad. When you select Edit Log, the Notepad window containing the connection log appears (see fig. 6.7). The Clear Log option in the Connection Log dialog box erases the contents of the log file.

To exit the Connection Log dialog box and save the current options chosen in the box, choose OK. Choose Cancel to exit the box and return the selection to its previous state.

Information on the individual Notepad commands is covered in the next section. To exit Notepad, choose Exit from Notepad's File menu.

Using the Notepad Editor Commands

The next several sections explain the commands on the Notepad editor menu bar. The "feel" of this editor is similar to most modern word processors. In fact, the Notepad editor is much like the DOS 5.0 Editor.

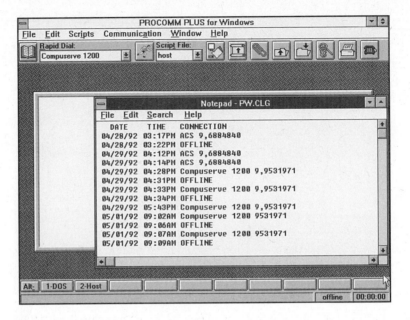

FIG. 6.7

Using Notepad to edit
the connection log.

Unless you are capable of error-free typing, you need Notepad's editing
capabilities. The sections that follow discuss methods available in
Notepad for typing over, inserting, deleting, copying, and moving text in
the Notepad working screen. The keystrokes used for editing are given in
table 6.1.

Table 6.1. Cursor-Movement and Editing Keys for Notepad

Key	Effect
←	Moves cursor one space to the left
→	Moves cursor one space to the right
↑	Moves cursor up one line
↓	Moves cursor down one line
Enter	Moves cursor to the next line, adds a new line if insert is on, or moves to the end of the file
Home	Moves cursor to the first character at the left end of the line
End	Moves cursor to the end of the line
Ctrl-Home	Moves cursor to the beginning of the document

Key	Effect
Ctrl-End	Moves cursor to the end of the document
Backspace	Deletes character to the left of the cursor
Tab	Goes to next tab stop
Del	Deletes character at current cursor position
PgUp	Moves cursor up 21 lines
PgDn	Moves cursor down 21 lines
F3	Enables you to find occurrences of text within a file
F5	Time/Date - Types current system time and date into file at cursor position
Alt-Backspace	Undo - Cancels last change made to a line
Shift-Del	Cut - Cuts currently highlighted text and places it into the Windows Clipboard
Ctrl-Ins	Copy - Copies contents of highlighted text into Windows Clipboard
Shift-Ins	Paste - Inserts contents of Clipboard into file at cursor position

Descriptions of the commands available from Notepad's menu bar, which includes File, Edit, Search, and Help, are included in the following sections.

Getting Help in Notepad

If you are familiar with using a word processor (particularly if it is Windows-based), you should have no trouble using Notepad immediately. You may, however, have questions about some of the commands in Notepad. Notepad contains an extensive help system, so you can get information quickly about using the editor.

You open the Help window in Notepad just as you display a help screen in PROCOMM PLUS for Windows. Select the Help option on the menu line. Then choose from the options Index, Keyboard, Commands, Procedures, or Using Help. The About option displays copyright information about Notepad. The Notepad Index Help window is shown in figure 6.8. As you can see, you can choose from a number of options on this first Help screen.

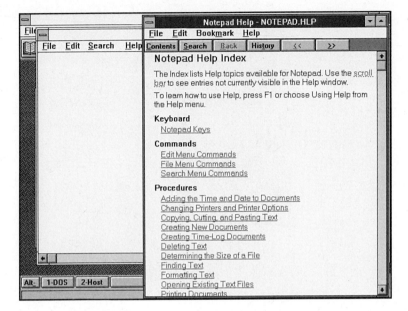

FIG. 6.8

The Notepad Help window.

Notepad's help system works exactly like the main PROCOMM PLUS for Windows help system described in Chapter 2, "Getting Around in PROCOMM PLUS for Windows." Briefly, to display help on any under-lined item in the index, click the underlined word. A description of that item then is displayed.

The last option on the Help menu is the About option. This option displays copyright information about Notepad and tells you the current size of your file in bytes. The maximum size for a Notepad file is about 50,000 characters (bytes).

Using the Notepad File Menu

The first item on the Notepad menu bar, as in most Windows applications, is File. To extend this menu, select File. The extended File menu is shown in figure 6.9.

The New option on the File menu causes Notepad to clear all the current information in the window. Then a blank Notepad window appears, en-abling you to enter new information. Be careful not to erase information you have not saved.

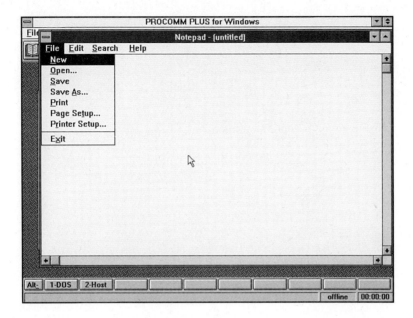

FIG. 6.9

Notepad's File menu
extended.

The Open option on the File menu enables you to open a file—in other
words, edit a file that already exists on disk. When you select Open, a
dialog box appears from which you choose the file you want to open and
edit.

With the Save and Save As options, you can save the contents of the
Notepad editor to a disk file. When you select Save, the file is saved
under the current name of the file. If you have not yet named the file,
you are prompted to enter a name. If you select the Save As option, you
also are prompted to enter the name of the file. The Save As option also
is handy for making a backup copy of a file. If you want to edit the
HOST.WAS file, for example, you can bring it into the editor and save the
file as HOSTBAK.WAS. You can always recover the original file by using
the backup copy.

The Print option enables you to print the contents of Notepad to the
printer. To set the margins, header, and footer for your printout, you use
the Page Setup option. When you select Page Setup, you see a dialog box
similar to the one in figure 6.10. The header and footer can be text, such
as "This is my Script File for Logging on to CompuServe," or can contain
codes as detailed in table 6.2. You also can use a combination of text and
codes for the header and footer. When you print the file, your defined
headers and footers are printed on each page of the output. The margins
determine how the contents of the file are printed when you choose the
Print option from the File menu.

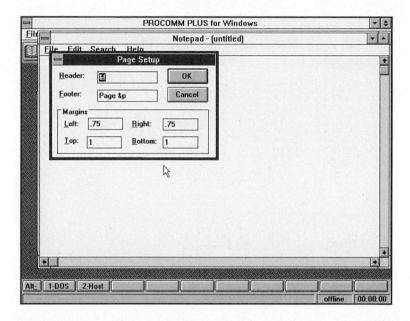

FIG. 6.10

The Page Setup dialog box.

Table 6.2. Header and Footer Codes for the Notepad Editor

Code	Effect
&d	Prints the current date
&p	Prints the page number on each page
&f	Prints the current file name
&l	Prints the text following this code justified left
&r	Prints the text following this code justified right
&c	Prints the text following this code centered
&t	Prints the current time

To change a header, footer, or margin setting, click the appropriate option in the Page Setup dialog box, or press Tab to move to that option, and then type the change. To save the changes, click OK or press Enter. To cancel any changes you have made, click Cancel or press Esc.

The Printer Setup option on the File menu enables you to specify what printer you are using. This information determines how the file is sent to the printer. Figure 6.11 shows the Printer Setup dialog box for an HP LaserJet printer. This printer is the default as chosen in the installation procedure or in the Setup window. You may have a different printer window on your setup of PROCOMM PLUS for Windows.

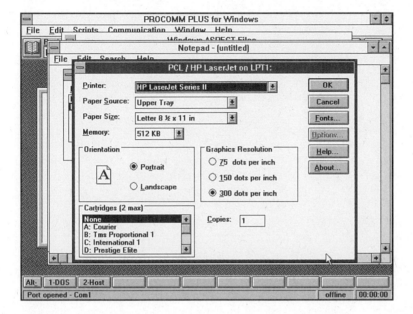

FIG. 6.11

The Printer Setup
dialog box.

From this window, you can choose, among other items, how many copies to print and whether to print in landscape or portrait mode. If your printer supports different fonts, you can choose what font to use when printing the contents of the file. Some of the printer options should have no particular effect in printing the contents of an ASCII file. For more information on setting up your default printer options, see Chapter 8, "Tailoring PROCOMM PLUS for Windows."

The File menu's Exit option enables you to exit Notepad. Make sure that you have saved information you want to keep before exiting the Notepad window.

Using the Notepad Edit Menu

The Notepad Edit menu contains commands related to changing, copying, and editing text in the editor. The extended Edit menu is shown in figure 6.12. Notice that most of these commands also have shortcut commands associated with them. The shortcut command for Undo, for example, is Alt-Backspace. (These shortcut commands also are documented in table 6.1.)

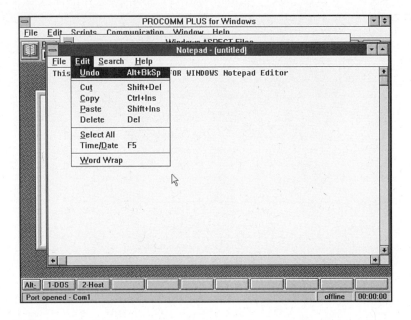

FIG. 6.12

The Edit menu
extended.

The Undo command (Alt-Backspace) enables you to recover from the last information you have changed. If you begin editing a line and then discover that it is all wrong, for example, you can select Undo, and the line reverts back to its original state before you began editing it. Keep in mind, however, that Undo redoes only your last change.

One of the more popular features of word processing programs is the capability to "cut" a block of text from one position in a file and "paste" the block to a different position in the file. Notepad includes this cut-and-paste capability, as well as the capability to copy or delete a block of text.

The Cut and Copy commands are related. Before cutting or copying text in the file, you must select that text. To select a block of text, place your mouse pointer on the first character you want to select. Hold down the mouse pointer and drag it to the last character you want to select. The characters between the first and last characters become highlighted. If you are using keyboard commands rather than the mouse, place your cursor on the first character to select, hold down the Shift key, and press the arrow keys to move the cursor to the last character. Again, the text appears highlighted.

After you have selected some text, you can choose Cut or Copy from the Edit menu (or press Shift-Del or Ctrl-Ins). If you choose Cut, the selected text disappears and is placed into the Windows Clipboard. If you choose Copy, the text is placed in the Windows Clipboard, but the selected text is not erased.

When you have text in the Windows Clipboard, you then can paste that information anywhere in the file. To paste information, place your cursor where you want to insert the information and choose Paste from the Edit menu (or press Shift-Ins). The contents of the Windows Clipboard are pasted into the file at the location of your cursor.

The Delete option also takes advantage of selected text. To delete a range of text, first select it and then choose Delete from the Edit menu or press Del.

The Select All option on the Edit menu enables you to select the entire contents of the currently opened file in Notepad. This feature comes in handy if you want to place the contents of the editor into the Windows Clipboard, in anticipation of pasting the text into another window. You can paste the text from one Notepad file to another, for example.

With the Time/Date (F5) option on the Edit menu, you can enter the current time and date at the cursor's location.

Text-editing programs like Notepad traditionally are used by programmers to write lines of codes rather than for true word processing. Consequently, these programs do not always provide the word processing features that you may take for granted. Notepad does contain some of the features you find in a word processing program, however, such as word wrap and margin setting. Because you can use Notepad for programming and word processing, an option is provided so that you can choose whether you want to use word wrap. With the Word Wrap option on the Edit menu, you can toggle word wrap on and off. If you are typing in sentences and paragraphs, you probably want to have word wrap on, as is usually the case in a word processor. If you are writing lines of programming code, you probably want the feature turned off. Each time you select the Word Wrap option, it toggles to the opposite state. If Word Wrap is on, a check appears to the left of the option in the extended Edit menu.

Using the Notepad Search Menu

If you are editing a long file, you may want to locate a particular word or phrase quickly. The Find and Find Next options on the Search menu enable you to do just that. The extended Search menu is shown in figure 6.13. To locate a word or phrase, choose the Find option. Notepad prompts you to enter the search string in the Find dialog box (see fig. 6.14).

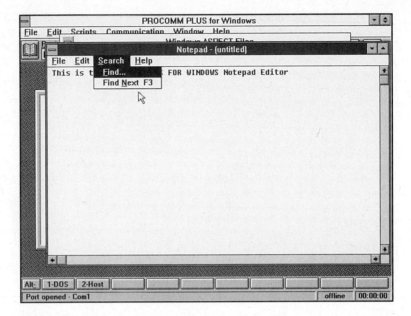

FIG. 6.13

The Notepad Search menu.

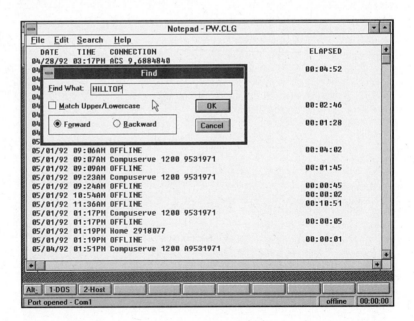

FIG. 6.14

The Notepad Find dialog box.

In this dialog box, you can choose to search from the cursor forward in the file or from the cursor backward in the file by selecting the Forward (Alt-O) or Backward (Alt-B) button. You also can choose to match upper- and lowercase letters in the search (Alt-M). Suppose that you want to find the word *HILLTOP* (no matter what case) in the file. You enter *hilltop* as the search string in the Find What box, do not select the Match Upper/Lowercase option, and select the Forward button. Notepad begins searching from the current location of the cursor forward in the file until locating a match for the word. Notepad then highlights the word and displays the section around the word in the Notepad window. If this occurrence of the word is not the one you are looking for, select Find Next (F3) from the Search menu to locate the next match. A message tells you if Notepad cannot find any more matches to the string.

Reviewing Save Techniques

As you work with Notepad, the file displayed on-screen is held in your computer's random-access memory (RAM). RAM is temporary; when you quit Notepad, the text is removed from memory. To preserve a screen file, you must save it to a disk file. Notepad provides several methods for completing this task.

Anytime you are working on a file in Notepad (or any other text editor or word processor), save the file to disk periodically (perhaps every 15 minutes) by selecting Save from the File menu. You then can continue working on the same file. This practice ensures that a power outage or some other premature termination of Notepad does not destroy your work. Changes made up to the last time you saved the file to disk are secure.

When you finish with the file and want to return to PROCOMM PLUS for Windows, save the file and then choose Exit from the File menu. You return to the window you were in when you started Notepad.

Occasionally, you may want to abandon the file or the changes you have made in Notepad. To quit Notepad without saving the file to disk, choose Exit from the File menu (without saving). Notepad asks whether you want to save the current contents of the file. Answer No to the prompt.

Using a Different Editor

Although Notepad is handy, you may have another editor that you prefer. With PROCOMM PLUS for Windows, you easily can tell the program to use a substitute editor. For this task, you use the System Settings dialog box shown in figure 6.15. To get to this screen, click the Setup Action icon or choose Setup from the Window menu. Then choose System Settings from the Setup menu.

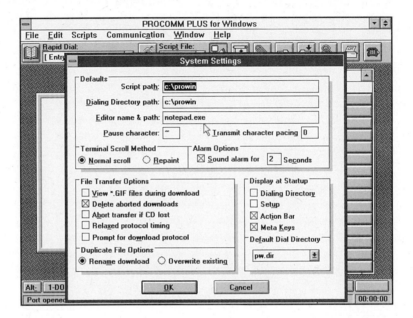

Suppose that you want to use an editor named NU-Edit (a hypothetical text editor). To specify this program as the editor to use, add the start-up command for NU-Edit to the Editor Name & Path field in the System Settings dialog box. In this example, the start-up command is NU-EDIT, so you must substitute this command for NOTEPAD.EXE in the Editor Name & Path option of the System Settings dialog box.

After you add the proper start-up command for your editor to the Editor Name & Path field, exit the System Settings dialog box by selecting OK. To save the settings, choose Save and then choose Exit from the File menu.

Starting Notepad from Windows

Because Notepad is a standard part of Microsoft Windows, you can run the editor as a stand-alone program from Windows. If you want to work on some editing of a script, a note file, or any other ASCII file, you can use Notepad without first entering PROCOMM PLUS for Windows. To begin Notepad from Windows, first make sure that the Accessories window is in view in the Windows Program Manager screen, as shown in figure 6.16. Your Program Manager screen probably looks somewhat different. If the Accessories window is not in view, it is probably a minimized icon at the bottom of the screen, like the Norton Desktop for DOS and Games icons at the bottom of the screen in figure 6.16. To open a minimized icon, click it twice. Then click the Notepad icon in the Accessories window twice. The Notepad program starts, and a blank Notepad window appears on-screen.

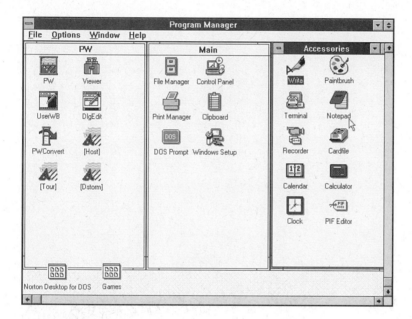

FIG. 6.16

The Program Manager with the Accessories window in view.

Summary

This chapter described how to use Windows' text editor Notepad, used with PROCOMM PLUS for Windows, to create and edit ASCII files. You also learned how to enter text; move around a file; make changes to the text in an existing file; copy, move, or delete portions of the text; search for character strings; and save ASCII text to a disk file.

One of the major uses for Notepad is to edit PROCOMM PLUS for Windows scripts. Turn to Chapter 7 to learn how to automate PROCOMM PLUS for Windows with meta keys and PROCOMM PLUS for Windows scripts.

Automating PROCOMM PLUS for Windows with Meta Keys and Script Files

When you discover a task that you perform repeatedly on your computer, look for a way to get the computer to do most of the work. Your computer can perform most tasks faster than you can, and computers don't make mistakes. PROCOMM PLUS for Windows provides two different features you can use to take advantage of the computer's capability to perform repetitive tasks quickly and correctly. These features are *meta keys* and *script files*.

PROCOMM PLUS for Windows offers three kinds of meta keys: text, script, and program. You can use meta keys to define a string of characters to be transmitted to a remote computer, begin a script with a single keystroke, and begin an external program from PROCOMM PLUS for Windows.

In this chapter, you learn how to create, edit, save, and use the three different types of meta keys and how to create one or more meta key files, each containing up to 40 meta key definitions for use in PROCOMM PLUS for Windows.

A PROCOMM PLUS for Windows script file is a short program written in the Windows ASPECT script (programming) language. This chapter demonstrates how to create a simple Windows ASPECT script without programming, explains how to create a script by simply recording keystrokes, discusses a sample script file that DATASTORM distributes with PROCOMM PLUS for Windows, and explains how to customize scripts for your own use. Finally, this chapter describes the methods for activating PROCOMM PLUS for Windows scripts. This chapter is only an introduction to PROCOMM PLUS for Windows scripts. After you are comfortable with the script techniques presented in this chapter, read Chapter 11, "An Overview of the Windows ASPECT Script Language."

Working with Meta Keys

Many aspects of PC communications become routine; you type certain words or phrases frequently. You log on to an on-line computer service, for example, by typing your identification number and then a password. Every time you log on to a bulletin board, you have to type your name and a password. Typing these entries is not hard work, but it does take time and holds a potential for typing errors. If your ID number is 2974,ARQ, for example, you may type 2947,AQR by mistake.

To help you save time and keystrokes and to reduce typographical errors, PROCOMM PLUS for Windows enables you to assign any string of up to 80 characters (including spaces) to a keystroke combination referred to as a text meta key. Three types of meta keys are available:

- *Text meta key*. Defines a string of characters that you type in, such as a logon code or a command to a remote computer. By using text meta keys, for example, you can condense to a meta key a text entry that you otherwise would have to type. When you are prompted to enter the information you stored in the meta key, you simply press the meta key associated with the prompt, and PROCOMM PLUS for Windows types the saved response on-screen for you.

- *Script meta key*. Starts up a Windows ASPECT script. When you define a meta key as a Script type, you can begin the script with a single keystroke combination. If you have a script called LOGON, for example, which logs on to your company's computer, you can define a meta key (Alt-5, for example) as the command LOGON. You simply press the meta key (such as Alt-5) while in Terminal mode to start the script. (The meta key Alt-2 already is defined as "Host," which begins the Host script that was provided on the PROCOMM PLUS for Windows disk.)

■ *Program meta key*. Runs an external program from PROCOMM PLUS for Windows. When you define a meta key as a Program type, you can begin the external program with a single keystroke combination. Suppose that you have a program called CONDENSE.EXE that you sometimes want to run while you are logged on to your company's database. You can associate the command CONDENSE with a meta key (Alt-6, for example). You simply press the meta key (Alt-6) while in Terminal mode to begin the CONDENSE program. When the program finishes, you are returned to the PROCOMM PLUS for Windows Terminal mode. (The meta key Alt-1 was defined when you installed PROCOMM PLUS for Windows as a program meta key that begins a second command [DOS] processor using COMMAND.COM.)

The meta key information you define is stored in a file on the disk and is available to be "played back" with one keystroke combination or one click. Ten meta key buttons usually appear at the bottom of the Terminal Display window. To "play" a key, you simply click the key, or press the assigned Alt-key combination plus the meta key number. Each button has four meanings. Alt-3 is one command, for example, but you also can define meanings for Alt-Shift-3, Alt-Ctrl-3, and Alt-Shift-Ctrl-3. Thus, you can define a total of 40 meta key commands.

The paragraphs that follow describe how to create, modify, save to disk, and use PROCOMM PLUS for Windows meta keys.

Defining a Meta Key

Meta keys are stored in a file on disk. You can store up to 40 meta key definitions in a single Meta Key file in the Current Setup menu. The extension to a meta key file is KEY. When you install PROCOMM PLUS for Windows on your disk, a meta key file called DEFAULT.KEY is placed in your default PPW directory. This file is the meta key file used by PROCOMM PLUS for Windows unless you specify some other meta key file in the Dialing Directory or in the Current Setup menu.

To create a new meta key file, first display the Current Setup menu (see fig. 7.1) by clicking the Setup Action icon, or select Setup from the Window menu. Notice on this screen the option Meta Key: default.key. This tells you that the file called default.key is the current default meta key file. To select the Meta Key option on the Current Setup menu, press Alt-M or click the Meta Key option. A drop-down menu appears. Select the Create option on the Meta Key drop-down box list. You are prompted to enter a name for the new meta key file. Enter a file name and press Enter. Choose Advanced! at the top of the Current Setup menu. The PROCOMM PLUS Meta Key Mapper screen appears (see fig. 7.2).

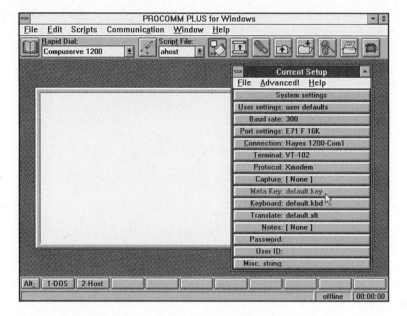

FIG. 7.1

The Current Setup menu.

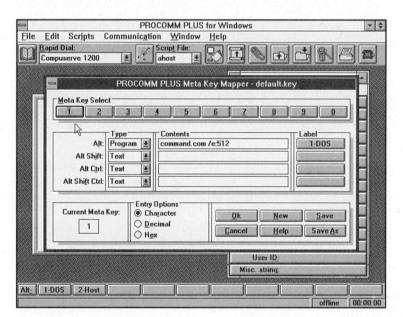

FIG. 7.2

The Meta Key Mapper screen.

At the top of the Meta Key Mapper screen is a series of 10 buttons labeled from 1 to 0. These refer to the 10 meta keys that appear at the bottom of the Terminal Display window. To add or edit a meta key, you first must indicate which key by selecting the appropriate button in the Meta Key Select section of the Meta Key Mapper screen. To edit meta key 3, for example, click button 3 or press Alt-3. In the bottom left corner of the screen is a box labeled Current Meta Key. This box tells you which key you currently are editing.

The middle of the screen contains the area where you enter or edit the meaning of the meta keys. Four keystroke types are included for each button, labeled Alt, Alt-Shift, Alt-Ctrl, and Alt-Shift-Ctrl. These labels refer to the keystroke needed to activate the meta key, such as Alt-3 or Alt-Shift-3.

The three fields that you use to define a meta key are the Type field, the Contents field, and the Label field. The Type field enables you to choose the kind of meta command—Text, Script, or Program—for each of the four meta keys you can assign to each meta key button. This field contains a drop-down box, as shown in figure 7.3. To extend this Type box, click the down arrow at the right side of the box, or press Tab until the box is highlighted and then press the space bar. To choose an option from the drop-down box, click the item, or press the up- and down-arrow keys to highlight your choice and then press Tab to move to the next field.

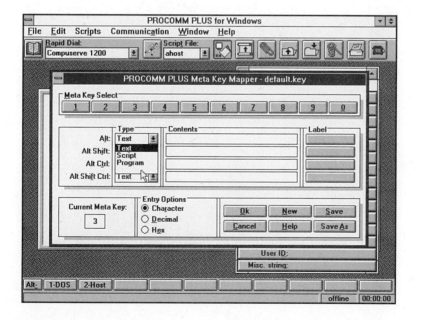

FIG. 7.3

Extending the Type field's drop-down box.

The Contents field is where you enter the meta key command. When you later execute the meta key, letters and numbers translate into their corresponding keystrokes (see "Executing Meta Keys" later in this chapter).

To enter information in the Contents field, highlight the Contents field and type the information you want the meta key to type when it is executed. Suppose that you type *BR549*. Later, when you execute the meta key, PROCOMM PLUS for Windows types the same characters: BR549.

The Entry Options box at the bottom of the screen enables you to choose how the contents of a meta key are displayed in the Contents box. Usually, you want this option set to Character, which means that you can use the characters on the keyboard to enter the meta key information. The Decimal option causes the contents to be displayed as decimal ASCII characters. Rather than the letter A, for example, the ASCII code 65 appears. The Hex option causes the characters to appear as hexadecimal codes. The letter A, for example, appears in hexadecimal as a 41. (See Appendix C for a table of ASCII, decimal, and hexadecimal codes.)

A number of special meta key codes are referred to as *control codes* because the first character in each code, the caret (^), represents the Ctrl key on the keyboard. When you execute a meta key that contains the characters ^C, for example, PROCOMM PLUS for Windows does not type the caret (^) and then the letter C. Instead, PROCOMM PLUS for Windows transmits to the remote computer the same code that is sent if you press Ctrl-C, a keystroke combination that may have a special meaning to a particular on-line service or bulletin board. Many on-line services and bulletin boards use Ctrl-key combinations, such as Ctrl-C, Ctrl-X, Ctrl-S, and Ctrl-Q, to enable you to control the flow of information across your screen or to cancel an operation in midstream.

In general, you can create any Ctrl-key combination by typing in the meta key entry area the caret (^) followed by a letter (A through Z, upper- or lowercase) or one of the following characters:

[ ] \ ^ _

Several of the meta key control codes translate into keystrokes that you normally would not expect and that do not involve the Ctrl key. Suppose that you type the characters ^M in a meta key entry. When you execute the meta key, PROCOMM PLUS for Windows sends a carriage return to the remote computer for the ^M. In other words, when you want the meta key to "press" Enter, use the code ^M. Several special control codes are listed in table 7.1.

Table 7.1. Special Meta Key Control Codes

Code	Executed keystroke
^M	Enter
^H	Backspace
^I	Horizontal tab (Tab key)
^J	Line feed
^K	Vertical tab
^[	Esc

Another special key you can use when defining a meta command is the vertical bar key (|). Use this key when you want to insert a literal caret (^) in the contents. If you enter ^C, for example, it normally is interpreted as Ctrl-C, but if you enter ^|C, it is interpreted as the characters ^C. To include a literal vertical bar in the contents, use two consecutive bars. ^|M||, for example, is interpreted as ^M|.

Control keys, such as ^M, are ASCII characters whose decimal codes are less then 32. (32 is the blank character.) ^A is ASCII character 1, ^B is ASCII character 2, and so on. If you need to enter an ASCII code less than 32 into a Contents field, you can use this technique. If you need to enter an ASCII character greater than 126 (characters not on the keyboard), you can use another technique. You can enter any character into the Contents field by pressing the Alt key and then entering 0 and the number's ASCII code from the numeric keypad. The Greek letter beta (β), for example, is ASCII character 225. To enter this character into the Contents field, hold down the Alt key and type *0225* on the numeric keypad. When you release the Alt key, a β appears. Although this technique is particularly useful for extended ASCII characters from 127 to 255, you can use it for any ASCII character. ^M, for example, is the same as ASCII character 013.

Another way to enter nonkeyboard characters is to use the Decimal or Hex entry options. When you choose the Decimal option in the Entry Options box, for example, the current entry in the Contents field is displayed as decimal ASCII codes. The letter A appears as 065, for example. Therefore, if you are in <u>D</u>ecimal mode, you can enter *0225* in the Contents area, switch back to Character mode, and see the Greek beta character appear where you typed the decimal code. You can use a similar technique with the H<u>e</u>x option if you know the hexadecimal code for a character.

In the Label field, you enter the name of the meta key button as you want it to appear at the bottom of the Terminal Display screen. To enter a label, highlight the Label field and enter the label you want to assign to the meta button.

You may, for example, want to create a meta key to enter a computer account number. Suppose that your ID is 75,1020. To create the account meta key as Alt-3, choose the 3 button, choose Text in the Type field, enter *75,1010^M* in the Contents field, and type *3-Account* in the Label field, as shown in figure 7.4.

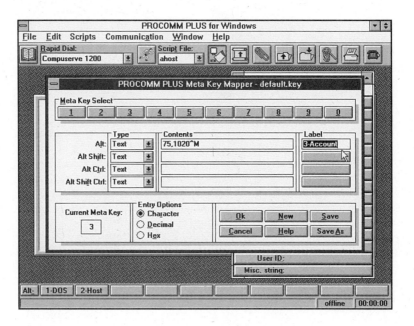

Entering meta key information.

The buttons in the bottom right corner of the Meta Key Mapper dialog box contain several options. The OK button exits the box and retains changes (but does not save them to disk). The New button erases all information from the current Meta Key Mapper screen and enables you to begin with a new meta key file. The Save option saves the information to disk, using the name of the file at the top of the screen (DEFAULT.KEY, for example, in fig. 7.2). The Cancel button exits the screen and cancels all changes you have made. The Help button displays the Help window. The Save As button enables you to save the information in the Meta Key Mapper screen to a new key file. For more on the save options, see the next section.

Saving Meta Keys to a Meta Key File

When you enter a meta key definition, PROCOMM PLUS for Windows stores the meta key in memory (RAM). The meta key is not saved automatically to a disk file. Unless you take steps to save the meta key to disk, you can use the meta key for the current PROCOMM PLUS for Windows session only.

To save the current meta key entry or entries, as they appear on the Meta Key Mapper screen, choose the Save As or Save button. If you choose Save, the information is saved in the current file. If you choose Save As, you can save the information in a different file.

You may, for example, want to use one group of 10 meta keys only when connected to the CompuServe on-line service. Perhaps each of these meta keys takes you directly to a different service of CompuServe. Because these meta keys are of no use for any other purpose, they need to be accessible only while you are using CompuServe. The CompuServe system uses a GO command to move from one part of the system to another. To go to the electronic mail system you type *go mail*; to go to the IBM PC Application forum, you type *go ibmapp*, and so on. If you create a CompuServe dialing directory entry, you also may want to create a CompuServe set of meta keys that automates these GO commands.

To create and save a CompuServe meta file (call it CSERVE.KEY), first display the Meta Key Mapper screen. You may want to start with the DEFAULT.KEY file, change it, and save it as your new file. In the Meta Key Mapper screen, enter each GO command. Figure 7.5 shows the command `GO IBMAPP^M` entered for meta key 3, with the label `3-IBMAPP`.

After you have entered all of the GO commands you want to define, choose the Save As option. The Meta Key File Save As dialog box appears (see fig. 7.6). Enter any legal DOS file name. You do not have to enter a file extension because PROCOMM PLUS for Windows adds the KEY extension for you. In figure 7.6, the file name CSERVE has been entered. Choose OK. This saves to the file the current contents of the Meta Key Mapper screen, exits the Mapper screen, and returns you to the Current Setup menu. Select Exit from the File menu to return to the Terminal Display screen.

Using a Meta Key File

After you have defined a meta key file, you can make it the current file from the Current Setup menu, or you can place the meta key file in a dialing directory entry.

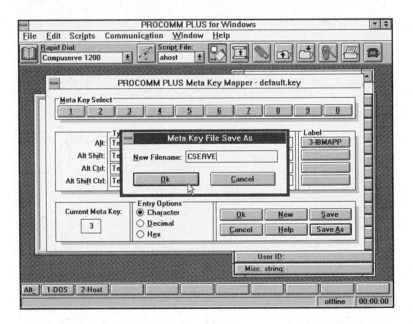

FIG. 7.5

Entering CompuServe
GO commands as
meta keys.

FIG. 7.6

Saving a Meta Key
file.

To make the CSERVE.KEY meta key file the current file, for example, display the Current Setup menu by clicking the Setup Action icon or by pressing Alt-W, then S. Select the Meta Key option. Select the CSERVE.KEY file from the drop-down list. Exit Current Setup by selecting the Exit option from the File menu. The Terminal Display window then shows the labels you have defined for each meta key on the buttons at the bottom of the screen, as shown in figure 7.7.

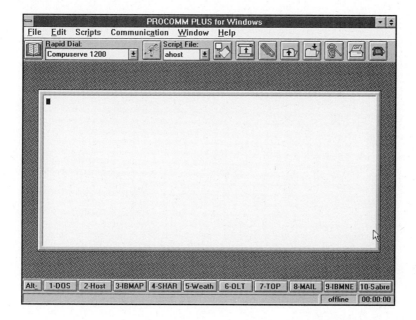

FIG. 7.7

CompuServe meta key buttons displaying in the Terminal Display window.

If you want the CSERVE.KEY meta keys to always be available when you dial into CompuServe, choose the CSERVE.KEY file in the CompuServe entry in your dialing directory. Then, when you dial CompuServe from the dialing directory, the CSERVE meta keys become active.

Modifying a Meta Key

The procedure for modifying a meta key you have created is almost the same as the procedure for creating a meta key. Display the Current Setup menu by clicking the Setup Action icon or by pressing Alt-W, then S. Select the Meta Key option. You also can press Alt-M from the Terminal windows. A drop-down menu containing all the KEY files appears. Select the file you want to edit.

The Meta Key Mapper screen appears. Just as when you added a new definition, you need to choose the button number to edit and then change the Contents or Label field to your liking.

Don't forget to save the modified version of the meta key entry to the disk file by choosing the Save or Save As button.

Loading a Meta Key File

Each time you start PROCOMM PLUS for Windows, it reads only the meta key file you have selected in the Current Setup. When you want to use a different set of meta keys, you must load into memory the meta key file that contains the set of meta keys you need. You can use only those meta key commands that are associated with the current meta file in memory, and you can have only one meta key file in memory at one time.

To load a meta key file, click the Setup Action icon or press Alt-W, then S. Select the Meta Key menu item. A drop-down menu containing all the KEY files appears. Select the file you want to load. Exit the Current Setup menu by selecting Exit from the File menu. Do not use the Save & Exit option from the File menu unless you want this file to become the permanent default file.

Executing a Meta Key

After you create a meta key, using it is simple. To execute a meta key, click the meta key button at the bottom of the Terminal Display screen or press the Alt-key combination associated with the key. The buttons in the Terminal Display screen normally display only the Alt-keystroke versions of the meta keys. To display other Alt-key combinations, click the far left button. This button causes the meta keys to cycle through the four Alt-key combinations. Of course, if you remember the specific Alt-key combination, you can press those keystrokes and access the meta key even if it is not a currently displayed button.

Creating PROCOMM PLUS for Windows Scripts

The next step in automating PROCOMM PLUS for Windows is the use of *scripts* (called command files in the original ProComm). A text meta key enables you to condense no more than 80 keystrokes into each Alt-key combination. A PROCOMM PLUS for Windows script can execute any number of keystrokes. A script is essentially a computer program, and Windows ASPECT is essentially a computer programming language. You can design the script to do much more than press keys. A script, for example, can wait for a particular prompt from the remote computer before executing a set of keystrokes. You can even write a script to automate PROCOMM PLUS for Windows completely. You can connect to other computers, read mail, upload and download files, and perform other functions, all by selecting options from menus of your own design. You also can set scripts to run unattended at a predetermined time.

As your introduction to PROCOMM PLUS for Windows scripts, this portion of the Chapter demonstrates two easy ways to create a script: by recording your keystrokes and by customizing a script supplied by DATASTORM on the PROCOMM PLUS for Windows disk.

Recording a Script

When you create a meta key, you are in a sense "teaching" it a sequence of keystrokes. PROCOMM PLUS for Windows enables you to create simple scripts in a similar way. Rather than type the keystrokes in a meta key entry space, you turn on PROCOMM PLUS for Windows' Record mode, a keystroke recorder that keeps track of your keystrokes while you are on-line to a remote computer. Not only does PROCOMM PLUS for Windows record your keystrokes, but it also records the remote system's prompts.

The Record mode records keystrokes only while you are connected to another computer. You can record the logon sequence needed to connect to another computer by starting the recorder just before dialing the connection. The keystroke recorder probably is used most often to record a logon sequence.

To activate Record mode, select Start Recorder (Alt-]) from the Scripts menu, as shown in figure 7.8. PROCOMM PLUS for Windows begins recording the information in a file named RECORD.WAS.

While Record mode is active and you are on-line to a remote computer, PROCOMM PLUS for Windows continues to record all your keystrokes as well as the remote computer's prompts. (When you later execute the script, PROCOMM PLUS for Windows plays back only your keystrokes when it gets the matching prompt from the remote computer.) To finish recording keystrokes, press Alt-] (Record Mode) again.

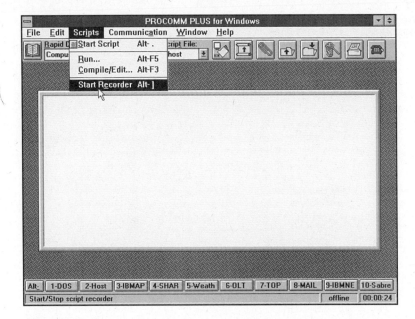

FIG. 7.8

The Scripts menu
extended.

Suppose that you want to record your logon sequence to connect to a
corporate computer for Big Corporation. Select Start Recorder (Alt-])
from the Scripts menu. Then begin the logon sequence to connect to the
computer. The progression of this sample logon is shown in figure 7.9.

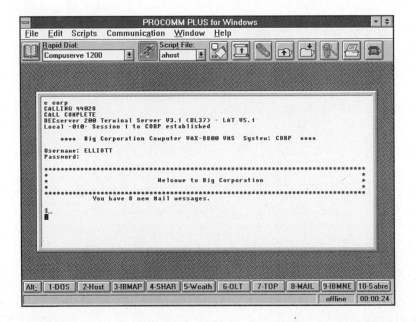

FIG. 7.9

Recording a logon
sequence.

In this case, the first message you type is *c corp*, which is your communication system's way of calling the computer named CORP. The message Calling 44028 on-screen tells you that the CORP computer is being called. (This particular computer is not using the Hayes command set for calling.) A CALL COMPLETE message is flashed as well as some additional information; then you are prompted to enter your user name. In response, you type your user name and press Enter. The remote computer then prompts you to enter a password.

Type the password (it usually does not appear on-screen as you type, so no one looking over your shoulder can see it) and press Enter. The logon procedure now is completed, and the remote computer displays a message and a $ prompt (a VAX computer prompt).

After you finish your logon sequence, you can turn off the recorder by selecting Stop Recorder (Alt-]) from the Scripts menu. A Save Recorded Script dialog box appears. From this box, you can choose to save the file as RECORD.WAS or enter a new name for the file and save. PROCOMM PLUS for Windows saves the script and returns to the Terminal Display screen.

You can associate a script with an entry in your dialing directory by entering the name of the script in the Script field of a particular entry. Then, when you dial that entry from the dialing directory, the script executes automatically.

Modifying the Recorded Script File

When you use Record mode to record a PROCOMM PLUS for Windows script, you may need to fine-tune the script later. You may, for example, be able to delete unnecessary commands. To display the script for editing, you can use the Notepad text editor or your own favorite ASCII text editor. When you select the Compile/Edit option from the Scripts menu, the editor specified in the Current Setup, System Settings dialog box is used to edit the script file.

To edit the recorded script, select Compile/Edit from the Scripts menu or press Alt-F3. Figure 7.10 shows the Windows ASPECT Files dialog box that appears. From this dialog box, you can choose what file to edit or compile. First, select the file from the File Name list at the left of the screen. In the figure, the file RECORD.WAS is selected. To edit the selected file, click Edit or press Alt-E.

The current RECORD.WAS script file then appears in the Notepad editor window. Figure 7.11, for example, shows the RECORD.WAS file generated by PROCOMM PLUS for Windows' Record mode keystroke recorder in the preceding example.

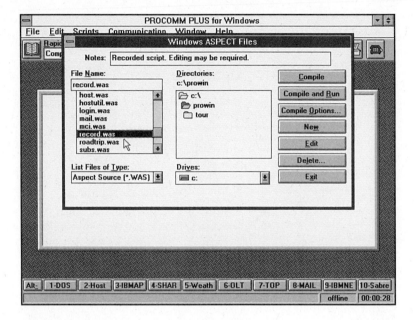

FIG. 7.10

The dialog box that
appears when you
select <u>C</u>ompile/Edit.

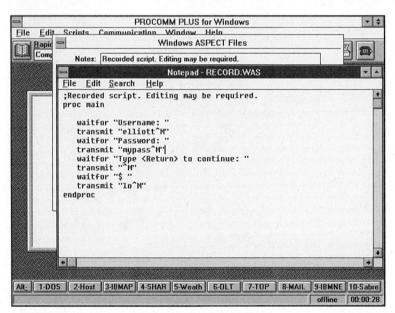

FIG. 7.11

The RECORD.WAS
script file created by
the Record mode
keystroke recorder.

A PROCOMM PLUS for Windows script file consists of one or more lines
of ASCII characters. Each line contains one command from the Windows
ASPECT script language. When you play the script, PROCOMM PLUS for

Windows executes these commands one by one from top to bottom, unless the program encounters a command that causes the execution to branch to some other portion of the script (see Chapter 11 for a list of such commands).

Because the script shown in figure 7.11 is generated by the Record mode keystroke recorder, the script contains no branching commands. PROCOMM PLUS for Windows' Record mode generates only a few commands of the Windows ASPECT script command language. Figure 7.11 demonstrates some of these Windows ASPECT commands:

- ■ PROC MAIN and ENDPROC. The first Windows ASPECT command in the script is PROC MAIN. This command tells Windows ASPECT that the following information is the starting command list for this script. At the end of this series of commands is the command ENDPROC, which signals the end of this procedure.

- ■ WAITFOR. This command causes the script to pause (do nothing) until a specified character string is received from the remote computer. When your computer receives the anticipated character string, PROCOMM PLUS for Windows continues with the next command in the script. The Record mode places in a WAITFOR command the last 15 characters received from the remote computer before you typed a particular response. In the RECORD.WAS example, the remote computer sent this prompt:

    Username:

    The Record mode keystroke recorder generated the following command in the script:

    waitfor "Username: "

- ■ TRANSMIT. This command sends a specified string of characters to the remote computer. The effect of this command is equivalent to executing a keyboard meta key containing the same string of characters. While you are in Record mode, the program generates a TRANSMIT command every time you type a string of characters terminated by a carriage return (Enter). In the example, the user name was the first thing typed after connection to the remote computer. The Record mode therefore generated the following Windows ASPECT command line:

    TRANSMIT "elliott^M"

Any text or other characters that appear on a line to the right of a semicolon (;) and are not enclosed in quotation marks are ignored when PROCOMM PLUS for Windows executes the script. You can use this feature to place comments, often called *internal documentation*, into the script for your future reference. The first line of RECORD.WAS indicates that this script is a recorded script and that editing may be necessary. This message was placed automatically in the file by the record procedure.

The script shown in figure 7.11 works as required, automating the procedure for logging on to a PC that is running PROCOMM PLUS for Windows in Host mode. With some editing, however, you can make this script easier to follow. You can modify the script using the Notepad editor, as shown in figure 7.12, deleting unnecessary text commands and adding comments that explain each step of the script. (For information on using the Notepad editor, see Chapter 6.)

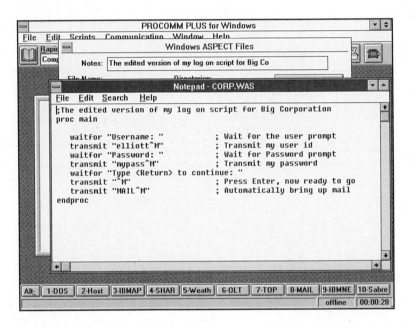

FIG. 7.12

An edited version of the recorded script.

When you customize the script, you probably should save it under a new name. To save the file, choose Save As from the Notepad File menu; then enter the new name for the file. Use the extension WAS to identify the file as a Windows ASPECT file.

Customizing a Predefined Script

If you read the section on "Recording a Script" earlier in this chapter, you learned that the Record mode generates scripts from only a limited number of script commands, plus the commands PROC MAIN and ENDPROC. These simple scripts are best suited for automating logon sequences. The Windows ASPECT script language, however, contains more than 400 commands. To take full advantage of its robust capabilities, you must go beyond Record mode.

One alternative to using Record mode is to write a script from scratch. This method is certainly possible and may be preferable after you are familiar with the Windows ASPECT script language. Sometimes you can find examples, provided by DATASTORM and others, for example, that you can tailor to your needs. By customizing a script that an experienced PROCOMM PLUS for Windows user has designed, you can save time and discover many useful Windows ASPECT programming techniques.

The PROCOMM PLUS for Windows Program disk, for example, contains a sample Windows ASPECT script file, MCI.WAS, which can automate the process of dialing and logging on to the MCI electronic mail service. Figure 7.13 shows a portion of this file. To edit the file, select Compile/Edit from the Scripts menu. Then select the file named MCI.WAS from the File Name list and choose Edit.

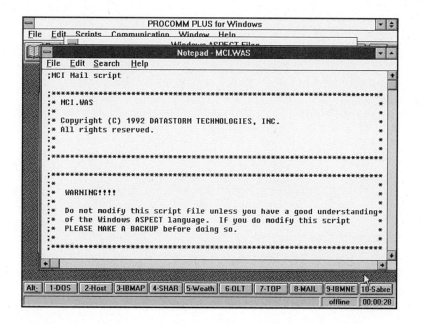

FIG. 7.13

The MCI.WAS script supplied on the PROCOMM PLUS for Windows distribution disks.

If changes need to be made to the script to fit your needs, you can change them and compile the new script. Scripts like the MCI script included with PROCOMM PLUS for Windows should be usable right away with no changes made. The first time you run the script, you will be prompted to enter your account number and password. From then on, the script will remember that information.

The best way to make changes to a predefined script is to make a copy under a different name and then modify the copy. After you have brought the file into the Notepad editor window, select Save As from the File menu and save the file under a new name. Then select Open and retrieve the file with the name you just assigned. That way, the original script is intact, and you are modifying a copy of itact. Or you can use the DOS COPY command or the Windows File Manager, for example, to make a copy of the script and give it a new name. You can make a copy of MCI.WAS, for example, named MYMCI.WAS. You then can modify MYMCI.WAS by adding the correct dialing code, your user ID number, and so on. Modifying the copy enables you to customize the script as necessary to fit your requirements without affecting the original. By following this practice, you have the DATASTORM version always readily available for comparison. You should never modify any script or other file on the original distribution disk. Always work from your hard disk or from a working copy of the distribution disk. For more information on modifying a script, refer to Chapter 11.

Compiling a Script

Before you can use a script, you must compile it. The compiling process translates the script from the English-like commands you used to build the script into a series of commands that the computer more easily understands. Thus, after a script is compiled, it can run faster because it "speaks the language" of the computer. When you compile a script, a new file is created with a WAX extension rather than the WAS extension. The WAS version of the program contains the original script, and the WAX version contains the compiled version of the script.

The screen you used to choose a script file to edit is the same one you use to choose a script to compile (refer to fig. 7.10). To compile a script, select Compile/Edit from the Scripts menu or press Alt-F3. From the File Name list in the Windows ASPECT Files dialog box that appears, choose the name of the file you want to compile.

Three commands in the Windows ASPECT Files dialog box are related to compiling scripts: Compile, Compile and Run, and Compile Options. When you select Compile Options, a screen like the one in figure 7.14 appears. This screen enables you to set up options for how the compilation is to take place. The Warning Level options enable you to choose how warnings about errors in the script code will be reported. You can choose one of three levels: to display no warning messages; display messages about unreferenced variables and labels; or display messages about unreferenced variables, labels, and procedures. The options in the Other Options box deal with items that help you as you are creating and correcting errors in the script. More information about compiling scripts is given in Chapter 11.

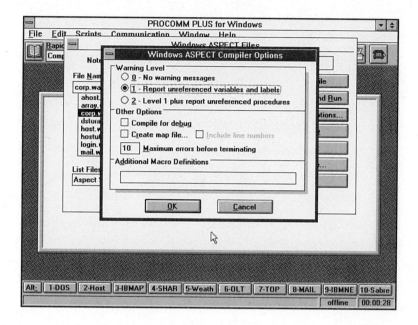

FIG. 7.14

The Windows ASPECT
Compiler Options
screen.

When you select the Compile option from the Windows ASPECT Files
dialog box, the currently highlighted file is compiled. During the compilation process, a screen like the one in figure 7.15 appears. This screen
gives you information about the compiler's progress and displays any
errors or warnings about the compile. If no errors are found in the compilation, this screen displays the message Script file successfully
compiled!. If errors are found, you must correct the errors by editing
the file, and then recompile the file.

At the bottom of the screen are four option buttons. Choose OK to exit
this screen. Choose Compile to begin the compilation process again
(usually after you have edited the file). Choose Edit Source File to return
to the editor to make changes in the file. This option is handy if an error
is detected. You can return quickly to the editor by choosing this option,
fix the problem, return to this screen, and recompile. You use the Edit
Error File option to look at the error file created by the compiler. This
file contains information about what, if any, errors were found in the
script.

The Compile and Run option you choose from the Windows ASPECT
Files dialog box enables you to compile the program quickly and then
begins running the program immediately. Use this option when you
know that the script will compile without errors (for example, when you
have copied the same file from another computer).

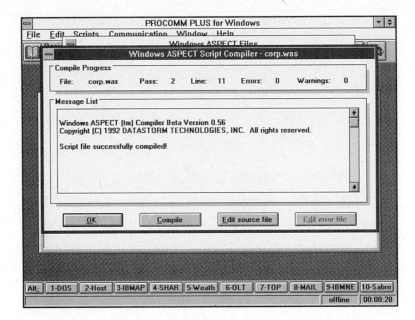

FIG. 7.15

Tracking the progress
as a script is compiled.

Running a Script

After you have compiled a script successfully, a file containing the compiled program is stored with the WAX file extension.

PROCOMM PLUS for Windows provides three ways to run a Windows ASPECT script: you can cause a script to run immediately after PROCOMM PLUS for Windows begins; you can execute a script by dialing an entry from the Dialing Directory screen; or you can run a script directly from the Terminal Display screen. The purpose of a script usually dictates the method you employ to activate it.

Running a Script at Start-Up

Using the Windows ASPECT script language, you can write a script to control a PROCOMM PLUS for Windows session from start to finish. Such a script normally displays a menu from which the user selects an action. Because you want this type of script to control access to PROCOMM PLUS for Windows, activating the script with the program makes sense.

To cause a script to run immediately after entering a command at the DOS prompt, enter the following command:

WIN \PROWIN\PW.EXE scr-name.wax

WIN is the command to begin Windows, \PROWIN is the directory containing the PROCOMM PLUS for Windows program, PW.EXE is the name of the PROCOMM PLUS FOR WINDOWS program file, and scr-name.wax is the name of the script to start. To begin the MCI.WAX script, for example, you would use the following command:

WIN \PROWIN\PW.EXE MCI.WAX

Your command may differ a little if you have stored the PROCOMM PLUS for Windows program in a different directory. With this command, when PROCOMM PLUS for Windows starts, it automatically begins the MCI script, as shown in figure 7.16. If you are familiar with batch files, you could place this command in a batch file and begin the script by using a shorter DOS (batch file) command. For more information on batch files, see Que's book *Using MS-DOS 5,* Special Edition.

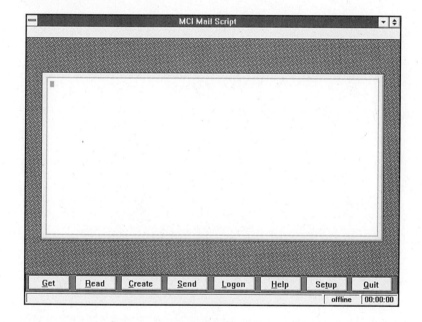

FIG. 7.16

The MCI script running.

Running a Script from the Dialing Directory Screen

The most frequently used method for activating a script is through a dialing directory entry. As you recall from Chapter 3, "Building Your Dialing Directory," you can assign a script to each entry in a dialing directory. When you use a dialing directory entry to which you have assigned a script, PROCOMM PLUS for Windows runs the script immediately after connecting to the remote computer. Such a script is used primarily to log on to the remote computer.

To execute a script you have assigned to a dialing directory entry, click the Rapid Dial drop box and choose the directory entry you want. (See Chapter 3 for a discussion of several ways to select and dial a directory entry.) PROCOMM PLUS for Windows dials the entry's telephone number. After your computer connects with the remote computer, PROCOMM PLUS for Windows executes the assigned script.

Suppose that you assign to a dialing directory entry a script named RBBS-PC.WAX, which logs you onto a bulletin board. To execute the script, you simply choose RBBS-PC from the Rapid Dial menu. PROCOMM PLUS for Windows dials the specified telephone number associated with the entry. When your computer connects, PROCOMM PLUS for Windows executes the RBBS-PC script, logging you on to the bulletin board.

Running a Script from the Terminal Mode Screen

The third way to execute a Windows ASPECT script is from the Terminal Display screen. Click the Script File drop box to display the available scripts. An example extended Script File drop box is shown in figure 7.17. Click the script you want, and then click the Script Action icon. You also can use the up- and down-arrow keys to highlight the script you want to run, then press Enter. The script will begin, and the runner in the Script Action icon will begin running.

Canceling the Execution of a Script

After executing a script, you may decide that you don't want to run it after all. To abort the script in midstream, click the Runner icon or select Stop Script from the Scripts menu. This terminates the script and returns you to the main Windows screen.

Some programs may have a built-in method of terminating the script. For example, at the bottom of the MCI menu is a button called Quit (see fig. 7.16). To end the MCI script, you can click Quit or press Alt-Q.

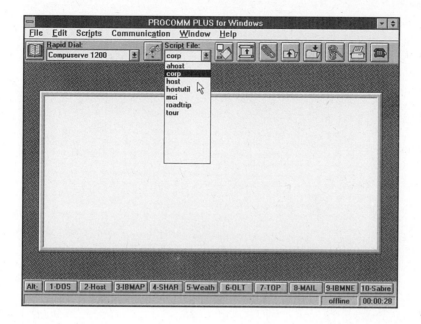

FIG. 7.17

The Script File drop box.

Summary

This chapter showed you two easy ways to make your computer work for you: by using meta keys and script files. The text described how to store up to 80 keystrokes as a meta key that you can play back at the touch of a single keystroke combination. You also learned how to automate such tasks as logging on to an on-line service simply by recording your keystrokes in a PROCOMM PLUS for Windows script file. This chapter is only an introduction to the automation of PROCOMM PLUS for Windows. After you are comfortable with meta keys and the script techniques presented in this chapter, see Chapter 11, "An Overview of the Windows ASPECT Script Language," to discover more of the capabilities of the PROCOMM PLUS for Windows command language.

This chapter is the last one in Part II. You now should be well acquainted with PROCOMM PLUS for Windows, so you are ready to move on to Part III to learn how to become a PROCOMM PLUS for Windows expert.

Becoming a PROCOMM PLUS for Windows Expert

PART III

OUTLINE

Tailoring PROCOMM PLUS for Windows

This chapter teaches you how to customize the many program settings that control the intricacies of PROCOMM PLUS for Windows' operation.

PROCOMM PLUS for Windows works so well "right out of the box" that you may not believe customizing is necessary. As you become an experienced PROCOMM PLUS for Windows user, however, you may begin to think of ways you want to tailor the program's features to meet your specific needs.

You control the setup for PROCOMM PLUS for Windows through the Current Setup menu. You can access this menu from the Terminal Display screen by clicking the Setup Action icon, by selecting Setup from the Window menu, or by pressing Alt-S. The Current Setup menu is shown in figure 8.1. (Your current setup screen may appear different depending on your particular system.)

To choose one of the options from the Current Setup menu, click the option or press the up- and down-arrow keys to highlight the option and then press the space bar. Some of the options directly access a dialog box in which you can change various settings, and other options access a simple drop-down list from which you can select a new setting.

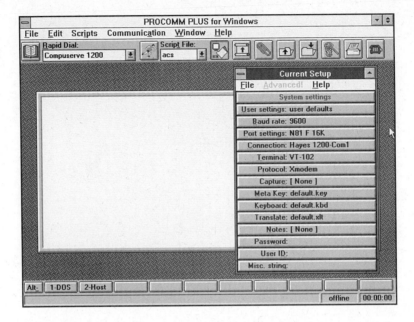

FIG. 8.1

The Current Setup menu.

When you decide to fine-tune a PROCOMM PLUS for Windows feature, you can, with few exceptions, change one setting while leaving all other settings unchanged. This chapter is arranged so that you can easily find the feature in which you are interested. This chapter describes in detail most of the items on this menu. Two options on this menu, Translate and Keyboard, are discussed in Chapter 10, "Terminal Emulation."

Note that the Current Setup menu bar contains three options: File, Advanced!, and Help. The Advanced! option is active for only some of the menu items in the Current Setup menu. When you choose an item from the Current Setup menu that has advanced options, the Advanced! item on the menu appears in dark lettering. If no advanced setup options exist for the current menu item, Advanced! displays in gray, as shown in figure 8.1. The other options, File and Help, are discussed in the following sections.

Using the Current Setup File Menu

The Current Setup File menu contains four options, as shown in figure 8.2. Select File to open the File menu. To choose one of the options from the extended menu, click the item or press the underlined key for the item.

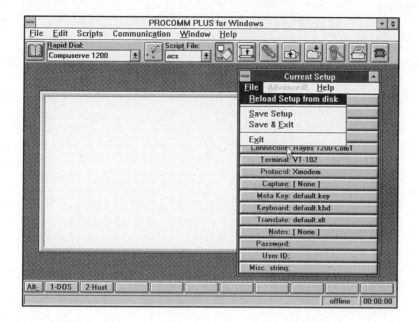

FIG. 8.2

The Current Setup File
menu extended.

The Reload Setup from Disk option enables you to return all settings in the Current Setup menu to the original default conditions that were active when you began PROCOMM PLUS for Windows. This feature is helpful if you have changed options in the setup and want to return quickly to the original setup options. This also enables you to experiment with the options, knowing that you can return easily to the setup defaults.

The Save Setup option on the File menu enables you to save to disk all changes you have made. Then, when you begin PROCOMM PLUS for Windows again, all the setup changes you have saved become the default settings in the setup. When you select Save Setup, the information is saved, but you remain in the Current Setup menu. When you select the Save & Exit option, however, the information is saved and then the Current Setup menu is closed.

The Exit option closes the Current Setup menu. If you have changed setup options, they remain in effect. After you end PROCOMM PLUS for Windows and return again, however, the old default settings are in effect. In other words, exiting does not save the changes you have made to disk. Sometimes making a change that you want to use only for the current session is necessary. With the Exit option, you can do so and exit Current Setup without permanently saving the change.

Using the Current Setup Help Option

When you choose the <u>H</u>elp option from the Current Setup menu bar, you enter the Windows help system for the Current Setup menu. A copy of the Current Setup menu is displayed, and you can click any of the menu items to display a brief description of that item. Figure 8.3, for example, shows the window that appears when you click the S<u>y</u>stem Settings menu option (the top option on the Current Setup menu). To exit the description, click again, and it disappears. To exit the help system, open the Help window's <u>F</u>ile menu and choose E<u>x</u>it. More information on using the options within the help system is given in Chapter 2, "Getting Around in PROCOMM PLUS for Windows."

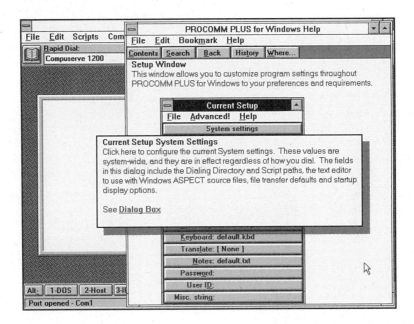

FIG. 8.3

A window in the Current Setup menu's help system.

T I P You frequently need to choose dialog box options to complete the setup for PROCOMM PLUS for Windows. The following briefly reviews how to use Windows dialog boxes:

To move your cursor to an option in a dialog box, you can press Alt plus the underlined character in the option name, click the item with the mouse, or press the Tab key to move from option to option.

In a PROCOMM PLUS for Windows dialog box, options marked with small circles within a boxed area are called *radio buttons*. In this list of options, you can choose only one button. When you select one button, all other buttons in the box are deselected. To select a button, press Alt plus the underlined character in the option name, or click the item with the mouse.

Some options in a dialog box are marked with small squares. These options are called *check boxes*. You can select and deselect each of these options independently. Move to the option using the Tab key, then press the space bar to select or deselect it. Or press Alt plus the underlined character in the option name.

An entry field that has a down-arrow button on the right can be extended into a *drop-down box*. To select this field and extend the drop-down box, press Alt plus the underlined letter of the option name and then press Alt-down arrow. Or simply click the down arrow at the right end of the box. Use the up- and down-arrow keys to highlight an option in the drop-down box and then press Alt-up arrow to select the option and close the extended box. Using the mouse, just click an option in the drop-down box to select the option and close the extended box.

Rectangular entry fields enable you to type in entries. Move to the option by holding down the Alt key and pressing the underlined character of the option name, or use the Tab key to move to a field. Then type the information. To use the mouse, click the box and then type your entry.

To exit the dialog box and save the changes, click OK or press Alt-O. To exit the box and discard any changes, click Cancel or press Alt-C.

Assigning System Options

The System Settings option on the Current Setup menu enables you to set or change a number of options related to global defaults within the PROCOMM PLUS for Windows system. When you choose System Settings, the dialog box shown in figure 8.4 appears. The following paragraphs explain the options in this dialog box.

When you're finished choosing options, exit the dialog box and retain the changes you have made by choosing OK, or exit the dialog box without retaining any changes by choosing Cancel.

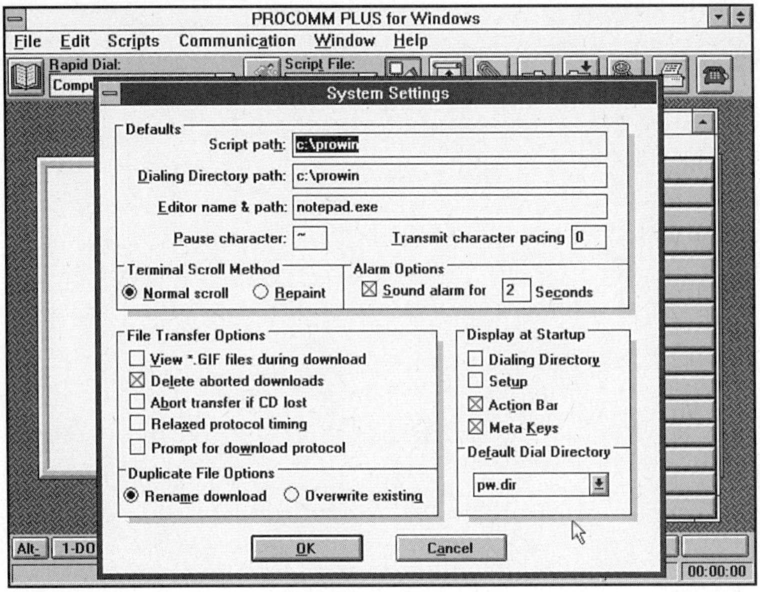

FIG. 8.4

The System Settings
dialog box.

Changing Default Path Names

The Script Path and Dialing Directory Path fields contain DOS path names specifying where on your computer's disks you normally store scripts and dialing directories. When you are in Terminal Display mode and choose the Script Path or Dialing Directory Path option, the path specified here determines where on your disk PROCOMM PLUS for Windows looks to locate the script or directory. If you want to keep your main \PROWIN directory uncluttered with these kinds of files, you can specify other paths such as \PROWIN\SCRIPTS for your scripts files and \PROWIN\DIR for your directory files.

The Editor Name & Path option specifies what editor is used when you choose to edit scripts, note files, or the connection log. Normally, the Windows Notepad editor (NOTEPAD.EXE) is entered in this field. You can, however, choose to use your own editor. If you prefer to use WordPerfect 5.1, for example, and it is in the \WP51 directory, place the path \WP51\WP.EXE in the Editor Name & Path field. Then when you choose an option in PROCOMM PLUS for Windows that normally brings up Notepad, the option brings up WordPerfect instead. You must be careful when you substitute an editor here, because files used by PROCOMM PLUS for Windows should be standard text (ASCII) files. When you use WordPerfect, for example, you need to save files by using the WordPerfect Text In/Out (Ctrl-F5) text file option instead of the

WordPerfect Save option (F10). If you save a script as a WordPerfect file rather than a text file, for example, PROCOMM PLUS for Windows is not able to compile the script for execution.

Changing the Pause Character

The *pause character* is used in keyboard meta keys and in the Hangup, Answer On, and Answer Off commands. (The Hangup, Answer On, and Answer Off commands are specified in the Modem Setup dialog box described later in this chapter, in the section "Specifying Modem Commands.") This character causes PROCOMM PLUS for Windows to pause processing for one-half second. As shown in figure 8.4, the default pause character is the tilde (~). The tilde is used as the pause character because the tilde is seldom used for any other purpose. For some special application, however, you may need to use the tilde in a keyboard meta key to represent an actual tilde. In that case, you need to change the pause character. To do so, select Pause Character from the System Settings dialog box and then type the character you want to use for the pause character. If you change the pause character, don't forget to edit the Hangup and Answer On and Answer Off commands in the Modem Options dialog box to replace each tilde in those commands with the new pause character.

Changing the Transmit Character Pacing Option

PROCOMM PLUS for Windows normally does not insert any time delay between transmitted characters. Some host computers, however, may have difficulty processing character strings and terminal-control sequences sent by a meta key or by terminal-emulation keyboard mapping without at least a slight delay between characters. If you think that you may be having this problem, try increasing the value in the Transmit Character Pacing option of the System Settings dialog box. Normally, the default is 0 (milliseconds). To change this setting, select Transmit Character Pacing and enter the number of milliseconds to pause.

Changing the Terminal Scroll Method

You can choose one of two methods of terminal scrolling to determine how the Terminal Display window is updated on-screen. If you are using a fast computer (a 386 or higher), use the Repaint option. On 386 and 486 computers, Repaint allows a faster updating of the screen than the normal scroll method. If you are using a slower machine, use the Normal Scroll option.

Changing the Alarm Option

PROCOMM PLUS for Windows by default uses a "beep-beep" sound to alert you to certain events. When your modem successfully connects to another modem, for example, or when a file transfer is completed or aborted, this alarm may sound. These alarms are normally a convenient feature. You may, for example, start downloading a large file from a bulletin board (a process that you know will take at least 20 minutes). Rather than doze off at your keyboard, you can go about your business around the office or house or in Windows because PROCOMM PLUS for Windows sounds the alarm as soon as the transfer is complete. Your spouse may not appreciate this feature, however, if you are downloading a file at 3:00 a.m. You can deselect the Alarm Sound option on the System Settings screen to prevent PROCOMM PLUS for Windows from sounding the alarm at all.

Use the Alarm Options area of the System Settings dialog box to modify the length of time that PROCOMM PLUS for Windows sounds an alarm signal, or whether you want the alarm to sound at all. By default, PROCOMM PLUS for Windows sounds the alarm for two seconds. The program causes your computer to generate a "beep" tone once each second for two seconds. To turn the alarm on or off, select the Sound Alarm For option to toggle the setting on and off. To change the duration of the alarm, choose the Seconds field, type an integer, and press Enter. If you change the value to 5, for example, the next time you download a file, PROCOMM PLUS for Windows sounds the alarm for five seconds.

Changing the File Transfer Options

The File Transfer Options area of the System Settings dialog box enables you to select several options concerning actions PROCOMM PLUS for Windows will or will not take during a download. The following sections explain each of these file transfer options in more detail.

Viewing GIF Files during Download

The first option in the File Transfer Options box is View *.GIF Files During Download. This option is selected by default. If this box is selected, when you download a GIF file (Graphics Interchange File), the graphic is displayed in a GIF window as the file is downloaded. This enables you to view the graphic as it is being downloaded. If you do not want to view the graphic during download, deselect this option.

Dealing with Partially Downloaded Files

When you begin a download, using a PROCOMM PLUS for Windows file-transfer protocol, PROCOMM PLUS for Windows opens a file on your disk to receive the downloaded data. As the transfer progresses, PROCOMM PLUS for Windows periodically adds data to this download file. The program closes the download file at the completion of the transfer. By default, if a file transfer is aborted before the entire original file is received, PROCOMM PLUS for Windows closes the download file even though it contains only a portion of the original file. PROCOMM PLUS for Windows keeps the download file on disk; this file contains all data that was received before the transfer was aborted.

In many cases, a partial file is of little use. A spreadsheet file, for example, is of no benefit unless you have the whole file. Your spreadsheet program cannot load a partial spreadsheet—and such an abbreviated spreadsheet is unlikely to be meaningful, even if it could be loaded. PROCOMM PLUS for Windows therefore provides an option that causes the program simply to eliminate incomplete download files.

The Delete Aborted Downloads option in the File Transfer Options area of the System Settings dialog box tells PROCOMM PLUS for Windows what to do with a file transfer that is canceled before successful completion. If this option is deselected, it tells PROCOMM PLUS for Windows to keep the downloaded partial file. If the option is selected (the default), it tells PROCOMM PLUS for Windows to delete partial files.

Dealing with CD Loss during Transfer

If a file is being transferred and the Carrier Detect (CD) is lost (which usually means that the connection is lost), PROCOMM PLUS for Windows no longer receives information from the remote computer. If you select the Abort Transfer if CD Lost option in the System Settings dialog box, PROCOMM PLUS for Windows cancels the transfer—either upload or download—when the loss of CD is detected. You usually want PROCOMM PLUS for Windows to react this way. If two computers are attached by a null modem, however, PROCOMM PLUS for Windows may detect a premature CD loss, or your cable may even lack a CD line. If PROCOMM PLUS for Windows is detecting a premature CD loss, deselect the Abort Transfer if CD Lost option. For more information on CD, see "Editing the Initialization Command" later in this chapter.

Setting Relaxed Protocol Timing

If you are experiencing problems with too many errors in downloads when using an XMODEM protocol, select the Relaxed Protocol Timing option in the System Settings dialog box. This option doubles the transmit time-out for XMODEM-type transfers, which gives the system more time to process transmitted information before deciding that a transmit error has occurred.

Controlling the Prompt for Download Protocol

Normally, PROCOMM PLUS for Windows assumes that you will use the currently selected file-transfer protocol when you begin receiving a downloaded file. But you may have a default selected (such as ZMODEM) that is not supported on some bulletin boards. Thus, even though your default mode is ZMODEM, you may be forced to use another, such as YMODEM, to perform a download. If you select the Prompt for Download Protocol option, PROCOMM PLUS for Windows prompts you to choose what protocol to use before each download begins.

Dealing with Duplicate File Names

When you request a file to be downloaded, and you already have a file by that name on your disk, a name collision occurs. Two files cannot have the same name. The Duplicate File Options section of the System Settings dialog box enables you to specify how to handle that situation. By default, PROCOMM PLUS for Windows uses the Rename Download option. If you already have a file named REPORT.WP5 on your disk, and you download a file with the same name, PROCOMM PLUS for Windows renames the new file $EPORT.WP5. If you are using the download procedure to update a number of files on your hard disk and want the downloaded files to overwrite the current files, select the Overwrite Existing option. This option has no effect on the ZMODEM or CIS-B+ protocols because they have built-in mechanisms for handling name collisions.

Changing the Display at Start-up Options

When you first begin PROCOMM PLUS for Windows, the Terminal Display window appears. You can customize what other information appears on that screen by using the following Display at Startup options in the System Settings dialog box:

■ *Dialing Directory*. Causes the dialing directory to appear on the start-up screen. This option is deselected by default.

■ *Setup.* Causes the Current Setup menu to appear on the start-up screen. This option is deselected by default.

■ *Action Bar.* Causes the Action Bar icons to appear on the start-up screen. This option is selected by default.

■ *Meta Keys.* Causes the meta key option buttons to appear at the bottom of the start-up screen. This option is selected by default.

You also can select what default directory you want to be active when you begin the program. Normally, the PW.DIR directory is the default. To change this option, choose Default Dial Directory, extend the drop-down list, and select the directory name you want from the list.

Choosing User Settings

The User Settings option on the Current Setup menu enables you to set or change options related to your personal preferences about file transfers, Chat mode, mouse options, and other options. When you select User Settings, a drop-down list appears containing names of stored user settings. When you first load PROCOMM PLUS for Windows, only one default user setting exists. You can save alternate default values, however, and then choose those settings to activate a new set of defaults. To set the user defaults, select Advanced! from the Current Setup menu bar to bring up the User Settings dialog box shown in figure 8.5.

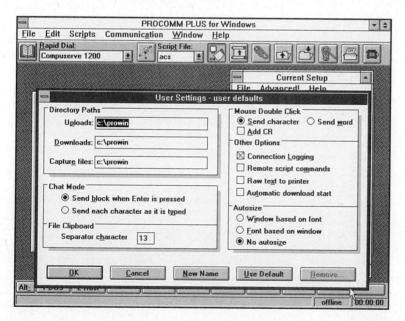

FIG. 8.5

The User Settings dialog box.

The User Settings dialog box contains six major parts: Directory Paths, Chat Mode, File Clipboard, Mouse Double Click, Other Options, and Autosize. The following sections describe how to set options within each of these areas.

Setting Directory Paths

The Directory Paths box contains path names in which you can designate where uploads, downloads, and capture files will be stored. If you want these files stored in the same directory as the program, you can specify the \PROWIN directory for each. If you do not want to clutter this directory with these files, you can specify a different directory for each option. You might want to store uploads in the \PROWIN\UPLOAD directory, downloads in a \PROWIN\DNLOAD directory, and capture files in a \PROWIN\CAPTURE directory. By default, these directories are what you choose during installation. To change the path in any of these fields, choose the appropriate field and type the path name you want to use for that option. If you enter the name of a directory that doesn't exist, a new directory is created.

Setting Chat Mode Options

The Chat Mode group of options enables you to specify whether information you type to the screen is sent immediately to the connected computer (Send Each Character As It Is Typed) or whether the program waits until Enter is pressed before sending a line of information (Send Block When Enter Is Pressed). Usually, the Send Block When Enter Is Pressed option is best. With this setting on, you can make corrections by backing up the cursor and retyping a word or phrase before that information is sent to the connected computer. This way, if you are a lousy typist, the person on the other end never finds out.

Setting the Separator Character

The single File Clipboard option in the User Settings dialog box, Separator Character, enables you to choose what default separator character you want the program to send between files names stored in the Clipboard. (You use the File Clipboard window to capture file names from one screen so that you can use them later to paste back onto another screen in response to a prompt for a file name to upload, download, and so on. See Chapter 5, "Transferring Files," for more information.)

Often a carriage return (which is ASCII character 13) is the separator character between file names. If your situation calls for another separator character, such as 32 for blank, you can change this default. (You also can change this character temporarily while you are in the File Clipboard window.) If the semicolon (;) is the separator character you want to use, for example, you enter the ASCII code 59. To change the entry in the Separator Character field, select the option and then enter the ASCII code value. See Appendix C for a list of decimal ASCII codes for characters.

Controlling the Effects of a Mouse Double-Click

You use the Mouse Double Click options in the User Settings dialog box to control how PROCOMM PLUS for Windows reacts when you double-click text in the Terminal Display window. If you select the Send Character option, double-clicking a character causes that character to be transmitted to the connected computer. This method is handy when you are dealing with menus on the Terminal Display screen, in which you are expected to respond to the window by entering a single character choice. If you select the Send Word option, double-clicking a word in the Terminal Display window causes that entire word to be transmitted to the connected computer. This method can come in handy if the host computer expects you to type in a command from a menu, and that command is displayed on-screen.

Optionally, you can choose the Add CR option, which sends a carriage return with either the single character or word sent as a result of a mouse double-click on text.

Setting Other User Options

The Other Options area of the User Settings dialog box enables you to set any of four options. The Connection Logging option, when selected, tells the program to capture the date and time to the connection log each time a successful connection is made. See Chapter 4, "A Session with PROCOMM PLUS for Windows," for more information about the connection log.

The Remote Script Commands option, when selected, enables remote computers to send ASPECT commands to your computer. Then PROCOMM PLUS for Windows acts on those commands. This feature is a powerful one, but you need to be aware of security risks because it gives the remote user access to virtually every aspect of your computer.

The Raw Text to Printer option, when selected, tells PROCOMM PLUS for Windows to send characters to the printer directly rather than through the Windows printer driver. This method can be useful if the characters being sent contain specific commands for the printer—for example, codes to place the printer into modes such as compressed type or underline. If the information is sent through the Windows printer driver, these codes may be interpreted differently.

The Automatic Download Start option refers to the ZMODEM and KERMIT protocols. When this option is selected, these protocols are enabled to begin downloads automatically. Another protocol that you can set for automatic download is CIS-B+. To set CIS-B+ for automatic download, use the CIS-B+ Enquiry option in the Terminal Settings dialog box, as discussed later in this chapter, in the section "Setting Terminal Enquiry."

Setting the Autosize Options

The Autosize options in the User Settings dialog box enable you to specify how the size of the Terminal Display window is set. If you select the Window Based on Font setting, PROCOMM PLUS for Windows sizes the Terminal Display window to match the font you have chosen. This enables you to select a small font to create a small terminal screen, for example, or to select a large font to make the displayed information more readable. If the font is large, however, not all the information on a line can be displayed at once. If you select Font Based on Window, an appropriate font is chosen when you size the Terminal Display window (see "Setting Terminal Size and the Scrollback Buffer" later in this chapter). This option ensures that the incoming information will be viewable on the screen, but the font being displayed may be difficult to read. Normally, the No Autosize option is selected. This option sets the Terminal Display window at its default maximum size, no matter what font is used.

Managing the User Settings Options

At the bottom of the User Settings box are five option buttons. When you choose the OK button, all changes you have made in this dialog box are retained, and you return to the Current Setup menu. If you choose Cancel, any changes you have made are reset to their original values, and you are returned to the Current Setup menu.

The New Name option enables you to specify a new name for the settings in the User Settings box. As mentioned previously, you may want to save several alternate versions of settings that you can later choose from the

User Settings drop-down list. You might, for example, use one version of these settings when using CompuServe, and another when connected to your company's mainframe. Figure 8.6 shows the prompt for a new name for user settings that appears when you choose the New Name button. The name must be a legal DOS file name.

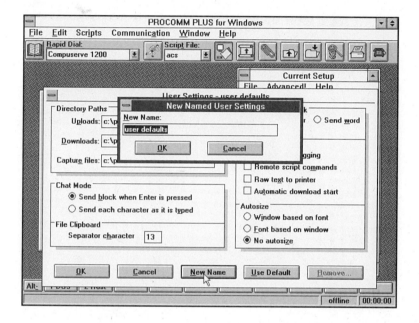

FIG. 8.6

Entering a new name for user settings.

The Use Default button returns all settings in the User Settings dialog box to their default state. Use this option if you have made changes but want to revert back to all the defaults. This option enables you to experiment with the settings without worrying about not being able to return to the original settings. The Remove option removes the current user settings name from the User Settings drop-down list. This currently used name appears in the name bar at the top of the dialog box. In figure 8.5, for example, the current name is user defaults.

Choosing the Baud Rate

The Baud Rate option on the Current Setup menu enables you to select what default baud rate is to be used when you're communicating with other computers. When you select Baud Rate, a drop-down list appears, containing the available baud rate options (see fig. 8.7). A discussion of baud is found in Chapter 1, "A Communications Primer." The baud rate choices for PROCOMM PLUS for Windows are 300, 600, 1200, 2400, 4800, 9600, 19200, 38400, 57600, and 115200. The most popular modems use 1200, 2400, or 9600 baud. When you are connected by a direct cable to another computer, you usually can use the higher baud rates. If you use a high baud rate and see that many errors occur in the transmission, the telephone line or one of the computers may not be able to handle the rate of transfer. In that case, you should try the next lower rate.

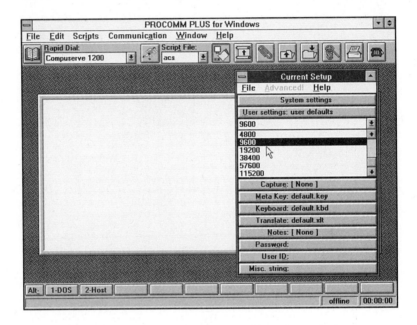

FIG. 8.7

The Baud Rate selection list box.

Choosing Port Settings

The Port Settings option enables you to control communication settings, specifying how your computer communicates with the connected computer. The first time you start PROCOMM PLUS for Windows, it uses the port settings that you specified during installation. See Appendix A for more information about the installation. As explained in Chapter 3, "Building Your Dialing Directory," you also can change port settings by using a dialing directory entry. Each time you dial another computer by using a dialing directory entry, PROCOMM PLUS for Windows uses line settings specified in that entry.

The current port settings are displayed on the Current Setup menu's Port Settings line. A current setting, for example, may be N81 F 16. This setting means that the computer's port settings are currently no parity, 8 data bits, 1 stop bit, and a 16K Com buffer.

From time to time, you may need to reassign the port settings without using a dialing directory entry—perhaps after you are already on-line. You may be connected to another computer, for example, but the characters you see are unintelligible—made up mostly of foreign-language symbols and box-drawing characters. You realize that the port settings should have been E71, but your dialing directory entry contains the setting N81. You could hang up, fix the dialing entry, and redial. But instead, you can bring up the Port Settings dialog box from the Terminal Display window by selecting Setup and then selecting Port Settings from the Current Setup menu. The Port Settings dialog box is shown in figure 8.8.

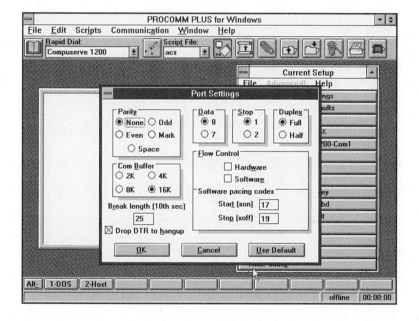

A simple rule of thumb is to use N81 for PC-to-PC or PC-to-bulletin board connections. All PCs need eight-bit bytes to represent the full IBM character set. Also, with eight data bits, no room is left for a parity bit. On the other hand, when calling another mainframe system or an on-line service such as CompuServe, use E71. Most such systems are run on computers that can handle only seven data bits per byte, always leaving one bit for a parity bit. Mainframe systems usually use even parity.

After you make changes in the Port Settings dialog box, you can exit the box and retain the current settings by choosing OK. To exit the dialog box and cancel all changes you have made, choose Cancel. To return all the settings in this box to their default values, choose Use Default. The following sections explain the Port Settings dialog box options in detail.

Setting Communication Options

The Port Settings dialog box is divided into six boxed sections—Parity, Data, Stop, Duplex, Com Buffer, Flow Control, and Software Pacing Codes—and the Break Length and Drop DTR to Hangup options.

The Parity, Data, Stop, Duplex, and Com Buffer boxes contain radio button options that you can use to set transmission control options. To choose an option from one of these boxes, hold down the Alt key and press the underlined letter of the box name. Then use the arrow keys to move from one radio button to the next within that box. Press the space bar to select one of the radio buttons. A discussion about the parity, data bits, stop bits, duplex, and the Com buffer is found in Chapter 1, "A Communications Primer."

Controlling the Flow

Many remote systems, including most on-line services and bulletin boards, support a flow-control method known as XON/XOFF. These systems stop transmitting information when they receive an ASCII character referred to as XOFF. This character is the same as the character you generate by pressing Ctrl-S on your keyboard. When the remote system receives the ASCII character known as XON, the remote system continues its transmission. The XON character is the same as the character you generate when you press Ctrl-Q.

When you select Software in the Flow Control option section, PROCOMM PLUS for Windows in Terminal Display mode and Host mode suspends the transmission of characters to the remote computer when XOFF is received from the remote computer and resumes transmission when XON is received. (The default setting is for software flow control to be deselected.)

 NOTE   PROCOMM PLUS for Windows sends XON and XOFF when you use the Alt-P (Screen Pause) feature described in Chapter 4, "A Session with PROCOMM PLUS for Windows," regardless of this Terminal Options setting.

You should select Hardware as the Flow Control option if you are using a modem that performs error control or data compression (such as MNP-capable modems, Hayes V-series modems, and CCITT V.42-compliant modems).

Setting the Software Pacing Codes

As described in the preceding section, you can use the XON and XOFF codes to control the flow of information transmitted. Usually, these codes are set to ASCII characters 17 (Ctrl-Q) for XON and 19 (Ctrl-S) for XOFF. These characters are the defaults, as shown in figure 8.8. If you have an unusual connection setup that requires another XON/XOFF setting, you can change the setting here. To change XON, select the Start field and enter the new ASCII code for the XON code. To change XOFF, select the Stop field and enter the new ASCII code for the XOFF code.

Setting the Break Length

A *break* is a signal that is sent to the computer to get its attention. If you press Alt-B (Break Key), PROCOMM PLUS for Windows temporarily interrupts the data transmission with a space condition on the transmit line for at least the length of a data word, which usually is a start bit (0), the byte itself, a stop bit (1), and perhaps a parity bit. The default length of the delay is 25 tenths of a second. Usually, a break of 25 tenths of a second is enough to get the other computer's attention. The Break Length option on the Port Settings dialog box enables you to change the duration of the break.

To change the length of the delay, select Break Length (10th sec) and then type an integer for the number of tenths of a second you want to set the delay.

Dropping the DTR Signal

The DTR (Data Terminal Ready) line is one of the circuits defined by the RS-232 standard. (Refer to Appendix B for a description of the RS-232 standard.) While you are on-line to another computer, your computer continuously asserts (sends a voltage over) the DTR line to the modem. If you select Hangup from the Terminal Display screen (by clicking the Hangup Action icon, for example), by default PROCOMM PLUS for Windows turns off this DTR signal, thus informing the modem that the computer no longer is going to send data. In response, the modem hangs up the phone line (assuming that your modem is watching the status of the DTR line).

PROCOMM PLUS for Windows can cause your modem to hang up the telephone line regardless of whether you turn off the DTR command. If you do not use the DTR method (the option is deselected), PROCOMM PLUS for Windows instead must send a hangup command to the modem (see "Setting the Hangup Command" later in this chapter). If you use DTR, the modem may not initiate its own hangup. If not, PROCOMM PLUS for Windows detects this situation and sends its own hangup command to the modem.

Choosing Connection Options

The Connection option on the Current Setup menu enables you to indicate what modem you are using and to specify certain setup parameters for that modem. When you select Connection, a drop-down list appears, containing names of modems you selected during the installation process or defined in the Connection dialog box. Select what modem you want to use.

To modify this list and settings for the modems on the list, choose Advanced! from the Current Setup menu bar to display the Connection dialog box, as shown in figure 8.9.

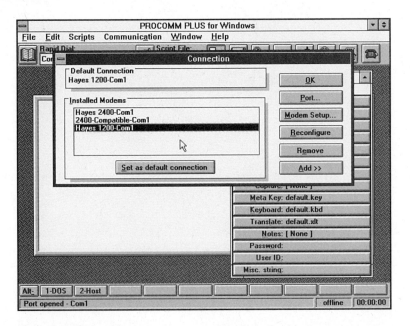

FIG. 8.9

The Connection dialog box.

Like the drop-down list, the Connection dialog box contains a list of the installed modems. This list comes from the selections you made during installation (see Appendix A) or from adding new modems from this dialog box. The modem listed in the Default Connection box is the one that appears on the Current Setup menu. To make one of the modems in the Installed Modems list the default, select your choice, and then choose the Set As Default Connection button.

The Connection dialog box contains six other option buttons along the right side of the screen. Use the OK option to exit back to the Current Setup menu and retain any changes you have made. The Remove option removes the currently highlighted modem from the Installed Modems list. When you choose the Reconfigure option, the program sends the initialization string to the modem. When you choose the Add option, a list of modems like the one that appeared during installation (see Appendix A) appears. You can choose modems from this list to add to the list of installed modems. When you choose the Port or Modem Setup option, a new dialog box appears. The Select Port and Modem Setup dialog boxes are described in the next two sections.

Using the Select Port Dialog Box

The Select Port dialog box enables you to choose what communications (serial) port is used to communicate with another computer, as shown in figure 8.10. To display this screen from the Connection dialog box, choose the Port button.

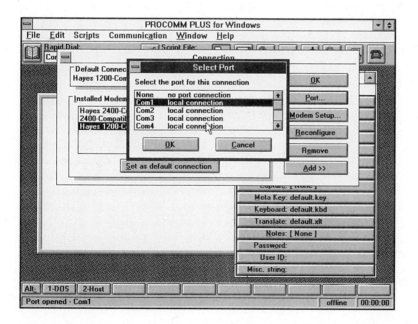

FIG. 8.10

The Select Port dialog box.

PROCOMM PLUS for Windows is one of the few communications programs that enables you to use serial ports above COM4, even though no version of DOS explicitly supports serial ports beyond COM4 (and many versions of DOS don't support COM3 or COM4).

If your computer has only one COM port, it is COM port number 1. If you have two COM ports, your first port may be used for a mouse, printer, or some other device. If so, you need to use the second COM port for communications. PROCOMM PLUS for Windows can be configured to use any COM port from 1 to 4. You also can choose from several dynamic link connections that are listed as INT4:1 to INT4:4 and EBIOS:1 to EBIOS:4.

Select which port to use, and then choose OK to return to the Connection screen.

CAUTION: Do not switch COM ports while on-line to another computer. If you do, PROCOMM PLUS for Windows drops the connection.

Using the Modem Setup Dialog Box

The Modem Setup dialog box enables you to choose options for a particular modem. To display this dialog box, choose Modem Setup from the Connection screen. Figure 8.11 shows the default values for a Hayes 1200 modem. The information on your screen may be different, but it reflects the default values for the particular modem you are using.

Notice the four option buttons in the lower right corner of the Modem Setup screen. After you have edited information on this screen, as described in the following sections, exit the screen and retain the changes by choosing OK. To exit and discard the changes, choose Cancel. If you want to assign a new name for this modem (change Hayes 2400 to the name of a clone modem you are using, for example), choose New Name. You are prompted to enter a new name. If you change the options and decide you want to return to the original settings, choose Use Default.

Specifying Modem Commands

The Commands area of the Modem Setup dialog box contains options to specify the modem's initialization command; the dialing command and suffix; and the Hangup, Answer On, and Answer Off commands. You also can choose whether to use hardware flow control and can set the baud rate. The following sections explain how to set the options in the Commands box.

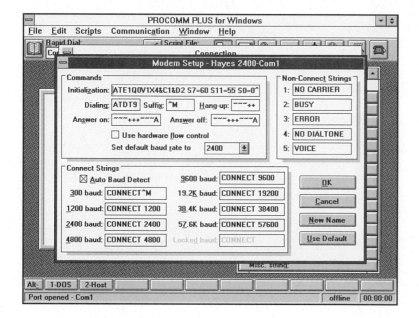

FIG. 8.11

The Modem Setup dialog box for a Hayes 1200 modem.

Editing the Initialization Command

Each time you start PROCOMM PLUS for Windows, it sends a software wake-up call, known as an *initialization command*, to your modem. The Initialization option in the Modem Setup dialog box enables you to customize this command.

The Initialization option activates a number of the modem's built-in features. Hayes-compatible modems, for example, are capable of sending back to your screen progress reports, usually referred to as connect strings, status messages, result messages, or result codes. A portion of PROCOMM PLUS for Windows's initialization command activates the modem's connect string feature. These connect strings and result codes inform you of telephone-line conditions. The result code (nonconnect string) RING, for example, means that the telephone line to which the modem is connected is ringing. The result code CONNECT 2400 means that your modem has connected to another modem at a speed of 2400 bps.

The initialization command is established first by the installation utility (see Appendix A). During the installation procedure, you choose from a list of many well-known modems. After you select a modem, the installation utility inserts the appropriate initialization command for that modem into the Modem Setup dialog box. The initialization command shown in figure 8.11 (it goes off the edge of the field, so you cannot see the whole command) is intended for use with a Hayes 2400 modem and includes these default initialization parameters:

```
ATE1Q0V1X4&C1&D2 S7=60 S11=55 S0=0^M
```

These parameters are standard for a Hayes-compatible modem.

The initialization command is not a single command but a series of commands. The initialization command shown in figure 8.11, for example, includes the following command components:

- *AT*. Stands for attention. These letters alert the modem that a command follows. All Hayes-compatible modems recognize this command. Most modems enable you to list several commands after AT.

- *E1*. Causes your modem to echo the characters back to the screen as you type, but only while the modem is in Command mode. In Command mode, the modem recognizes and responds to commands typed at the keyboard. The E1 command has no effect while your modem is on-line and communicating with another modem.

- *Q0*. Controls the modem's display of result codes. If the command is set to Q1, the modem sends no result codes, verbal or numeric. PROCOMM PLUS for Windows uses result codes, so this portion of the initialization command should always be Q0.

- *V1*. Causes the modem to use verbal result codes (result messages) rather than numeric result codes. The verbal result code (connect string) CONNECT 1200, for example, is equivalent to the numeric result code 5. PROCOMM PLUS for Windows uses the verbal result codes as it monitors the dialing process. You use the command V0 if you want to specify numeric codes.

- *X4*. Selects the result message codes that are sent to PROCOMM PLUS for Windows. Each result code set monitors a different group of line conditions. With set 1 chosen, for example, the modem detects modem speeds of 300, 1200, and 2400 baud and sends messages such as CONNECT 1200 to PROCOMM PLUS for Windows when a connection is made. X4 is sometimes preferred because it causes the modem to wait for a dial tone before dialing and to detect busy signals. The X4 option is appropriate in most situations, but on some telephone systems, the dial tone may be so faint that the modem cannot detect the tone. In those cases, X1, which does not detect a tone (called blind dialing), must be used. Other codes include X0, which means use the message CONNECT for all speeds with no dial tone detection; X2, which means wait for dial tone and use the same connect messages as X1; and X3, which means detect a busy signal and use the same connect messages as X1.

■ *&C1*. Turns on the DCD (Data Carrier Detect) signal when the modem detects a carrier signal from the modem at the other end of the line. If another modem is not detected, the DCD signal is turned off. An &CO command keeps the DCD signal on at all times.

■ *&D2*. Causes the modem to monitor the DTR (Data Terminal Ready) signal. If the modem detects an on-to-off transition of DTR, it responds to Hayes-type AT commands. An &DO command causes the modem to use a DTR setting at all times. An &D1 setting causes the modem to detect an on-to-off transition of DTR by ignoring AT commands and to detect an off-to-on transition by again responding to AT commands.

■ *S7=60*. Sets the number of seconds your modem waits before disconnecting and issuing the NO CARRIER nonconnect string. The default value is 30 seconds. Setting S7 to 60 increases the time to 60 seconds.

■ *S11=55*. Sets the duration, in milliseconds, of the touch-tones generated when your modem dials a number. Setting S11 to 55 causes each tone to last 55 milliseconds. The result is fast dialing.

■ *S0=0*. Disables the Answer On command in the Modem Setup dialog box. This option ensures that your modem does not answer the phone except when PROCOMM PLUS for Windows is in Host mode or when you execute the Answer On command.

■ *^M*. Causes PROCOMM PLUS for Windows to send the ASCII carriage-return character. (See Chapter 7, "Automating PROCOMM PLUS for Windows with Meta Keys and Script Files," for other PROCOMM PLUS for Windows control codes.) The carriage-return character causes the modem to process the initialization command by telling the modem that the command is complete.

At times, you may want to customize the initialization command. To make changes to this command, make sure that the Initialization option is selected in the Modem Setup dialog box. Use the left- and right-arrow keys to move the cursor within the entry and make necessary modifications.

Refer to the manual that was distributed with your modem to find further explanation of the component commands of the initialization command and to determine whether you need to modify the initialization command inserted by PROCOMM PLUS for Windows' installation utility (see Appendix A).

Understanding the Dialing Command and Suffix

Below the Initialization option in the Modem Setup dialog box, the setup utility lists two options that determine the command PROCOMM PLUS for Windows sends to your modem when you use the program to dial a telephone number. The options are Dialing and Suffix. To edit the current dialing code, choose the Dialing field and type a dialing code. To edit the current Suffix code, select the Suffix field and type the suffix code.

The dialing command shown in figure 8.11 is ATDT9. Another common dialing command is ATDT. The AT is the Hayes-modem command "ATtention," and the DT command stands for "Dial Tone." DT is recognized by all Hayes-compatible modems to mean use touch-tone to dial the telephone. When the telephone service in your area supports only pulse (rotary) dialing, select the Dialing option in the Modem Setup dialog box and edit the entry to change the second T to the letter P (that is, change the command to ATDP). The 9 in the command is used to "dial out" when you are using a company phone system, just as you must dial 9 manually before dialing an outside phone number.

After you issue a PROCOMM PLUS for Windows command to dial a specific telephone number, PROCOMM PLUS for Windows sends to the modem the dialing command listed in the Dialing entry of the Modem Setup dialog box, followed by the telephone number you specify in the Dialing Directory screen. If you issue a PROCOMM PLUS for Windows command to dial the number 555-4391 (assuming touch-tone service), for example, PROCOMM PLUS for Windows sends the following command to your modem:

    ATDT95554391

To specify characters to add to the end of each dialing command, use the Suffix option in the Modem Setup dialog box. PROCOMM PLUS for Windows then adds to the end of the dialing command the characters you specify in this entry. Hayes-compatible modems expect all commands to end with a carriage return, so the Suffix entry must be a carriage-return character. As explained in "Editing the Initialization Command" earlier in this chapter, the control code ^M causes PROCOMM PLUS for Windows to send a carriage-return character. ^M thus is normally the dialing command suffix, as shown in figure 8.11. Some company phone systems require that you use another suffix; however, the ^M suffix is almost universal.

Understanding the Hangup Command

Occasionally, you must execute the Hangup command (click the Hangup Action icon or press Alt-F2) to disconnect from a communications session. When you issue this command, PROCOMM PLUS for Windows first tries to hang up the line by dropping the DTR signal. (This setting is the default condition, but refer also to "Editing the Initialization Command" and "Dropping the DTR Signal," both in this chapter.) If this attempt is not successful, PROCOMM PLUS for Windows sends to the modem the command specified at the Hang-up option on the Modem Setup dialog box.

The default Hangup command is

~~~+++~~~ATH0^M

You can see only the first part of this command in the Hang-up field in figure 8.11. The first character in this modem command, repeated three times, is the tilde (~). The tilde is the default pause character. PROCOMM PLUS for Windows translates this character into a pause of one-half second. The three tildes therefore result in a pause of one and one-half seconds. In other words, no characters are sent or received by the modem for one and one-half seconds.

Following the three tildes in the Hang-up command are three plus signs (+++) followed by three more tildes (~~~). Three pluses together, preceded and followed by at least one character-free second (no characters are sent or received by the modem for at least one second), cause a Hayes-compatible modem to go from On-line mode to Command mode. (These three pluses are sometimes called an *escape code*.) In On-line mode, the modem ignores commands from PROCOMM PLUS for Windows. When the modem is in Command mode, the modem recognizes the AT commands PROCOMM PLUS for Windows sends.

The command that causes the modem to hang up the telephone (go on hook) is ATH0. This modem command follows the second trio of tildes. A carriage return also must be sent to cause the modem to process the command, so the control code ^M appears at the end of the Hang-up command.

Editing Answer On and Answer Off

Chapter 4, "A Session with PROCOMM PLUS for Windows," explains how to use the Auto Answer command to place your modem in Answer mode. If you press Alt-F3 and compile and run the HOST.WAS host mode script, PROCOMM PLUS for Windows sends to your modem the command that is specified at the Answer On option in the Modem Setup dialog box. You use the Answer Off option to define the command that turns off the Auto Answer feature. The default Answer On command is

~~~+++~~~ATS0=1^M

You cannot see the whole command in figure 8.11 because the command is longer than the entry field. As explained in the preceding section, the first portion of the command (~~~+++~~~) places your modem in Command mode so that the modem is expecting a command from PROCOMM PLUS for Windows. The remainder of the Auto Answer command (ATS0=1) instructs the modem to switch to Answer mode and to answer any incoming call on the first ring. As in the other commands, the ^M code sends a carriage-return character to the modem, causing it to process the command.

In some situations, you may prefer that the modem not answer on the first ring. To modify the Answer On command, select the Answer On field and then type your change. For example, ATSO=2 means to answer on the second ring.

The Answer Off command is similar to the Answer On command, except that Answer Off contains the command ATSO=0, which instructs the modem to turn off the Auto Answer feature. PROCOMM PLUS for Windows uses the Answer Off command after you exit Host mode. To modify Answer Off, select the Answer Off field and then enter your change.

Setting Hardware Flow Control

You should select the Use Hardware Flow Control option in the Commands area of the Modem Setup dialog box if you are using a modem that performs error control or data compression (such as MNP-capable modems, Hayes V-series modems, and CCITT V.42-compliant modems). This option normally is unselected by default.

Choosing the Default Baud Rate

You can choose the default baud rate for this modem in the last option in the Commands box. To do so, select the Set Default Baud Rate To field, extend its drop-down box, and select a baud rate from the list.

Specifying Result Messages

When you use the installation utility to install PROCOMM PLUS for Windows on your computer, the utility asks you to indicate the brand and model of the modem you are using. Based on your response to this question, the installation program inserts values into the entry spaces in the Connect Strings and Non-Connect Strings boxes of the Modem Setup dialog box. These values are known as *result messages* because they display the result of some event. Figure 8.11 shows the messages the installation utility inserts for a Hayes 2400 modem.

Hayes-compatible modems usually can generate more than one set of result messages. The modem command ATXn, where n is a positive integer, determines which result message set the modem uses. This command usually is a part of your initialization command. Refer to your modem manual and to "Editing the Initialization Command" earlier in this chapter for information on how to select a result message set.

The messages displayed in the Connect Strings and Non-Connect Strings boxes must match the result message set your modem is returning. Otherwise, some of PROCOMM PLUS for Windows's features, such as Auto Baud Detect, may not work properly. Check your modem manual to make sure that the messages listed in the Connect Strings and Non-Connect Strings fields match the messages generated by your modem. If a result message is incorrect, select a string field in the Connect Strings box or the Non-Connect Strings box, and then type the information you want to appear in the selected field.

To change the message PROCOMM PLUS for Windows expects for a 2400-baud connection, for example, press Alt-2 to select 2400 baud and then type the necessary changes.

At the top left of the Connect Strings box is an option called Auto Baud Detect. Sometimes when you use PROCOMM PLUS for Windows to dial a remote computer, you aren't sure of the remote modem's transmission speed. At other times, you think that you know the other modem's speed but are mistaken. PROCOMM PLUS for Windows can handle either situation with its Auto Baud Detect option.

To activate the Auto Baud Detect option, just select it (this option is usually selected by default). In figure 8.11 the option currently is selected (an X is in the box). When Auto Baud Detect is on, PROCOMM PLUS for Windows detects the transmission speed at which your modem connects to the remote modem. If the connect speed is different from your computer's current transmission speed setting—set by the dialing directory entry or by the Alt-P (Line/Port Setup) command—PROCOMM PLUS for Windows adjusts your computer's transmission speed setting. If you have not activated the Auto Baud Detect option, even though the modems communicate, your computer displays only gibberish on-screen. To remedy the situation, you must change the computer's line setting by choosing Baud Rate from the Current Setup menu. If you are using a modem that supports using a higher baud rate between a modem and computer than between the two modems—for example, your modem can operate using two different baud rates at the same time—you should set Auto Baud Detect to off (unselected). This is the case with many MNP and V.42 modems.

If you are using a 2400-bps modem to call a remote computer, and you have turned on the Auto Baud Detect option, set your modem to its highest transmission speed—2400 bps. Use this setting even if you think that the other computer may be using a 1200-bps modem. When two modems connect and attempt to communicate, they go through a "negotiation" process to determine a transmission speed at which both can operate. During this negotiation process, one modem may have to decrease its transmission speed, but neither modem increases its transmission speed. If your modem contains a speaker, you may be able to hear a change in pitch as the modems attempt to decide on the best baud rate to use.

Suppose that you have a 2400-bps modem. You set it to 1200 bps to dial a computer you think is operating at 1200 bps. When the modems connect, they never negotiate a connect speed higher than 1200 bps, even if the remote modem also is set to 2400 bps. On the other hand, if you call the remote computer with your modem set to 2400 bps—your modem's fastest speed—the modems negotiate a connect speed of 2400 bps or 1200 bps, depending on the speed of the remote modem.

For the Auto Baud Detect feature to work effectively, the connect strings must be set correctly. PROCOMM PLUS for Windows can adjust the transmission rate to match a particular connect speed only if the corresponding connect message on the Connect Strings box is spelled exactly the same way the modem sends the connect message. For a Hayes-compatible modem, for example, make sure that the 300-baud connect message reads CONNECT^M, not just CONNECT. The other messages don't need the ^M.

Setting the Default Terminal Emulation and Settings

The Terminal option on the Current Setup menu enables you to choose what default terminal emulation is used to display information on the Terminal Display window. When you select Terminal, a drop-down box appears, showing the possible emulations from which you can choose (see fig. 8.12). Use the up- and down-arrow keys to choose the emulation you want, or point to the emulation with the mouse pointer and click. You can override the default terminal emulation by specifying a different terminal emulation in a dialing directory entry (see Chapter 3, "Building Your Dialing Directory").

After you have selected a terminal emulation from the Current Setup menu, select Advanced! from the menu bar to change settings for that emulation. Figure 8.13 shows the Terminal Settings dialog box that appears for a VT-102 terminal emulation. The following paragraphs describe how to set options for the VT-102 terminal, which is a popular emulation. Other terminals have different options. Refer to Chapter 10, "Terminal Emulation," for more information about specific emulations and terminal settings.

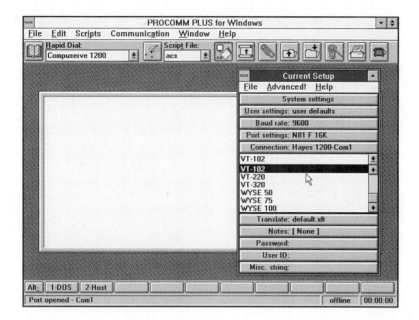

FIG. 8.12

Selecting a terminal emulation.

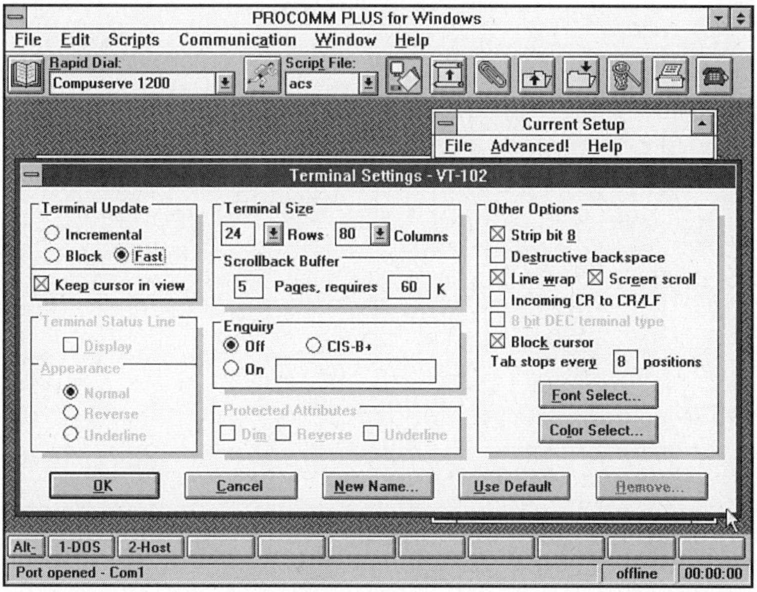

FIG. 8.13

Settings options for a VT-102 emulation.

After you make changes in the Terminal Settings dialog box, you can exit the box and retain the current settings by choosing OK. To exit this box and cancel all changes you have made, choose Cancel. To choose a new name for these terminal settings (other than the current VT-102, for example) choose New Name. You then are prompted to enter a new name. If you have experimented with these settings and you want to return all the settings in this box to their default values, choose Use Defaults.

Setting the Terminal Update Method

The Terminal Update options in the Terminal Settings dialog box determine how the Terminal Display screen displays characters. The Incremental option causes the screen to display each character as it is received. The Block option causes the screen to wait until a block of characters is received and then display the entire block at once with a continuous scrolling effect. The Fast option reduces scrolling by buffering a number of characters until a large number of characters can be displayed at once. Usually, you want to use the Fast option. The Incremental option may be preferred if you often access bulletin board systems that display animated ANSI screens.

The Keep Cursor in View option is relevant only if your terminal display is larger than what can be displayed on your screen. If this option is selected, it causes the display to scroll so that the cursor is always in view. Thus, if your screen shows only 70 characters (on a normally 80-character-wide screen), the display scrolls if the cursor moves past the 70th character.

Setting the Terminal Status Line

The Terminal Status Line options control the appearance of the status line displayed on-screen. This option is available only for terminal emulations that support a status line. If it is not supported, this box appears in gray and is unselectable in the Terminal Settings dialog box, as in figure 8.13.

You can select or deselect the Display option to control whether the status line is displayed. You also can choose the appearance of the status line as Normal, Reverse, or Underlined.

Setting Terminal Size and the Scrollback Buffer

The Terminal Size settings enable you to choose the number of rows and columns that are displayed in the Terminal Display area. The most common display has 24 rows by 80 columns. Depending on the terminal emulation and your monitor type, however, you may be able to display 132-character-wide screens. The Rows and Columns options contain drop-down boxes. To open a box, press Alt-Z, press the arrow keys to select Row or Column, and press Alt-down arrow. In the extended box, use the up- and down-arrow keys to select the row or column value; then press Alt-up arrow to close the drop-down box. If you're using the mouse, just click the down arrow to the right of the entry box you want to open and click the value you want to choose.

The Scrollback Buffer settings determine how much information is stored in the terminal display's buffer. The information in this buffer can be searched, captured, or printed. This buffer comes in handy when something scrolls off the screen, and you want to scroll back to reread the information. The buffer can contain a maximum of 30 pages, depending on the terminal emulation. To change the number of pages, choose the Pages field and then enter a number from 1 to 30. The Requires field displays the amount of memory required to buffer that much information.

Setting Terminal Enquiry

The Enquiry options in the Terminal Settings dialog box specify how PROCOMM PLUS for Windows responds to an incoming ENQ (ASCII decimal 5) character. By default, this feature is set to Off, and PROCOMM PLUS for Windows doesn't respond at all to the ENQ character. You do, however, have two other choices:

- If you set Enquiry (ENQ) to On, PROCOMM PLUS for Windows transmits the contents of the String field displayed beside the On button in the Enquiry box when the ENQ character is received. (Refer to Chapter 7, "Automating PROCOMM PLUS for Windows with Meta Keys and Script Files," for more information on meta keys.)

- If you set Enquiry (ENQ) to CIS B+, PROCOMM PLUS for Windows begins file-transfer procedures by using the COMPUSERVE B+ file-transfer protocol whenever PROCOMM PLUS for Windows receives the ENQ character (see Chapter 5, "Transferring Files").

The following Windows ASPECT script command has the same effect as setting the Enquiry (ENQ) option to CISB:

    SET ENQ CISB

Using this method enables you to keep the Enquiry (ENQ) option set to Off so that errant ENQ characters don't cause the File-Transfer Progress window to appear. The CIS-B+ option should be used only when connecting to CompuServe.

T I P   If you set the Enquiry (ENQ) option to CIS B+, you occasionally may have a problem with the File-Transfer Progress window popping up when you log on to or are connected to CompuServe. This problem results from CompuServe's sending of the ENQ character. To prevent this situation, change your CompuServe on-line terminal settings. While on-line to CompuServe, type *go terminal*. This command takes you to the Terminal/Service Options area. Select the Change Permanent Settings option and then Terminal Type/Parameters. Change the Micro Inquiry Sequence at Logon setting to No. Finally, select Make Session Settings Permanent.

Setting Protected Attributes

The Protected Attributes options in the Terminal Settings dialog box determine whether protected text is displayed as dim, reversed, or underlined. Protected text is a text display feature of certain terminal emulations, such as the Telewide and Wyse emulations. If the terminal you have selected does not support this feature, the Protected Attributes box of the Terminal Settings dialog box is gray and cannot be selected.

Stripping the Eighth Bit

The IBM character set is different from the ASCII character set recognized by other computers—referred to in this chapter as the generic ASCII character set—in two important ways. The generic ASCII character set includes only the first 128 characters of the IBM character set (decimal values 0 through 127) and can be represented by using just seven of the eight bits available in each byte of a PC's memory (RAM) or storage (disk).

In practical use, however, these two distinctions between the generic ASCII character set and the IBM character set seldom create a problem. Most people do not use the extended IBM characters (decimal 128 through 255) in normal correspondence. PROCOMM PLUS for Windows, however, enables you to perform ASCII transfers while using the full IBM character set as long as the Strip Bit 8 option on the Terminal Settings dialog box is deselected. If you have to upload a file that uses the full IBM character set (for example, a WordStar file or a file containing IBM box-drawing characters) to a system that supports only the generic ASCII character set, you can select this option. You also can select this option if you want to download a WordStar file and "translate it down" to generic ASCII.

When you use the ASCII file-transfer protocol to send an ASCII file to a computer that can handle only seven data bits, deselect the Strip Bit 8 option.

Setting the Destructive Backspace

The Destructive Backspace option in the Terminal Settings dialog box enables you to specify how PROCOMM PLUS for Windows translates the Backspace character on the Terminal Display screen. If you select this option, the Backspace key becomes destructive—in other words, pressing Backspace moves the cursor one space to the left and deletes any character there. If the option is deselected, pressing the Backspace key does not erase the preceding character.

Most host systems (on-line services and bulletin boards) use the Backspace key as a destructive backspace. Occasionally, however, you may connect to a host system in which the Backspace key is not intended to delete the character to the left of the cursor. If so, you should deselect the Destructive Backspace option. (Note: This setting does not affect the operation of Chat mode.)

Setting Line Wrap

If the Line Wrap option in the Terminal Settings dialog box is selected (the default setting), PROCOMM PLUS for Windows splits long lines to fit within the screen's margins when the program receives characters in a continuous stream with no carriage returns (from you or the remote computer). The typical PC screen is 80 characters wide, so when PROCOMM PLUS for Windows receives the 80th character or space, the line is filled. At this point, PROCOMM PLUS for Windows moves the cursor down one line (line feed) and returns the cursor to the left side of the screen (carriage return) before placing the next character or space on-screen. In 132-column video mode, a line can contain 132 characters before the cursor is repositioned on the next line. With the Line Wrap option turned off, the 81st character (or 133rd character, in 132-column mode) and all subsequent characters overwrite the 80th (or 132nd) character. Refer to Chapter 4, "A Session with PROCOMM PLUS for Windows," for a full discussion of this topic.

Setting Screen Scroll

If the Screen Scroll option in the Terminal Settings dialog box is selected (the default setting), PROCOMM PLUS for Windows scrolls the contents of the Terminal mode screen up one line when the cursor is in the last line on-screen, and an additional line of characters is received. Any characters on line 1 of the screen scroll off the top. Turning off this option causes the last and subsequent lines of characters to overwrite characters on the last line of the screen. (Note: This setting does not affect the operation of Chat mode.)

Setting Incoming CR to CR/LF

The Incoming CR to CR/LF option in the Terminal Settings dialog box specifies whether an incoming CR (Carriage Return) received from a remote computer is translated as a CR/LF (Carriage Return/Line Feed) on the Terminal Display screen. The default setting is no conversion (deselected). (Note: This setting does not affect the operation of Chat mode.)

Most host computers, such as on-line services and bulletin boards (including PROCOMM PLUS for Windows Host mode acting as a simple bulletin board), add a line feed to each carriage return. If PROCOMM PLUS for Windows also adds a line feed, everything on your screen is double-spaced. Therefore, you usually should leave the Incoming CR to CR/LF option set to off to leave CR alone.

If you plan to connect to a PC that is not operating as a bulletin board (including PROCOMM PLUS for Windows Host mode), or if you are connecting to any system that sends carriage returns without line feeds, you can set CR translation to CR/LF. Select CR Translation from the Terminal Settings screen.

Because you probably will connect to on-line services and bulletin boards more often than to a PC, the easier choice is to leave the default Incoming CR to CR/LF option deselected. Then, if you need the translation, you can select it from the Terminal Settings dialog box after you connect to the remote computer. You easily can tell when you need to change this option. Any time all lines of characters you type or receive from another computer continually overwrite the preceding lines, you need to toggle the Incoming CR To CR/LF option.

Setting the DEC Terminal Type

The 8 Bit DEC Terminal Type option in the Terminal Settings dialog box is available when your emulation is either a VT-220 or VT-320 terminal. This option specifies whether seven- or eight-bit escape sequences are sent by the terminal to the connected computer. This option matches a similar option on the VT-220 and VT-320 terminals.

Setting the Block Cursor Option

The Block Cursor option determines whether the cursor on the Terminal Display screen appears as a small underline or a block. Often, when you are using a laptop computer, the display is not as sharp as a normal display, and the cursor can be easily lost on-screen. If you choose the Block Cursor option, the cursor is easier to locate. On the other hand, if you are used to the smaller cursor and prefer it, you may not want the larger cursor to be used. The default is for Block Cursor to be selected.

Setting the Tab Stops Option

The Tab Stops Every option determines how many characters the cursor is moved when you press the Tab key in the Terminal Display mode. Normally, this option is set to 8. If you want to change this number, choose the option and type an integer value in the entry box.

Selecting a Font

A *font* is the style of character used to display information in the Terminal Display screen. When you choose the Font Select button in the Terminal Settings dialog box, a screen like the one in figure 8.14 appears.

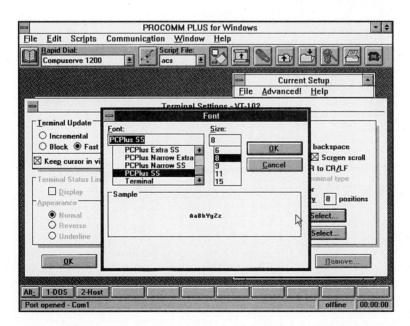

FIG. 8.14

The Font dialog box.

The Font dialog box consists of three major parts: the Font selection list, the Size selection list, and the Sample area. The Font and Size options are list boxes, and the Sample box shows you what text will look like in the font and size you have selected.

When you choose a font and size, you need to consider carefully how information will be displayed on the Terminal Display screen. You can use the font types to select a character design that is easy for you to read or is pleasing to you. You want a size large enough to enable you to read the information on-screen, but keep in mind that if you choose too large a font size, a normal 80-character screen cannot be displayed all at one time. Thus, you may have to scroll left and right to see information that is hidden off-screen.

To choose a font, select the Font option and then select the font you want or choose OK to accept. Use the same method to choose a size. Sample text in the selected font type and size is displayed in the Sample box. When you are satisfied with your selections, choose OK to lock in your choice or choose Cancel to exit this box and cancel any changes.

Selecting Colors

You use the Color Select button in the Terminal Settings dialog box to specify what colors are used on the Terminal Display screen for background and text. When you choose this option, a screen like the one in figure 8.15 appears.

This screen contains two dialog boxes. The box on the left is called the Color Display box. Notice on the name line for this box is the designation Type 1. This designation has to do with the terminal emulation. Because different emulations support different features, a different terminal emulation (other than VT-102) may bring up a slightly different Color Display dialog box. The box on the right is called the Color Selector box. This box contains 256 different color options in a 16-by-16 matrix.

To select the color to be used in the Terminal Display window, use the arrow keys to move the indicator box (currently at the bottom left) to the color combination you want to use. Or just click the appropriate color combination.

As you choose different color combinations, notice that the colors in the Attribute Display box change to reflect your color choice. This Attribute Display box contains the varieties of ways the color selection will be used to display information in the Terminal Display window. Therefore, you can choose the color combination that best matches your preferences. If you want to restore colors to the current default value (the value last saved in Current Setup), choose the Restore button.

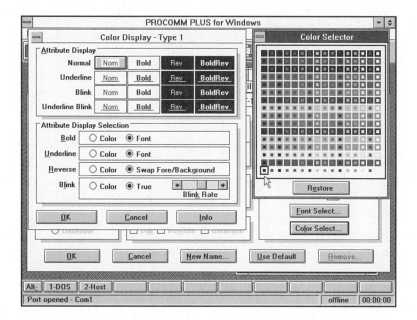

FIG. 8.15

The Color Display and Color Selector dialog boxes.

The Attribute Display Selection box contains four types of selections that affect the attribute display. The Bold attribute enables you to choose to display bold by displaying a bold color or a bold font. In a similar way, you can choose for the Underline attribute to be represented by a font or a color. The Reverse option enables you to choose for the reverse color to be an actual reverse caused by swapping the foreground and background color or to be represented by a simple change in color.

With the Blink option, you determine whether a blink is a true blink (you see the text blinking in the Attribute Display box) or is represented by a nonblinking color. If you select the blink (True) option, you can adjust the blink rate from slow to fast. To set the blink rate, select the Blink Rate option and then press the left- or right-arrow key to change the rate. If you prefer to use the mouse, point to the control box in the Blink Rate scale and drag the control to the right or left. The rate of blink is reflected in the Blink and Underline Blink lines of the Attribute Display box.

Choosing the Info button at the bottom of the Color Display dialog box produces a list of the terminal emulations that use the Type 1 color display. If this dialog box were a Color Display Type 2 dialog box, this option would list the terminal emulations that use Type 2 colors.

After you make changes in the Color Display dialog box, you can exit the box and retain the current settings by choosing OK. To exit the box and cancel all changes you have made, choose Cancel. You are returned to the Terminal Settings dialog box.

Selecting the Transfer Protocol

The Protocol option on the Current Setup menu enables you to specify the default file-transfer protocol that is used when you send or receive (upload or download) files to or from another computer. When you select Protocol, a drop-down list box appears (see fig. 8.16).

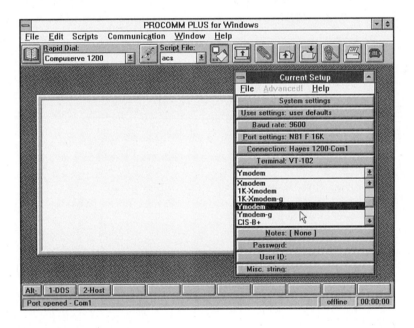

FIG. 8.16

The Protocol drop-
down list box.

The protocols available in PROCOMM PLUS for Windows include the following:

    ZMODEM
    KERMIT
    XMODEM
    1K-XMODEM
    1K-XMODEM-g

YMODEM
YMODEM-g
CIS-B+
ASCII
RAW ASCII

A complete description of how the protocols work and which one is best in certain circumstances is covered in Chapter 5, "Transferring Files."

Setting Capture File Options

The Capture option on the Current Setup menu enables you to choose several options concerning how capture files are handled by the program. A capture file is a file that contains text information from the Terminal Display window that was captured from the screen as it was displayed, and then placed into the capture file. When you select Capture, the Capture File Options dialog box appears (see fig. 8.17).

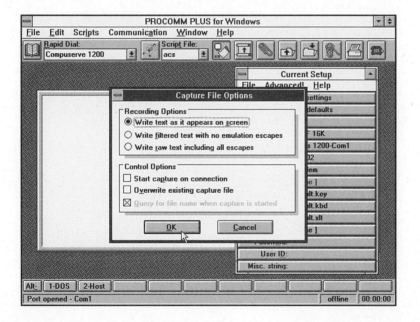

FIG. 8.17

The Capture File Options dialog box.

In the Capture File Options dialog box, you can choose from one of three Recording Options. The Write Text As It Appears On Screen (default) option causes information to be recorded exactly as it appears on the Terminal Display window. This option captures each line as it scrolls off the top of the screen. Therefore, if lines have been wrapped, they are captured as such, and not as a long line that would flow past the edge of the screen. This method is usually how you want to capture information. The Write Filtered Text with No Emulation Escapes option enables you to record information while filtering out any escape emulation codes used by some emulations. Therefore, if you are connected with a BBS that displays graphics by sending Escape code, these codes will be filtered out and not sent to the capture file. The Write Raw Text Including All Escapes option enables you to record the information exactly as it is communicated to the computer, which may not be exactly what appears on-screen. Therefore, graphics escape codes and unwrapped lines are captured as is into the file.

The Control Options box on the Capture File Options dialog box contains three additional Capture File options. If you want the capture to begin immediately upon connection so that you don't have to initiate it manually, select the Start Capture On Connection. This option is unselected by default. If you want a capture to overwrite an existing capture file, select the Overwrite Existing Capture File option. If this option is not selected, captured information is appended to existing information in the capture file. By default, this option is unselected. The third option in the Control Options box is Query For File Name When Capture Is Started. When this option is selected, a file box will appear on-screen before a capture file is opened, enabling you to specify the capture file name. This option is selected by default.

Choosing a Meta Key File

The Meta Key option on the Current Setup menu enables you to choose a file containing information about the definitions of meta keys. When you select Meta Key, a drop-down list box similar to the one shown in figure 8.18 appears.

A detailed discussion of how to define meta keys is found in Chapter 7, "Automating PROCOMM PLUS for Windows with Meta Keys and Script Files."

Setting Keyboard and Translate Options

The Keyboard and Translate options on the Current Setup menu enable you to choose a file containing descriptions of keyboard mapping and translation codes for a terminal emulation. A detailed discussion of these two options is covered in Chapter 10, "Terminal Emulation."

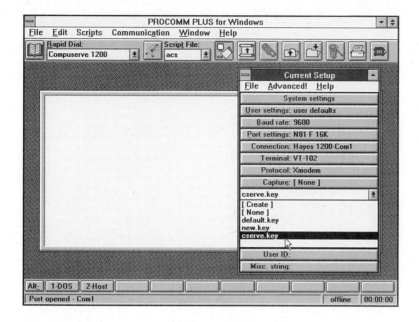

FIG. 8.18

The Meta Key list box.

Choosing a Note File

The Notes option on the Current Setup menu enables you to choose what default note files to use in the Terminal Display window. When you select Notes, a drop-down list box similar to the one shown in figure 8.19 appears.

A discussion of creating and editing note files is found in Chapter 6, "Using the Windows Notepad Editor."

Setting a Password

The Password option on the Current Setup menu enables you to enter a default password for use in a Windows ASPECT script. This password is similar to the password used in a dialing directory entry, as discussed in Chapter 3, "Building Your Dialing Directory." To enter a password in this field, select Password, type a password, and press Enter. For more information on using a password with an ASPECT script, refer to Chapters 11 and 12.

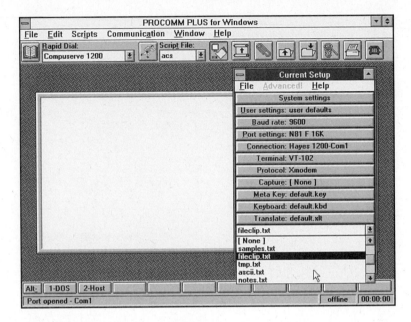

FIG. 8.19

The Notes list box.

Setting a User ID

The User ID option on the Current Setup menu enables you to enter a default user ID for use in a Windows ASPECT script. This user ID is similar to the user ID used in a dialing directory entry, as discussed in Chapter 3, "Building Your Dialing Directory." To enter a user ID in this field, select User ID, type a user ID, and press Enter. For more information on using a user ID in an ASPECT script, refer to Chapters 11 and 12.

Entering a Miscellaneous String

The Misc. String option on the Current Setup menu enables you to enter a default miscellaneous string for use in a Windows ASPECT script. This miscellaneous string is similar to the miscellaneous string used in a dialing directory entry, as discussed in Chapter 3, "Building Your Dialing Directory." To enter a miscellaneous string in this field, select Misc. String, type a miscellaneous string, and press Enter. For more information on using a miscellaneous string with an ASPECT script, refer to Chapters 11 and 12.

Setting Window Colors

In addition to the options that you can change from the Current Setup menu, you can select certain colors used in the Terminal Display window by choosing the Custom Color option from the Window menu. The PROCOMM PLUS for Windows Colors dialog box appears (see fig. 8.20).

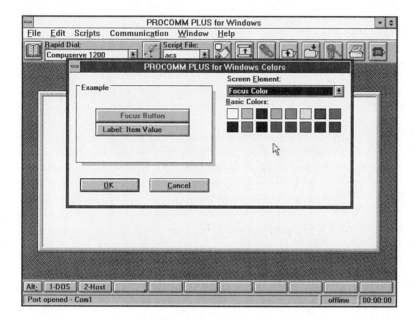

FIG. 8.20

The PROCOMM PLUS for Windows Colors dialog box.

From this dialog box, you can choose colors for a number of items called *screen elements*. To choose a screen element, select the Screen Element field and extend its drop-down list box. The extended list of screen elements is shown in figure 8.21. The following elements are available:

> Focus Color
> Label Text
> Value Text
> Dialing Directory
> Scrollback Scrollbar
> Terminal Workspace
> Monitor/Chat Send Text Color
> Monitor Receive Text Color

When you scroll up and down this Screen Element list, you see the sample display change in the Example box. You can see how changing a color changes the way the element appears on-screen.

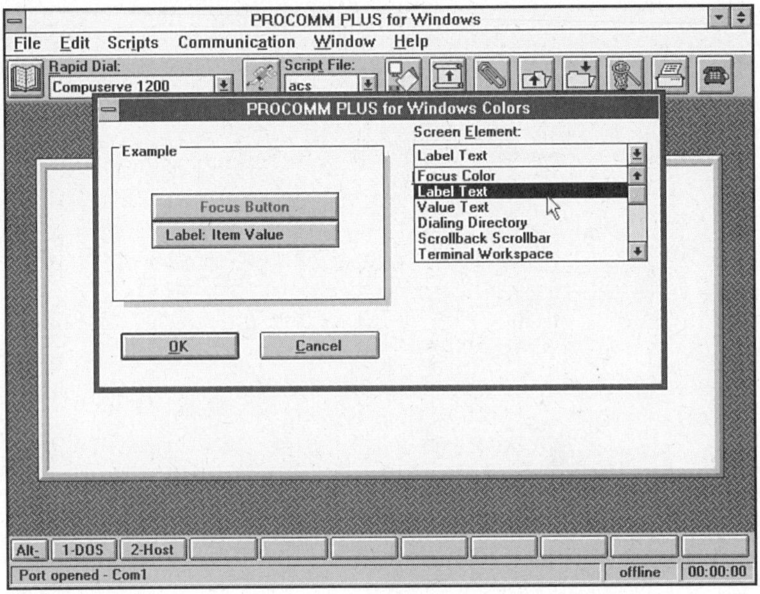

FIG. 8.21

The Screen Element
drop-down list box.

After you have chosen an element, you can choose what color to use for that element. In figure 8.20, you can see the Basic Colors boxes, which show the possible colors for the currently selected element.

You can choose a color for most elements, but the color choices for different elements may be different. The Terminal Workspace option in the Screen Element box contains additional choices. When you select Terminal Workspace, you see a screen similar to figure 8.22. Notice the Patterns and Display Terminal Frame options. The Patterns option enables you to choose what pattern appears at the edge of the Terminal Display area. Select Patterns and extend its drop-down box to see these available patterns:

None
Boxes
Paisley
Weave (the default)
Waffle
Tulip
Spinner
Scottie
Critters
Quilt
Diamonds
Thatches

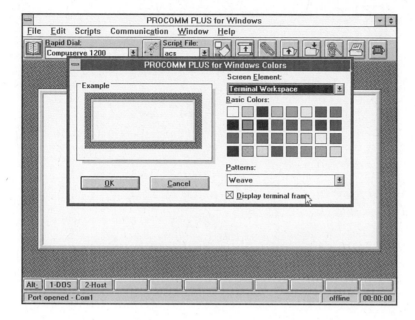

FIG. 8.22

The Terminal
Workspace options.

The Display Terminal Frame option enables you to turn the frame off
and on. When this option is selected, the frame is displayed. When it is
deselected, the frame does not appear on the Terminal Display screen.

Summary

This chapter showed you how to customize the many program settings
that control the way PROCOMM PLUS for Windows operates. You
learned how to use the Current Setup menu to set system settings, user
settings, the baud rate, port settings, connections, the terminal type, the
protocol type, the capture file, the meta key file, the note file, and the
password, user ID, and miscellaneous string for a Windows ASPECT
script. You also learned how to use the Custom Color option to choose
color settings for a variety of window screen elements. As you no doubt
have discovered by now, PROCOMM PLUS for Windows works pretty
well right off the rack. Now that you know how to tailor its many features, however, you should be able to make adjustments until
PROCOMM PLUS for Windows fits your needs like a designer suit.

Using Host Mode

One of the most popular uses for PROCOMM PLUS for Windows and other personal computer-based communications programs is to connect to electronic bulletin board systems. Traditionally, these bulletin board systems are run by computer hobbyists for computer hobbyists. A growing number of businesses, however, are discovering that PC-based bulletin boards can provide a convenient and inexpensive company-wide electronic mail service. A centrally located PC running bulletin board software can serve as an unattended electronic post office for a company. By means of a telephone line, the bulletin board receives electronic mail and files from across town, across the country, or around the world. This chapter describes Host mode—the rudimentary bulletin board system built into PROCOMM PLUS for Windows.

This chapter first describes the steps you should take before opening your electronic post office. These preliminary steps include specifying a welcome message, establishing a list of registered users, and deciding whether the system is to be open or closed to new, unregistered users. Then you learn several ways to invoke and operate in Host mode, first from a user's perspective and then from your perspective as the Host mode system operator. The text explains how to log on to the system and describes the Host mode features available to a remote user, including the uploading and downloading of files and electronic mail. The chapter then describes the functions the system operator can perform in Host mode. Finally, you learn about administrative matters, including the management of Host mode files and the administration of the Host mode electronic mail facility. After you complete this chapter, you will be ready to use PROCOMM PLUS for Windows to set up your own bulletin board system.

Preparing Host Mode

As with nearly every other feature of PROCOMM PLUS for Windows, you can use PROCOMM PLUS for Windows' built-in bulletin board system with no special preparation. Because the program is set up to run a host script and a host utility program when you take it out of the box, you can invoke Host mode, quickly set up the necessary options, and immediately enable users to call in, log on, and use this system as an electronic bulletin board. To maintain reasonable control over your computer's resources, however, you probably will want to take certain actions before permitting a user to log on to Host mode.

Before running Host mode the first time, you can specify certain setup options by running the Host Utility program. Figure 9.1 shows the Terminal Display screen with the Script File drop-down box extended and the hostutil script highlighted. To extend this box, point to the down arrow at the right side of the Script File field and click, or press Alt-T. To begin the script, select hostutil.

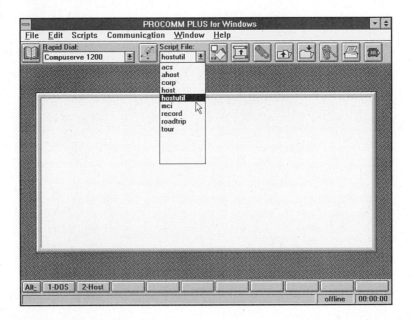

FIG. 9.1

The Script File drop-
down box extended.

You use the PROCOMM PLUS for Windows HOSTUTIL Host Mode Utility dialog box to modify several Host mode parameters. The Host Mode Utility displays the screen shown in figure 9.2. To change one of the three entry fields at the top of this dialog box, click the appropriate entry box or press Tab until your highlight is in the field (the highlight should be in the first entry field when you first open the screen); then type your entry. To change one of the radio button settings, click the button you want to select; or press Tab to get to the appropriate option box, use the up- and down-arrow keys to highlight the button you want to choose, and press the space bar to lock in the option. The following few sections describe when you might want to modify the options on this screen; then you learn how to set up the user file, HOST.USR.

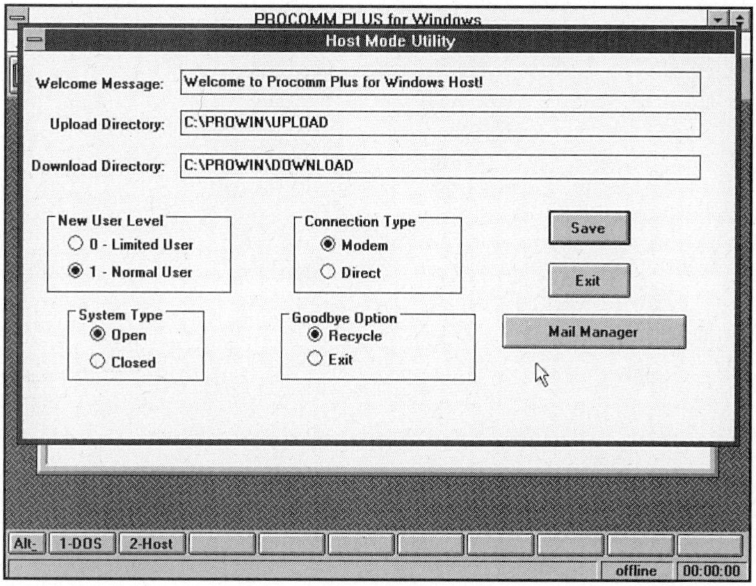

FIG. 9.2

The Host Mode Utility
dialog box.

Modifying the Host Mode Welcome Message

Each time a user logs on to Host mode, PROCOMM PLUS for Windows displays a welcome message on the user's screen. The default message is

```
Welcome to Procomm Plus for Windows Host!
```

You certainly can think of a more appropriate welcome message for your bulletin board system. Suppose, for example, that you are the national sales manager for Terry's T-Shirts, Inc. You are tired of playing telephone tag, so you want to set up PROCOMM PLUS for Windows Host mode to act as an electronic post office for your four regional sales offices. An appropriate welcome message for your bulletin board may be

```
You are connected to Terry's T-Shirts, Inc., BBS
```

To make this message the Host mode welcome message, select the Welcome Message field of the Host Mode Utility dialog box and type your message. The entry space accommodates a message of up to 256 characters.

In addition to the welcome message, PROCOMM PLUS for Windows enables you to create a logon message of unlimited length. See "Creating a Logon Message File" later in this chapter for more information.

Specifying Upload and Download Directories

Below the Welcome Message field in the Host Mode Utility dialog box is an option that enables you to assign a DOS directory into which users can send files. Because users will be uploading these files to the bulletin board, this directory is referred to as the *Upload Directory*. Similarly, the next field enables you to assign a directory from which users can download files, referred to as the *Download Directory*.

When you first display the Host Mode Utility dialog box, the contents of these two fields are shown on-screen. By default, the upload directory is C:\PROWIN\UPLOAD and the download directory is C:\PROWIN\DNLOAD.

If the upload and download directories were named the same, say C:\PROWIN\SHARE, any file uploaded by one user could be downloaded by any subsequent user. The capability to assign separate upload and download directories solves this obvious system security problem. All user-uploaded files go exclusively into the designated upload directory, and users can download files only from the specified download directory. (***Note:*** This limitation does not apply to privileged users—level 2 users. See "Understanding User Privileges" later in this chapter for more information.)

Suppose that the current working directory is C:\PROWIN, and you want to create a DOS directory named C:\PROWIN\HOST-UP as the Host mode upload directory, and a directory C:\PROWIN\HOST-DN for use as the Host mode download directory. To specify an upload directory, select the Upload Directory field and type the directory path *c:\prowin\host-up*. Similarly, to designate a download directory, type *c:\prowin\host-dn* in the Download Directory field. Then when a user sends (uploads) a file to the bulletin board, PROCOMM PLUS for Windows places the file in the directory C:\PROWIN\HOST-UP. Users can download files only from the directory C:\PROWIN\HOST-DN.

Specifying the New-User Privilege Level

When you have an open system (see the next section), PROCOMM PLUS for Windows enables each new user to specify the user's name and password. The program then enters the name into the HOST.USR file as a new user. The New User Level option in the Host Mode Utility dialog box enables you to specify the security level for a new user. Options are 0 and 1. A level 0 user (limited user) can connect, list files, chat, read mail, and leave mail but cannot upload or download files. A level 1 user (normal user) can access level 0 options and also upload or download files.

Setting the System Type

The System Type options in the Host Mode Utility dialog box enable you to choose between an open and a closed system. The default value is Open—the least restrictive bulletin board system type. When your Host mode system is open, anyone who connects to your computer (while it is running PROCOMM PLUS for Windows in Host mode) can log on and use the bulletin board.

For many systems, however, like the Terry's T-Shirts' bulletin board, an open system is not appropriate. A closed system gives you more control over who can access your bulletin board. When your Host mode system is closed, only users whose names you included in the HOST.USR file can log on to your bulletin board. (HOST.USR is an ASCII file that contains a list of authorized users. See "Building the User File" later in this chapter for information on adding users to the HOST.USR file.)

To switch to a closed system, select (fill in) the Closed option button in the Host Mode Utility dialog box.

Setting the Connection Type

The Connection Type option in the Host Mode Utility dialog box specifies whether the user will be connected by modem (Modem) or directly (Direct). Most often you use the PROCOMM PLUS for Windows Host mode to permit remote users to connect to your computer through modems over telephone lines. In most situations, therefore, the Connection Type option setting should be Modem (the default).

Occasionally, however, you may want to transfer data between two computers that are physically close enough to be connected by a short cable (50 feet or less). Such a connection is referred to as a *direct connection*. In this case, you need to change to the Direct setting.

A direct connection requires a special type of cable. If you connect the two computers with a standard RS-232 serial cable, they cannot communicate; instead, you must connect the serial ports of the computers with a special cable known as a *null modem* (which means literally "no modem"). This connection sometimes is referred to as *hard wiring* the computers together. A null modem looks like a normal serial cable but is configured to connect two DTE (data terminal equipment) RS-232 devices. A PC's serial port normally is configured as a DTE device. (See Appendix B, "Installing a Modem," for a description of the RS-232 standard and a diagram that shows how to construct a null-modem cable.)

Suppose that your desktop PC has a 5 1/4-inch floppy disk drive, but your laptop PC has a 3 1/2-inch disk drive. How can you trade files between the two machines? You could buy a 3 1/2-inch drive for the desktop PC or perhaps an external 5 1/4-inch drive for the laptop PC. Either of these solutions, however, probably would cost at least $100—more if you pay full retail, and even more if you don't want to install the new drive yourself. As an alternative, you can buy a null-modem cable for as little as a $7 mail order and no more than $30 full retail. You then can use PROCOMM PLUS for Windows to send files in either direction over the null-modem cable between the two computers.

After you connect two PCs with a null-modem cable, load PROCOMM PLUS for Windows on both machines. With the Connection Type option set to Direct on one PC, activate Host mode (see "Invoking and Exiting Host Mode" later in this chapter). PROCOMM PLUS for Windows on the Host mode machine immediately sends the welcome message to the other machine. You then control the session from the user computer (the one not running in Host mode).

More than likely, you will use the Current Setup menu to set the COM port and transmission speed (see Chapter 8, "Tailoring PROCOMM PLUS for Windows"). When using a null-modem cable to connect to another PC, you must specify the COM port to which the cable is connected. Unless you disconnected your modem and are using the same COM port, you have to change the COM port setting.

Because you are not using a modem, you are not constrained by the modem's maximum speed. You can use the fastest transmission speed that both computers can accommodate. The easiest way to determine the maximum transmission speed between a pair of computers is by trial and error. Set both computers to PROCOMM PLUS for Windows' fastest speed, 115,200 bps, and attempt a file transfer. If the file transfer aborts, try a slower speed. After you complete a successful transfer, you discover the maximum mutual speed. Use this speed when you transfer files between these two computers over a null-modem cable.

If you attempt to transfer files through a null-modem hookup, and the transfer aborts quickly, you may need to set the Abort Transfer if CD Lost option in the System Settings dialog box. See Chapter 8, "Tailoring PROCOMM PLUS for Windows." The reason is that some null modems do not transmit a CD (carrier detect) signal properly, so PROCOMM PLUS for Windows thinks it has been dropped and thus aborts the transfer. Another item to check if transfers are not working properly is the FILES command in the CONFIG.SYS file. Make sure that your command is set to 30 or higher.

Setting the Goodbye Option

When a disconnection from the remote computer is made—by the remote sending a "good-bye" or through Host time-out—PROCOMM PLUS for Windows recycles, hangs up, or exits. (Recycle is the default.) The Recycle setting in the Goodbye Option box of the Host Mode Utility dialog box tells PROCOMM PLUS for Windows to disconnect the current user and wait for the next call. The Exit button instructs PROCOMM PLUS for Windows to turn control back to Terminal Display mode.

Exiting the Host Mode Utility Dialog Box

After you modify the Host mode options, choose Save to save the new Host mode settings and return to the Terminal Display screen. To exit without saving changes, choose Exit. (The Mail Manager button that accompanies the Save and Exit buttons is discussed later in this chapter, in the section "Administering the Electronic Mail Facility.")

Building the User File

As explained in the earlier section on "Setting the System Type," you can set up Host mode as an open system or a closed system. When the system is open (the default condition), anyone can log on to the Host mode bulletin board. As soon as any new user specifies a first name, a last name, and a password, that user is given immediate access to the system. On the other hand, a closed system is just the opposite. No user can log on remotely to a closed Host mode system until the system operator adds the user's name and password to the list of authorized users. This list is kept in a user file called HOST.USR.

In an open or a closed system, a user file must be maintained. In an open system, PROCOMM PLUS for Windows helps you maintain this file by automatically adding each new name when a new user logs on for the first time. In a closed system, the system operator must maintain the user file. Even in an open system, however, you should keep control over the user file because it includes every user's name and password.

The Host mode user file is an ASCII file kept in the directory that contains the other PROCOMM PLUS for Windows program files (usually C:\PROWIN). A sample file is shown in figure 9.3.

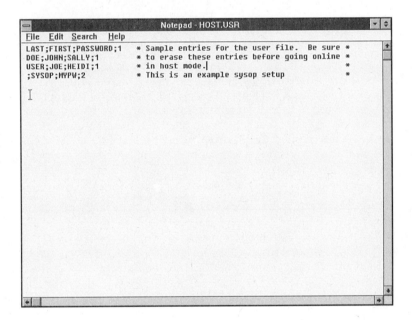

FIG. 9.3

The HOST.USR user file with four sample entries.

Each line, or entry, in the user file represents one authorized user. Each entry consists of four fields separated by semicolons in the format

```
lastname;firstname;password;n
```

where `lastname` is the user's last name, `firstname` is the user's first name, `password` is the user's password, and `n` is a single digit (0, 1, or 2) that represents the user's privilege level. The user's privilege level is assigned by the system operator and determines which Host mode features are available to that user. The last entry in figure 9.3 is a special type of user, discussed later in this section.

The lastname and firstname fields each can contain from 1 to 30 characters, but their combined length can be no more than 30 characters. Both names must be stored in the user file in all uppercase letters. The user password field can contain from 1 to 8 characters. The password also is stored in all uppercase letters.

As shown in figure 9.3, you also can add text to the right of each entry. PROCOMM PLUS for Windows ignores any text to the right of the privilege number. You can use this area of the file to store comments about each entry. When PROCOMM PLUS for Windows adds a new user to the user file, the program places this comment to the right of the new entry:

```
* NEW USER *
```

To edit the user file, you can use the Windows Notepad editor or any other text editor or word processor program that is capable of editing an ASCII file (see Chapter 6, "Using the Windows Notepad Editor"). Before you use Host mode, you should use a text editor or word processor to specify the users who need access to your system.

As shown in figure 9.3, you can have one entry in the user file with an empty lastname field. This entry typically is used for the system operator, which usually has the abbreviated name SYSOP. To indicate an empty lastname field, start the entry with a semicolon. You can add the following entry, for example, to your user file:

```
;SYSOP;MYPW;2
```

This entry enables you to log on as SYSOP by using the password MYPW. Your privilege level is 2 whenever you log on as SYSOP (see "Understanding User Privileges" later in this chapter for more information about privilege levels).

Refer also to the "Testing the System" section later in this chapter for another method of adding users to the user file.

Invoking and Exiting Host Mode

You invoke Host mode from the Terminal Display screen, normally before you are on-line to a remote user. To begin the Host mode script, click the Host meta key at the bottom of the Terminal Display screen or press Alt-2. You also can select the Script File drop-down box and then select the host script. If you have altered meta keys, you may need to run the Host script by pressing Alt-F3, selecting HOST.WAS, and selecting Compile & Run from the menu. After the script begins, you see some commands appear on-screen. These are the modem initializing codes that place the modem in Answer mode (see Chapter 8, "Tailoring PROCOMM PLUS for Windows"). After the modem is in Answer mode, ready to pick up the next incoming call, you see the Host Mode Waiting for Call box (see fig. 9.4). This box shows the status of the host session. If a caller has connected, the statistics box contains information about the last caller, when the caller logged on, and when the caller logged off.

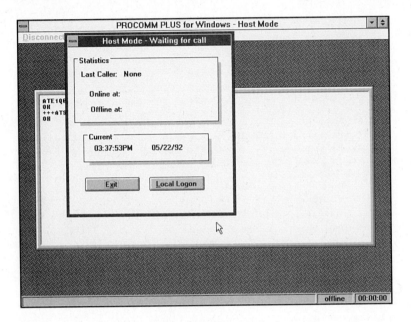

If a user named John Doe connects to your computer, for example, the status line at the top of the screen displays the message Remote User JOHN DOE online (see fig. 9.5).

During logon and throughout the Host mode session, you can see the messages Host mode sends to the user and the user's responses. Figure 9.5 shows the first part of a dialog in which a user named John Doe has logged on.

After the user logs off, PROCOMM PLUS for Windows "hangs up" the telephone line and again places the modem in Answer mode. The program displays the message Recycling (if Recycle has been set as the Goodbye Option in the Host Mode Utility dialog box; otherwise, Host mode exits). When the modem is ready to accept another call, PROCOMM PLUS for Windows again displays the Host mode box containing the message Waiting for Call.

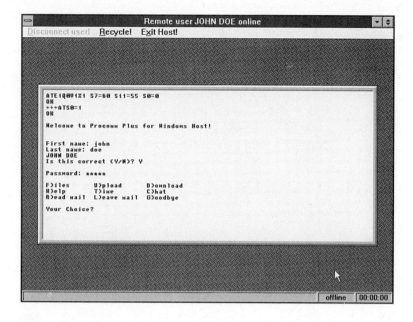

ATE1Q0V1X1 S7=60 S11=55 S0=0
OK
+++ATS0=1
OK

Welcome to Procomm Plus for Windows Host!

First name: john
Last name: doe
JOHN DOE
Is this correct (Y/N)? Y

Password: *****

F)iles   U)pload   D)ownload
H)elp   T)ime   C)hat
R)ead mail   L)eave mail G)oodbye

Your Choice?

Remote user JOHN DOE online

Disconnect user!   Recycle!   Exit Host!

offline   00:00:00

FIG. 9.5

The Host mode screen,
indicating that a user
is logged on.

 NOTE   You also can recycle or exit manually by selecting the
Recycle! or Exit Host! options in the menu bar of the Host
mode screen (refer to fig. 9.5).

PROCOMM PLUS for Windows also enables you to start Host mode after
you are connected to another PC. When you begin Host Mode (from a
meta key or script menu), PROCOMM PLUS for Windows switches to
Host mode without disconnecting the remote user. Host mode prompts
the user for a first name. The user then must log on in order to use Host
mode.

When you finish using Host mode and are in the Host Mode Waiting for
Call screen (refer to fig. 9.4), choose Exit to exit. PROCOMM PLUS for
Windows then returns to the Terminal mode screen.

Logging On to Host Mode

PROCOMM PLUS for Windows Host mode is intended to be used as a
small-scale unattended bulletin board system. When PROCOMM PLUS
for Windows is in Host mode, most commands are issued by a user at
a remote PC. The steps required to call and connect to a PC running
PROCOMM PLUS for Windows Host mode are similar to the steps

required to call and connect to any PC-based bulletin board. (See Chapters 3 and 4 for information on using PROCOMM PLUS for Windows to dial and connect to an electronic bulletin board.) To connect to your Host mode bulletin board, a user's computer can be running almost any communications software. In other words, a remote user does not have to be running PROCOMM PLUS for Windows in order to connect to and use PROCOMM PLUS for Windows running in Host mode on your PC.

After a remote user connects to your computer, Host mode sends the welcome message and prompts for the user's first name, as shown in figure 9.6. The user then types a name. The name can contain from 1 to 30 characters, including letters, numbers, and other displayable keyboard characters. Host mode does not distinguish between upper- and lowercase letters.

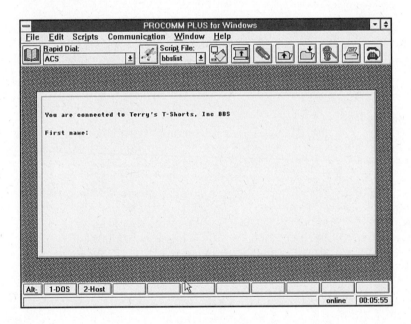

FIG. 9.6

Logging on to Host mode.

After the user types the first name and presses Enter, Host mode prompts the user for the last name. Again, the user types a name of from 1 to 30 characters (letters, numbers, and other displayable keyboard characters). When the user presses Enter after typing the last name, Host mode displays the first and last names in all uppercase letters and asks for the user's confirmation, as shown in figure 9.7.

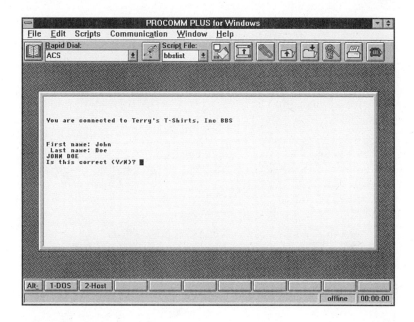

FIG. 9.7

Confirming first and
last names.

> **T I P**
>
> As a shortcut, the user can type both the first and last names at the
> First name prompt, separating the names by a space or a semicolon.
> Host mode then skips the Last name prompt and immediately asks
> whether the full name is correct.

If the displayed user name is not correct, the user presses *N* for No, and
Host mode again prompts the user to enter the first name and then the
last name.

If the caller confirms that the user name is typed correctly, PROCOMM
PLUS for Windows checks this name against the user file. If PROCOMM
PLUS for Windows cannot find the caller's name in the user file, what
occurs next depends on whether the system is closed or open.

In a closed system, only users whose names the system operator already
has added to the user file—authorized users—may log on to the system.
PROCOMM PLUS for Windows disconnects unauthorized users (anyone
whose name is not found in the user file).

In an open system, PROCOMM PLUS for Windows enables any user to log
on. If a caller enters a name not already in the user file, PROCOMM PLUS
for Windows prompts the user to enter a password. The user can type
any string of characters consisting of one to eight characters and then

press Enter. This string of characters becomes the user's personal password for use each time the user logs on to the system (unless the Host mode operator changes that password in the HOST.USR file).

As the user types the password, Host mode echoes only asterisks (*) to the user's screen. This security precaution helps the user keep the password private. PROCOMM PLUS for Windows Host mode then displays the prompt Please verify:.

To *verify* means to enter the password a second time to ensure that Host mode received the password correctly the first time. After the user enters the password the second time and presses Enter, PROCOMM PLUS for Windows adds the caller as a new user in the user file and displays the Host mode main menu, shown near the bottom of the screen in figure 9.8.

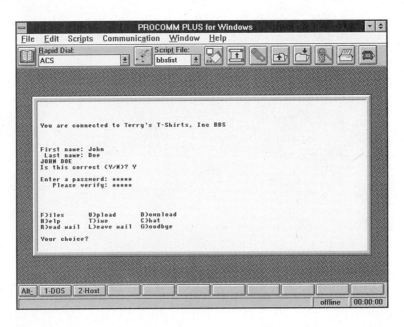

FIG. 9.8

The logon procedure for a new user on an open Host mode system.

Whether a caller is logging on to a closed system or an open system, PROCOMM PLUS for Windows prompts a previously authorized caller to enter a password. The caller gets three chances to enter the correct password. PROCOMM PLUS for Windows disconnects any caller who cannot in three tries enter the password stored in the user file with the caller's name. An authorized user does not have to enter the password a second time for verification (compare fig. 9.9 with fig. 9.8).

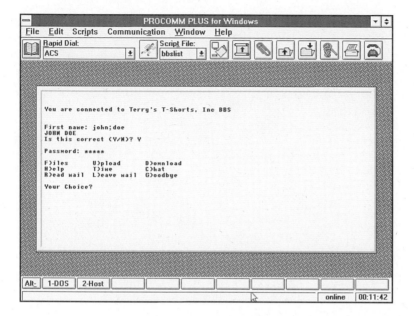

FIG. 9.9

The logon procedure
for an authorized user
on an open or a
closed Host mode
system.

You also can display the same logon message to every user by creating a
file named HOST.NWS and placing this file in the directory that contains
the PROCOMM PLUS for Windows program files. PROCOMM PLUS for
Windows displays this message after a caller logs on, just before the
program displays the Host mode main menu. Refer to "Creating a Logon
Message File" later in this chapter for more information.

Understanding User Privileges

After the caller enters the correct password, PROCOMM PLUS for Windows displays one of two Host mode menus, depending on the user's
privilege level. Any new user logging on to an open system for the first
time is assigned privilege level 0 or 1, according to the New User Level
setting in the Host Mode Utility dialog box. These users, called *limited
users* (0) or *normal users* (1), see the following menu:

```
F)iles          U)pload        D)ownload
H)elp           T)ime          C)hat
R)ead mail      L)eave mail    G)oodbye

Your choice?
```

A user with level 0 choosing Upload or Download gets a message indicating that access is not available for those options.

When the user has privilege level 2, a user referred to as a *privileged user* or a *superuser*, PROCOMM PLUS for Windows adds two more options to the menu seen by a normal user:

```
S)witch Directory
A)bort (SHUT DOWN host mode)
```

You designate a privileged user by using a text editor to add an entry or to modify the privilege-level number of an existing entry in the HOST.USR file. You often grant the system operator privileged user status. (See "Building the User File" earlier in this chapter for more information.)

T I P   If you want to log on using the user ID SYSOP, you must enter the name *sysop* followed by a blank space at the First name prompt.

The next section discusses the function of each menu option available on either version of the Host mode main menu.

Using the Host Mode Main Menu

As explained in the preceding section, the Host mode main menu for a limited or normal user contains nine options (although limited users cannot access Upload or Download). The Host mode main menu for a privileged user (superuser) contains two additional options. To choose an option, the user presses the first letter of the option. To enter Chat mode, for example, the remote user presses C for Chat at the Your choice? prompt. The following paragraphs explain, from the user's perspective, how to use each option.

Viewing the Download Directory

A primary reason for using Host mode is to enable remote users to up-load and download files easily to and from your computer without you having to be there. The first command on the Host mode main menu, Files, displays a list of all the files available for downloading. When a remote user selects Files from the Host mode main menu, PROCOMM PLUS for Windows Host mode displays the following prompt on the user's screen:

```
Enter FILE SPEC: (Carriage Return = *.*)
>
```

At this prompt, the caller presses Enter to see a list of all the files in the Host mode download directory. If you did not specify a download directory in the Host Mode Utility dialog box, Host mode lists files from your current working directory (see "Specifying Upload and Download Directories" earlier in this chapter). The user also can use the DOS wild-card characters * and ? to display only a subset of the files in this directory. When Host mode has listed all matching file names, it returns the user to the Host mode main menu.

Suppose that the sales manager for your company's southern region has logged on to Host mode and wants to download a copy of the consolidated sales report for August 1992 but cannot remember the name of the file. She first selects Files from the Host mode main menu. Then she types *.wk1 to the right of the prompt and presses Enter. Host mode lists all the files in the download directory that have the file-name extension WK1. (Files with this extension can be received by the remote user.)

In this case, suppose that two WK1 files, SALES792.WK1 and SALES892.WK1, are in the download directory (see fig. 9.10). The SALES892.WK1 file is apparently the August '92 spreadsheet the regional sales manager needs.

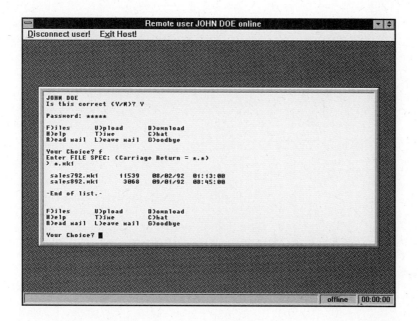

FIG. 9.10

Listing all files in the download directory with the file name extension WK1.

Sometimes more files may be in the download directory than will fit vertically on-screen. To give the caller a chance to review all the file names before they scroll off the screen, Host mode displays the maximum number of file names that fit on-screen (depending on the font used) and then pauses. The message -MORE- displayed after the last file name indicates that more file names follow. The user can press any key to continue the display.

The user can cancel the Files command before it finishes listing all requested file names. As soon as the user presses Ctrl-C, Host mode stops listing file names and returns to the Host mode main menu.

T I P   When the caller is a privileged user—having privilege level 2—the Files command lists the host system's current working directory rather than the download directory. Also, when Host mode asks for a file spec, a privileged user can specify any directory on the host system by typing the complete DOS path.

Downloading a File

Downloading a file from Host mode is similar to downloading a file from most other bulletin board systems. The user first selects Download from the Host mode main menu. Host mode then prompts the user to choose from among seven file-transfer protocols:

K) Kermit   X) Xmodem
O) 1K-Xmodem   E) 1K-Xmodem-G
Y) Ymodem   G) Ymodem-G (Batch)
Z) Zmodem

The user must choose a file-transfer protocol that also is supported by the user's communications program (see Chapter 5, "Transferring Files," for guidelines on deciding which protocol to use).

After the caller selects a file-transfer protocol, Host mode prompts for a file name to download. If the user chooses KERMIT, YMODEM-G (Batch), or ZMODEM, the user can specify multiple files in the file specification by using the DOS wild-card characters, as in *.wk1. With any of the seven protocols, the user can specify a single file name to download. A privileged user (superuser) can specify a file from any directory on the host system by including the complete DOS path. Normal users can download files only from the current working directory or from the download directory if one is specified. Host mode then gives the user this prompt:

```
Begin your transfer procedure... (CTRL-X aborts)
```

The caller executes the proper commands at the remote computer to begin the download procedure, using the same file-transfer protocol that the host system was instructed to use. If the caller is using ZMODEM and using PROCOMM PLUS for DOS or Windows on the other end, the transfer is initiated automatically.

Suppose that the southern region sales manager is ready to download the August 1992 sales report—the file SALES892.WK1. From the Host mode main menu, she selects Download. Host mode displays the list of seven available file-transfer protocols. She is using PROCOMM PLUS for Windows on her computer, which supports the ZMODEM file-transfer protocol, so she presses Z to select the Zmodem option. Host mode prompts her for a file name. In response, the sales manager types the file name *sales892.wk1* and presses Enter. Host mode displays the following prompt:

```
Begin your ZMODEM transfer procedure...  (CTRL-X aborts)
```

The sales manager then issues the appropriate command to her communications software to begin downloading the file, using the ZMODEM file-transfer protocol. Because she is using ZMODEM, which normally supports Auto Download, she may not have to give her communications software any command. This is controlled by the Automatic Download Start setting in the User Settings dialog box from the Current Settings menu. While the transfer is taking place, she sees a progress window on-screen, similar to figure 9.11. When the transfer is complete, she is returned to the Host mode main menu.

See Chapter 5, "Transferring Files," for a discussion of how to use PROCOMM PLUS for Windows and a file-transfer protocol to download files.

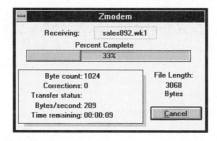

FIG. 9.11

The download progress window for a ZMODEM file transfer.

Uploading a File

Uploading a file to Host mode is similar to uploading a file to most other bulletin board systems. The user first selects Upload from the Host mode main menu. Host mode then prompts the user to choose from among seven file-transfer protocols:

K) Kermit   X) Xmodem
O) 1K-Xmodem   E) 1K-Xmodem-G
Y) Ymodem   G) Ymodem-G (Batch)
Z) Zmodem

The user must choose a file-transfer protocol that also is supported by the user's communications program (see Chapter 5, "Transferring Files," for guidelines on deciding which protocol to use).

After the caller selects a file-transfer protocol, Host mode prompts for a file name. If the user chooses KERMIT, YMODEM-G (Batch), or ZMODEM, the user can specify multiple files by using the DOS wild-card characters. With any of the seven protocols, the user can specify a single file name and then press Enter. A privileged user (superuser) can upload a file to any directory on the host system by including the complete DOS path. Normal users can upload files only to the current directory or to the upload directory if one is specified. Protocols capable of sending multiple files will transfer files to the current directory or to the upload directory if one is specified, no matter what the user specifies at the File name prompt and regardless of the user's privilege level.

After the user enters the name of the file to upload, the system gives the user this prompt:

```
Begin your transfer procedure (CTRL-X aborts)
```

The caller then executes the proper commands to begin the upload procedure on the user's own computer, using the same file-transfer protocol that the host system was instructed to use. If the user is using a copy of PROCOMM PLUS for Windows and is uploading a file using the YMODEM protocol, for example, a screen similar to figure 9.12 appears on the user's screen. This screen enables the user to specify what file to upload. Notice that the file sales992.wk1 has been selected in the File Name list box. This box lists the files in the \PROWIN\UPLOAD directory, which is specified as the upload directory for this system. After the file to be uploaded has been specified, the user chooses OK to begin the file transfer. A progress screen similar to figure 9.11 (except saying "Sending" rather than "Receiving") appears on the remote user's screen. When the transfer is compete, the user returns to the Host mode main menu.

Host mode next displays a progress window while the transfer is being made. See Chapter 5, "Transferring Files," for a complete discussion of how to use PROCOMM PLUS for Windows and a file-transfer protocol to upload files.

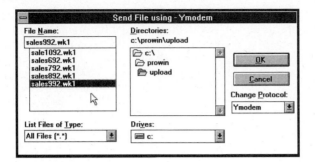

FIG. 9.12

Sending a file with the
YMODEM protocol.

Getting Help

Someone may—in fact, someone probably will—log on to your Host
mode system without knowing how to use it. The Host mode main menu
therefore includes the Help option. When the user selects Help from the
Host mode main menu, Host mode displays the first of several screens of
information. This information explains, from the user's perspective, how
the Host mode system operates. The help information is stored in the
file HOST.HLP, which is an ASCII text file that you can edit, add to, and
change to meet the specific needs of your system. An example help
screen is displayed in figure 9.13.

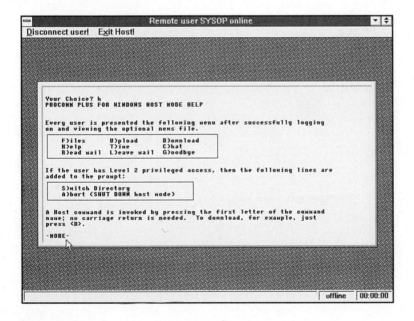

FIG. 9.13

An example help
screen displayed by
the Host mode system,
from the remote user's
perspective.

Consider advising users of your system to capture to disk and print a copy of all help screens displayed by the Help command. This copy can provide a handy reference manual for people who log on to your Host mode system. When the help file is displayed, only the first 23 lines are shown. The notice at the bottom of the screen, -MORE-, indicates that more information is included. When the user presses Enter, the next 23 lines are shown. This process continues until the entire help file has been displayed.

For information on customizing your system's help file, refer to "Customizing the Help File" later in this chapter.

Checking the Time

Depending on the purpose of your bulletin board, a user may be calling long distance and therefore may be interested in how long the connection has lasted. Or you may have many users competing for time on the system, so you may have to impose a time limit on each connection. For whatever the reason, PROCOMM PLUS for Windows Host mode enables a caller to determine the time at which the connection was made as well as the current time of day. When the caller selects Time from the Host mode main menu, Host mode displays the message

```
Online at: hh:mm:ssx
It is now: hh:mm:ssx
```

where hh is hours, mm is minutes, ss is seconds, and x is AM or PM. Figure 9.14 shows the screen of a user who connected at 04:06:14 A.M. and is still on-line at 04:11:39 A.M. This user has been on-line for about five minutes.

The Host mode log file, HOST.LOG, keeps a running log of all Host mode transactions, including the times each user logs on and logs off. For more information, refer to "Viewing and Editing the Host Log File" later in this chapter.

Chatting with the Host Mode Operator

Although PROCOMM PLUS for Windows Host mode is intended as a simple, unattended bulletin board system, someone probably is within the vicinity of your computer during significant portions of the day. PROCOMM PLUS for Windows therefore provides the Chat feature, through which the user can page the host system's operator.

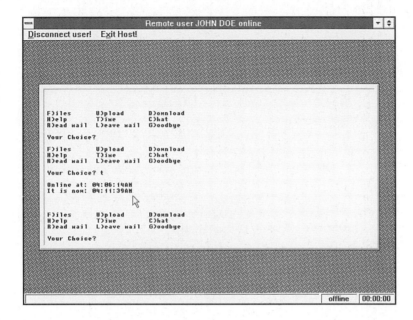

```
                    Remote user JOHN DOE online
 Disconnect user!   Exit Host!



      F)iles       U)pload       D)ownload
      H)elp        T)ime         C)hat
      R)ead mail   L)eave mail   G)oodbye

      Your Choice?

      F)iles       U)pload       D)ownload
      H)elp        T)ime         C)hat
      R)ead mail   L)eave mail   G)oodbye

      Your Choice? t

      Online at: 04:06:14AM
      It is now: 04:11:39AM


      F)iles       U)pload       D)ownload
      H)elp        T)ime         C)hat
      R)ead mail   L)eave mail   G)oodbye

      Your Choice?




                                              offline  00:00:00
```

FIG. 9.14

Checking the time.

When the remote user wants to "converse" interactively with the host system's operator, the user selects Chat from the Host mode main menu. Host mode displays the message Paging Host operator... on the user's screen and sounds a beep on the host system once each second for 10 seconds. If the operator does not come on-line within 10 seconds, Host mode sends this message to the caller:

Host operator is not available!

The caller then is returned to the Host mode main menu.

When the remote user requests a chat, the message Remote User is requesting to chat is displayed on the host computer. If the host system operator chooses OK in response to the message, Host mode sends the message Host operator is online! to the caller's screen. The operator (you or someone else at your computer) and the caller then can type and receive information interactively. (See Chapter 4, "A Session with PROCOMM PLUS for Windows," and this chapter's later section on "Interacting with a User On-line" for more information.) When the user and operator finish their on-line conversation, either can terminate Chat mode by pressing Esc. Host mode then returns to the Host mode main menu.

Sending Electronic Mail

One of the most impressive capabilities of PROCOMM PLUS for Windows Host mode is the electronic mail, or E-Mail, feature. This feature enables a user to send public and private messages. A public message can be read by any user, but a private message is accessible only to the user to whom the message is addressed and to the user who created it.

When a user wants to send a public or private message (mail), the user selects Leave Mail from the Host mode main menu. Host mode first displays a To prompt, asking the user for the addressee. The user types the first and last name of the individual who is to receive the mail and presses Enter. (If you have a user entry for SYSOP, as described in "Building the User File" earlier in this chapter, the user can send mail to the system operator by using the single name SYSOP.)

After the user specifies the addressee, Host mode asks for the subject. Although this information is not required, the user can type a description of the subject (all displayable characters are acceptable). The user then presses Enter, and Host mode displays the following message:

```
Private Mail (Y/N)?
```

The user presses Y if the message should be read only by the addressee, or N if the message is to be available to any user on the system. The Host mode E-Mail system then displays the user's entries so far, as in this example:

```
To: addresseename
From: username
Subj: subject
```

addresseename is the name of the intended recipient of the message, username is the name of the current user, and subject is the subject of the message, if any, specified by the user. Host mode then asks

```
Is this correct (Y/N/Q)?
```

The user presses N if any line is incorrect. Otherwise, the user presses Y to indicate that the information is correct. The user presses Q to quit the message procedure without leaving a message.

Host mode then displays 1: at the beginning of a new line. This line is the first message entry line.

Suppose that your assistant, John Doe, is sending a message to Victor Laslo, manager of the eastern sales region, concerning the upcoming October sales meeting. John selects Leave Mail from the Host mode main menu, types *Victor Laslo* at the To prompt, and presses Enter. John then types *October Sales Meeting* at the Subj. prompt and again presses

Enter. Finally, John indicates that the message is intended only for Victor by responding Y to the `Private Mail (Y/N)?` prompt. Host mode displays the information John has entered so far and asks whether the information is correct. John responds Y, so Host mode displays the first message entry line. This entire sequence is shown in figure 9.15.

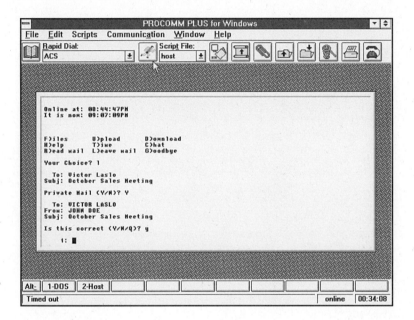

FIG. 9.15

Preparing to leave a mail message.

After Host mode displays the first message entry line, the user can type the message line by line or can use the ASCII file-transfer protocol (or the equivalent, if the user is not using PROCOMM PLUS for Windows) to send a previously typed ASCII message to the host system.

If the user types the message while on-line, only the current line can be edited. The user must press Enter at the end of each line and then no longer can change that line. Host mode interprets a blank line as the end of the message.

To include a blank line within the message, the user must press the space bar before pressing Enter, causing the blank space character (ASCII decimal 32) to be sent to Host mode.

T I P

After the user finishes the message and presses Enter at a blank line, Host mode displays the Leave Mail menu, which contains the following four options (see fig. 9.16):

- *Save*. The sender chooses this option to save the message and send it to the addressee. The message is saved to a file named HOST.MSG on the host system's disk (see "Administering the Electronic Mail Facility" later in this chapter). Host mode displays the message `Saving message...` and then returns the caller to the Host mode main menu.

- *Abort*. If the sender selects this option, Host mode asks for confirmation that the user wants to abort the message. To return to the Host mode main menu without saving the message, the user presses Y. The user may select this option by mistake, however, but can press N to answer No and remain in the Leave Mail menu.

- *Display*. Sometimes a message is too long to display all on one screen. By the time the user types the last line, the first portion of the message has scrolled off the screen. If the user chooses Display, Host mode displays the entire message, 23 lines at a time, starting at the beginning of the message. At the end of each screen, Host mode displays the message `-MORE-`, and the user can press any key to see the next screen. After displaying the entire message, Host mode returns the caller to the Leave Mail menu.

- *Continue*. This option enables the user to continue entering text at the end of the message. Host mode places the cursor at the beginning of a blank line. The user should choose this option in order to finish typing the message—for example, after accidentally pressing Enter at a completely blank line or pressing Enter on purpose and then choosing Display to display the first part of the message.

Ultimately, the user sends or aborts the message, and Host mode then returns the user to the Host mode main menu.

Reading Electronic Mail

Like many dedicated electronic mail systems and many bulletin board systems, PROCOMM PLUS for Windows Host mode notifies a user if mail is waiting for that user. After the user has entered the logon password, this message appears on-screen if new mail is waiting for that user:

        You have mail waiting!

To check and read mail, the caller selects Read Mail from the Host mode main menu. Host mode first indicates the number of messages currently stored on the system. All private and public messages are included in this number, but all messages are not always accessible to every user. Host mode messages that are accessible to a particular user include all public messages, any private message addressed to that user, and any private message sent by that user.

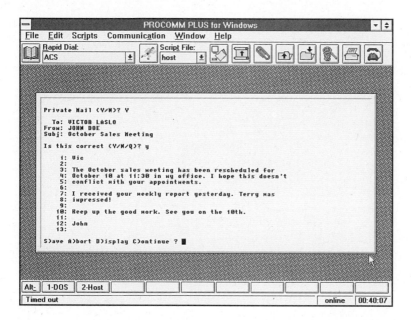

FIG. 9.16

Completing a message and viewing the Leave Mail menu.

After Host mode displays the number of messages, the Read Mail menu appears, containing the following options:

```
F)orward Read
N)ew Mail
S)earch Mail
Q)uit
```

To return to the Host mode main menu, the user selects Quit. The other options are discussed in the following sections.

Reading Messages in Sequence

The user selects Forward Read to read multiple messages in sequence. This option is used frequently on a system in which the majority of messages are public and users normally read all messages. If a user selects Forward Read, Host mode displays the following prompt:

```
Starting message number (<CR> for first):
```

The user can type the number of the first message the user wants to read, and then press Enter, or can just press Enter to see all accessible messages, beginning with message number 1. After the user responds to this prompt, Host mode displays the first accessible message specified.

T I P   Messages are stored in chronological order. Host mode indicates on the same line as the message number the date and time the message was sent (see fig. 9.17).

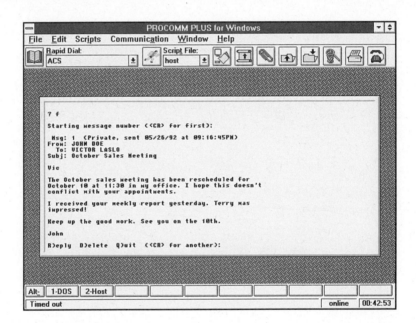

FIG. 9.17

Reading message number 1.

At the end of each message, Host mode gives the user these four options, as shown in figure 9.17:

- *Reply*. After choosing this option, the user can send back to the message's author a message on the same subject. You see a line number 1: prompt. Enter the message as described in the "Sending Electronic Mail" section, but don't specify the To: address.

- *Delete*. This option enables the user to delete the message. Only the user who wrote the message or the user to whom it is addressed can issue this command. Host mode then displays a prompt telling the user that the message has been deleted. A deleted message

remains in the HOST.MSG file until removed by the system operator, but the message no longer can be displayed by the Read Mail
options.

- *Quit.* This option enables the user to quit reading messages and
return to the Host mode main menu.

- *(<CR> for another).* By pressing Enter, the user can display the next
accessible message without replying to the current message.

Some messages are too long to display all on one screen. If a message
contains more lines than can fit on-screen (this limit is determined by
the font size being used), Host mode displays the maximum number of
lines at a time and places the message -MORE- in the next line. The user
then must press any key to see the next group of lines in the message.
This procedure continues until the entire message is displayed.

After Host mode displays all accessible messages in the specified sequence, the program displays the message End of messages and then
returns to the Read Mail menu. Choose Quit from this menu to return to
the Host mode main menu.

Reading New Mail

If you receive the new mail message when you log on, you can read only
the new messages by choosing Read Mail from the Host mode main
menu and then choosing the New Mail option from the Read Mail menu.
Similar to the Forward Read option, the New Mail option displays all new
messages, beginning with the first one and continuing until no more new
messages are available.

Searching for Specific Messages

The Search Mail option on the Read Mail menu enables a user to find
specific messages to read. If a user chooses this option, Host mode displays the prompt Which field and lists three options: To, From, and
Subject. Each option corresponds to one of the first three entries, or
fields, in a Host mode message: To, From, and Subj.

A user chooses From, for example, when looking for accessible messages
from a particular user. After the user selects this option, Host mode asks
for the search string. The user then types the name and presses Enter.
Host mode searches the message file for all mail from the specified user
and displays any messages found, beginning with the first message.

Suppose that Victor Laslo, manager of the eastern sales region, logs on to Host mode to check his electronic mail. He selects Read Mail from the Host mode main menu and then Search Mail from the Read Mail menu. When asked which field, Victor chooses To, and types *Victor Laslo* as the search string. He presses Enter, and Host mode searches for his mail. If he does not search for specific mail, all public messages are displayed using the Forward Read method. He can use this search method to avoid reading the other messages. Host mode displays his first message.

If Host mode finds no matching message at all, the program displays the message End of messages.

Using a procedure similar to that used with the To option, a user can read all messages sent by a particular user or on a given subject by using the From and Subject options at the Which field prompt.

Changing to a New Directory on the Remote Computer

One of the two additional options available on a privileged user's Host mode main menu is the Switch Directory option. This option enables a privileged user operating from a remote computer to switch to any directory of the host system and then display a file list of the files found in that directory. Figure 9.18 shows what happens if a privileged user selects Switch Directory from the Host mode main menu. After you switch directories, use the File option to list files in that directory.

 NOTE If you are familiar with PROCOMM PLUS for DOS, you may recognize that this option is different in the Windows version. In the DOS version, the option is Shell to DOS, which enables the user to type a DOS command and see the results from the host computer. This capability is not available in the Windows version.

Aborting Host Mode from a Remote Computer

The second option on the Host mode main menu available exclusively to privileged users is the Abort option. This option enables a privileged user to abort Host mode, returning the host system to PROCOMM PLUS for Windows' Terminal mode.

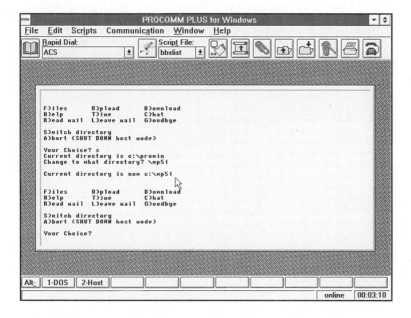

FIG. 9.18

Selecting the Switch
Directory option.

If a privileged user selects Abort, Host mode displays the following
prompt:

```
Abort Host mode (Y/N)
```

The user presses Y to cause Host mode to abort and to return
PROCOMM PLUS for Windows to Terminal mode. This response has the
same effect as if the host system's operator had pressed Alt-X (Exit).
Host mode displays the message Aborting... and then returns the host
computer to the Terminal Display screen. This feature is a convenient
way to prevent subsequent callers from connecting with Host mode. You
may want to use this feature as a safety measure.

Saying Goodbye

When the remote user is ready to disconnect from Host mode, the user
selects Goodbye from the Host mode main menu. Host mode sends the
following message to the remote user's screen:

```
Online at: hh:mm:ssx
It is now: hh:mm:ssx
```

where hh is hours, mm is minutes, ss is seconds, and x is AM or PM.

Host mode then causes its modem to "hang up" the telephone and prepares the modem for answering the next call. The status line message on the host system's screen again says `Waiting for call`. If the user hangs up without "saying good-bye" or if the telephone connection is lost for some other reason, your modem sends to Host mode a message that the modem no longer detects a carrier signal. In response, Host mode recycles, displays the `Waiting for call` message in the status line, and sends to the modem a command that prepares it to answer the next call.

Understanding Operator Rights and Responsibilities

PROCOMM PLUS for Windows' Host mode is intended to provide access to remote users, but someone who has direct access to the host computer must be given the responsibility to perform certain administrative tasks in order to keep the system running efficiently. This individual often is referred to as the system operator, or SYSOP.

As far as PROCOMM PLUS for Windows is concerned, anyone who has access to the host system's keyboard is the system operator. In other words, PROCOMM PLUS for Windows assumes that any command executed at the host computer's keyboard is performed by the system operator.

The system operator's duties are fairly simple. Obviously, someone must be responsible for turning on Host mode when users are expected to call (see "Invoking and Exiting Host Mode" earlier in this chapter). Also, to encourage efficient use, someone must be available (within reasonable limits) while new users are on-line to help them get comfortable with Host mode's features. Finally, someone periodically must check the various important system files for needed maintenance.

The commands available to the system operator from the host computer's keyboard are Disconnect Remote User (Alt-D), Exit (Alt-X), and Recycle (Alt-R).

Interacting with a User On-line

During the time a user is on-line to Host mode, the host computer's screen displays an exact copy of what the user sees on the remote computer's screen. When you are in the vicinity of the host computer, you can monitor the activity of a caller by watching the host system's screen.

Be aware, however, that while a user is on-line to Host mode, the host computer's keyboard and the remote keyboard are in "lock step." If you touch one of the displayable keys (letters, numbers, or symbols), the corresponding character displays on both the host system's screen and the remote user's screen. This character display occurs only while PROCOMM PLUS for Windows has the active focus. The remote user can use other applications while the host system operates.

Occasionally, a user may have a question for the system operator while the user is on-line. The user can select Chat from the Host mode main menu to page the system operator. Host mode displays a message such as Remote user JOHN DOE is requesting to chat and sounds a beep on the host system for 10 seconds. If the operator does not come on-line within 10 seconds by clicking on OK, Host mode returns to the Host mode main menu. To exit Chat mode, the host or the remote user can press Esc. The system then returns to the Files, Upload menu.

Testing the System

From time to time, you may want to test Host mode, but you probably don't want to go to the trouble of calling in from a remote computer. PROCOMM PLUS for Windows enables you to log on directly from the host computer's keyboard just for this purpose. When you begin the host script and see the Host Mode - Waiting For Call dialog box (see fig. 9.4), choose the Local Logon (Alt-L) option to logon locally.

No user can be on-line when you log on to Host mode from the host system's keyboard. When you initiate Host mode from the host computer, you can log onto the computer like any user, including logging on as a privileged user. If you log on locally, however, you cannot upload, download, or initiate a chat session.

Testing the logon procedure locally also provides a convenient way to add a new user's name to the user file (HOST.USR) for an open system. Rather than log on as SYSOP, log on with the name of a user. If the name doesn't already exist in the HOST.USR file, PROCOMM PLUS for Windows adds the name. The next time you view the contents of HOST.USR, it contains the new user's name, password, and the default new user privilege level, with the note * NEW USER *.

After you test the system, perhaps reading messages or leaving mail, you select Goodbye from the Host mode main menu to log off. Host mode then recycles and prepares to answer the next call.

Maintaining Host Mode Files

Several files stored on the host computer are important to your Host mode bulletin board system. These include the logon message file, the new user file, the help file, the host log file, and the mail files, which are described in the following sections.

Creating a Logon Message File

In addition to the Host mode welcome message, which can be no longer than 256 characters, you can create a logon message of unlimited length. Use a text editor, such as Windows Notepad, to create an ASCII file named HOST.NWS. Store the file in the directory that contains the PROCOMM PLUS for Windows program files. Host mode displays this file, if it exists, immediately after a user logs on to the system. If the file is longer than the number of lines that can be displayed on-screen, Host mode displays the maximum number of lines at a time, adding the notation -MORE- as the last line. The user can press any key to see the next screen of information. The Host mode main menu appears after the entire message has been displayed.

 NOTE If you set the connection type in the Host Mode Utility dialog box (hostutil script) to Direct, the Host Mode - Waiting For Call dialog box does not appear and you cannot log on locally. In order to choose the Local Logon option, you must have the connection type set to Modem.

As suggested by the file name extension NWS, this file is convenient for distributing news—information that is of interest to the majority of your users. You can even cause the message to display in color by including ANSI escape sequences (see your DOS manual for more information about ANSI). Users must use ANSI terminal emulation in order to see any color enhancements to Host mode screens.

Creating a New User File

When you have an open system, and a user logs on for the first time, you may want to display a particular message to that person. In the same way that you create the HOST.NWS file (see the preceding section, "Creating a Logon Message File"), you can create a file named HOST.NUF as a new user file. This file is displayed like the HOST.NWS file, but only the first time a new user logs onto the system.

Customizing the Help File

As explained in "Getting Help" earlier in this chapter, the Help option on the Host mode main menu enables you to provide to users helpful information about your host system. These help messages offer good information about how to use Host mode, but they are not specific to your bulletin board. Consequently, PROCOMM PLUS for Windows enables you to modify, enhance, or replace this file so that you can supply your users with more pertinent information.

To edit or create a new HOST.HLP file, use Windows Notepad or another text editor. You can modify this file, adding or deleting information as you see fit in order to tailor the message to the needs of your users. If you prefer, you can replace the file with an entirely different help message, but be sure to use the same file name. A convenient practice is to write a short user's manual for your system, using the distributed HOST.HLP file as a model. Then use your manual as the help message file. Encourage users to capture the file to disk and print the file as a handy reference.

Viewing and Editing the Host Log File

Every time a user logs on to your Host mode system, PROCOMM PLUS for Windows adds information to a file named HOST.LOG, the Host mode log file. In HOST.LOG, Host mode records the following information:

- The date and time you start Host mode

- The date and time you exit Host mode

- The date, time, and user name when a remote user logs on

- The date, time, and user name when a remote user logs off

- The date, time, and user name when a remote user issues the Abort command

- The date, time, and user name when a remote user requests the Chat mode

- The date, time, user name, and names of files downloaded when a remote user downloads files

- The date, time, user name, message number, and information about a new message entered

- The date, time, and first and last name of a user entering three consecutive incorrect passwords while trying to log on

■ The date, time, and user name when a carrier is lost during a call

When a remote user uploads a file, the following information is recorded:

■ The name of the uploaded file

■ The name of the user who uploaded the file

■ Any comments entered by the user who uploaded the file

■ The date and time of the upload

> **WARNING:** If a user chooses the YMODEM or ZMODEM protocol to transfer a file, the file name under which the uploaded file is stored may differ from the upload name stored in the HOST.LOG file. These protocols will rename a file if an existing file has that name.

Figure 9.19 shows some of the types of entries created in a sample HOST.LOG during a period of time on May 31, 1992.

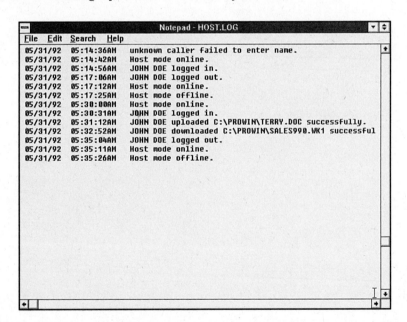

```
                          Notepad - HOST.LOG
 File  Edit  Search  Help
 05/31/92   05:14:36AM    unknown caller failed to enter name.
 05/31/92   05:14:42AM    Host mode online.
 05/31/92   05:14:56AM    JOHN DOE logged in.
 05/31/92   05:17:06AM    JOHN DOE logged out.
 05/31/92   05:17:12AM    Host mode online.
 05/31/92   05:17:25AM    Host mode offline.
 05/31/92   05:30:00AM    Host mode online.
 05/31/92   05:30:31AM    JOHN DOE logged in.
 05/31/92   05:31:12AM    JOHN DOE uploaded C:\PROWIN\TERRY.DOC successfully.
 05/31/92   05:32:52AM    JOHN DOE downloaded C:\PROWIN\SALES990.WK1 successful
 05/31/92   05:35:04AM    JOHN DOE logged out.
 05/31/92   05:35:11AM    Host mode online.
 05/31/92   05:35:26AM    Host mode offline.
```

FIG. 9.19

An example of the Host mode log file, HOST.LOG.

You can view the log file by editing it in the Windows Notepad editor or in some other editor, such as your word processor. If you operate a busy Host mode system, however, this log file can grow quickly. Use an ASCII text editor routinely to delete the old entries from this file.

Administering the Electronic Mail Facility

Unlike the other Host mode-related files, the files that contain messages left on the Host mode electronic mail system cannot be maintained by using an ASCII text editor. Instead, PROCOMM PLUS for Windows includes a utility program called the Mail Manager, which enables you to perform a number of maintenance functions on the Host mode mail files.

The Mail Manager is intended to operate on two files: HOST.MSG (the message file) and HOST.HDR (the header file). Together HOST.MSG and HOST.HDR constitute the Host mode message base. The message file, HOST.MSG, contains the text of the messages. The header file, HOST.HDR, contains for each message the sender's name, the addressee's name, the subject, the date and time, and a notation indicating whether the message is private or deleted.

PROCOMM PLUS for Windows creates these two files on the working directory the first time a Host mode user leaves mail. PROCOMM PLUS for Windows then updates the files as users add and delete electronic mail messages, using Host mode. The Mail Manager enables you, as the system operator, to review, add, and remove permanently messages on this message base.

Before you can start Mail Manager, you must be in the HOSTUTIL program. (Choose hostutil from the list of scripts; see "Preparing Host Mode" in this chapter for more information.) In the Host Mode Utility dialog box, you can choose the option Mail Manager, which displays the dialog box shown in figure 9.20.

The Mail Manager enables you to review the contents of each mail message, to mark messages for deletion, and to pack the message file. The left part of the screen contains information about the message currently being displayed in the box at the bottom of the screen. In figure 9.20, for example, a total of four messages are in the system, and the screen is currently showing message number 4, the note from John Doe to Victor Laslo. The Received option is set to No, which means that the message has not yet been read, and the Marked for Delete option also is set to No.

To view other messages, you can choose Next or Goto. If you choose Next, the next message in the system is displayed on a similar screen. If you want to go to a specific message, choose Goto. You are prompted to enter the number of the message; then it is displayed.

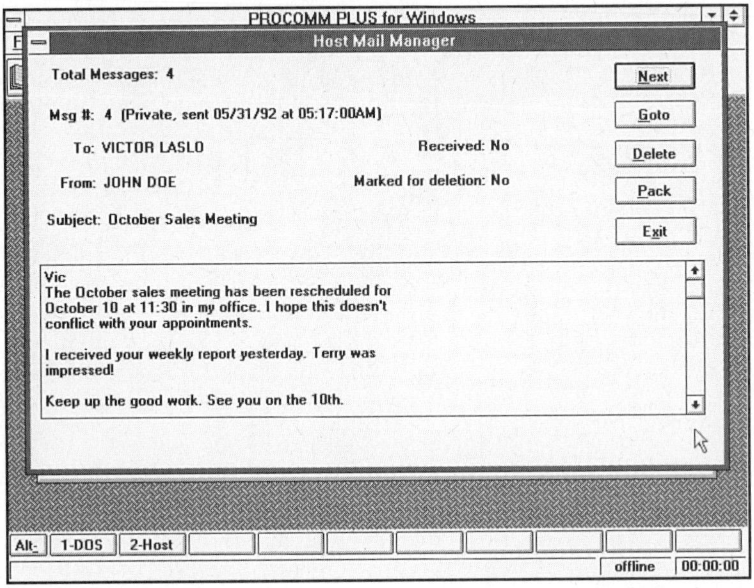

FIG. 9.20

The Host Mail
Manager dialog box.

You use the <u>D</u>elete and <u>P</u>ack options to clean out old messages from the system. When a message is deleted, it is "marked for deletion." It is still in the message system until you choose the <u>P</u>ack option. The <u>P</u>ack option deletes all messages marked for deletion. Thus, you often can read "deleted" messages before they are erased from the system. When packing the message base, the Mail Manager renumbers the messages having numbers that follow a removed message. Suppose, for example, that message number 2 is marked for deletion, but messages 1 and 3 are not. When you execute the <u>P</u>ack option, the original message number 2 is permanently removed, and the original message number 3 becomes message number 2.

The E<u>x</u>it option exits the Mail Manager and returns you to the Host Mode Utility dialog box.

Summary

This chapter described the rudimentary bulletin board system built into PROCOMM PLUS for Windows and known as Host mode. You learned how to prepare Host mode for use by others, including how to specify a welcome message, establish a list of registered users, and designate the system as open or closed to new unregistered users. The chapter also described several ways to invoke Host mode and explored Host mode first from a user's perspective and then from your perspective as the host system operator. You learned how a user logs on to the system and studied the Host mode features available to the user, including the uploading and downloading of files and electronic mail. The chapter also described the functions the system operator can perform in Host mode and discussed a number of administrative functions that the system operator must perform, including managing Host mode files and administrating the Host mode electronic mail facility. Now that you have completed this chapter, you are ready to set up your own bulletin board system, using PROCOMM PLUS for Windows.

Terminal Emulation

Terminals have the sole purpose of connecting to a larger computer for entry and retrieval of data. When PROCOMM PLUS for Windows emulates a particular type of terminal, PROCOMM PLUS for Windows "impersonates" that terminal in order to communicate with a host computer that expects only certain types of terminals to be connected. This chapter describes the 34 terminal emulations available in PROCOMM PLUS for Windows: ADDS 60, 90; ADM 31, 3A, 5; ANSI BBS; ATT 4410, 605; DG D100, D200, D210; ESPRIT 3; HEATH 19; IBM 3101, 3161, 3270, IBM PC; TTY; TVI 910, 912, 920, 922, 925, 950, 955; VIDTEX; VT 52, 100, 102, 220, 320; WYSE 50, 75, 100. Many of these terminals are similar and are basically the same emulation, such as the VT100 and VT102. This chapter also explains how you can customize a terminal emulation by modifying the keyboard mapping, the translation table, or both.

Understanding Terminal Emulation

Terminal emulation performs a function analogous to that of a United Nations translator. If you have ever seen or read about the United Nations General Assembly, you probably are aware that an army of translators are always at work so that representatives of all nationalities can understand what is being said, regardless of the language spoken. Each representative can listen with ear phones to a simultaneous translation of the proceedings into his or her native language.

When PROCOMM PLUS for Windows is emulating a particular type of terminal, PROCOMM PLUS for Windows is performing a simultaneous translation between different "languages," but PROCOMM PLUS for Windows translates in two directions at once. Each time you press a key on your keyboard, PROCOMM PLUS for Windows converts the keystroke into the code that would be generated by a real terminal; this code is the "language" the host minicomputer or mainframe computer expects to receive. This conversion of outgoing keystrokes is referred to as keyboard mapping. At the same time, the host computer is sending to your computer codes intended to control the screen and printer of a real terminal; these codes are in a "language" the terminal understands. PROCOMM PLUS for Windows also translates these incoming codes into codes your PC understands.

Just as the United Nations needs translators for more than one pair of spoken languages, PROCOMM PLUS for Windows also needs to emulate more than one type of terminal. Terminals from different manufacturers often don't speak exactly the same language, and not all host computers are designed to work with the same type of terminal. Unless PROCOMM PLUS for Windows emulates a terminal that speaks and understands the language spoken and understood by the host computer to which your computer is connected, effective communication cannot take place. PROCOMM PLUS for Windows therefore gives you 34 terminal emulations from which to choose, in an effort to provide at least one emulation that each host computer can understand.

Each emulation maps your PC's keyboard in a different way and expects a different set of screen (and sometimes printer) control signals from the host computer. Standard typewriter keys, A through Z and 0 through 9, are understood universally by other computers, regardless of the type of terminal PROCOMM PLUS for Windows is emulating. This understanding is possible because all terminals emulated by PROCOMM PLUS for Windows send the generic ASCII character codes for these keys. The remaining, so-called special keys on the keyboard, however, are the crux of the issue. You can use these keys alone, or with another key (Shift, Ctrl, or Shift-Ctrl) to program (or map) so that you can send a different code to the remote computer for each different type of terminal emulation. Table 10.1 lists the PC keystrokes that are mappable by PROCOMM PLUS for Windows.

Table 10.1. PROCOMM PLUS for Windows Mappable PC Keystrokes

PC, PC AT, and Enhanced type keyboards	Enhanced keyboard only
Tab	
Shift-Tab (Backtab)	
Ins	Gray Insert
Del	Gray Delete
Backspace	
Home	Gray Home
End	Gray End
PgUp	Gray PgUp
PgDn	Gray PgDn
Enter	
Num Lock	
Scroll Lock	
↑	Gray ↑
↓	Gray ↓
←	Gray ←
→	Gray →
Ctrl-Home	
Ctrl-End	
Ctrl-PgUp	
Ctrl-PgDn	
Ctrl-Backspace	

Keypad characters:

*

-

+

.

/

Enter

0 through 9

continues

Table 10.1. Continued

PC, PC AT, and Enhanced type keyboards	Enhanced keyboard only
Function keys:	
F1 through F10	
F11 and F12	
Shift-F1 through Shift-F10	
Shift-F11 and Shift-F12	
Ctrl-F1 through Ctrl-F10	
Ctrl-F11 and Ctrl-F12	
Shift-Ctrl-F1 through F10	
Shift-Ctrl-F11 and F12	

Each key listed in table 10.1 can be programmed, or mapped, to send a special code (refer also to "Changing the Keyboard Mapping," later in this chapter). Through this mapping, PROCOMM PLUS for Windows makes your keyboard act like the keyboard of a real terminal. Each time you press a mapped key, PROCOMM PLUS for Windows sends the code that would be sent by pressing a corresponding key on a real terminal's keyboard. Each of PROCOMM PLUS for Windows' 34 terminal emulations uses a particular keyboard mapping (listed later in this chapter). All the mappings are stored together on the disk in the file DEFAULT.KBD in the same directory as the PROCOMM PLUS for Windows program files.

Always keep in mind that terminal emulation is never 100 percent effective. Just as all PCs are not alike, each type of terminal has its own special features and capabilities. Although the power and flexibility of your PC enables programmers to make it act like many different types of terminals, your PC cannot always perform every special function of every type of terminal.

When you install PROCOMM PLUS for Windows by using the installation utility, the default terminal is set to ANSI BBS. You can change this default setting by using the Current Setup option (refer to Chapter 8), and you can override a default setting by choosing a different terminal emulation in a dialing directory entry (see Chapter 3).

Choosing a Terminal Emulation

The sections that follow describe briefly each terminal emulation available in PROCOMM PLUS for Windows and list the standard and special features. Use these descriptions to decide which emulation is appropriate in each case. Each section also includes a keyboard mapping used by PROCOMM PLUS for Windows for that terminal emulation. Knowing which key on your PC's keyboard is mapped to each key on a real terminal's keyboard is important.

Ultimately, the terminal emulation you select for any communications session is determined by the computer with which you want to communicate. Make sure that the terminal emulation you select is supported by the host computer. Many host computers or the protocol converters that act as translators at the host computer are capable of supporting several different terminal types, so you also may have to tell the host computer which emulation you are using.

T I P

If possible, obtain the following materials:

- A manual or some other form of instructions for the type of terminal you have told PROCOMM PLUS for Windows to emulate. A diagram of the terminal's keyboard especially is helpful.

- Instructions from the operator of the host computer. These instructions should explain how to use the terminal effectively with the host computer.

Compare the terminal's documentation with the corresponding keyboard mapping table listed in this chapter to determine which keys on your keyboard correspond to the keys on the real terminal's keyboard. The keyboard mappings, including the hexadecimal codes transmitted to the host, also are listed in the PROCOMM PLUS for Windows Help file. To display a table for a keyboard, choose the Keyboard option from the Help pull-down menu. The Help menu displaying the Keyboard options is shown in figure 10.1. Choose either the 101 keyboard or 84 keyboard option. A list of available terminal emulations appears, as shown in figure 10.2 (for the 101 keyboard). Select the terminal emulation type you want to see, and a listing of the keyboard mapping appears. Figure 10.3 shows this mapping for a VT-52 terminal emulation. If you want a printed copy of the keymapping, choose the Print option from the File menu, and a copy of the displayed mapping will be output to your printer.

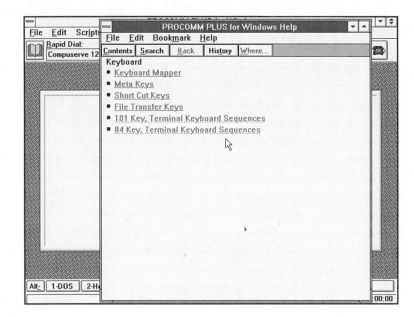

FIG. 10.1

The Keyboard options from the Help menu.

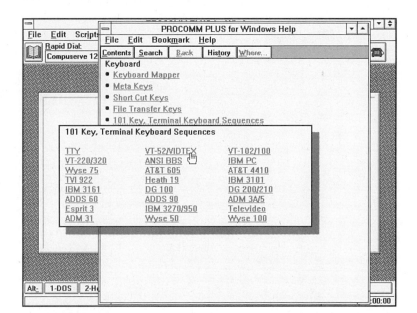

FIG. 10.2

101 Key Keyboard Emulations options.

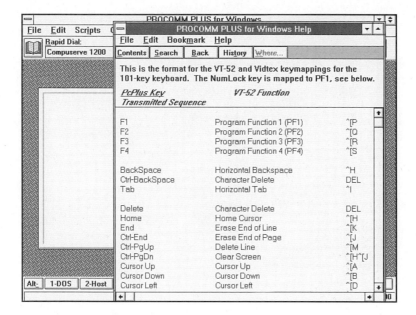

FIG. 10.3

Listing of VT-52
101 key keyboard
mappings from the
Help menu.

Because you can easily display the keyboard mappings, they are not all listed here. Several common keyboard mappings are described in the following sections, however, so that you can examine and compare mappings for these common emulations.

Keyboard Mapping for ANSI BBS

When you use PROCOMM PLUS for Windows primarily to access electronic bulletin boards, you should set the default terminal emulation to ANSI BBS. ANSI stands for American National Standards Institute, but in this context, ANSI refers to the terminal emulation standard recommended by the American National Standards Institute. BBS stands for Bulletin Board System. The ANSI standard's widespread use by bulletin boards stems from its capability to create colorful screens and to provide full-screen control over the cursor.

ANSI's special display attributes are accomplished through the host computer's use of a set of codes known collectively as ANSI escape sequences. The codes are called *escape sequences* because each begins with the ASCII Esc character (ASCII decimal 27). The ANSI escape sequence to set the screen to white characters (foreground) on a blue background, for example, follows:

    ESC[37;44m

DOS (IBM PC DOS or Microsoft MS-DOS) is distributed with a driver file named ANSI.SYS. This file normally defines the ANSI escape sequences that can be recognized and acted on by your computer. (Refer to your DOS manual for a complete explanation of ANSI.SYS and ANSI escape sequences.) PROCOMM PLUS for Windows, however, doesn't use the ANSI driver provided by DOS; PROCOMM PLUS for Windows uses its own emulation of ANSI.SYS, which is essentially the same as the DOS ANSI 3.x device driver. PROCOMM PLUS for Windows responds to ANSI escape sequences sent by a host computer in the same manner as DOS' ANSI.SYS responds, with a few minor exceptions.

NOTE The code ^[translates into the ASCII character Esc; therefore, when you are using the ANSI BBS terminal emulation and press F1, PROCOMM PLUS for Windows sends to the remote computer the Esc character followed by the letters OP.

The keyboard mapping for ANSI BBS (101 keyboard) is listed in table 10.2. Note that the Num Lock key is not mapped.

Table 10.2. ANSI BBS 101 Keyboard Mapping

PcPlus key	ANSI function	Transmitted sequence
F1	Program Function 1 (PF1)	^[OP
F2	Program Function 2 (PF2)	^[OQ
F3	Program Function 3 (PF3)	^[OR
F4	Program Function 4 (PF4)	^[OS
Backspace	Backspace	^H
Shift Backspace	Character Delete	DEL [7F]
Ctrl-Backspace	Ctrl-Backspace	^X
Tab	Tab	^I
Enter	Return	^M
Keypad /	Keypad /	/
Keypad *	Keypad *	*
Keypad -	Keypad -	-

PcPlus key	ANSI function	Transmitted sequence
Keypad +	Keypad +	+
Shift Keypad +	Keypad MINUS	-
Keypad End	Erase End of Line	^[[K
Keypad Cursor Down	Cursor Down	^[[B
Keypad PgDn	Clear Screen	^[[H^[[2J
Keypad Cursor Left	Cursor Left	^[[D
Keypad Cursor Right	Cursor Right	^[[C
Keypad Home	Home Cursor	^[[H
Keypad Cursor Up	Cursor Up	^[[A
Keypad PgUp	Delete Line	^[[M
Keypad Delete	Character Delete	DEL [7F]
Keypad Enter	Enter	^M
Shift Home	7	7
Shift Cursor Up	8	8
Shift PgUp	9	9
Shift Cursor Left	4	4
Shift Keypad 5	5	5
Shift Cursor Right	6	6
Shift End	1	1
Shift Cursor Down	2	2
Shift PgDn	3	3
Shift Delete	.	.
Shift Insert	0	0
Shift Ctrl-Home	Insert Line	^[[L
Ctrl-Keypad -	Keypad Application MINUS	^[Om

continues

Table 10.2. Continued

PcPlus key	ANSI function	Transmitted sequence
Ctrl-Keypad +	Keypad Application COMMA	^[O1
Ctrl-Insert	Keypad Application 0	^[Op
Ctrl-End	Keypad Application 1	^[Oq
Ctrl-Cursor Down	Keypad Application 2	^[Or
Ctrl-PgDn	Keypad Application 3	^[Os
Ctrl-Cursor Left	Keypad Application 4	^[Ot
Ctrl-Keypad 5	Keypad Application 5	^[Ou
Ctrl-Cursor Right	Keypad Application 6	^[Ov
Ctrl-Home	Keypad Application 7	^[Ow
Ctrl-Cursor Up	Keypad Application 8	^[Ox
Ctrl-PgUp	Keypad Application 9	^[Oy
Ctrl-Delete	Keypad Application PERIOD	^[On
Ctrl-Enter	Keypad Application Enter	^[OM
Gray Delete	Delete Character	DEL [7F]
Gray Home	Home Cursor	^[[H
Gray End	Erase End of Line	^[[K
Ctrl-Gray Home	Insert Line	^[[L
Ctrl-Gray PgUp	Delete Line	^[[M
Ctrl-Gray PgDn	Clear Screen	^[[H^[[2J
Gray Cursor Up	Cursor Up	^[[A
Gray Cursor Down	Cursor Down	^[[B
Gray Cursor Left	Cursor Left	^[[D
Gray Cursor Right	Cursor Right	^[[C

DEC VT52, VT100, VT102/Wyse 75, VT220/320/Televideo 922, and VIDTEX

Digital Equipment Corporation (DEC) has for many years been a primary manufacturer of minicomputers. DEC computers are used widely in business, industry, government, and education; DEC computers support several different DEC terminals. PROCOMM PLUS for Windows can emulate five of the most popular DEC terminals: VT52, VT100, VT102, VT220, and VT320. The Televideo 922 is similar to the VT220 and VT320, the WYSE 75 is similar to the VT102, and the VIDEX is similar to the VT52.

The PROCOMM PLUS for Windows VT52 emulation supports the following VT52 features:

- Full-duplex mode

- Half-duplex mode

- Keypad Application mode

- Full-screen cursor control

- Erase functions

- Printer control functions, including printing to printer only or to printer and screen

- Full-display attributes

The VT52 emulation enables you to use the numbers on your numeric keypad and gives you access to the VT52 Keypad Application mode. The emulation accomplishes this capability by mapping the Ctrl-keyboard combinations to the VT52 numeric Keypad Application mode.

You can use the PROCOMM PLUS for Windows VT102 emulation when the host computer expects a DEC VT100 terminal or a VT102 terminal. These two terminals are similar, but VT102 has a few more features. Both terminals are more powerful than the VT52 terminal. The following functions are supported by the PROCOMM PLUS for Windows VT100 and VT102 emulations, as well as WYSE 75 and VIDTEX:

- Full-duplex mode

- Half-duplex mode

- Set/Reset modes

- Scroll region

- Special graphics character set

- United States and United Kingdom character sets

- Keypad Application mode

- Full-screen cursor control

- Erase functions

- Insert/delete lines

- Programmable tabs

- True double-high and/or double-wide character font (VT100/102/ 220/320)

- Host-programmable function keys (VT 220/320, TVI 922)

- Printer control functions, including printing to printer only or to printer and screen

- Full-display attributes

The VT 100/102, WYSE 75, and VIDTEX emulations handle the ENQ option in a special way (see Chapter 8 for more information). Set the Enquiry (ENQ) option on the Current Setup, Terminal Settings, Enquiry option to On. The Enquiry (ENQ) option on the Terminal Options screen specifies the way that PROCOMM PLUS for Windows responds to the ENQ (ASCII decimal 5) character (generated by pressing Ctrl-E at either end of the connection). By default, the Enquiry option is set to CIS-B, causing PROCOMM PLUS for Windows to begin a CIS-B+ transfer when the enquiry is received. If you set this option to On, PROCOMM PLUS for Windows transmits the Enquiry string configured in the Terminal Settings, Enquiry option when the program receives the ENQ character. This response often is called an answerback message.

PROCOMM PLUS for Windows' VT102 keyboard mapping of the Keypad Application mode is not the same as the mapping for VT52. The VT102 emulation mapping is listed in table 10.3.

Table 10.3. 101-Keyboard Mapping for VT102/100 Emulation

PcPlus key	VT102/100 function	Transmitted sequence
F1	Program Function 1 (PFl)	^[OP
F2	Program Function 2 (PF2)	^[OQ
F3	Program Function 3 (PF3)	^[OR
F4	Program Function 4 (PF4)	^[OS

PcPlus key	VT102/100 function	Transmitted sequence
Backspace	Backspace	^H
Shift Backspace	Character Delete	DEL [7F]
Ctrl-Backspace	Ctrl-Backspace	^X
Tab	Tab	^I
Enter	Return	^M
Num Lock	Program Function 1 (PFI)	^[OP
Keypad /	Program Function 2 (PF2)	^[OQ
Keypad *	Program Function 3 (PF3)	^[OR
Keypad -	Program Function 4 (PF4)	^[OS
Keypad +	Keypad COMMA	,
Shift Keypad +	Keypad MINUS	-
Keypad End	1	1
Keypad Cursor Down	2	2
Keypad PgDn	3	3
Keypad Cursor Left	4	4
Keypad 5	5	5
Keypad Cursor Right	6	6
Keypad Home	7	7
Keypad Cursor Up	8	8
Keypad PgUp	9	9
Keypad Delete	.	.
Keypad Enter	Enter	^M
Shift Home	Home Cursor	^[[H
Shift Cursor Up	Cursor Up	^[[A
Shift PgUp	Delete Line	^[[M

continues

Table 10.3. Continued

PcPlus key	VT102/100 function	Transmitted sequence
Shift Cursor Left	Cursor Left	^[[D
Shift Cursor Right	Cursor Right	^[[C
Shift End	Erase End of Line	^[[K
Shift Cursor Down	Cursor Down	^[[B
Shift PgDn	Clear Screen	^[[H^[[2J
Shift Delete	Character Delete	DEL [7F]
Shift Ctrl-Home	Insert Line	^[[L
Ctrl-Keypad -	Keypad Application MINUS	^[Om
Ctrl-Keypad +	Keypad Application COMMA	^[Ol
Ctrl-Insert	Keypad Application 0	^[Op
Ctrl-End	Keypad Application 1	^[Oq
Ctrl-Cursor Down	Keypad Application 2	^[Or
Ctrl-PgDn	Keypad Application 3	^[Os
Ctrl-Cursor Left	Keypad Application 4	^[Ot
Ctrl-5	Keypad Application 5	^[Ou
Ctrl-Cursor Right	Keypad Application 6	^[Ov
Ctrl-Home	Keypad Application 7	^[Ow
Ctrl-Cursor Up	Keypad Application 8	^[Ox
Ctrl-PgUp	Keypad Application 9	^[Oy
Ctrl-Delete	Keypad Application PERIOD	^[On
Ctrl-Enter	Keypad Application Enter	^[OM
Shift Ctrl-Up	Application Cursor Up	^[OA
Shift Ctrl-Down	Application Cursor Down	^[OB
Shift Ctrl-Left	Application Cursor Left	^[OD

PcPlus key	VT102/100 function	Transmitted sequence
Shift Ctrl-Right	Application Cursor Right	^[OC
Gray Delete	Delete Character	DEL [7F]
Gray Home	Home Cursor	^[[H
Gray End	Erase End of Line	^[[K
Ctrl-Gray Home	Insert Line	^[[L
Ctrl-Gray PgUp	Delete Line	^[[M
Ctrl-Gray PgDn	Clear Screen	^[[H^[[2J
Gray Cursor Up	Cursor Up	^[[A
Gray Cursor Down	Cursor Down	^[[B
Gray Cursor Left	Cursor Left	^[[D
Gray Cursor Right	Cursor Right	^[[C
Ctrl-Gray Up	Application Cursor Up	^[OA
Ctrl-Gray Down	Application Cursor Down	^[OB
Ctrl-Gray Left	Application Cursor Left	^[OD
Ctrl-Gray Right	Application Cursor Right	^[OC

You can use the PROCOMM PLUS for Windows VT220/320 emulation when the host computer expects a DEC VT220 or VT320 terminal. These terminals are similar, but VT320 has a few more features. All of these terminals are more powerful than the VT52 and VT102 terminals. The keyboard mapping supported by the PROCOMM PLUS for Windows VT220/320 emulation can be displayed by choosing the Keyboard option from the Help menu, as described in the earlier section, "Choosing a Terminal Emulation."

IBM 3101 and 3161

A popular asynchronous IBM terminal is the IBM 3101 series. These terminals normally are used with IBM's Time Sharing Option (TSO).

PROCOMM PLUS for Windows's emulation of the IBM 3101 terminals supports the most commonly used features of Model 1x and Model 2x IBM 3101 series terminals, including the following features:

- Full-duplex mode
- Half-duplex mode
- Full IBM character set
- Scroll on/off
- Program function keys
- Erase functions
- Cursor control

Block mode transfer of data to and from the host computer, however, is not supported by the PROCOMM PLUS for Windows 3101 emulation. Data is sent and received one character at a time.

Keyboard mapping for the IBM 3101 and 3161 can be displayed by choosing the Keyboard option from the Help menu, as described in the earlier section, "Choosing a Terminal Emulation."

IBM 3270/950

The IBM 3270/950 terminal emulation actually doesn't emulate one terminal, but two. The keyboard mapping emulates an IBM 3270, and the screen-handling features emulate a TeleVideo 950 terminal. To understand the logic behind this "hybrid" emulation, you need a little background information.

Real IBM 3270 terminals connect by synchronous modem to IBM mainframe computers and afford many advanced features. Complete emulation of a 3270 terminal using a PC, however, requires you to purchase a synchronous modem and a "terminal on a card" integrated circuit board for installation in your PC. Emulation of the 3270 terminal also may require you to use a special, more costly telephone line, known as a *leased line*.

Sometimes the benefits of true 3270 emulation justify the cost. If you plan to use your PC exclusively or primarily as a terminal to an IBM mainframe, consider going all the way. Data transfer is several times faster, and you have access to all the 3270 features. If you only occasionally need to connect to a host computer that supports a 3270 terminal and you more often connect to systems that support asynchronous communications, PROCOMM PLUS for Windows' emulation may suit your needs well.

In order to connect your PC to an IBM mainframe through an asynchronous modem, you must go through a protocol converter. The protocol converter changes your computer's asynchronous signal into the synchronous signal required by the mainframe computer.

A protocol converter also performs terminal emulation. The protocol converter enables many different types of terminals to dial in, and then the protocol converter performs a two-way translation between the mainframe and each terminal. An IBM 7171 protocol converter, for example, can accept connections from DEC VT102 terminals, TeleVideo 950 terminals, and IBM 3101 terminals (among many others) and can make all these terminals look to the mainframe computer like IBM 3270 terminals. At the same time, the protocol converter translates signals sent by the mainframe into signals the different terminals can interpret and act on.

The PROCOMM PLUS for Windows IBM 3270/950 emulation is intended for use through a protocol converter. The keyboard mapping enables you to send through an IBM 7171 protocol converter the codes necessary to emulate all the keys on a 3270 keyboard.

IBM 3270 keyboards have 24 function keys. Figure 10.4 shows how the PROCOMM PLUS for Windows 3270/950 emulation maps the function keys on your computer's keyboard to these 24 function keys. The label on the top of each key in the figure represents the PC keystroke. The label on the front of each key in the figure represents the equivalent function key on the 3270 terminal's keyboard. When two labels are on the top of a key, the second is optional and is available only on an Enhanced keyboard.

FIG. 10.4

Mapping of PC function keys to IBM 3270 function keys.

The 3270 functions are mapped to your computer's keys, as listed in table 10.4.

Table 10.4. 101 Keymapping for IBM 3270/950 Emulation

PcPlus key	IBM 3270/950 function	Transmitted sequence
F1	Program Function 1 (PF1)	^A@^M
F2	Program Function 2 (PF2)	^AA^M
F3	Program Function 3 (PF3)	^AB^M
F4	Program Function 4 (PF4)	^AC^M
F5	Program Function 5 (PF5)	^AD^M
F6	Program Function 6 (PF6)	^AE^M
F7 or Gray PgUp	Program Function 7 (PF7)	^AF^M
F8 or Gray PgDn	Program Function 8 (PF8)	^AG^M
F9	Program Function 9 (PF9)	^AH^M
F10	Program Function 10 (PF10)	^AI^M
F11	Program Function 11 (PF11)	^AJ^M
F12	Program Function 12 (PF12)	^[Q
Shift F1	Program Function 13 (PF13)	^A'^M
Shift F2	Program Function 14 (PF14)	^Aa^M
Shift F3	Program Function 15 (PF15)	^Ab^M
Shift F4	Program Function 16 (PF16)	^Ac^M
Shift F5	Program Function 17 (PF17)	^Ad^M
Shift F6	Program Function 18 (PF18)	^Ae^M

PcPlus key	IBM 3270/950 function	Transmitted sequence
Shift F7	Program Function 19 (PF19)	^Af^M
Shift F8	Program Function 20 (PF20)	^Ag^M
Shift F9	Program Function 21 (PF21)	^Ah^M
Shift F10	Program Function 22 (PF22)	^Ai^M
Shift F11	Program Function 23 (PF23)	^Aj^M
Shift F12	Program Function 24 (PF24)	^[q
Ctrl-F5	Program Application 1 (PA1)	^A'^M
Ctrl-F6	Program Application 2 (PA2)	^A.^M
Ctrl-F7	Program Application 3 (PA3)	^A/^M
Ctrl-F8	Erase Input	^[^[R
Ctrl-F9	Column Tab	^I
Ctrl-F10	Column Back Tab	^[I
Backspace	Backspace	^H
Tab	Field Tab	^[T
Shift Tab	Shift Tab	^[t
Ctrl-Enter or Ctrl-J	Newline	^J
Keypad *	Keypad	^Ae^M [01 8A 0D]
Home	Home	^^ [1E]
Ctrl-Home	Clear	^Z or Keypad + or Keypad Enter
Cursor Up	Cursor Up	^K
Cursor Left	Cursor Left	^H
Cursor Right	Cursor Right	^L
End or Ctrl-End	Erase End of Field	^[R

continues

Table 10.4. Continued

PcPlus key	IBM 3270/950 function	Transmitted sequence
Cursor Down	Cursor Down	^V
Insert or Gray Insert	Insert	^[E
Delete or Ctrl-Backspace or Gray Del	Delete Character	DEL [7F]
Ctrl-PgUp	Indent	,,^[Y
Ctrl-PgDn	Unindent	^[y
Ctrl-X	Type Ahead Purge	^X
Ctrl-S	Pacing Start	^S
Ctrl-Q	Pacing Stop	^Q
Ctrl-T	Keyboard Unlock	^T
Ctrl-R	Char-error Reset	^R
Ctrl-G	Master Reset	^G
Pause	Redisplay	^[*

For addressing and controlling your PC's screen, this emulation uses the TeleVideo 950 protocol. You therefore must inform the protocol converter that you are using a TeleVideo 950 terminal. PROCOMM PLUS for Windows then takes advantage of the protocol converter's capability to translate screen-handling commands from the mainframe into the proper codes for a TeleVideo 950 terminal. PROCOMM PLUS for Windows, in turn, performs a second translation and sends the proper screen- and printer-control commands to your PC's hardware.

IBM PC

The IBM PC emulation enables you to use a PC host doorway to simulate the actual key codes generated by a PC keyboard. Door programs are used on a number of BBSs to enable the remote user to interact with the host computer by using a special programmed interface rather than the normal PROCOMM PLUS for Windows remote user interface. As expected, the function codes match the PC keyboard, including function keys F1 through F12, Shift-F1 to Shift-F12, and Ctrl-F1 to Ctrl-F12.

Lear Siegler ADM 3A/5 and 31

Another popular series of terminals is manufactured by Lear Siegler. The PROCOMM PLUS for Windows ADM 3A/5 and 31 emulations are used for the Lear Siegler ADM-3A/5 and 31 series terminals. The ADM 3A/5 and 31 emulations support the following functions:

- Full-duplex mode
- Half-duplex mode
- Full-character set
- Erase functions
- Full-screen cursor control

Key mappings for the ADM 3A/5 and 31 emulations can be displayed by choosing the Keyboard option from the Help menu, as described in the earlier section, "Choosing a Terminal Emulation."

TTY

A TTY, or Teletype, terminal is a video display terminal version of the original one-line-at-a-time typewriter-style terminal. If you have never used one of these old Teletype-style terminals, you may have seen one. They look much like a typewriter, having a keyboard on the front and a paper feed and printer on the back. As you type a command to the host computer, the command is printed on the paper. Any response from the host also is printed on the paper. When a line scrolls up past the printing element, the line cannot be recovered.

The familiar DOS command line uses a TTY approach. Even though your computer's screen can display at least 25 lines of text, the DOS command line uses only one line at a time. When you press Enter, the cursor moves to the next command line, and you cannot go back up to correct a mistake.

When you select PROCOMM PLUS for Windows' TTY terminal emulation, you get basic one-line-at-a-time control of your screen, with no special screen attributes, such as line drawing or color. The only special keys mapped specifically by PROCOMM PLUS for Windows are Tab, Backspace, and Enter. The keys available on your numeric keypad with Num Lock activated follow:

    0 through 9 / * - + . Enter

Use TTY emulation only if absolutely required by the host you are calling.

Changing the Keyboard Mapping

Sometimes a terminal emulation's keyboard mapping doesn't include a function you need. This omission may occur because the host computer's support of a particular type of terminal is slightly different from what PROCOMM PLUS for Windows expects, because you are dialing in through a protocol converter that is performing a second-level terminal emulation, or simply because you want to add a function that is not part of the terminal emulation. Whatever the reason, PROCOMM PLUS for Windows enables you to customize any terminal emulation keyboard mapping. As mentioned previously, all the terminal emulation mappings are stored on the disk in the file DEFAULT.KBD, in the same directory as the PROCOMM PLUS for Windows program files.

CAUTION: Before you make any changes to DEFAULT.KBD, make a disk copy of the file. Then you can easily return the file to its default settings. Of course, you should never change the DEFAULT.KBD file or any other file on the distributed PROCOMM PLUS for Windows disks. Always work from an installed copy of the original disks.

NOTE   PROCOMM PLUS for Windows will re-create its DEFAULT.KBD file if the original is deleted.

To alter a keyboard mapping, select the Setup Action icon from the Terminal Display screen, select Keyboard (usually the file DEFAULT.KBD) from the Current Setup menu, and then select Advanced! from the Current Setup menu bar. Alternatively, press Alt-F8 from the Terminal Display screen. PROCOMM PLUS for Windows displays a Keyboard Mapper dialog box for the currently selected terminal. The Keyboard Mapper dialog box in figure 10.5, for example, shows the mapping for the VT102 terminal emulation.

Editing the Transmit Codes

A *transmit code* is one or more ASCII characters sent from your computer to the connected computer.

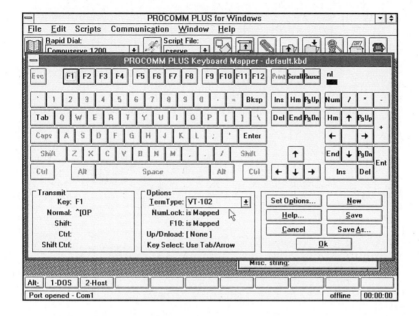

FIG. 10.5

The Keyboard Mapper
dialog box showing
the mapping for the
VT102 terminal
emulation.

The dialog box in figure 10.5 contains a picture of the IBM enhanced
keyboard, with some keys in bold and some keys in light gray. The gray
keys cannot be programmed, and the bold keys can be programmed. At
the bottom left of the screen is the Transmit box. This box shows the
settings for the currently selected key. Figure 10.5, for example, indicates
that the currently selected key is F1. For the Normal setting (the keystroke that is transmitted when F1 is pressed), the code ^[OP is listed.
The code ^[translates into the ASCII character Esc; therefore, when you
are using the VT102 terminal emulation and press F1, PROCOMM PLUS
for Windows sends to the remote computer the Esc character followed
by the letters OP. In this box, no transmit codes are listed for the keystrokes Shift-F1, Ctrl-F1, or Shift-Ctrl-F1 because they currently aren't
mapped in the VT102 terminal emulation.

To move to and select another key in the dialog box diagram, press Tab
or the right-arrow key (or click the key you want to edit). The current
information on that key appears in the Transmit box.

To edit the transmit information, double-click the key to edit, or highlight the key and then press the space bar. A dialog box named Edit
Mapped Key appears (see fig. 10.6). This dialog box contains four entry
fields: Normal, Shift, Ctrl, and Shift Ctrl. To edit or enter information in a
field, select the field, and then enter the code you want transmitted
when that key is pressed. Refer to Chapter 7, "Automating PROCOMM

PLUS for Windows with Meta Keys and Script Files," for information on keystroke codes. The code ^[means Esc, for example, and ^M means Enter.

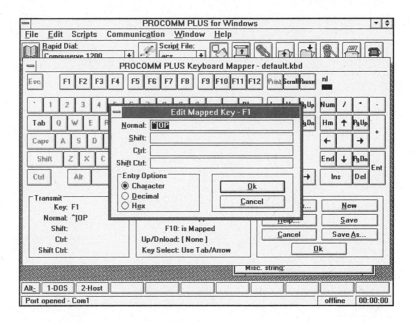

FIG. 10.6

The Edit Mapped Key dialog box.

If you want to see the transmit codes in decimal or hexadecimal format, choose the Decimal or Hex button. Viewing and editing in Decimal or Hex mode enables you to enter the transmit codes as decimal or hexadecimal numbers. You can enter the letter A, for example, as code 065. See Appendix C for a list of ASCII characters and their decimal and hexadecimal codes. Choosing Character returns the display to normal Character mode. Choose OK to exit the Edit Mapped Key dialog box and return to the Keyboard Mapper dialog box.

Selecting a Different Emulation

The Options box to the right of the Transmit box in the Keyboard Mapper dialog box contains information about the current terminal emulation. The TermType field contains the name of the terminal emulation currently being edited. To choose another emulation, extend the list box and then select a name.

In the Keyboard Mapper dialog box, you can view the keyboard mappings for all 34 available terminal emulations by selecting the various emulations from the TermType list box. The keyboard mappings are arranged in the following order:

ADDS 60
ADDS 90
ADM 31
ADM 3A
ADM 5
ANSI BBS
ATT 4410
ATT 605
DG D100
DG D200
DG D210
ESPRIT 3
HEATH 19
IBM 3101
IBM 3161
IBM 3270
IBM PC
TTY
TVI 910
TVI 912
TVI 920
TVI 922
TVI 925
TVI 950
TVI 955
VIDTEX
VT 52
VT 100
VT 102
VT 220
VT 320
WYSE 50
WYSE 75
WYSE 100

In figure 10.5, the settings Numlock:is Mapped and F10:is Mapped mean that the Num Lock key and the F10 key are currently mapped with a transmit code. The Up/Dnload [None] setting indicates that no upload and download keystrokes are defined. The Key Select:Use Tab/Arrow setting indicates that you can use the Tab or arrow keys to select which key to edit. An alternate setting is by keypress. For information on how to modify all these settings by using the Set Options button, see the next section, "Setting Special Options." For information on how to use the other buttons in the bottom right corner, see the section "Selecting Other Command Buttons."

Setting Special Options

You use the Set Options button in the Keyboard Mapper dialog box to select several special options related to a terminal emulation that cannot be set on the main Keyboard Mapper screen. Choose this button to display the Set Options dialog box, as shown in figure 10.7.

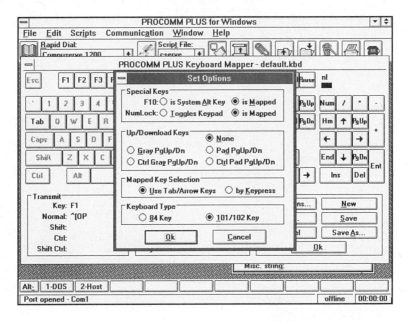

The Special Keys options enable you to choose the status of the F10 and Num Lock keys. If the Is Mapped option is selected (the button is filled), the specified key is defined in the emulation. To reselect F10 for use as the system Alt key, select the Is System Alt Key button. To reselect Num Lock so that it toggles the keypad, select the Toggles Keypad button.

In the DOS version of PROCOMM PLUS, the PgUp and PgDn keys typically are used to initiate an upload or download. Using the Up/Download Keys section of the Set Options dialog box, you can specify what keys, if any, are to be used to initiate an upload or a download. The Gray PgUp/PgDn key refers to the Page Up and Page Down keys on the enhanced keyboard, not on the cursor pad. The Pad PgUp/PgDn keys are the PgUp and PgDn keys on the numeric (cursor) keypad.

In the Keyboard Mapper dialog box, the default way to select what key to edit (using the keyboard) is to press Tab or the arrow keys to highlight the key. Using the Mapped Key Selection area of the Set Options dialog box, you can change the selection method so that pressing a key on the keyboard selects that key in the Keyboard Mapper dialog box. To make this change, select the By Keypress option.

The default keyboard shown in the Keyboard Mapper dialog box is the IBM Enhanced (101/102-key) keyboard. If you are using the older PC keyboard, select the 84 Key option to cause that keyboard to be shown in the dialog box instead.

After you have made your selections in the Set Options dialog box, choose OK to retain your choices and return to the Keyboard Mapper dialog box, or choose Cancel to exit to the Keyboard Mapper dialog box and discard changes you have made in this dialog box.

Selecting Other Command Buttons

Note that in addition to the Set Options button, the Keyboard Mapper dialog box contains six other buttons in its lower right corner: Help, Cancel, New, Save, Save As, and OK.

Choose the Help button to display the Help window. Accessing the help system was described fully in Chapter 2, "Getting Around in PROCOMM PLUS for Windows."

The Cancel button enables you to exit the screen and discard any changes you have made to this terminal emulation file.

With the New button, you can create a new keyboard file. After choosing this button, you are prompted to enter the name for the new file. Usually, instead of creating a new file (which contains all blank transmit codes), you should start by selecting a file (like DEFAULT.KBD) that contains codes similar to the ones you want to set. Then you can choose the Save As button to save the file under a new name, edit the transmit codes in the new file, and use the Save button to save the changes you have made to the file under its new name.

Suppose that you log on to a system for which you want to use the VT102 emulation, but you want to include some special keyboard mapping codes. On other occasions, you log on to other systems with which you use the VT102 emulation, but you require different keyboard mapping codes for these systems. The answer to this situation is to create a special keyboard mapping for each system to which you want to log on.

The OK button in the Keyboard Mapper dialog box enables you to exit back to the Current Setup menu and retain the changes you have made to the mappings. Unless you first choose the Save option in the Keyboard Mapper dialog box, however, these changes are not permanent.

Creating Keystroke Macros

Most keyboard mappings do not use all the programmable keys. You can assign keyboard mapping codes to any keystrokes that are not used by a terminal emulation. Indeed, you can create a set of mappings for use exclusively with a terminal emulation. Use the Keyboard Mapper dialog box to display the standard keyboard mapping for the terminal emulation; then assign new keyboard mapping codes to keystrokes that are not already used. When you later select this emulation, PROCOMM PLUS for Windows also loads the new mappings.

You may find, for example, that when you are using PROCOMM PLUS for Windows to communicate with electronic bulletin board systems, you routinely type the word *open*. This word, followed by a number, is usually the command required to use the DOORS feature, which is available on many popular BBSs. You normally have the ANSI terminal emulation active when you connect to a BBS, and you notice that the Ctrl-F1 keystroke is not used by the emulation's standard keyboard mapping. You decide to add to the keyboard mapping a new mapping code that types the word *open*.

To add this macro, display the Keyboard Mapper dialog box and select the ANSI BBS keyboard mapping from the TermType list box. Then press Ctrl-F1 and the space bar to display the Edit Mapped Key dialog box. Edit the F1 key, and enter the word *open* in the Ctrl-F1 field of the Edit Mapped Key dialog box. Exit the box by choosing OK. Save the changed keyboard file by pressing Alt-S. The next time you connect to a bulletin board while using the ANSI terminal emulation, you can just press Ctrl-F1 to cause PROCOMM PLUS for Windows to type your open command.

Changing the Translation Table

In addition to controlling outgoing characters with keyboard mapping, you can use PROCOMM PLUS for Windows to control the display of incoming characters on your screen. Normally, the current terminal emulation interprets data coming in from a host computer and displays the appropriate characters. Occasionally, however, you may want to display characters that are different from the characters being transmitted. When you want PROCOMM PLUS for Windows to perform such a translation, select the Translate option from the Current Setup menu and then choose Advanced! from the menu bar. The Translate Table dialog box for the DEFAULT.XLT file is shown in figure 10.8.

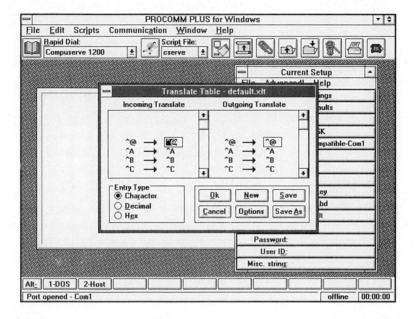

FIG. 10.8

The Translate Table
dialog box.

The translation table consists of a total of 256 entries in two lists. The left list is labeled Incoming Translate, and the right list is labeled Outgoing Translate. Within each list is an ASCII character (or representation), an arrow, and another ASCII character. The first set of characters is ^@, for example, which is the ASCII character null, or Ctrl-@. This entry means that when a ^@ comes through the program the character is translated as a ^@ (no change). Similarly, in the right side list, a ^@ entered at the keyboard is transmitted as a ^@.

To change the translation values in the translation table, press Tab to highlight the code to change and then enter the new code. Or click the code to change, and then enter the new code.

To scroll through the codes in the list box, make sure that your highlighter is in the list you want and then press the up- and down-arrow keys. To use the mouse, click the up or down arrow at the right of the list box to move the list up and down.

If you want to display the codes in decimal or hexadecimal format, choose Decimal or Hex in the Entry Type area of the dialog box. To return to the character display, choose Character. Viewing and editing in Decimal or Hex mode enables you to enter the transmit codes as decimal or hexadecimal numbers. You can enter the letter A, for example, as code 065. See Appendix C in this book for a list of ASCII characters and their decimal and hexadecimal codes.

The Options button in the bottom right corner of the Translate Table dialog box enables you to choose from three scrolling options for the Incoming and Outgoing lists. When you choose Options, the Scrolling Options dialog box appears (see fig. 10.9). When the Independent option is selected, the two lists are scrolled independently of one another. When the Move Together option is selected, you can move the Incoming Translate list up or down and have the Outgoing Translate list move also. With the Mirror Image option selected, the two lists move together as in the Move Together option, plus if you change a code in one list, the code for the same character is changed in the other list. Choose OK from the Scrolling Options dialog box to return to the Translate Table dialog box.

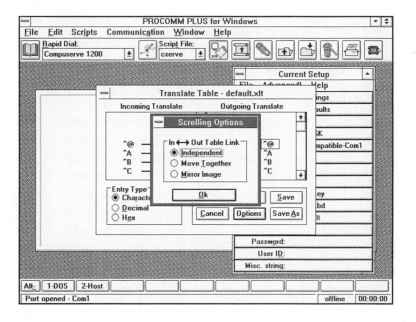

FIG. 10.9

The Scrolling Options dialog box.

The translation table normally is set as the DEFAULT.XLT table, which translates each character to the identical character. To create another translation, you must alter the DEFAULT.XLT file or create a new file and then place that file in the default settings by choosing the file in the Keyboard setting in the Current Setup window, or activate that file in a dialing directory entry.

To save the information in the translation table to a new file, choose Save As. The program prompts you for a new file name. To save the changes to the current file (listed in the name line at the top of the Translate Table dialog box), just choose Save. The New option enables you to create a new file with initial default settings that translate each character to itself.

Choose OK to exit the Translate Table dialog box and retain the current settings. (If you have not saved these settings to a file, however, they are lost when you end the program.) Choose the Cancel option to exit the Translate Table dialog box and discard any changes you have made to the table.

Summary

This chapter described the 34 terminal emulations available in PROCOMM PLUS for Windows and listed the keyboard mappings associated with each emulation. This chapter also described how you can customize a terminal emulation by modifying the keyboard mapping and the translation table.

Turn now to Chapter 11 to read an overview of the Windows ASPECT script language. Chapter 11 discusses the commands available and offers some suggestions on how to develop scripts with Windows ASPECT.

An Overview of the Windows ASPECT Script Language

This chapter provides an overview of the programmable capabilities available through the PROCOMM PLUS for Windows script language, Windows ASPECT. In Chapter 7, you learned how to record scripts that automate the logon sequence to connect to another computer. This chapter introduces you to all the major features of the Windows ASPECT programming language. You learn some basic techniques of using the Windows ASPECT language in planning and programming a script file. For more information on the Windows ASPECT language, refer to the *PROCOMM PLUS for Windows Windows ASPECT Script Language Reference Manual.*

The Windows ASPECT script language is a high-level communication programming language suitable for developing full-featured communications applications. Although extensive coverage of this language is beyond the scope of this book, this chapter helps you develop a good feel for the overall capabilities of Windows ASPECT. This chapter then helps you begin writing your own scripts.

Use this chapter to learn the basic ways that you can create, run, and debug (correct errors) in Windows ASPECT programs and to discover the wide array of Windows ASPECT commands that are available. This information gives you a good start at learning to program with Windows ASPECT.

Defining Windows ASPECT

Windows ASPECT is a high-level communication programming language that enables you to create structured programs that control PROCOMM PLUS for Windows.

Windows ASPECT is the language used by the PROCOMM PLUS for Windows Record mode, which is discussed in Chapter 7. By modifying scripts created by Record mode and writing your own scripts, you can develop many useful communications applications.

The Windows ASPECT script language is similar to the QuickBASIC programming language. If you are experienced at programming in QuickBASIC, the structure and commands of Windows ASPECT should be easy for you to understand. If you are a novice at programming, however, you need to learn some fundamental programming concepts before trying to develop a complex script with Windows ASPECT.

Understanding Windows ASPECT Scripts

Windows ASPECT programs are referred to as *scripts*. Chapter 7 introduces you to scripts and demonstrates how to record, as a script, the logon sequence to connect to another computer. Chapter 7 also discusses several sample script files that are distributed on the PROCOMM PLUS for Windows disks. In addition, Chapter 7 explains how to edit a script and run a script from start-up, from the Dialing Directory, and from the menu or Action Bar. This chapter picks up where Chapter 7 leaves off by introducing you to the commands and capabilities available in Windows ASPECT.

A PROCOMM PLUS for Windows script file consists of a series of lines of ASCII characters, with each line containing one command from the Windows ASPECT script language. Chapter 7 introduces you to several of these commands: ENDPROC, PAUSE, PROC, TRANSMIT, and WAITFOR. PROCOMM PLUS for Windows essentially executes commands one-by-one from top to bottom unless the program encounters a command that causes execution to branch to some other portion of the script.

Every Windows ASPECT script must have a main procedure that begins with the PROC MAIN command and ends with the ENDPROC command.

When PROCOMM PLUS for Windows executes the script, any text or other characters that appear to the right of a semicolon (;) are ignored—except when the semicolon is within a quoted string. Use this text to incorporate comments (called *internal documentation*) into the script for future reference.

The DOS file name of each Windows ASPECT script must end in the extension WAS. When a script is compiled, the PROCOMM PLUS for Windows compiler assigns the script a WAX extension.

Use Windows ASPECT scripts to control and automate the operation of PROCOMM PLUS for Windows. The scripts further simplify the use of this already easy-to-use communications program. You can create several scripts, for example, executed through the Dialing Directory, each of which logs on to a different computer system. You also can create a single script that condenses the use of PROCOMM PLUS for Windows down to selecting options from a menu system of your own design. You can even create scripts that prompt the user for textual entry, which PROCOMM PLUS for Windows then uses in the script.

Windows ASPECT contains additional commands and some structural differences from the PROCOMM PLUS ASPECT versions. If you have ASPECT scripts written in previous versions of PROCOMM PLUS, you can convert these scripts into Windows ASPECT scripts. See Chapter 12 to learn more about the differences between the versions of ASPECT.

Comparing Windows ASPECT to Other Languages

The Windows ASPECT programming language is similar in many ways to traditional programming languages like QuickBASIC. Windows ASPECT has three important similarities to these traditional languages:

- *Command placement.* Windows ASPECT is a free-form programming language. Because you can start a command anywhere on a line, you can indent commands to enhance code readability. Except when using commands that set the success/failure flag in conditional expressions, you cannot place more than one Windows ASPECT command on one line. You can extend a line, however, by placing a backslash at the end of the line and continuing the command on the next line.

- *Modularization.* Windows ASPECT enables you to modularize your programs. In other words, you can break the program into more manageable pieces by using procedure blocks, as explained in more detail in Chapter 12. You also can modularize your programs by using one script to execute one or more other scripts. In Windows ASPECT, this technique is referred to as *chaining* script files.

- *Structure.* You can use Windows ASPECT program control commands to create structured programs, which are scripts that are modularized internally. Each Windows ASPECT script must contain a main procedure (which begins with the command PROC MAIN). You can call on other procedures (similar to subroutines) to perform specific operations or to return some value to the main procedure.

Despite these similarities, Windows ASPECT is not exactly like every other programming language. To learn to use Windows ASPECT successfully and efficiently, you need to become familiar with its features and capabilities. The only way to learn the program is to roll up your sleeves and write programs. This chapter helps you get started.

Creating a Windows ASPECT Script

PROCOMM PLUS for Windows provides two ways to create a Windows ASPECT script. You can use PROCOMM PLUS for Windows Record mode, or you can use a text editor to modify an existing script or to write a script from scratch.

Record mode records your keystrokes while you are on-line to a remote computer. Record mode also records the remote system's prompts. This mode is ideal for recording the logon sequence for connecting to another computer. (See Chapter 7 for a complete discussion of using the Record mode.)

You can write a script from scratch or edit a script by using Windows Notepad or any other text editor or word processor that can produce an ASCII file. The file-name extension of each script file must be WAS.

Because you can start a command anywhere on a line, you can enhance code readability by indenting some commands. You cannot, however, include more than one Windows ASPECT command on one line except when using commands that set the success/failure flag in conditional expressions.

If a command line is long, you can break up one command line into several lines by placing a backslash (\) as the last character in a line. The backslash tells Windows ASPECT to use the information on the next line as if it were added onto the current line. The maximum length of any command line is 320 Characters (including CR-LF and null).

You can type Windows ASPECT commands in upper- or lowercase letters, but the commands must be spelled out completely.

This chapter introduces the available Windows ASPECT commands. All the commands are listed and thoroughly explained in the *PROCOMM PLUS for Windows Windows ASPECT Script Language Reference Manual*.

Internally documenting—explaining the operation of—the script is easy because PROCOMM PLUS for Windows ignores anything typed to the right of a semicolon (;) unless the semicolon is part of text enclosed in double quotation marks (for example, "Sam;Spade;Falcon"). You cannot, however, include a comment on an extended line (that ends with a \). Because blank lines do not affect the operation of a script, you can use them as often as you like to make the script more readable.

Windows ASPECT enables you to define large blocks of text as comments by bracketing the lines of text between #COMMENT and #ENDCOMMENT statements. If the first line of the script begins with a semicolon, the comments following are shown in the Notes section of the Run and Compile/Edit dialog boxes.

You may want to look at the scripts on the PROCOMM PLUS for Windows disks and at the examples presented in this chapter to get a better idea of how to use Windows ASPECT. The distribution disks include the following scripts:

- *ARRAY.WAS*. Enables you to manipulate integer or character arrays of up to three dimensions.

- *BBSLIST.WAS*. Enables you to add dialing directory entries from the Darwin BBS list, which can be downloaded from many BBSs.

- *DEMO.WAS*. Demonstrates many of the capabilities of Windows ASPECT. DEMO.WAS is the script that saves and restores PROCOMM PLUS for Windows status and launches the other demo modules. These files are installed in the ASPECT\DEMO subdirectory if this option was selected during installation.

- *HOST.WAS*. Emulates the Host Mode of PROCOMM PLUS, DOS version.

   HOSTUTIL.WAS. Configures the Host Mode operating parameters.

   MAIL.WAS. Mail routines for the Host Mode script.

   SUBS.WAS. Subroutines for the Host Mode script.

- *LOGIN.WAS*. Creates login scripts for CompuServe, Dow Jones, Genie, the DATASTORM BBS, and BIX. The file CSIPHONE.TXT contains telephone access numbers and is used by the script when creating the login script for CompuServe.

- *MCI.WAS*. Accesses and navigates MCI Mail.

- *README.WAS*. Displays the PROCOMM PLUS for Windows READ.ME file.

- *ROADTRIP.WAS*. Processes your Dialing Directory to insert or remove area codes when you are not in your "home" area code.

■ *PCBOARD.WAS, RA.WAS, TBBS.WAS,* and *WILDCAT.WAS.* Generic login scripts for the indicated bulletin board systems. These scripts must be edited to include the Dialing Directory entry, your user name, password, and other information required by the BBS during login.

Each of these scripts contains insights about how you can use Windows ASPECT to accomplish a number of tasks. Before beginning to program with Windows ASPECT, print these files and study the flow of the program and how certain commands are used. Liberally use the procedures included in these examples to build your own Windows ASPECT scripts. A detailed discussion of many of these scripts is found in the next chapter.

Compiling a Script

For PROCOMM PLUS for Windows to obey the instructions that you place in a script file, it must interpret each command and option, then act upon them. If a script is complicated, interpreting the script may require a great deal of time and may slow the script execution. To avoid this problem, PROCOMM PLUS for Windows enables you to compile the script.

The compilation process changes the English-like Windows ASPECT script commands into codes that are much easier for PROCOMM PLUS for Windows to read and execute. When you compile a Windows ASPECT script, which has a WAS extension, a new file is created with a WAX extension. PROCOMM PLUS for Windows can read and execute the new WAX script quickly. This compilation process also encrypts information—such as passwords—to prohibit unauthorized persons from reading that information. Of course, the WAS version of the script still contains the original script commands.

The Compile/Edit dialog box is used to set up options for the compiler and to compile WAS files (see fig. 11.1). This dialog box is displayed by selecting Compile/Edit from the Scripts menu, pressing Alt-F3, or clicking the Tools icon on the Action Bar.

NOTE Depending on the user's video resolutions and display, the user may not see the Tools icon.

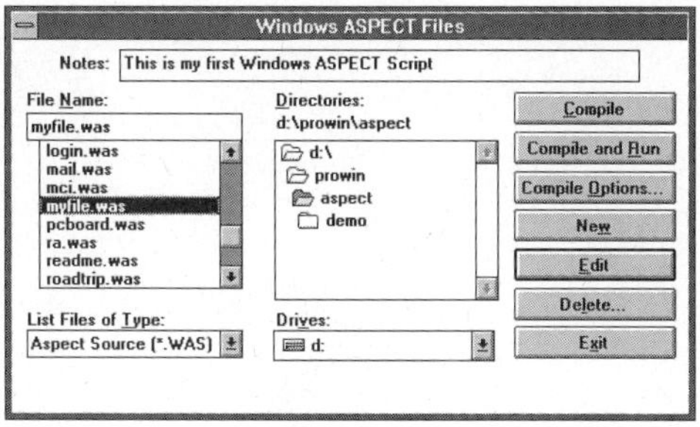

FIG. 11.1

The Compile/Edit
dialog box.

Creating and Compiling a Windows ASPECT Script

The following paragraphs show you how to write and compile a Windows ASPECT script. To create a simple script file named MYFILE.WAS, follow these steps:

1. Display the Compile/Edit dialog box and choose the New button.

   PROCOMM PLUS for Windows uses the Windows Notepad as the default text editor. To select the text editor of your choice, change this option in the Current Setup, System Settings dialog box.

2. In the editor, enter the following lines (comments are optional, but the first comment line will appear in the Notes field of the Compile/ Edit dialog box):

```
           ;This is my first Windows ASPECT Script
PROC MAIN ; Every Windows ASPECT script has a main procedure
CLEAR     ; Clear the screen
USERMSG "This is my first Windows ASPECT script!"
END PROC  ; End the main procedure
```

3. Save this file as MYFILE.WAS.

   Note that the file as created here contains an error. The END PROC command should be one word—ENDPROC.

4. Select the Compile and Run button on the Compile/Edit dialog box.

   The message shown in figure 11.2 appears. These two error messages are caused by the incorrect END PROC command.

5. To correct the error, choose the Edit Source File button and change END PROC to ENDPROC.

6. Save the file.

7. Choose the Compile button.

   This time the script compiles successfully and displays the message box shown in figure 11.3.

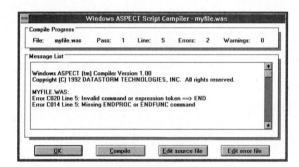

FIG. 11.2

The Compiler Dialog Box showing the script errors.

FIG. 11.3

The message box from your first Windows ASPECT script.

Using Other Methods To Run a Script

In addition to the method shown above, PROCOMM PLUS for Windows provides several options for executing, or running, a script:

- From the Program Manager at the PROCOMM PLUS for Windows start-up
- From the File Manager using Drag and Drop
- From the Dialing Directory when an entry is selected
- From the Terminal window
- From within another script
- From another computer (before you run a Windows ASPECT script, you may want to compile it)

If you run a noncompiled Windows ASPECT script, PROCOMM PLUS for Windows compiles it first and then runs the script. Compiling a script before it is run is a good practice because it reduces the time required before script execution begins. Precompiling also ensures that the script is free of syntax errors.

If the Action Bar is displayed, the name of the executing script appears in the Script File drop-down list.

From the Windows Program Manager

PROCOMM PLUS for Windows provides a way to run a script from the the Windows Program Manager. This method causes a script to run immediately when you start PROCOMM PLUS for Windows by double-clicking on an icon displayed in the Program Manager. To run a Windows ASPECT script from the Program Manager, you first must set up the Program Item or icon in the Program Group. Select or make active the Program Group where you want the icon to appear. Select the File, New menu in the Program Manager, and choose the Program Item option. Type the following in the Command Line edit box of the Program Item Properties dialog:

> *pwpath***pw.exe** *scriptname.wa?*

In the Command Line, replace *pwpath* with the directory path of PW.EXE. Replace *scriptname* with the file name of the script, including the WAS or WAX extension. If the script is an uncompiled WAS version, PROCOMM PLUS for Windows compiles the script each time the Program Item is run, then executes the WAX version.

By default, the Program Item Properties dialog uses the first icon in the PW.EXE file and displays it in the Program Group after the OK button is selected. PW.EXE includes several icons that can be used for display in a Program Group. To view the other icons in PW.EXE, select the Change icon button after the Command Line is typed. Refer to the Windows documentation or Que's *Using Windows 3.1,* Special Edition to learn how to use other icons in the Program Manager.

To create a Program Item to run the script MYFILE.WAX (which is the script created in "Compiling a Script"), type the following in the Command Line edit box of the Program Item Properties dialog:

> *pwpath***pw.exe myfile**

Change the icon if you want and select the OK button. When the new icon has the focus and the enter key is pressed or the icon is double-clicked, PROCOMM PLUS for Windows runs, the script is executed, and your message box is displayed. The script continues to run until the OK button is selected in the message box.

You can use this technique to create Program Items for each of your logon scripts and then connect to any service by double-clicking on its icon.

From the Dialing Directory

If you want PROCOMM PLUS for Windows to run a script from the Dialing Directory, select the name of the script in the Script File field of the Dialing Directory entry. PROCOMM PLUS for Windows runs the script every time you connect to the remote computer or when the entry is selected, depending on the Scripts, Run option selected.

PROCOMM PLUS for Windows provides two advanced options for running scripts associated with a directory entry. To display the Advanced option dialog for a Dialing Directory script, highlight the script name and select the Advanced button. If you have a login script that you want to run after PROCOMM PLUS for Windows connects to another computer, select the Start Script When Connection Is Made option. If your script requires user input before the number is dialed, select the Start Script When Entry Is Dialed option. When the latter option is selected, the program expects the script to initiate the call.

The system variable $FROMDDIR can be tested to determine if the script was started from the Dialing Directory.

From the Terminal Screen

You have four ways to start a script when the PROCOMM PLUS for Windows terminal screen is displayed.

■ If the Action Bar is displayed, you can start the script displayed in the Script File: drop-down list box by selecting the Run Script icon. You can run any other compiled script by selecting the drop-down button to the right of the list and then selecting the script file name. You can stop the script by selecting the Run Script icon again. Pressing Alt-. (period) has the same effect as selecting the Run Script icon.

■ If you have a meta key configured to execute a script, you can press its displayed button or use its key combo. See Chapter 7 for more information on meta keys.

■ Press Alt-F5.

■ Select Run from the Scripts menu.

If you run the script using one of the last two methods, the Windows ASPECT Run dialog box appears (see fig. 11.4).

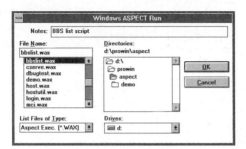

FIG. 11.4

The Windows ASPECT Run dialog box.

You can run your new script named MYFILE, for example, by displaying the dialog box, selecting *myfile* from the File Name list, and pressing Enter. The script clears the screen and displays your message box.

Notice that the List Files of Type list shows only type WAX. You can, however, type the script file name in the File Name edit box with or without a WAS extension. PROCOMM PLUS for Windows will run the WAX version of the script if it exists. If only a WAS version exists, PROCOMM PLUS for Windows will compile it and run the WAX version.

From within Another Script

You also can run a script from within another script; this technique is sometimes called *chaining* or *spawning* scripts. The script that causes another script to run is called the *parent*. The script that is run is called the *child*. Windows ASPECT provides two commands for running other scripts from within a script: CHAIN and EXECUTE.

CHAIN (similar to the PROCOMM PLUS EXECUTE command) does not allow a return from the chained-to script. When one Windows ASPECT script CHAINs to another Windows ASPECT script, the first script no longer is active. The following Windows ASPECT command plays the script named MYSCRIPT (be sure to enclose the script name in quotation marks):

CHAIN "myscript"

You can use this command to chain together an unlimited number of Windows ASPECT scripts. The first script can call a second script, the second script can call a third, and so on. You have no limitation on the number of scripts that can be chained one after another because PROCOMM PLUS for Windows does not need to keep information from the parent script.

EXECUTE, on the other hand, does allow the chained-to (child) script to return to the original (parent) script. PROCOMM PLUS for Windows saves the state of the original script when the EXECUTE command is encountered and restores it when the chained-to script terminates. The following Windows ASPECT program plays SCRIPT1, then SCRIPT2, and then ends.

```
PROC MAIN
    EXECUTE "SCRIPT1"
    EXECUTE "SCRIPT2"
ENDPROC
```

The program has no absolute limitation on the number of scripts that can be executed one to the next to the next (nested) without a return to the previous. Because PROCOMM PLUS for Windows does need to keep information from each parent script without a return, good programming practice would require that scripts not be nested too deeply.

The end result of the CHAIN and EXECUTE commands is that you can break Windows ASPECT scripts into smaller, easier-to-manage modules instead of having to program an entire application in one script. Creating programs in small, manageable scripts is sometimes referred to as *modularization.*

The system variable $CHAINED can be tested to determine if the script was started from a CHAIN command. The system variable $CHILD can be tested to determine if the script was started from an EXECUTE command.

When you use the EXECUTE or CHAIN command, Windows ASPECT always looks for a WAX version of the script. If only an uncompiled WAS version exists, Windows ASPECT attempts to compile the WAS version, and then executes the resulting WAX file. If PROCOMM PLUS for Windows cannot compile the WAS script, execution terminates in the case of a chain or passes back to the parent in the case of an execute.

Terminating the Execution of a Script

From time to time, you may decide that you do not want to run a script after all. To terminate a script in midstream, press Alt-. (period). If the script currently running has a parent script, PROCOMM PLUS for Windows displays the dialog box asking Halt all parent scripts, too? (see fig. 11.5).

FIG. 11.5

The Halt Script dialog.

If you choose No, the script returns to the parent; if you choose Yes, all script execution ends.

A script terminates, of course, when it encounters the ENDPROC command of the main procedure. The EXIT command also can be used to terminate script execution anywhere within a script. If the script is a child script started with an EXECUTE command, the EXIT command has an optional integer argument that can be used to pass a value to the parent script. This value can be tested in the parent script by using the $EXITCODE system variable.

Debugging a Script

While creating a Windows ASPECT program, you may need to debug the script. That is, your script may contain errors—such as syntax errors found when attempting to compile the script. (Refer to the errors reported in the "Compiling a Script" section earlier in this chapter.) Using the information provided from the Windows ASPECT compiler, you should be able to locate and correct the source of the syntax error.

Sometimes a script compiles without any syntax errors and still does not work properly. Errors in assigning a value to the wrong variable or just basic errors in the logic of the script may cause invalid results.

While running the script, PROCOMM PLUS for Windows may encounter a condition that does not allow the execution to proceed properly. A value may be passed to a command that is not within the range that it can handle, for example. This is called a run-time error.

Run-time errors fall into two categories; critical and noncritical. Critical errors are those that cause PROCOMM PLUS for Windows to terminate the script. Noncritical errors do not terminate automatically but display a dialog box requesting whether the script should continue to run. In either case, the errors must be found and corrected.

ASPECT includes several techniques for troubleshooting programs. One of the simplest is to add USERMSG commands at various places throughout the script. Text in the USERMSG box can indicate where the script currently is executing and display the values of variables that are of interest. The most helpful method of troubleshooting is to use some of the advanced options available in the compiler. To display the Compiler Options dialog box, select Alt-F3 and Alt-O. The dialog box shown in figure 11.6 appears.

FIG 11.6

The Windows ASPECT Compiler Options dialog box.

The Create Map File option creates a file that includes statistical information about the compiled script. If the Include Line Numbers option is checked, a line number (source file) to offset (compiled file) cross reference is added to the map file. This information can be very useful—especially when debugging very large script files.

By far the most powerful method of debugging a script is to use the Compile For Debug option. When this option is checked and a script is compiled, additional information is added to the WAX file. This information is used in the Windows ASPECT Run-Time Debugger window during script execution.

When a script (compiled with the Compile For Debug option on) is running and Ctrl-Break is pressed or script execution encounters a BREAKPOINT command, the debugging window is displayed. Like the USERMSG described above, the BREAKPOINT command can be inserted at places within the script where you want to know the values of variables or where you want to follow the logic flow of the program.

Display the Compile/Edit dialog box (Alt-F3), select New, and enter the following program into the text editor:

```
;Debugging test
PROC MAIN
INTEGER incno                        ;Define local vars
STRING outstr
    CLEAR                            ;Clear the screen
BREAKPOINT "Breakpoint 1"           ;Show debugging window
    FOR incno = 1 UPTO 10           ;Loop for 10 times
        STRFMT outstr "testing %i`r`n" incno ;Format outstr
        TERMWRITES outstr           ;Display outstr
    ENDFOR
ENDPROC
```

Save the script as DBUGTEST.WAS. Select the Options button in the Compile/Edit dialog box, check the Compile For Debug check box, and choose OK. Now compile and run DBUGTEST.WAS. Select DBUGTEST.WAS from the File Name list in the Compile/Edit dialog box and Choose the Compile And Run button. The dialog box shown in figure 11.7 appears.

FIG. 11.7

The Windows ASPECT Run-Time Debugger dialog box.

Notice that the string Breakpoint 1 in the BREAKPOINT source command now appears in the Message field of the dialog box. If this were a much larger script, you could use different BREAKPOINT messages to indicate which breakpoint had been encountered. The Procedure Name is main because main is the only procedure in the test program. Also shown is the Target File Offset, which is the currently executing position in the WAX file. Of more benefit are the Source Line Number and Source Line Text, which tell you the next statement to be executed.

Choose the Step button. Notice that the Source Line Number increments and the Source Line Text changes from the FOR statement to the STRFMT statement. Choose the Step button several times and observe the Source Line Text and the output strings as they appear in the Terminal window. By stepping through a program in this manner, you can uncover errors in program flow logic.

Now select the drop-down button for the Variable list. You see the MAIN PROC local variables incno and outstr as well as the predefined global variables. (The predefined global variables are comprised of 10 strings, longs, floats, and integers. Predefined global variables are available to any procedure without any previous definition.) Select the incno variable and notice that its current value is displayed. Step the program several times and watch the value change. Do the same with the outstr variable.

You can see from this simple exercise that the Windows ASPECT Run-Time Debugger is indispensable for debugging large complex scripts.

An Overview of the Windows ASPECT Commands

PROCOMM PLUS for Windows provides more than 300 Windows ASPECT script commands, more than 160 SET/FETCH commands, and approximately 100 system variables. The SET/FETCH statements are special Windows ASPECT commands used to control and obtain internal system values. They provide the script programmer with the ability to set all values that are available through the user interface and to control internal script operation. System variables are used to return values of internal variables. These commands and variables are used to develop Windows ASPECT scripts and fall into 26 groups:

ASPECT
Clipboard
Communications
Conditional Compilation and Macro
Conversion
Dynamic Data Exchange
Dialing and Dialing Directory
Dialog Box Controls and Objects
Dialog Boxes, predefined
Disk File and Path
Execution Control, Branching, and Looping
File Input/Output
File Transfer
General Operation
Math
Menu
Modem
Operating System Hardware and Memory
Packet Transfer
Printer
Script Control
Setup
String Processing
Terminal
User Window
Windows

The rest of this chapter briefly introduces you to these commands to help you gain a general understanding of the types of the commands that are available. Refer to the *PROCOMM PLUS for Windows Windows ASPECT Script Language Reference Manual* for a more complete description.

Syntax Conventions

■ Parameters enclosed in square brackets ([ ]) are optional.

■ Parameters enclosed in curly brackets ({}) are required when several choices are available.

■ Parameters separated by a vertical bar (|) indicate that one option is to be selected from the choices.

■ Command words are shown in capital italics.

■ Other words in capitals are keywords and should be typed as they appear.

■ SET/FETCH commands should be followed with the SET command word to assign the value and the FETCH command word to retrieve the value.

■ System variables can be used as a variable in any expression.

ASPECT Commands

The ASPECT command group consists of SET/FETCH commands that control how PROCOMM PLUS for Windows operates when running a script.

ASPECT SET/FETCH Commands

■ *ASPECT CONTROL* OFF | ON: Enables and disables the Start Script/ Stop Script menu item and the Action Bar Run Script icon. ON is normal operation.

■ *ASPECT DECIMAL* integer: Sets the number of digits to the right of the decimal point to print for floating point numbers.

■ *ASPECT DEFAULTPATH* pathname: Determines default path that Windows ASPECT commands will use.

■ *ASPECT DIALINGBOX* OFF | ON: Controls whether the Dialing window is displayed after a DIAL, DIALNAME, DIALNUMBER, or DIALQUEUE command.

■ *ASPECT DISPLAY* OFF | ON: Controls whether characters received are displayed.

- *ASPECT FILEXFERBOX* OFF | ON: Determines whether PROCOMM PLUS for Windows will display the file transfer statistics box during a SENDFILE or GETFILE operation.

- *ASPECT HELPFILE* filespec: Specifies the name of an alternate Help file to use with on-line help. Typically, this is a custom help file written especially for a script.

- *ASPECT KEYS* OFF | ON: Controls whether the script or PROCOMM PLUS for Windows processes all keystrokes. The default is OFF; characters are sent to the terminal.

- *ASPECT RANGECHK* OFF | ON: Determines whether out-of-range value will issue an error message during execution. The default is ON.

- *ASPECT REMOTECMD* OFF | ON: Determines whether PROCOMM PLUS for Windows will accept script commands sent by a remote PC.

- *ASPECT RGETCHAR* character: Specifies the character that will terminate an active RGET command.

- *ASPECT RXDATA* {OFF [UNTIL WHENTARGET index]} | ON: Controls whether the script or PROCOMM PLUS for Windows processes characters received through the com port. The default is OFF, which means characters are sent to the terminal. If the UNTIL WHENTARGET option is used and a target string is matched by an active WHEN TARGET, PROCOMM PLUS for Windows will automatically turn RXDATA ON.

- *ASPECT SCRIPTPATH* pathname: Specifies the DOS path where Windows ASPECT programs are located and compiled.

- *ASPECT SPAWN* OFF | ON: Controls whether scripts can be spawned automatically from a dialing directory entry, meta key, or the DDEEXECUTE command as well as from the Action Bar Start Script icon, the Script Menu Start Script command, or the Start Script drop-down list box. The default is OFF.

- *ASPECT STRFINDCASE* OFF | ON: Sets case sensitivity OFF or ON for the STRFIND command.

- *ASPECT SWITCHCASE* OFF | ON: Sets case sensitivity OFF or ON when the SWITCH command is using string values.

- *ASPECT WAITFORCASE* OFF | ON: Sets case sensitivity OFF or ON for the WAITFOR command.

- *ASPECT WHENCASE* OFF | ON: Sets case sensitivity OFF or ON for the WHEN TARGET command.

- *CAPTURE PATH* pathname: Specifies the default path for Capture files.

ASPECT Global Variables

- *$CHAINED*: Returns TRUE (1) if the current script task was chained from another script.

- *$CHILD*: Returns TRUE (1) if the current script task has a "parent" script.

- *$SCRIPT*: The name of the currently executing script.

Clipboard Commands

These commands are used to store and retrieve data in the Windows Clipboard.

- *CLIPTOFILE* BITMAP | METAFILE | TEXT filespec: Saves the contents of the Windows Clipboard in the specified file. The data in the Clipboard must be of the specified type.

- *FILETOCLIP* BITMAP | METAFILE | TEXT filespec: Loads the contents of the specified file into the Windows Clipboard. The data in the file must be of the specified type.

- *PASTETEXT*: Sends the text contents of the Windows Clipboard out the COM port.

Communications Commands

The Communications commands are used to monitor and control the communication port and to send, receive, and process characters through the communication port.

- *BREAK*: Sends break to remote.

- *CLEARXOFF*: Clears an XOFF condition.

- *COMGETC* intvar [integer]: Assigns an integer variable the value of the next character in the communications buffer, or a zero if the buffer is empty.

- *COMGETS* strvar length [integer]: Assigns a string variable the value of the next number of characters in the communications buffer specified by length, or null if the buffer is empty.

- *COMPUTC* character: Sends a character out the active communications port.

- *COMPUTS* string length: Sends a string of characters out the active communications port. The number of characters sent is specified by length.

- *CRC16* string integer intvar: Calculates the CRC value of string and returns the value in intvar. The integer is used to initialize the CRC value.

- *HANGUP*: Disconnects the call.

- *RGET* strvar [length [integer]]: Receives characters from remote computer and assigns them to a string variable.

- *RXFLUSH*: Flushes or removes all characters from the receive buffer.

- *TRANSMIT* string: Sends specified string to remote computer.

- *TXFLUSH*: Flushes or removes all characters from the transmit buffer.

- *WAITFOR* string [integer | FOREVER]: Suspends execution until a specified string is received or a specified period of time has elapsed.

- *WAITQUIET* [integer [integer | FOREVER]]: Suspends execution until data line has been inactive for a specified period of time.

Communication SET/FETCH Commands

- *BAUDRATE* long | DEFAULT: Sets the baud rate. Valid values are displayed in the Setup Baud rate drop-down list.

- *CDINXFER* NO | YES: Determines whether carrier detect will be monitored in file transfer mode.

- *DNLDPROMPT* OFF | ON: Enables and disables the display of the file transfer dialog box.

- *DUPDNLDFILE* RENAME | OVERWRITE: Determines whether downloaded files that have duplicate names will be renamed or overwritten.

- *PORT BREAKLEN* integer: Sets the duration of a break in tenths of a second.

- *PORT COMBUFSIZE* integer: Sets the size of the Windows communications buffer. Values include 2, 4, 8, and 16 kilobytes.

- *PORT DATABITS* integer: Sets the data bits used. Possible values are 7 or 8.

■ *PORT DROPDTR* NO | YES: Controls whether PROCOMM PLUS for Windows will disconnect the modem by dropping the modem Data Terminal Ready signal.

■ *PORT DUPLEX* FULL | HALF: Sets the duplex mode.

■ *PORT HARDFLOW* OFF | ON: Enables and disables hardware flow control.

■ *PORT PARITY* NONE | ODD | EVEN | MARK | SPACE: Controls the parity setting.

■ *PORT SOFTFLOW* OFF | ON: Enables or disables software flow control.

■ *PORT STOPBITS* 1 | 2: Sets the number of stop bits for the com port.

■ *PORT XOFFCHAR* character: Specifies the software flow-control character that will pause the transmission of data.

■ *PORT XONCHAR* character: Specifies the character that will restart data paused by software flow control.

■ *TXPACE* integer: Determines the time in milliseconds between characters for outgoing characters.

Communication System Variables

■ *$CARRIER*: Returns the status of the modem carrier detect signal.

■ *$CNCTMSG*: Returns the message sent by the modem during a successful connection.

■ *$CONNECTION*: The integer ID of the current connection as it appears in the Modem Selection dialog.

■ *$FLOWSTATE*: Returns the status of software or hardware flow control.

■ *$RXCOUNT*: Returns the number of characters in the receive data buffer. These characters may not be available to the script if PROCOMM PLUS for Windows is not in terminal mode—for example, during a file transfer.

■ *$RXDATA*: Returns the number of characters in the receive data buffer that are available to the script.

■ *$TXDATA*: Returns the number of characters that can be sent to the transmit data buffer without causing an overflow.

■ *$TXCOUNT*: Returns the number of characters remaining in the transmit data buffer.

Conditional Compilation and Macro Commands

These statements are used to tell the compiler how to use text defined in a macro with the #DEFINE command. A macro is text that the compiler substitutes for the macro name when it is encountered during compilation. Other statements in this group enable testing for the existence of macros to include or exclude sections of the script based on their presence.

■ *#COMMENT*: Defines the beginning of a comment block. The compiler will ignore any lines of text between a #COMMENT and an #ENDCOMMENT command.

■ *#ENDCOMMENT*: Ends a comment block.

■ *#DEFINE* name text: Defines a macro name and the text to substitute for it during compile time.

■ *#UNDEF* name: Cancels a previous specified #DEFINE.

■ *#IFDEF* name: Tests for a specific #DEFINE and conditionally compiles based on its presence.

■ *#IFNDEF* name: Used with the #IFDEF statement to test for a specific #DEFINE and conditionally compile, based on its presence.

■ *#ELSE*: Used with the #IFDEF statement to test for a specific #DEFINE and conditionally compile, based on its presence.

■ *#ELIFDEF* name: Used with the #IFDEF statement to test for a specific #DEFINE and conditionally compile, based on its presence.

■ *#ELIFNDEF* name: Used with the #IFDEF statement to test for a specific #DEFINE and conditionally compile, based on its presence.

■ *#ENDIF*: Ends an #IFDEF statement group.

■ *#INCLUDE* "filespec": Specifies a file having additional #DEFINE commands, or additional procedures for inclusion in the current script, that are added during compilation.

Conversion Commands

You use the Windows ASPECT conversion commands to convert one type of variable to another. A program may read numeric information as a string variable, for example, and later need to use it as an integer number. ASPECT provides a command (ATOI) to convert an ASCII string into an integer. The following conversion commands are available:

- *ANSITOKEY* character intvar: Converts an ANSI character to its corresponding virtual key value and keyboard state.

- *ATOF* string floatvar: Converts numeric string from ASCII to float value.

- *ATOI* string intvar: Converts numeric string from ASCII to integer value.

- *ATOL* string longvar: Converts numeric string from ASCII to long value.

- *FTOA* float strvar: Converts float value to ASCII string.

- *HEXTONUM* string numvar: Converts a string representing a hexadecimal value and stores it in a numeric variable.

- *INTSLTIME* year month day hour min longvar: Converts integers representing date and time values to a long date time value.

- *ITOA* integer strvar: Converts integer value to ASCII string.

- *KEYTOASCII* integer intvar: Converts integer key code to its ASCII value, stored as a string value.

- *LTIMEINTS* long intvar intvar intvar intvar intvar: Converts long date time value to integers representing date and time values.

- *LTIMESTRING* long strvar: Converts long date time value to a time date string of the form Mon May 25 12:00:00 1992.

- *LTIMESTRS* long string string: Converts long date time value to time date strings of the form MM/DD/YY HH:MM:SS.

- *LTOA* long strvar: Converts a long string to an ASCII string.

- *NUMTOHEX* number string: Converts a number to a hexadecimal value and stores it in a string.

- *STRSLTIME* datestr timestr longvar: Converts date and time strings to a long date time value.

DDE (Dynamic Data Exchange) Commands

This group of commands is used to establish and maintain Dynamic Data Exchange (DDE) links with a DDE server application. DDE is used to transfer information between programs running under Windows. PROCOMM PLUS for Windows might retrieve information from an on-line service, for example, and use DDE to pass the data to a spreadsheet program. See also WHEN DDEADVISE.

■ *DDEADVISE* long string gdatavar [integer]: Establishes an advise on a server variable.

■ *DDEEXECUTE* long string: Used to execute a command in a server application.

■ *DDEINIT* longvar string string [integer]: Used to start a DDE conversation with a server application.

■ *DDEPOKE* long string data: Used to send data to a server application.

■ *DDEREQUEST* long string datavar: Used to obtain the value of an item in the server application.

■ *DDETERMINATE* long: Used to terminate a DDE conversation with a server application.

■ *DDEUNADVISE* long string: Terminates an advise on a server variable.

DDE System Variable

■ *$DDEADVISE*: Returns the ID of the last DDEADVISE statement to receive a new value.

Dialing and Dialing Directory Commands

The Dialing and Dialing Directory commands are used to dial numbers and entries in the Dialing Directory as well as to obtain information about entries in the directory. Note that the SET DIALDIR ACCESS command enables you to use the SET/FETCH statements listed in the Setup group to access Dialing Directory entries.

■ *DIAL* integer | "entry..." | strvar: Dials the specified entry(s) in the currently loaded Dialing Directory.

- *DIALADD* name phonenum [script] [intvar]: Adds an entry to the currently loaded Dialing Directory.

- *DIALCANCEL*: Cancels a current dialing operation.

- *DIALCREATE* filespec: Creates a new Dialing Directory of the specified name.

- *DIALDIR OFF|ON*: Displays or conceals dialing directory.

- *DIALFIND* string [intvar]: Returns a Dialing Directory index number corresponding to an entry name.

- *DIALLOAD* filespec: Loads the specified Dialing Directory.

- *DIALNAME* string: Dials the number of the entry with the name field matching the string argument.

- *DIALNUMBER* "[ldcode] phonenum [ldcode]" | strvar: Dials the specified phone number.

- *DIALQUEUE*: Dials the numbers in the dialing queue.

- *DIALSAVE* [filespec]: Saves the current contents of the Dialing Directory to a disk file.

Dialing Directory SET/FETCH Commands

- *DIALDIR CALLPAUSE* integer: Specifies the number of seconds PROCOMM PLUS for Windows will pause between numbers in a dialing queue.

- *DIALDIR DROPDTR* NO | YES: Specifies whether PROCOMM PLUS for Windows will drop DTR when you hang up a call made from the Dialing window.

- *DIALDIR MAXDIAL* integer: Determines the maximum number of times that PROCOMM PLUS for Windows will attempt to connect with a Dialing Directory entry.

- *DIALDIR PATH* pathname: Specifies the default path for your Dialing Directory files.

- *DIALDIR SENDCR* NO | YES: Specifies whether PROCOMM PLUS for Windows will send a carriage return between dial attempts.

- *DIALDIR STARTUPFILE* filespec: Specifies the Dialing Directory that PROCOMM PLUS for Windows will load when started.

- *DIALDIR WAITCNCT* integer: Specifies the number of seconds PROCOMM PLUS for Windows will wait after dialing before timing out.

Dialing Directory System Variables

- *$D_LASTDATE*: Returns a long time date value representing the last call time for the currently accessed Dialing Directory entry.

- *$D_NUMBER*: The phone number for the current Dialing Directory entry.

- *$D_NAME*: The name identifying the current Dialing Directory entry.

- *$D_SCRIPT*: The script name for the current Dialing Directory entry.

- *$D_TOTAL*: The total number of successful connections for the current Dialing Directory entry.

- *$DDIRFNAME*: Returns the name of the current Dialing Directory.

- *$DIALENTRY*: The directory entry number of the last Dialing Directory entry with a successful connection.

- *$DIALING*: Returns TRUE (1) if PROCOMM PLUS for Windows is dialing a queue of numbers.

- *$DIALCOUNT*: Returns the number of entries in the Dialing Directory.

- *$DIALQUEUE*: Returns the number of entries in the dialing queue.

- *$DIALCHANGED*: Returns TRUE (1) if the current Dialing Directory has been modified and not saved to disk.

- *$FROMDDIR*: Returns TRUE (1) if the current script was started by a Dialing Directory entry; FALSE (0) otherwise.

Dialog Box Controls and Objects

This group of statements is used to create and control Windows ASPECT dialog boxes. Windows ASPECT dialog boxes are the main method for prompting and providing user input for Windows ASPECT scripts. The *position* parameters in the statements below refer to four integer values that define the top left position and the width and height of the control in dialog units. Windows ASPECT dialog boxes are easily created using the PROCOMM PLUS for Windows Dialog Editor. See also WHEN DIALOG.

- *BITMAP* position filespec: Displays a bit map in a Windows ASPECT dialog box.

- *CHECKBOX* position strcon gintvar: Adds a check box to a Windows ASPECT dialog box.

- *COMBOBOX* id position itemlist gstrvar [SORT]: Adds a combo box to a Windows ASPECT dialog box.

- *DESTROYDLG*: Destroys a Windows ASPECT dialog box.

- *DIALOGBOX* left top width height type [strcon] [HELPID gintvar]: The first statement in a Windows ASPECT dialog box statement group.

- *DIRLISTBOX* id position filespec {MULTIPLE filespec} | {SINGLE gstrvar}: Adds a directory list box to a Windows ASPECT dialog box.

- *DIRPATH* position: Displays the current path of the files displayed in the DIRLISTBOX. Must follow a DIRLISTBOX command.

- *EDITBOX* position gstrvar [MASKED] [length]: Adds an edit box to a Windows ASPECT dialog box.

- *ENDDIALOG*: The last statement in a Windows ASPECT dialog box statement group.

- *FCOMBOBOX* id position filespec [offset[length]] gstrvar [SORT]: Adds a file combo box to a Windows ASPECT dialog box. The list displayed in combo box is contained in the specified file.

- *FEDITBOX* position filespec [HSCROLL]: Adds a file edit box to a Windows ASPECT dialog box. The file edited by the FEDITBOX is *filespec*.

- *FLISTBOX* position filespec [offset[length]][tabstring] {MULTIPLE filespec} | {SINGLE gstrvar} [SORT]: Adds a file list box to a Windows ASPECT dialog box. The list displayed in list box is contained in the specified file.

- *FTEXT* position filespec [HSCROLL] [long]: Adds a scrollable text display box showing the contents of the specified file to a Windows ASPECT dialog box.

- *GROUPBOX* position [title] [SHADOW]: Adds a black rectangle with optional text to a Windows ASPECT dialog box.

- *ICON* left top gstrvar gintvar: Displays an icon in a Windows ASPECT dialog box.

- *ICONBUTTON* left top gstrvar gstrvar gintvar [DEFAULT]: Displays an icon button in a Windows ASPECT dialog box. An icon button can be selected by the operator much the same way as a PUSHBUTTON.

- *LISTBOX* position itemlist gstrvar [SORT]: Adds a list box to a Windows ASPECT dialog box.

- *METAFILE* position filespec: Displays a meta file in a Windows ASPECT dialog box.

- *PUSHBUTTON* position strcon NORMAL | CANCEL | UPDATE [DEFAULT]: Adds a push button to a Windows ASPECT dialog box.

- *RADIOBUTTON* position strcon [gintvar ENDGROUP]: Adds a radio button to a Windows ASPECT dialog box.

- *TEXT* position LEFT | CENTER | RIGHT strcon: Adds a static text field to a Windows ASPECT dialog box.

- *UPDATEDLG* integer: Used to update the values displayed in a Windows ASPECT dialog box.

- *VTEXT* position LEFT | CENTER | RIGHT gstrvar: Adds a text field displaying the contents of a string variable to a Windows ASPECT dialog box.

Dialog Box System Variable

- *$DIALOG*: Returns a value indicating an item has been selected or a change has occurred in a Windows ASPECT dialog box. The values returned are listed in the following table.

Value returned in $DIALOG	Windows ASPECT dialog event	Value returned in $DIALOG	Windows ASPECT dialog event
0	No dialog event	130 - 133	FLISTBOX item selected
1	Cancel PUSHBUTTON Pressed	150	DIRLISTBOX item selected
10 - 25	Normal PUSHBUTTON Pressed	170 - 185	COMBO BOX item selected
30 - 45	Update PUSHBUTTON Pressed	190 - 193	FCOMBOBOX item selected
50 - 57	RADIOBUTTON changed	210 - 225	ICONBUTTON selected in a group
70 - 85	CHECKBOX state toggled	230 - 245	EDITBOX contents changed
110 - 117	LISTBOX item selected	250	FEDITBOX contents changed

Dialog Boxes, Predefined

These commands display predefined dialog boxes that can be used to name and select files, display messages, and obtain user input. Unlike Windows ASPECT dialog boxes created using the statements above, script execution suspends while the predefined dialog box is displayed.

- *ERRORMSG* formatstr [arglist]: Displays a message with the exclamation icon.

- *SDLGFOPEN* title filespec strvar: Displays a standard File Open dialog box.

- *SDLGINPUT* title string strvar [DEFAULT]: Displays a message box that allows user input.

- *SDLGMSGBOX* title string icon button intvar [integer] [BEEP]: Displays a message box with a specified icon and message text.

- *SDLGSAVEAS* title filespec strvar: Displays a standard File Save As dialog box.

- *USERMSG* formatstr [arglist]: Displays a message with the information icon.

Disk File and Path Commands

The Windows ASPECT disk file and path commands enable you to access information from the disk. Some of these commands mimic DOS commands, enabling you to change directories, make a directory, remove a directory, rename a file, and so on. Other commands give you more access to disk information than you can get from DOS.

- *ADDFILENAME* pathname filename: Returns a fully qualified path from a path and file name.

- *CHDIR* pathname: Changes the current directory to the specified path.

- *COPYFILE* filespec filespec: Copies a file to the specified file or path.

- *DELFILE* filespec: Deletes the specified file.

- *DIR* filespec [strvar]: Displays the files in the specified path.

- *DISKFREE* integer longvar: Returns free space on specified drive.

- *FINDFIRST* filespec [string]: Locates file or files matching file specification.

- *FINDNEXT*: Locates next file that matches the specification used in FINDFIRST.

- *FULLPATH* filespec strvar: Returns the fully qualified drive and path of the specified file.

- *GETDIR* disk strvar: Returns the current directory path of the specified disk.

- *GETDISK* strvar: Returns the current default disk drive.

- *GETFATTR* filespec strvar: Returns attributes of specified file.

- *GETFDATE* filespec strvar: Returns date stamp of specified file.

- *GETFLTIME* filespec longvar: Returns date and time stamp of specified file in long date time variable form.

- *GETFSIZE* filespec longvar: Returns size of specified file in bytes.

- *GETFTIME* filespec strvar: Returns time stamp of specified file.

- *ISFILE* filespec: Determines if file exists given specified path.

- *MKDIR* filespec: Makes (creates) a new DOS directory.

- *RENAME* filespec filespec: Renames an existing file or moves a file to a different directory.

- *RMDIR* filespec: Removes empty existing directory.

- *SETFATTR* filespec string: Sets file attributes.

- *SETFDATE* filespec string: Sets file date stamp.

- *SETFLTIME* filespec long: Sets file time and date stamp using a long date time variable.

- *SETFSIZE* filespec long: Sets the specified file size.

- *SETFTIME* filespec string: Sets file time stamp.

- *TYPE* filespec: Displays the text contents of a file.

Disk File and Path System Variables

- *$DEFAULTPATH*: Returns the current contents of the default path specified with the SET DEFAULTPATH command.

- *$DISK*: Returns the current disk drive; 1 indicates drive A, 2 indicates drive B, and so on.

- *$FATTR*: The attribute characters of the last file found by a FINDFIRST or FINDNEXT command.

- *$FDATE*: Returns the creation date of the last file found by a FINDFIRST or FINDNEXT command in the format mm/dd/yy. A string value.

- *$FEXT*: Returns the extension of the last file found by a FINDFIRST or FINDNEXT command.

- *$FILENAME*: The full file name of the last file found by a FINDFIRST or FINDNEXT command.

- *$FLTIME*: Returns the long time date value of last file found by a FINDFIRST or FINDNEXT command.

- *$FNAME*: The file name without extension of the last file returned by a FINDFIRST or FINDNEXT command.

- *$FSIZE*: Returns a long value indicating the size of the last file returned by a FINDFIRST or FINDNEXT command.

- *$FTIME*: Returns a string in the format HH:MM:SS, indicating the creation time for the last file found by a FINDFIRST or FINDNEXT command.

- *$PATHNAME*: Returns the current directory path.

Execution Control, Branching, and Looping Commands

The Windows ASPECT execution control, branching, and looping commands enable you to control the sequence in which script commands are executed. Without these commands, scripts execute from top to bottom, just as you read a printed page. You can use these branching commands to cause script execution to branch to another line in the script, to cause script execution to perform commands in another portion of the script and return, or to run another Windows ASPECT script. Looping commands allow portions of the script to be repeated until a condition is satisfied.

Conditional, FOR

- *FOR* numvar[=expression] UPTO | DOWNTO number [BY number]: Executes a statement or series of statements a given number of times.

- *ENDFOR*: Ends a FOR statement group.

- *EXITFOR*: Passes execution to the statement following the ENDFOR.

- *LOOPFOR*: When encountered within a FOR loop will increment or decrement the control variable and continue execution following the FOR statement.

Conditional, IF

- *IF* condition: Executes a command or series of commands if a condition is met.

- *ELSEIF* condition: Used within an IF statement group to test another condition to execute a different set of commands if the condition is met.

- *ELSE*: Used following an IF or ELSEIF to group commands to be executed if the condition is not met.

- *ENDIF*: Ends an IF statement group.

Conditional, SWITCH

- *SWITCH* string | integer: Enables a variable to be tested and different code segments executed based on the value of the variable.

- *CASE* string | integer: Marks the beginning of a code segment to execute if the value of the variable matches the CASE value.

- *ENDCASE*: Ends a CASE statement group.

- *ENDSWITCH*: Ends a SWITCH statement group.

- *DEFAULT*: Marks the beginning of a code segment to execute if the value of the variable does not match any of the CASE values.

- *EXITSWITCH*: Transfers control to the statement following the ENDSWITCH.

Conditional, WHILE

- *WHILE* condition: Executes a statement or group of statements while a condition is true.

- *ENDWHILE*: Ends a WHILE statement group.

- *EXITWHILE*: Transfers control to the statement following the ENDWHILE.

- *LOOPWHILE*: Jumps to the conditional test specified in the WHILE command.

Unconditional

- *CALL* name [with data...]: Passes control to another procedure, returns, and executes next command following the CALL.

- *CHAIN* filespec: Executes another Windows ASPECT script with no return.

- *EXECUTE*: Passes control to another script, returns, and executes next command following the EXECUTE.

- *GOTO* name: An unconditional jump in program flow to a label within the current procedure.

- *LONGJMP* index integer: Returns control to a previously marked SETJMP location.

- *RETURN* [string | expression]: Returns execution control to the calling procedure at the statement immediately following the CALL statement.

- *SETJMP* index intvar: Creates a location to be used with LONGJMP.

Execution Control System Variable

- *$EXITCODE*: Contains the return code of an EXIT command after returning to the parent from a child script.

File Input/Output Commands

These Windows ASPECT commands enable you to control and to read and write data in disk files. Commands are available to read and write strings, binary data, lines of text, and any variable type.

- *FCLEAR* index: Clears end-of-file and error flags for the input file.

- *FCLOSE* index: Closes a file. See the example in FOPEN.

- *FEOF* index intvar: Tests for end-of-file condition.

- *FERROR* index intvar: Tests to see whether the last disk operation created an error condition.

- *FFLUSH* index: Writes the current contents of the I/O buffer to an output file.

- *FGETC* index intvar: Reads a character from the input file and assigns it to an integer variable.

- *FGETF* index floatvar: Reads a float from the input file and assigns it to a float variable.

- *FGETI* index intvar: Reads an integer from the input file and assigns it to an integer variable.

- *FGETL* index longvar: Reads a long from the input file and assigns it to a long variable.

- *FGETS* index strvar: Reads a string from the input file and assigns it to a string variable.

- *FOPEN* index filespec read | write | r/w | create [text]: Opens a file.

- *FPUTC* index character: Writes character to output file.

- *FPUTF* index float: Writes a float value to output file.

- *FPUTI* index integer: Writes an integer value to output file.

- *FPUTL* index long: Writes a long value to output file.

- *FPUTS* index string: Writes a string to output file.

- *FREAD* index strvar length intvar: Reads a block of data from the input file and assigns it to a string variable.

- *FSEEK* index long integer: Repositions file pointer.

- *FSTRFMT* index formatstr [data]...: Writes formatted string to output file.

- *FTELL* index longvar: Returns file pointer position.

- *FWRITE* index string length: Writes block of data from a string to an output file.

- *REWIND* index: Places file pointer at beginning of file.

File Transfer Commands

The Windows ASPECT file transfer commands are used to start file transfers and select file transfer options from within a script. See also WHEN FILEXFER.

- *GETFILE* protocol | string | default [filespec]: Initiates specified protocol to retrieve a file from a remote computer.

- *SENDFILE* protocol | string | default [filespec]: Initiates a file sent to a remote computer.

- *XFERCANCEL*: Cancels any protocol file transfer in progress.

File Transfer SET/FETCH Commands

- *ABORTDNLD* KEEP | DELETE: Specifies whether incomplete and aborted downloads will be deleted or saved.

- *ASCII BLANKEXPAND* OFF | ON: Controls expansion of blank lines during ASCII uploads.

- *ASCII CHARPACE* integer: Sets the character pacing in milliseconds (valid values range from 0 to 999).

- *ASCII DNLD_CR* STRIP | CR_LF | CR: Controls translation of incoming carriage returns during ASCII downloads.

- *ASCII DNLD_ECHO* OFF | ON: Controls whether characters will be displayed during ASCII uploads.

- *ASCII DNLD_LF* STRIP | CR_LF | LF: Controls translation of during ASCII downloads.

- *ASCII DNLD_TIMEOUT* integer: Sets the time-out delay in seconds between characters for ASCII downloads.

- *ASCII LINEPACE* integer: Sets the time in 1/10 seconds PROCOMM PLUS for Windows waits between lines during an ASCII upload.

- *ASCII PACECHAR* character: Sets the pace character used during an ASCII upload.

- *ASCII STRIPBIT8* OFF | ON: Strips the 8th bit from each character sent or received during an ASCII file transfer.

- *ASCII TABEXPAND* OFF | ON: Determines whether tab characters will be converted to eight spaces during ASCII uploads.

- *ASCII UPLD_CR* STRIP | CR_LF | CR: Determines whether carriage returns are stripped or appended with a line feed in ASCII uploads.

- *ASCII UPLD_ECHO* OFF | ON: Controls whether characters will be displayed during ASCII uploads.

- *ASCII UPLD_LF* STRIP | CR_LF | LF: Determines whether line feeds are stripped or a carriage return is added in ASCII uploads.

- *ASCII USEPACECHAR* NO | YES: Controls whether PROCOMM PLUS for Windows will use the pace character method of flow control during ASCII uploads.

- *DUPDNLDFILE* RENAME | OVERWRITE: Determines whether a duplicate file will be overwritten or renamed during a download. This value affects all protocols except ZMODEM and CIS-B+.

■ *KERMIT BIT8QUOTE* character: Selects the 8th bit quote character. Valid values range from 33 to 126.

■ *KERMIT BLOCKCHECK* 1 | 2 | 3: Selects the block check type, where 1 is a 1-byte checksum, 2 is a 2-byte checksum, and 3 is a 3-byte CRC.

■ *KERMIT EOLCHAR* character: Selects the Kermit end-of-line character. Valid values range from 0 to 127.

■ *KERMIT FILETYPE* TEXT | BINARY: Selects the Kermit transfer file type. FETCH returns a 0 for TEXT and a 1 for BINARY.

■ *KERMIT HANDSHAKE* character: Selects the Kermit handshake character. Valid values range from 0 to 31.

■ *KERMIT PACKETSIZE* integer: Sets the Kermit maximum packet size. Valid values range from 20 to 1024.

■ *KERMIT PADCHAR* character: Selects the pad character. Valid values range from 0 to 127.

■ *KERMIT PADNUM* integer: Sets the number of pad characters. Valid values range from 0 to 127.

■ *KERMIT QUOTECHAR* character: Sets the Kermit control quote character. Valid values range from 32 to 127.

■ *KERMIT STARTCHAR* character: Specifies the Kermit block start character. Valid values range from 0 to 127.

■ *RAWASCII CHARPACE* integer: Sets the character pacing in milliseconds. Valid values range from 0 to 999.

■ *RAWASCII DNLD_ECHO* OFF | ON: Controls whether characters will be displayed during RAW ASCII uploads.

■ *RAWASCII DNLD_TIMEOUT* integer: Sets the time-out delay for RAW ASCII downloads The value can range from 0 to 99 seconds between received characters.

■ *RAWASCII LINEPACE* integer: Sets the time in 1/10 seconds PROCOMM PLUS for Windows waits between lines during a RAW ASCII upload.

■ *RAWASCII PACECHAR* character: Sets the pace character used during RAW ASCII uploads.

■ *RAWASCII UPLD_ECHO* OFF | ON: Controls whether characters will be displayed during RAW ASCII uploads.

■ *RAWASCII USEPACECHAR* NO | YES: Controls whether PROCOMM PLUS for Windows will use the pace character method of flow control during RAW ASCII uploads.

■ *RELAXED* OFF | ON: Relaxes the amount of time PROCOMM PLUS for Windows will wait for a block before timing out during an XMODEM-family file transfer.

■ *ZMODEM EOLCONVERT* ON | OFF: Controls whether the receiving end of a ZMODEM transfer should convert the end-of-line characters within a file to "native" mode.

■ *ZMODEM ERRDETECT* CRC16 | CRC32: Selects ZMODEM 16-bit or 32-bit CRC error detection.

■ *ZMODEM RECVCRASH* ON | OVERWRITE | NEGOTIATE | PROTECT: Determines ZMODEM crash recovery action for received files.

■ *ZMODEM SENDCRASH* ON | ONVERIFY | OVERWRITE | NEGOTIATE | PROTECT: Determines ZMODEM crash recovery action for files being sent to another computer.

■ *ZMODEM TIMESTAMP* OFF | ON: Sets ZMODEM time/date stamping ON or OFF.

■ *ZMODEM TXMETHOD* STREAMING | 2KWINDOW | 4KWINDOW: Selects ZMODEM window/streaming transmission method.

File Transfer System Variable

■ *$FILEXFER*: Returns the status of the current file transfer.

  0   No file transfer in progress

  1   File transfer in progress

  2   File transfer completed successfully

  3   File transfer aborted

General Operation Commands

These Windows ASPECT commands control the appearance of PROCOMM PLUS for Windows and define defaults used by the program.

■ *ACTIONBAR* OFF | ON: Controls the display of the Action Bar.

■ *ALARM* [integer]: Sounds an alarm for the default or a specified time period.

■ *BEEP*: Sounds the Windows default beep sound.

■ *CAPTURE* OFF | ON: Controls capturing of keyboard and com port data to a disk file.

- *CAPTURESTR* string: Writes the specified string to the capture file.
- *CLEAR*: Clears the terminal screen.
- *DIALDIR* OFF | ON: Controls the display of the Dialing Directory.
- *DISABLE* CTRL | MENU | PWMENU start_id [end_id]: Enables and disables PROCOMM PLUS for Windows menu items and Windows ASPECT dialog box and menu controls.
- *HELP* [integer]: Displays the Windows Help program with the specified topic.
- *KERMSERVE* {GET | SEND filespec} | FINISH | LOGOUT: Issues the specified Kermit server command.
- *KEYFLUSH*: Flushes or clears all keys in the keyboard buffer.
- *KEYGET* [intvar]: Reads a key from the keyboard buffer and optionally stores it in an integer variable.
- *KEYSTATE* integer intvar: Tests to see if a key corresponding to a virtual key code is currently pressed.
- *LOCATE* row column: Positions the cursor at a specific location on the terminal screen.
- *METAKEY* ALT | ALTSH | ALTCT | ALTCTSH int: The script equivalent of selecting a meta key.
- *METAKEYS* ON | OFF: Controls the display of the meta keys.
- *MONITORMODE* OFF | ON: Controls the display of the Monitor window.
- *PLAYBACK* OFF | filespec: Controls the playback of capture files.
- *SB.SAVE* CLIPBOARD | CAPTURE | {FILE filespec} | PRINTER: Writes the Scrollback Buffer to the specified destination.
- *SETUP* OFF | ON: Controls the display of the Current Setup window.
- *SNAPSHOT* CLIPBOARD | CAPTURE | {FILE filespec} | PRINTER: Writes the current screen to the specified location.
- *STATCLEAR*: Clears the Status Message Line.
- *STATMSG* formatstr [arglist] [BEEP]: Displays the specified text in the Status Message Line.
- *USERMSG* formatstr [arglist]: Displays a message box with the information icon.

General Operation SET/FETCH Commands

■ *ALARM* OFF | ON: Enables and disables the alarm sound.

■ *ALARMTIME* integer: Specifies the number of seconds the alarm will sound when activated.

■ *AUTODNLD* OFF | ON: Enables and disables auto-downloading for ZMODEM and Kermit file transfers.

■ *CAPTURE AUTOSTART* OFF | ON: Specifies whether PROCOMM PLUS for Windows will open the Capture file automatically while you're connected and close it automatically as you disconnect.

■ *CAPTURE FILE* filename | NONE | CURRENT: Specifies the default name for the capture file. Maximum length for the name of the file is 12 characters.

■ *CAPTURE MODE* {APPEND | CREATE} {RAW | FILTERED | VISUAL}: Determines whether data is captured to a new file or appended to an existing Capture file and how to handle emulation escape sequences.

■ *CAPTURE PATH* pathname: Specifies default path and directory for capture files.

■ *CAPTURE QUERY* OFF | ON: Specifies whether PROCOMM PLUS for Windows displays a dialog box prompting the user for a file name when the Capture file is enabled.

■ *CONNECTION LOGGING* OFF | ON: Controls whether PROCOMM PLUS for Windows will keep a record of each completed call.

■ *CONNECTION PORT* port | index | string | NONE: Specifies the com port to use, COM1 through COM4.

■ *CONNECTION STATMSG* OFF | ON: Determines whether PROCOMM PLUS for Windows will record all Terminal window status messages in the connection log.

■ *CONNECTION TYPE* index | string [DEFAULT]: Specifies a direct or modem connection.

■ *DNLDPATH* pathname: Specifies the path name where PROCOMM PLUS for Windows will save received files unless otherwise specified.

■ *EDITOR* filespec: Specifies the text editor to use with the Windows ASPECT Compile/Edit dialog.

- *MOUSEDBLCLK* WORD | CHARACTER: Specifies whether a single character or a whole word is sent when the user double-clicks a word on the terminal screen.

- *MOUSESENDCR* OFF | ON: Determines whether a carriage return will be added to the word or character when the user double-clicks in the Terminal window.

- *NOTESFILE* filename | NONE | CURRENT: Specifies a NOTES file for current setup.

- *PAUSECHAR* integer: Identifies the character PROCOMM PLUS for Windows translates into a half-second pause when sending characters to the modem.

- *UPLDPATH* pathname: Specifies the default path name where PROCOMM PLUS for Windows will look for files to send.

- *VIEWGIF* NO | YES: Determines whether the GIF viewer will display when GIF graphics are downloaded.

General Operation Global Variables

- *$ACTIONBAR*: Returns TRUE (1) if the Action Bar is displayed and FALSE (0) if it is hidden.

- *$DIALDIR*: Returns TRUE (1) if the Dialing Directory is displayed and FALSE (0) if it's hidden.

- *FAILURE*: Indicates if the last testable ASPECT operation was not successful.

- *FOUND*: Denotes that a matching file name has been found by a FINDFIRST or FINDNEXT statement or to indicate a match by a STRFIND statement.

- *$KEYHIT*: Returns the number of keys available in the keyboard buffer.

- *$LASTMSG*: Returns the current status line message.

- *$METAKEYS*: Returns TRUE (1) if the meta keys are displayed and FALSE (0) if they're hidden.

- *$MONITORMODE*: Returns TRUE (1) if the Monitor Mode is displayed and FALSE (0) if it's hidden.

- *$PWVER*: Returns a string giving the version number of PROCOMM PLUS for Windows.

- *$SERIALNUM*: Returns a string giving the serial number of this copy of PROCOMM PLUS for Windows.

- *$SETUP*: Returns TRUE (1) if the Setup window is displayed and FALSE (0) if it's hidden.

- *SUCCESS*: Indicates whether the last testable ASPECT operation completed successfully.

- *$TIME*: The current system time in the format HH:MM:SSAM or HH:MM:SSPM.

- *$TIME24*: The current system time in 24-hour format HH:MM:SS.

- *$USERNAME*: The name of the registered user of this copy of PROCOMM PLUS for Windows.

Math Commands

Occasionally, you want a script to manipulate numeric values. You may want the script to count the number of messages that it downloads from an electronic mail system, for example. PROCOMM PLUS for Windows provides the following Windows ASPECT commands that perform operations such as add, subtract, multiply, divide, increment, and decrement numeric values.

- *ADD* number number numvar: Adds two numbers.

- *AND* number number numvar: Performs bitwise comparison between two numbers.

- *ANDL* number number numvar: Performs logical AND comparison of two numbers.

- *CEIL* float numvar: Computes smallest integer value greater than or equal to a floating point number.

- *COMP* number numvar: Performs bitwise complement of number.

- *DEC* numvar: Decrements number by one.

- *DIV* number number numvar: Divides one number by another.

- *EQ* number number numvar: Tests two numbers for equality.

- *FLOOR* float numvar: Computes the largest integer value less than or equal to a floating point number.

- *GE* number number numvar: Performs greater-than or equal-to comparisons.

- *GT* number number numvar: Performs greater than comparisons.

- *INC* numvar: Increments a number by one.

- *INIT* numvar number: Sets the value of a numeric variable.

- *LE* number number numvar: Performs less-than or equal-to comparisons.

- *LT* number number numvar: Performs less-than comparisons.

- *MOD* number number numvar: Returns MOD value (remainder after division).

- *MUL* number number numvar: Multiplies two numbers.

- *NEG* number numvar: Negates a number.

- *NEQ* number number numvar: Performs not-equal-to comparisons.

- *NOT* number numvar: Performs logical NOT operations.

- *OR* number number numvar: Performs bitwise comparison of two values.

- *ORL* number number numvar: Performs logical OR comparisons.

- *SHL* number number numvar: Performs left-shift operations.

- *SHR* number number numvar: Performs right-shift operations.

- *SUB* number number numvar: Subtracts one number from another number.

- *XOR* number number numvar: Performs bitwise comparison of two numbers.

- *ZERO* number numvar: Compares a number with zero.

 NOTE   Many of the math commands have operator forms. A listing of the operator equivalents can be found in Appendix C of the *PROCOMM PLUS for Windows Windows ASPECT Script Language Reference Manual*.

Menu Commands

These commands are used to change the PROCOMM PLUS for Windows menu bar. The existing menu bar can be modified, or a totally new menu bar can be created.

■ *MENUBAR* intvar: Creates a new PROCOMM PLUS for Windows menu bar and returns an identifier for adding popups and items.

■ *MENUITEM* integer {integer string} | SEPARATOR: Adds a menu item to a popup or a menu bar.

■ *MENUPOPUP* integer string intvar: Adds a popup to the menu bar or to another popup.

■ *SHOWMENU* integer: Displays the menu bar with the specified ID.

Menu System Variables

■ *$MENU*: The ID of the last command selected by the user from a Windows ASPECT menu.

■ *$PWMENUBAR*: Contains the ID of the current PROCOMM PLUS for Windows menu bar.

Modem Commands

This group of modem SET/FETCH commands can be used to set up the command strings PROCOMM PLUS for Windows uses to control your modem. Normally these strings come from the WMODEMS.DAT file and are loaded when you install a modem.

Modem SET/FETCH Commands

■ *MODEM AUTOANSOFF* string: Contains the modem string to disable auto answer operation. Maximum length for this field is 24 characters.

■ *MODEM AUTOANSON* string: Contains the modem string to enable auto answer operation. Maximum length for this field is 24 characters.

■ *MODEM AUTOBAUD* OFF | ON: Sets auto baud detection ON or OFF.

■ *MODEM BAUDRATE* OFF | ON [long]: Selects a particular baud rate for an on-line connection. Valid values are 110, 300, 600, 1200, 2400, 4800, 9600, 19200, 38400, 57600, and 115200.

■ *MODEM CNCTLOCKED* string: Contains the message sent by the modem for a "locked" baud rate connection.

■ *MODEM CNCTXXXX* string: Contains the message sent by the modem for baud rate connections 300 through 57600 baud. Maximum length for each field is 15 characters. A modem connection string exists for 300, 1200, 2400, 4800, 9600, 19200, 38400, and 57600 bauds.

■ *MODEM DIALCMND* string: Contains the modem dialing command string.

■ *MODEM DIALSUFFIX* string: Contains the modem dialing command suffix string.

■ *MODEM HANGUP* string: Contains the hang-up command string.

■ *MODEM HARDFLOW* OFF | ON: Specifies whether PROCOMM PLUS for Windows will use hardware flow control to pace the flow of data between your PC and modem.

■ *MODEM INIT* String: Contains the modem initialization string.

■ *MODEM NOCNCT1, NOCNCT2, NOCNCT3, NOCNCT4, NOCNCT5* string: Strings sent by the modem indicating that no connection has been established with the system being called.

Operating System Hardware and Memory Commands

These commands are used to obtain information about the operating system, to run other programs, and to execute DOS commands.

■ *DATE* strvar: Returns the system date in the form MM/DD/YY.

■ *DOS* string [MINIMIZED | MAXIMIZED | HIDDEN] [intvar]: Executes a DOS internal or external command or runs a DOS program.

■ *GETENV* string strvar: Returns the contents of a DOS environment variable.

■ *MEMFREE* longvar: Returns the amount of Windows free memory.

■ *PUTENV* string: Sets the contents of a DOS environment variable.

■ *RUN* filespec [MINIMIZE | MAXIMIZE | HIDDEN] [intvar]: Executes any Windows or DOS external program.

■ *SHELL* [intvar]: Displays the DOS command prompt.

■ *TIME* strvar: Returns the system time in the form HH:MM:SSAM or HH:MM:SSPM.

■ *TIME24* strvar: Returns the system time in the 24-hour form HH:MM:SS.

Operating System Variables

■ *$DATE*: The current system date in the format mm/dd/yy.

■ *$LTIME*: A long value representing the number of seconds between midnight of January 1, 1970, and the current system time and date.

■ *$OS*: A string identifying the current operating system.

■ *$OSVER*: A string identifying the current operating system version.

Packet Transfer Commands

Packet transfer commands enable the script to send and receive string variables error-free. This greatly simplifies scripts that need to send small blocks of data to each other and to have the data arrive at the receiving script error-free. When a PKSEND statement is executed, PROCOMM PLUS for Windows automatically puts the string in a "packet," attaches a CRC, retries if errors occur, and notifies the script when the packet has been sent error-free. See also WHEN PKSEND and WHEN PKRECV.

■ *PKMODE* OFF | {ON txtimeout rxtimeout}: Controls PROCOMM PLUS for Windows packet mode.

■ *PKRECV* intvar strvar intvar [rxtimeout]: Puts PROCOMM PLUS for Windows in packet receive mode.

■ *PKSEND* integer string length [txtimeout]: Puts PROCOMM PLUS for Windows in packet send mode.

Packet Transfer System Variables

■ *$PKRECV*: Returns the status of a PKRECV command.

Possible values are:

0 - Packet not received or idle (default state)

1 - Packet received successfully

2 - Time-out occurred, packet not received

3 - Errors occurred, packet not received

- *$PKSEND*: Returns the status of a PKSEND command.

  Possible values are:

  0 - Packet send in progress or idle (default state)

  1 - Packet sent successfully

  2 - Time-out occurred, packet not sent

  3 - Errors occurred, packet not sent

  4 - Packet send canceled by receiver, packet not sent

Printer Commands

These commands set up the printer and define the margins, font, font size, and output characters to the printer. With these commands, output to the printer can be formatted with different fonts, font sizes, and styles to make output appear like it came from a word processing program.

- *PRINTALIGN* RIGHT | LEFT | CENTER: Specifies how the text will be aligned when sent to the printer with the PRINTCHAR and PRINTSTR statements.

- *PRINTATTR* NORMAL | {[BOLD] [ITALIC] [UNDERLINE]}: Specifies the character attributes of text sent to the printer with the PRINTCHAR, PRINTTABSTR, and PRINTSTR statements.

- *PRINTCAPTURE* OFF | ON: Controls print capturing.

- *PRINTCHAR* character: Prints a character to the open printer device.

- *PRINTER* OPEN | CLOSE | CANCEL: Controls the action of the printer device.

- *PRINTFIT* string [length]: Tests to see whether text will print on the current page.

- *PRINTFONT* font size charset: Specifies the font for characters sent to the printer.

- *PRINTMARGIN* left [right [top [bottom]]]: Sets the printer margins.

- *PRINTSELECT*: Displays the Windows printer selection dialog box.

- *PRINTSTR* string [length]: Prints a string of characters to the open printer device.

- *PRINTTABS* CLEAR | string: Sets the tabs in the open printer device for use with the PRINTTABSTR command.

■ *PRINTTABSTR* string [length]: Prints a tab-separated string using the tabs set with the PRINTTABS command.

Printer SET/FETCH Commands

■ *PRINT CHARSET* integer: Identifies the character set used for printing.

■ *PRINT DEVICE* string: The string that matches a selection from the Select Printer list defines the device to be used for printing.

■ *PRINT FONTNAME* string: The string that matches a selection from the Setup Printer Fonts defines the font to be used for printing.

■ *PRINT FONTSIZE* integer: The integer defines the size font to be used for printing.

■ *PRINT FOOTER* string: Specifies the text to print at the bottom of each page.

■ *PRINT HEADER* string: Specifies the text to print at the top of each page.

■ *PRINT MARGINS* left right top bottom: Float values that specify the margins for each printed page.

■ *PRINT ORIENTATION* PORTRAIT | LANDSCAPE: Determines the orientation of each printed page.

■ *PRINT RAW* OFF | ON: When set to ON, data is sent directly to the "open" printer without formatting, bypassing the Windows printer driver.

Script Control Commands

These commands form the basic structures of a Windows ASPECT script. Among other things, these commands are used to define procedures and functions, set breakpoints for debugging, and pause or exit the script.

■ *BREAKPOINT* formatstr [arglist]: Causes the Windows ASPECT debugging window to display if the script was compiled with the Compile For Debug option.

■ *CLOSEPW*: Halts the script and closes PROCOMM PLUS for Windows.

■ *ENDFUNC*: Denotes the end of a function procedure.

■ *ENDPROC*: Denotes the end of a procedure.

- *EXIT* [integer]: Terminates execution of the current script, and passes control back to a parent script if one exists.

- *FUNC* name datatype: Denotes the beginning of a function procedure and specifies the name and type of value to be returned.

- *HALT*: Terminates execution of the current script and any parent scripts if they exist.

- *MSPAUSE* integer: Pauses script execution for a specified number of milliseconds.

- *PAUSE* integer: Pauses script execution for a specified number of seconds.

- *PROC* name: Denotes the beginning of a procedure block.

- *SUSPEND UNTIL* timestr [datestr] hours minutes: Suspends script execution until the specified time and optional date.

Setup Commands

These commands are used to modify and obtain values for the variables stored in the PW.PRM file and for other internal variables used by PROCOMM PLUS for Windows. A "memory image" of PW.PRM is created when PROCOMM PLUS for Windows is started. The SET/FETCH commands in this group modify this memory image (unless SET DIALDIR ACCESS is in use). The changes made in memory can be saved to disk with the SAVESETUP command.

- *FETCH* param datavar: Returns the values of any SET parameter.

- *FINDITEM* {CONNECTION I PROTOCOL I TERMINAL I USERSET} name intvar: Returns an index associated with the specified named table item.

- *GETITEM* {CONNECTION I PROTOCOL I TERMINAL I USERSET} index strvar: Returns the name associated with the specified index.

- *NEWITEM* {PROTOCOL protocol I index I string} I {TERMINAL emulation I index I string} I {USERSET index I string} [intvar]: Adds a new named table item.

- *RESTSETUP*: Loads the Current Setup configuration from disk.

- *SAVESETUP*: Saves the Current Setup configuration.

- *SET* param data: Sets the specified system parameter.

Setup SET/FETCH Commands

- *DIALDIR ACCESS* OFF | index: Specifies whether SET and FETCH commands apply to the current Setup values or the Dialing Directory entry number.

- *KEYMAPFILE* filename | CURRENT: Specifies the name of the Keyboard Map file.

- *METAKEYFILE* filename | NONE | CURRENT: Specifies the name of the meta key file.

- *MISC* string: Sets the string from the Misc. String field in the Current Setup or Dialing Directory entry.

- *NOTESFILE* filename | NONE | CURRENT: Specifies the name of a Notes file for the Current Setup or Dialing Directory entry.

- *PASSWORD* string: Contains the string from the Password field in the Current Setup or Dialing Directory entry.

- *PROTOCOL* protocol | index | string: Selects a protocol for uploading and downloading.

- *TRANSLATE* filename | NONE | CURRENT: Specifies a Translate Table file to be used.

- *USERID* string: Contains the string from the User ID field in the Current Setup or Dialing Directory entry.

- *USERSET* index | string: Specifies the name or index of the User Settings entry for the Current Setup or Dialing Directory entry.

Setup System Variables

- *$MISC*: The contents of the Current Setup window Misc. String field.

- *$PASSWORD*: The contents of the Current Setup window Password field.

- *$PROTOCOL*: Returns the table index of the current protocol.

- *$USERID*: The contents of the Current Setup window User ID field.

- *$USERSET*: Returns the index number of the Current Setup window User Settings entry.

String Processing Commands

A *text string* (or *quoted string* or *string*) is a group of characters in a specific order. Communication between two computers by definition involves transfer of text strings in both directions, so Windows ASPECT provides several commands that manipulate these text strings. These commands are used to perform such operations as assigning a value to a string variable, combining text strings, comparing text strings, and extracting a portion of a string.

- *ASSIGN* strvar string [length]: Assigns a string to a string variable.

- *NULLSTR* string intvar: Tests the string for null contents (zero length).

- *RSTRCMP* string string length: Compares the contents of two raw strings up to the specified length, returns True if identical. The strings can contain values from 0 to 255.

- *STRCAT* strvar string [length]: Concatenates two strings.

- *STRCMP* string string [length]: Compares two strings, returns True if identical. Strings cannot contain nondisplayable characters.

- *STRCMPI* string string [length]: Compares two strings, returns True if identical. Strings cannot contain nondisplayable characters. The string compare is not case-sensitive.

- *STRCPY* strvar string [length]: Same as ASSIGN.

- *STRDELETE* strvar strindex length: Removes characters from within a string.

- *STREXTRACT* strvar string delimiter no: Returns a string from a list delimited by a common substring.

- *STRFIND* string string [intvar]: Tests for the occurrence of one string within another string.

- *STRFMT* strvar formatstr [data]...: Creates a formatted string using a template.

- *STRLEN* string intvar: Returns the length of a string.

- *STRLWR* strvar: Converts all characters in the string to lowercase.

- *STRPEEK* string strindex intvar: Returns integer value of a byte in a string.

- *STRPOKE* strvar strindex character: Sets a byte in a string to specified value.

- *STRQUOTE* strvar: Places the string in double quotes.

■ *STRREPLACE* strvar string [count]: Performs a "search and replace" on the string.

■ *STRRIGHT* strvar string length: Returns a specified number of characters from the right of a string.

■ *STRSEARCH* string string intvar: Searches a string for the occurrence of a substring.

■ *STRSET* strvar character length: Sets all characters in a string to a given value.

■ *STRUPDT* strvar string strindex length: Replaces characters in a string with another string.

■ *STRUPR* strvar: Converts all characters in a string to uppercase.

■ *SUBSTR* strvar string strindex length: Copies characters from one string to another, beginning at a given location.

String Processing System Variables

■ *$NULLSTR*: Returns a "null" (or empty) string.

■ *$STRCMP*: Returns a 0 if the last STRCMP or STRCMPI command resulted in both strings being identical.

Terminal Commands

The Windows ASPECT terminal emulation commands give you control over the terminal emulation options and enable you to send characters to and get characters from the screen.

■ *TERMGETC* row col intvar: Returns the ASCII value of the character at the specified location on the Terminal window.

■ *TERMGETS* row col strvar length: Returns an ASCII string beginning at the specified location on the Terminal window.

■ *TERMKEY* [kbdstate] vkey [EXTENDED]: Sends a key to the Terminal window just as if the key had been pressed.

■ *TERMRESET*: Clears the screen and resets the Terminal logic.

■ *TERMVKEY* keyval: Sends an encoded key value to the Terminal window just as if the key had been pressed.

■ *TERMWRITEC* character [RAW]: Sends a character to the Terminal window just as if the character had been received on the com port.

■ *TERMWRITES* string [RAW]: Sends a string to the Terminal window just as if the string had been received on the com port.

Terminal SET/FETCH Commands

■ *AUTOSIZE* WINDOW | FONT | OFF: Controls whether PROCOMM PLUS for Windows will automatically adjust the Terminal window based on the selected font size or will adjust the font size based on the Terminal window size.

■ *CHATMODE* BLOCK | CHARACTER: Specifies whether each character is sent as it is pressed or after a carriage return in chat mode.

■ *CLIPCHAR* character: Specifies the Clipboard file-name separator character.

■ *TERMINAL ANSI8BIT* OFF | ON: Specifies whether PROCOMM PLUS for Windows will process 8-bit ANSI Escape sequences for the VT220, VT320 terminal types.

■ *TERMINAL BACKSPACE* NONDEST | DEST: Controls whether a character will be destroyed when a backspace character is received.

■ *TERMINAL BLOCKCURSOR* OFF | ON: Specifies the type of cursor to display in the Terminal window.

■ *TERMINAL COLUMNS* 80 | 132: Controls whether PROCOMM PLUS for Windows will use an 80-column screen or a 132-column screen. Only the DEC VT family and WYSE 50 terminals support 132 columns.

■ *TERMINAL ENQUIRY* OFF | ON | CISB: Controls response to ENQ (ASCII 5).

■ *TERMINAL ENQUIRYSTR* string: Specifies the string to send when an ENQ character is received and SET TERMINAL ENQUIRY is ON.

■ *TERMINAL LINEWRAP* OFF | ON: Specifies whether PROCOMM PLUS for Windows will allow characters to extend past the right margin or wrap to the next line.

■ *TERMINAL ROWS* integer: Specifies the number of rows to be displayed within the Terminal window.

■ *TERMINAL RXCR* CR | CR_LF: Controls whether a line feed is added to a carriage return when it is received.

■ *TERMINAL SBPAGES* integer: Controls the size of the Terminal Scrollback Buffer.

- *TERMINAL SCROLL* OFF | ON: Determines whether characters or messages on the last row and column of the screen will scroll when the line wraps. This command has no effect if TERMINAL LINEWRAP is set OFF.

- *TERMINAL STATUSATTR* NORMAL | REVERSED | UNDERLINE: Determines the appearance of the Terminal status line for emulations that support it.

- *TERMINAL STATUSLINE* OFF | ON: Turns the Terminal emulation status line ON or OFF for emulations that support it.

- *TERMINAL STRIPBIT8* OFF | ON: Determines whether PROCOMM PLUS for Windows will strip the 8th (or high) bit from received data before displaying it.

- *TERMINAL TABSTOP* integer: Specifies the default tab stops for the current emulation.

- *TERMINAL TYPE* terminal | index | string: Sets the terminal emulation type.

- *TERMINAL UPDATE* INCREMENTAL | BLOCK | FAST: Determines how the terminal will display characters when they are received. INCREMENTAL displays each character as it is received. BLOCK Update displays blocks of characters. FAST Update buffers characters until a large group can be displayed at once.

- *TERMINAL VIEWCURSOR* YES | NO: Determines whether the cursor will be kept in view if the window size is smaller than logical terminal size.

Terminal System Variables

- *$COL*: The integer column cursor position within the Terminal window.

- *$ROW*: Returns the current row cursor position within the Terminal window.

- *$TERMCOLS*: Returns the number of columns supported by the current terminal (not the number of columns displaying).

- *$TERMINAL*: Returns the table index of the current terminal emulation.

- *$TERMROWS*: Returns the number of rows in the current terminal emulation (not the number of rows displaying).

User Window Commands

These commands are used to convert part or all of the PROCOMM PLUS for Windows Terminal display area into a graphics display area. The display area—called a User Window—can have a solid color, bit map, or metafile background. Graphic objects can be placed in the User Window, creating a graphic menu system. Another set of commands enables a dynamically linked library to draw in the User Window, allowing animation. See also WHEN OBJECT.

- *BITMAP* id left top label filespec BACKGROUND | USERWIN: Displays a Windows bit map in the User Window.

- *BITMAPBKG* CENTER | LEFT | RIGHT CENTER | TOP | BOTTOM MEMORY | DISK filespec: Displays a Windows bit map as a background in the User Window.

- *DEFUSERWIN* TOP | BOTTOM | LEFT | RIGHT | FULL | SCREEN | WINDOW | PIXELS int R G B BITMAP | METAFILE: Defines the size and properties of the User Window.

- *DLLOBJECT* id left top width height BACKGROUND | USERWIN: Specifies the position and size of the DLL object.

- *DLLOBJFILE* filespec: Defines a dynamically linked library (DLL) that places a DLL object in the User Window.

- *DLLOBJUPDT* id [arglist]: Calls the DLL to update the DLL object.

- *ENABLE* CTRL | MENU | PWMENU start_id [end_id]: Enables objects placed in the User Window which were previously disabled.

- *HOTSPOT* id left top width height BACKGROUND | USERWIN: Creates a hot spot that can be selected with the mouse.

- *ICONBUTTON* id left top label filespec index BACKGROUND | USERWIN: Displays an icon in the User Window. The icon can be selected like a button.

- *ICON* id left top filespec index BACKGROUND | USERWIN: Displays an icon in the User Window.

- *METAFILE* id left top width height filespec BACKGROUND | USERWIN: Displays a Windows metafile in the User Window.

- *METAFILEBKG* CENTER | LEFT | RIGHT CENTER | TOP | BOTTOM SCALE | EXACT filespec: Displays a Windows metafile as a background in the User Window.

- *MOVEOBJECT* id left top [NOPAINT]: Moves an object placed in the User Window.

- *PAINT*: Redraws the User Window.

- *PUSHBUTTON* id left top width height label BACKGROUND | USERWIN: Places a push button in the User Window.

- *REMOVE* {BACKGROUND | USERWIN} | {start_id [end_id]}: Removes a User Window object or background.

- *UWUTOWIN* intvar intvar BACKGROUND | USERWIN: Converts User Window units to Windows coordinates.

- *WINTOUWU* intvar intvar BACKGROUND | USERWIN: Converts Windows coordinates to User Window units.

User Windows Global Variables

- *$OBJECT*: Returns the ID of the last object selected in the User Window.

- *$USERWIN*: Returns the ID of the User window, FALSE (0) if it does not exist. A User window is created with the DEFUSERWIN command.

When Event Commands

When Event commands enable the script programmer to set up conditions that will call a procedure when something occurs. Although several programs may be running at the same time, Windows must be able to respond when an action needs to be taken. The When event statements enable Windows ASPECT programs to be structured in much the same way. The script may have a file transfer in progress, for example, but also may want to cancel the transfer if a key is pressed on the keyboard. The commands WHEN FILEXFER and WHEN ISKEY could be used to call procedures that would handle whichever "event" needs to be processed.

- *CLEARWHEN {TARGET index}* | *NOCARRIER* | *QUIET* | *FILEXFER* | *PKSEND* | *PKRECV* | *MENU* | *OBJECT* | *DIALOG* | *{ISKEY index}* | *ELAPSED* | *DDEADVISE* | *KEYHIT* | *RXDATA* | *USERSET* | *PKRECV* | *MOUSEEVENT*: Clears an active WHEN statement.

- *WHEN CDCHANGES* {CALL name}: Calls a procedure when the modem carrier detect status line changes.

- *WHEN DDEADVISE* {CALL name}: Calls a procedure when a DDEADVISE variable value has changed.

- *WHEN DIALOG* {CALL name}: Calls a procedure when the user has made a selection in a Windows ASPECT dialog box.

- *WHEN ELAPSED* {CALL name}: Calls a procedure when a specified period of time has elapsed.

- *WHEN FILEXFER* {CALL name}: Calls a procedure when the status of a file transfer protocol has changed.

- *WHEN ISKEY index value* {CALL name}: Calls a procedure when the specified key has been pressed on the keyboard.

- *WHEN KEYHIT* {CALL name}: Calls a procedure when a key has been pressed on the keyboard.

- *WHEN MENU* {CALL name}: Calls a procedure when the user has made a selection from a Windows ASPECT menu.

- *WHEN MOUSEEVENT* {CALL name}: Calls a procedure when the user clicks the left mouse button within the User Window.

- *WHEN OBJECT* {CALL name}: Calls a procedure when the user selects an object in the User Window.

- *WHEN PKRECV* {CALL name}: Calls a procedure when the status of a packet receive changes.

- *WHEN PKSEND* {CALL name}: Calls a procedure when the status of a packet send changes.

- *WHEN QUIET duration* {CALL name}: Calls a procedure when no characters are received over the com port for a specified time.

- *WHEN RXDATA* {CALL name}: Calls a procedure when a character is received through the com port.

- *WHEN TARGET index string* {CALL name}: Calls a procedure when characters matching a specified string are received on the com port.

- *WHEN USEREXIT* {CALL name}: Calls a procedure when the user stops the script.

Windows Commands

These commands are used to control and monitor Windows programs, control the mouse pointer, execute multimedia commands, and send keys to other Windows applications.

- *ACTIVATETASK* task: Activates the specified task.

- *ACTIVATEWIN* window | string: Activates the specified window.

- *CLOSEWIN* window: Closes the specified window.

- *DLLCALL* integer process [arglist]: Calls a process in a Windows ASPECT DLL.

- *DLLFREE* integer: Frees a Windows ASPECT DLL.

- *DLLLOAD* filename intvar: Loads a Windows ASPECT DLL.

- *EXITTASK* task: Exits the specified task.

- *EXITWINDOWS*: Exits Windows.

- *FIRSTTASK* intvar: Returns the first task in the Windows task list.

- *GETWINTEXT* window strvar: Returns the title bar text of the specified window.

- *HIDEWIN* window: Hides the specified window.

- *ISTASK* task: Used to determine whether a windows task still exists.

- *ISWINDOW* window: Used to determine whether a window still exists.

- *MAXIMIZE* window: Maximizes the specified window.

- *MCIEXEC* string: Executes a high-level Windows multimedia command.

- *MINIMIZE* window: Minimizes the specified window.

- *MOVEWIN* window left top: Moves the specified window.

- *NEXTTASK* intvar: Returns subsequent task IDs following the FIRSTTASK command.

- *PROFILERD* filespec string string strvar | intvar: Reads the specified item value from a file written with the PROFILEWR command.

- *PROFILEWR* filespec string string string | integer: Writes the specified item value to a file using the Windows INI format.

- *PWTITLEBAR* string: Specifies the text to display in the PROCOMM PLUS for Windows title bar.

- *RESTOREWIN* window: Restores the specified window.

- *SCREENTOWIN* window intvar intvar: Converts screen coordinates to application-relative coordinates.

- *SENDKEY* kbdstate vkey [EXTENDED]: Sends a key to the active window as if it had been pressed from the keyboard.

- *SENDKEYSTR* string: Sends keys to the active window as if they had been typed from the keyboard.

- *SENDVKEY* keyval: Sends an encoded key value to the active window as if it had been pressed from the keyboard.

- *SETFOCUS* integer | string: Sets the focus to the window ID or the application or window that matches the text string.

- *SETPOINTER* integer integer: Positions the mouse pointer at the specified screen coordinates.

- *SHOWWIN* window: Displays the specified window after being hidden with the HIDEWIN command.

- *SIZEWIN* window left top [width [height]]: Sizes and positions the specified window.

- *TASKNAME* integer strvar: Returns the name of the corresponding task ID.

- *TASKPATH* integer strvar: Returns the directory from which the task with the specified ID was started.

- *TASKWIN* integer intvar: Returns the window ID corresponding to the specified task ID.

- *WINCOORD* window left top [width [height]]: Returns the coordinates of the specified window.

- *WINTASK* integer intvar: Returns the task ID corresponding to the specified window ID.

- *WINTOSCREEN* integer intvar intvar: Converts application-relative coordinates to screen coordinates.

Windows Global Variables

- *$ACTIVEWIN*: Returns the integer ID of the currently active window.

- *$FOCUSWIN*: Returns the ID of the window that currently has the focus.

- *$MAINWIN*: Returns an integer ID of an application's main (top level) window.

- *$MOUSESTATE*: Returns TRUE (1) if the left mouse button is currently depressed.

- *$MOUSEX*: Contains the User Window X coordinate for the last mouse event within the User Window.

- *$MOUSEY*: Contains the User Window Y coordinate for the last mouse event within the User Window.

- *$NUMCOLORS*: The number of colors available from the current Windows display driver.

- *$NUMTASKS*: Returns the number of tasks currently running in Windows.

- *$POINTERTASK*: Returns an integer ID of the task over which the mouse pointer is currently positioned.

- *$POINTERWIN*: Returns an integer ID of the window over which the mouse pointer is currently positioned.

- *$POINTERX*: Returns an integer containing the screen X coordinate of the current mouse pointer.

- *$POINTERY*: Returns an integer containing the screen Y coordinate of the current mouse pointer.

- *$PWACTIVE*: Set to TRUE (1) if PROCOMM PLUS for Windows is active.

- *$PWMAINWIN*: Returns the integer window ID of the PROCOMM PLUS for Windows application window.

- *$PWTASK*: Returns the PROCOMM PLUS for Windows task ID that is executing this script.

- *$PWTASKPATH*: Returns the path where PROCOMM PLUS for Windows' EXE file is found.

- *$PWTITLEBAR*: Returns the PROCOMM PLUS for Windows application title bar text.

- *$TASK*: Contains the task ID of the active Windows application.

- *$TITLEBAR*: Returns the caption or title bar text of the active application.

- *$WINMODE*: The current Windows mode.

- *$WINPATH*: Returns the path name of the Windows directory.

- *$WINVER*: Returns the current Windows version number.

- *$XPIXELS*: The horizontal resolution of the current display screen in pixels.

- *$YPIXELS*: The vertical resolution of the current display screen in pixels.

Summary

In this chapter, you have written a couple of simple scripts, used the Windows ASPECT Compiler, changed some of the compiler options, and used the run-time debugger. You also have been exposed to the vast command set that makes up Windows ASPECT.

In the next chapter you take a look at some of the more advanced features of Windows ASPECT. To gain a better understanding of how to write well-designed complex scripts, you get a close look at some of the scripts included in the installation disks.

Examining Some Advanced Features of Windows ASPECT

This chapter covers the general script writing process and discusses the major components of a Windows ASPECT script. This chapter also includes a brief discussion about the differences between PROCOMM PLUS ASPECT scripts and Windows ASPECT scripts. Finally, this chapter covers several of the advanced features of Windows ASPECT, using sample scripts. The examples come from scripts found on the installation disks and sample code from the on-line Windows ASPECT help file and some that are provided here to help you understand the script writing process. We want to thank DATASTORM TECHNOLOGIES for their cooperation and permission in using this sample code.

Two of the sample scripts described also include a tutorial covering the operation of the Dialog Box editor and the User Window Builder programs. These programs, included with PROCOMM PLUS for Windows, enable you to create dialog boxes and design user windows graphically and paste the resultant Windows ASPECT commands into your scripts.

If you did not install the sample and demonstration scripts during PROCOMM PLUS for Windows initial installation, you need to do so now to follow the examples in this chapter. To install the sample scripts, run the installation program just as you did for the initial installation. At the Installation Options screen, remove all items from the Selected list except *Features demo* and *Sample scripts*, and then select Continue.

When using these installation options, the program will reinstall the WMODEMS.DAT and DEFAULT.KBD files. If you have updated either of these files since installation, temporarily rename them. Install the scripts by using the preceding procedure, and then rename the temporary files, using their original names.

Differences between PROCOMM PLUS ASPECT and Windows ASPECT

Windows ASPECT varies in several areas from PROCOMM PLUS ASPECT. The most noticeable are commands that deal with script-driven user interfaces. Commands like ATSAY and ATGET in PROCOMM PLUS ASPECT have been replaced with a whole new group of commands—the Windows ASPECT dialog box statements. A wide range of dialog box controls in Windows ASPECT are available that give the script writer a great amount of flexibility in designing the user interface.

A Windows ASPECT script also can define its own menus. The Windows ASPECT script can add menus to a standard PROCOMM PLUS for Windows menu bar or the script can create its own menu bar to completely replace it. Menu items also can be disabled and enabled under script control.

Another completely new set of statements that can greatly enhance the user interface are the User Window commands. These commands can display graphics and allow hypertext or hypergraphic menuing scripts to be developed. The script also can display high-resolution bit-map "pictures" for applications, such as a real estate program that can show a home visually rather than just describing it.

The WHEN commands have been expanded to a WHEN event group. Now 16 of these asynchronous event-driven commands reflect the multi-tasking operation of the Windows environment. These commands enable scripts to be modularized into process procedures and a main loop where the script waits until an event occurs. The WHEN command then automatically calls the process procedure to take the appropriate action. Most WHEN event commands also have a system variable which returns a value that gives additional information about the event. To send a file, for example, the script can set a WHEN FILEXFER event statement, and then issue the SENDFILE command. The script continues to run but when the status of the file transfer changes, the procedure specified in the WHEN FILEXFER statement is automatically called and the $FILEXFER system variable can be tested to determine what triggered the change.

The SET/FETCH commands and the system variables have been expanded and grouped into categories that closely match the parameters the user can set through the PROCOMM PLUS for Windows dialog boxes. Almost every internal variable PROCOMM PLUS for Windows uses during operation is available and can be set from within a script.

From a communications standpoint, a set of high-level commands have been added to Windows ASPECT that enable the script to transmit an error-free block of data to another script. These packet send and receive commands can be used for anything from transferring files to indicating chess moves in an on-line game.

Other areas of improvement in Windows ASPECT include additional string processing commands, user-defined functions, simplified call statements, and a more consistent use of syntax.

Converting ASPECT to Windows ASPECT scripts could be a relatively simple job if the scripts are simple login scripts that don't have any user interface commands. Complex scripts that use the PROCOMM PLUS ASPECT user interface statements may take considerable time to convert. Consideration also should be given to restructuring the script to take advantage of the new event-driven procedures. Chapter 6 of the Windows ASPECT manual thoroughly address the differences in the command set and make recommendations for commands that have been eliminated.

Learning the Script Writing Process

Each ASPECT script contains identifiable sections: definitions, the main procedure, called procedures, and called functions (see fig. 12.1). The main procedure is the only required section. Global variables can occur anywhere outside a procedure but usually are put at the beginning of the script. Another part of any script that may appear anywhere are comments. As mentioned in Chapter 11, scripts also can run other scripts. When scripts run other scripts, the execution can return to the parent, in the case of a spawn, or not return to the parent, in the case of a chain.

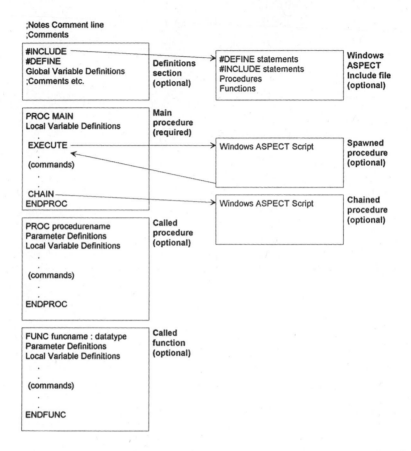

FIG. 12.1

General outline for
ASPECT scripts.

Creating a Definitions Section in a Windows ASPECT Script

The definitions section that appears first in the script defines macro
names. The #DEFINE command is used to define the macro names and
their values. Examples of this command are found in the following lines
of the file PCBOARD.WAS:

```
#define FIRSTNAME "First name"
#define LASTNAME  "Last name"
#define PASS  "password"
#define DIALN  "The specific board which you wish to call"
```

After you make these definitions, any use of the macro name is given the value that you specified in the define statement. For example, the command

    transmit FIRSTNAME

transmits the value of the macro named FIRSTNAME, or as shown in this example, First name.

The scripts PCBOARD.WAS, RA.WAS, TBBS.WAS, and WILDCAT.WAS (included with PROCOMM PLUS for Windows) are generic login scripts for the indicated bulletin board systems. These scripts use the #DEFINE command to create macros for the information required during the login process. Before you use the scripts, you must create a dialing directory entry for each bulletin board you intend to call. You then need to edit the #DEFINE statements in each script to include your name, password, and the name of the dialing directory entry. The scripts are designed to be used with an unmodified login procedure. If the SYSOP has changed the login procedure for the bulletin board, you need to modify the script to match the changes.

You can make declarations of global variables anywhere in a script outside a procedure. Generally, however, variables are placed at the beginning of a script. The four variable types recognized by ASPECT are *float*, *long*, *string*, and *integer*. You can define up to 128 of each type of global variable, adding to a total of 512 variables. Global variables are accessible within any procedure. If you change the value of a global variable within a procedure, the value is changed for all future references in any procedures. If these statements are used to define a variable within a procedure, they are considered to be *local* and are valid only within that procedure. Definitions of the four variable types follow:

- *float*. A floating point variable that can range in value from approximately $2.225e^{-308}$ to $1.797e^{+308}$.

- *long*. A long integer that can range in value from –2,147,483,648 to 2,147,483,647.

- *integer*. An integer that can range in value from –32,768 to 32,767.

- *string*. A string variable that can be up to 256 characters in length.

Examples of global variable declarations are found in the following lines of the file README.WAS:

```
string readme,icofile

integer done=0,icoindex,dlgsize=0
```

The first example defines two string variables. The second example defines three integer variables and initializes the value of done and dlgsize to zero.

ASPECT also contains a number of predefined string, long, float, and integer variables. If you use these variables, you do not need to define them at the beginning of your script or within any procedure. The predefined string variables are named S0 to S9, the predefined integer variables are named I0 to I9, the predefined long variables are named L0 to L9, and the predefined float variables are named F0 to F9. The predefined variables hold their values even when spawning and chaining scripts so that they can be used to pass variables from one script to another. After you have defined your variables, the next section of your script is the main procedure.

Creating a Main Procedure Section in a Windows ASPECT Script

Every script must have a main procedure. The main procedure begins with a PROC MAIN command and ends with an ENDPROC command. When an ASPECT script is executed, the main procedure is the starting point. Within the main procedure, you may define variables similar to how you defined global variables in the preceding section. Variables defined within a procedure, however, are local to the procedure. If a local variable is changed within a procedure, its value is not made available to other procedures unless it passes to another procedure by a call statement. You can have two variables with identical names in two separate procedures, and they will each have their own unique value.

You may examine the main procedure in any of the WAS files on disk. For many applications, all the programming can be performed in the main procedure. In the file PCBOARD.WAS, for example, except for the macro declarations outside the main procedure, the entire program is simply the execution of commands in the main procedure, beginning with the first command (WHILE $TXCOUNT) to the last (ENDIF).

In contrast, the main procedure in the file README.WAS consists of only a few lines. Its function is to initialize the global variables and call the procedure *display_files*. The call command relates to the third major section in an ASPECT script, the called procedures.

Creating Called Procedures in a Windows ASPECT Script

When an ASPECT script becomes complicated or performs some repetitious function, programmers often break the script into a main procedure and several called procedures. A *called procedure* is like a small program within the script; it begins with a PROC command and ends with ENDPROC. The first called procedure in the file README.WAS, for example, contains only six lines:

```
proc display_files
    dodlg()
    when dialog call action
    while not done
    endwhile
endproc
```

This procedure calls another procedure dodlg, sets up a WHEN event process, and waits in a WHILE loop until the variable done indicates the user is finished. Within the main procedure, you find the statement

```
display_files()
```

You will notice that this statement and the dodlg() call do not use the classic CALL DISPLAY_FILES statement construction. Windows ASPECT also supports a simplified calling convention that uses only the procedure name followed with parentheses. This call tells Windows ASPECT to perform the function within the called procedure and then resume executing the script at the next command after the call statement.

You can call a procedure three different ways. The first, as in the preceding example, is simply to call the procedure by using the procedure name. In this case, no information is passed between the calling procedure and the called procedure. The second method of calling involves passing information to the called procedure. If the preceding call wanted to pass a file name to the display_files procedure, the statement might look like this:

```
call display_files with filename
```

or using the simplified call:

```
display_files (filename)
```

In this call, the value of the string filename is passed to the procedure called display_files. This type of a call is termed a call *by value*. In this case, if the passed value is changed in the called procedure, it is *not* changed in the calling procedure. If the call had been

```
display_files (&filename)
```

this would be a *call by reference*. In this case, if the value of the passed variable is changed in the called procedure, it also is changed after returning to the calling procedure. The called procedure must "reserve space" for the values passed to it. This is accomplished by using the parameter variable definition statements *strparm*, *intparm*, *longparm*, and *floatparm*, based on the type of variable passed. The first two lines of the called procedure might look like this:

```
proc display_files
strparm filename
```

In this case, the variables in the calling and the called procedure use the same name. Because they are local variables (defined only within the procedures), however, they can have different names. If the call passes more than one variable, the parameter variable statements in the called procedure must be defined in the same sequence and of the proper variable type.

For example, the call

```
display_files (filename, filesize)
```

would require the called procedure to declare the parameter variables something like this:

```
proc display_files
strparm filename
longparm filesize
```

Creating a Function in a Windows ASPECT Script

PROCOMM PLUS for Windows also supports user-defined function calls. Functions and procedures are similar in that they are self-contained segments of code. The difference is that a function begins with the statement FUNC *funcname : datatype* and ends with the ENDFUNC statement. Notice that the FUNC command in addition to the function name includes a colon (:) followed by *datatype*. The datatype argument specifies the type of variable that will be returned by the function. A function might operate on system variables, global variables, or values passed to it through the call statement, and then return a value.

The following program, for example, uses the function *getword* to return a word based on its position in the sentence and display the word in a message box.

```
proc main
integer wordnum
string outword, strwordnum
string sentence = "Will this ever be finished?"
    sdlginput "Sample" "Which word to return?" strwordnum
```

```
    atoi strwordnum wordnum;string to integer
    wordnum --;decrement wordnum
    outword = getword (wordnum sentence);call function
    usermsg "The selected word was [%S]" outword
endproc

func getword : string
intparm numberword   ;parameter variables defined in same
strparm sentence     ;sequence as they are called
string returnword
    strextract returnword sentence " " numberword
    return returnword
endfunc
```

The outword = getword statement calls the function getword and passes it the arguments in parentheses, wordnum and sentence, and assigns the function value to outword upon return. The INTPARM statements in the function must be declared in the same sequence as they appear on the calling statement just as with parameter declaration statements in procedures. The variable wordnum is decremented by one using the -- operator because the function is "0 based"; in other words, the first word in the sentence is the zeroth word instead of the first.

Functions may be used in statements anywhere a constant value can be used. Functions cannot, however, be used as arguments in Windows ASPECT commands or as arguments to other procedures or functions. Functions can be extremely useful for repetitive operations in scripts where the same type of operation must be performed on variables of different values.

Windows ASPECT Include File

Windows ASPECT also supports a C-like include file. The include file can contain #DEFINE macros, procedures, and functions creating a library of commonly used items. To specify the file, the #INCLUDE command can be inserted anywhere in the script. When any macro or call appears in the source script contained in the file, the compiler will "include" the macro, procedure, or function in the resulting WAX file. The include file also can #INCLUDE other files with no limit to the number of included files. The Windows ASPECT compiler will add only the called or defined sections of the include file to the compiled script, resulting in a WAX file no larger than if the statements had been in the original script. One limitation of include files is that they cannot contain a PROC MAIN declaration.

Chaining and Spawning in a Windows ASPECT Script

Windows ASPECT, as mentioned in Chapter 11, provides two methods for running another script from within a script. The first method uses the CHAIN command in a "parent" script to execute a "child" script. Using this technique, all processing in the parent script should be complete because execution control will not return to it.

The second method uses the EXECUTE command to spawn the second script. When this occurs, PROCOMM PLUS for Windows stores the state of the parent script in a temporary data area. When the spawned script finishes from an EXIT command or the ENDPROC of the main procedure, the status of the parent will be restored and script execution will resume at the statement following the CALL statement. Information that is restored upon return to the parent includes all user-defined global variables, active WHEN commands, all open files, and all active SETJMP/ LONGJMP commands.

When a script is spawned or chained, any existing Windows ASPECT dialog boxes are destroyed and any client DDE statements are terminated. The spawned or chained script inherits the values of the system variables, the SET/FETCH values, the global variables, a User Window and its objects, and any Windows ASPECT menus as well as their status. If a parent script has created and displayed a new menu bar, for example, the child script should be able to process any menu selections made.

Designing a Windows ASPECT Script

Using the block diagram shown earlier in figure 12.1, you can design a Windows ASPECT script. Before actually writing any commands, you should outline your script. You may use the following steps in the process:

1. Decide if this script will be short enough to be contained in the main procedure, or if it can be modularized into a main procedure and one or more called procedures. If the script is extremely large, consider breaking it into separate scripts by using the chain or execute commands.

2. Decide if you need to define any global macros. Determine if you need to declare or initialize any variables.

3. If your main procedure will contain the entire program, create a step-by-step outline of the tasks you need to accomplish.

4. If your main procedure will call other procedures, decide on the function of each called procedure. What variables, if any, need to be passed to each procedure? Will they be passed by value or by reference or should they be defined as global variables?

5. Determine how you will exit the script. When the script is exited, should it do any "housekeeping" such as closing or deleting temporary files?

After you outline the script (you can do this on paper or in an editor), the next step is to begin substituting one or more commands for each task in the outline. On your first pass, you do not need to write every command syntactically correct. Many programmers write what is called a *pseudocode*—a script that contains ASPECT commands that are not yet fully "fleshed out." You may decide, for example, to play a sound, although you do not remember the exact syntax of the command. During this pass you may type the following:

    sound the system exclamation sound

After you write your pseudocode, go back and, using the *Windows AS-PECT Script Language Reference Manual*, correct any command syntax. On this pass, the sound command would become the following:

    mciexec "sound c:\windows\chord.wav"

After you write all commands into your script, attempt a compile using the Windows ASPECT compiler as described in Chapter 11. Unless you are a whiz at programming, you will receive error messages during the compile. Begin correcting the errors. When you can compile the program without errors, begin testing the program.

Testing the program should include a rigorous exercise that tests all of the programs options under as many conditions you can devise. Often, you will find logic errors that did not show up during compilation. Using the methods described in "Compiling a Script" in Chapter 11, work through the logic problems until you correct them. If you have time, test the program several days in a row, because a good night's sleep often gives you some insight into how a problem could be solved better. Be convinced that the script is working correctly before you make it available to other users.

Looking at Examples of Windows ASPECT Scripts

This part of the chapter takes an in depth look at several Windows AS-PECT scripts distributed with PROCOMM PLUS for Windows. We want to thank DATASTORM TECHNOLOGIES for their assistance and permission to use the scripts README.WAS, LOGIN.WAS, PKSEND.WAS, and PDRECV.WAS as shown in these examples. The scripts MENU.WAS and USERWIN.WAS as listed in the book are not part of the PROCOMM PLUS for Windows samples. The last two descriptions, USERWIN.WAS and LOGIN.WAS, take advantage of the User Window Builder and the Dialog Editor to help in writing the scripts. These are utility programs that come with PROCOMM PLUS for Windows.

In the following sections, the operation of each script is described briefly and a list of Windows ASPECT statements introduced in the sample are listed. The remainder of the description includes the listing of the program interspersed with comments describing the commands, how they are used, and the logic of the script.

Run each of these scripts before and as you read the explanation to help you follow the logic of the source code. For the samples that are included on the installation disks, you can view the complete listing in your text editor or print the file to follow the examples.

README.WAS

This script uses a Windows ASPECT dialog box to display the contents of the README.TXT file. You can select a button in the dialog box to change its size. Use this example as a sample if you need to display text files in dialog boxes or want to process Windows ASPECT dialog boxes using the WHEN DIALOG event command.

The following Windows ASPECT statements are introduced in this script:

```
$PWTASKPATH
ADDFILENAME
WHEN DIALOG
PUSHBUTTON NORMAL
PUSHBUTTON CANCEL
$DIALOG
```

```
    string readme,icofile
    integer done=0,icoindex,dlgsize=0
```

These variables are defined globally (outside of any procedure) because they are used by more than one procedure.

```
proc main
    readme = $pwtaskpath              ;initialize README to the
                                      ;location of PW.EXE
    addfilename readme "readme.txt"   ;add the filespec to the path
    icofile = $pwtaskpath             ;initialize ICOFILE to the
                                      ;location of PW.EXE
    addfilename icofile "pw.exe"      ;add PW.EXE filespec to ICOFILE
    icoindex=0                        ;we want the first icon in PW.EXE
    display_files()                   ;display the README.TMP file
    exit                              ;exit the script, finished
endproc
```

The global string variables are initialized by using the $PWTASKPATH global variable that returns the EXE directory path of PROCOMM PLUS for Windows. The ADDFILENAME command is used to append the README.TXT and PW.EXE file names to the contents of the global variables. The ADDFILENAME command is similar to the STRCAT command, except that it specifically deals with fully qualified file names. The variable icoindex is set to 0 and the display_files procedure is called.

```
    proc display_files
        dodlg()
        when dialog call action
        while not done
        endwhile
    endproc
```

This procedure immediately calls the dodlg procedure and upon return starts a WHEN DIALOG event process. The procedure then waits in a WHILE loop until the variable done indicates that the user is finished. When the user selects one of the buttons in the dialog box, the WHEN event statement calls the action procedure that changes the variable dlgsize if the Size button is selected or the variable done if the Done button is selected and execution returns to the WHILE loop.

```
    proc dodlg
        switch dlgsize
            case 0
            dialogbox 52 20 328 153 7 "Readme.txt"
                ftext 11 25 306 109 readme
                icon 41 0 icofile icoindex
                pushbutton 90 6 75 14 "&Done" cancel default
                pushbutton 190 6 76 14 "&Size" normal
            enddialog
            endcase
            case 1
            dialogbox 52 20 328 244 7 "Readme.txt"
```

```
        ftext 13 27 304 200 readme
        icon 41 0 icofile icoindex
        pushbutton 90 6 75 14 "&Done" cancel default
        pushbutton 190 6 76 14 "&Size" normal
    enddialog
    endcase
    case 2
    dialogbox 52 20 328 91 7 "Readme.txt"
        ftext 12 25 305 47 readme
        icon 41 0 icofile icoindex
        pushbutton 90 6 75 14 "&Done" cancel default
        pushbutton 190 6 76 14 "&Size" normal
    enddialog
    endcase
    case 3
    dialogbox 52 20 202 152 7 "Readme.txt"
        ftext 9 24 184 107 readme
        icon 10 0 icofile icoindex
        pushbutton 63 5 33 15 "&Done" cancel default
        pushbutton 121 5 33 14 "&Size" normal
    enddialog
    endcase
  endswitch
endproc
```

The dodlg procedure is repeatedly called by action and uses a SWITCH statement group to test the variable dlgsize and display one of four different dialog boxes based on its value. dlgsize is incremented in the action procedure each time it is called.

When the dodlg procedure is first called by PROC MAIN, the dialog box defined in CASE 0 will be displayed as shown in figure 12.2 because the value of dlgsize is initialized to 0 in the global definition statement.

```
proc action
  switch $dialog
    case 1                      ;end or cancel selected
      done=1                    ;set global done flag
    endcase
    case 10                     ;size button pressed
      dlgsize++
      if dlgsize==4             ;change dialog size
        dlgsize=0
      endif
      dodlg()                   ;redraw dialog at new size
    endcase
  endswitch
endproc
```

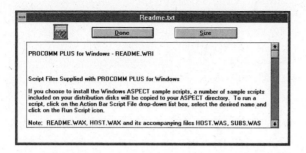

FIG. 12.2

The first dialog box
displayed by
README.WAS.

Like the `dodlg` procedure, the `action` procedure consists of a SWITCH statement group. This time the system variable $DIALOG is tested to determine what was selected in the dialog box. The only values tested are 1, indicating that the dialog box has received a Cancel command, and 10, indicating that a push button with the Normal option was selected. The cancel is issued by the user by pressing Alt-F4 or by selecting the push button with the `cancel` option defined as in this statement from the `dodlg` procedure:

```
pushbutton 90 6 75 14 "&Done" cancel default
```

Notice that the push button also has the `default` option specified. When the default option is used, the button is displayed with a dark border and will be the button selected when the user presses the Enter key. The default option can be used on any type of push button. A Windows ASPECT dialog box can have only one push button with the Cancel option defined but can have up to 16 push buttons with the Normal option defined. With the exception of the Cancel push button that always returns a 1, the system variable $DIALOG is assigned a value for each push button based on the sequence it appears in the dialog box statement group. When the first Normal push button appearing in the dialog box statement group is selected, 10 is returned in $DIALOG, 11 for the next normal push button in the statement group, and so on.

If the Done button is selected, the global variable `done` is assigned a value of 1 and execution returns to the `display_files` procedure. The statements in the `display_files` procedure:

```
while not done
endwhile
endproc
```

test the `done` variable and return to the calling procedure PROC MAIN, which ends the script with the following:

```
exit                ;exit the script, finished
endproc
```

If the Size button is selected, the `dlgsize` variable is incremented in the statement

```
dlgsize++
```

This statement is equivalent to the statement

```
dlgsize = dlgsize +1
```

but is a form that Windows ASPECT supports, making scripts simpler to write. The variable then is tested to determine if it exceeds the number of types of dialog boxes that can be displayed by the `dodlg` procedure; if so the variable is changed to zero, the value that will display the first dialog box.

The WHEN event statements are one of the most important group of commands in Windows ASPECT. They handle asynchronous events and call a specified procedure when the event occurs. PROCOMM PLUS for Windows has 16 different WHEN event statements you can use to greatly simplify scripts. For example, rather than periodically checking the value of $DIALOG to determine if something has been selected in the dialog box, you can execute a WHEN DIALOG event statement. When the dialog box event occurs, PROCOMM PLUS for Windows will automatically call the specified procedure. The called procedure then can test $DIALOG to determine what caused the event.

LOGIN.WAS

This script steps through a list of on-line services, requesting information for each service to create an automatic login script. The user is prompted to enter a user ID, password, and the dialing directory entry number for the service. If the entry doesn't exist, the user must create and enter an entry name and the service's telephone number. The script then will create the Windows ASPECT source file to automatically log into the service and create a dialing directory entry if necessary.

This script has examples of the statements necessary for creating and modifying dialing directory entries, for file output, and uses a different method of processing dialog boxes.

The following Windows ASPECT statements are introduced in this script:

```
WHEN USEREXIT
FETCH ASPECT SCRIPTPATH
FTEXT
PUSHBUTTON UPDATE
FAILURE
DIALADD
```

```
SET DIALDIR ACCESS
SET PORT PARITY, DATABITS, STOPBITS, DUPLEX
SET TERMINAL TYPE
SET PROTOCOL
FOPEN
FCLOSE
FPUTS
FLISTBOX
CHECKBOX
SUBSTR
STRCAT
VTEXT
UPDATEDLG
DDEINIT
DDEEXECUTE
DDETERMINATE
STRFMT
```

This script is much less complicated than it appears at first glance. The procedures GETINFO, GETLIST, and DEFAULTS are not used because the statements that call them have been commented out. With some modification to PROC MAIN, these procedures can be called to generate login scripts for some BBS services in addition to the commercial services the script now supports. The other procedure not used is DIS_CSERVE_N. This procedure originally was written to call an 800 number to obtain a local CompuServe phone number. The script, as it now operates, allows selection of the CompuServe number from a list box. The PROC MAIN calls five procedures in sequence and generates a login script for each service requested. The only procedure we will look at closely is the one for CompuServe, CSERVE, because it is representative of the other four.

As in the preceding script, this one also begins with global variable definitions.

```
integer    stat,entry,flg=0
string     introfile="LOGIN.int"
string     service
string     phone
string     uid,pass
string     user,passw,dialent
string     fullnm,firstnm,lastnm
string     scrname
integer    cisnumber
integer    longd,speed
string     cis1,cis2,cphone,localnum
string     cappath,msg
string     tabstr="130,180,360"
```

This is followed by the main procedure.

```
proc main
    string    tmp,spath=""
    when userexit call cleanup
```

The WHEN USEREXIT statement calls a procedure when the user stops the script by using the Script button on the Action Bar, by pressing Ctrl . (period), or by selecting the Scripts, Stop Script menu item. The WHEN USEREXIT command is very useful in scripts that create temporary files that should be deleted before the script halts.

```
fetch aspect scriptpath spath
strcat spath "\"
tmp=spath
strcat tmp introfile
introfile = tmp
```

These statements obtain the directory path for ASPECT files by using the FETCH ASPECT SCRIPTPATH command, create a fully qualified path and file by using the STRCAT statements, and assign the result to introfile. This section could be simplified by using the ADDFILENAME command as shown in the following sample.

```
fetch aspect scriptpath spath
addfilename spath introfile
introfile = spath
    call intro
    if stat==1
        call cleanup
    endif
```

The intro procedure is called and upon return stat is tested. To terminate the script, the user may select the Cancel button in a dialog box in which case, the script assigns the variable stat to 1. If stat is equal to 1, the cleanup procedure is called.

```
service = "CompuServe"
call cserve
if stat == 1
    call cleanup
endif
service = "BIX"
call bix
if stat == 1
    call cleanup
endif
service = "DATASTORM"
call dstorm
```

```
         if stat == 1
            call cleanup
         endif
         service = "Dow Jones"
         call dow
         if stat == 1
            call cleanup
         endif
         service = "GEnie"
         call genie
         if stat == 1
            call cleanup
         endif
         ;* Insert any additional bbs procedures here
         call cleanup
     endproc
```

The remainder of the main procedure assigns the variable `service` and calls each procedure in sequence to create the login script for the specified service. Once again, the `stat` variable is tested to see if the user selected Cancel.

```
     proc intro
         dialogbox 113 30 200 171 3 "LOGIN Introduction"
            ftext 14 8 176 114 introfile
            pushbutton 45 128 40 14 "C&ontinue" normal default
            pushbutton 107 128 40 14 "&Cancel" cancel
         enddialog
         stat=$DIALOG
         while stat != 10 && stat != 1
            stat=$DIALOG
         endwhile
     endproc
```

The `intro` procedure is called when the script is started and is used to display an introductory message using a Windows ASPECT dialog box (see fig. 12.3). The message text is contained in the file LOGIN.INT (the variable `introfile` contains the path and file name) and is displayed in the dialog box using the FTEXT statement. The FTEXT statement can display text files up to about 16K characters.

The dialog box is processed differently in this procedure than in the README.WAS example that uses the WHEN DIALOG statement and a separate procedure to determine the dialog box status. This procedure uses the $DIALOG system variable and assigns it to the global variable `stat` that is tested directly in the WHILE statement. When $DIALOG is evaluated, it returns to its default value of 0 to prevent the loss of a dialog event or to prevent the script from processing the same event more

402

than once. If you want to test the value of $DIALOG more than one time, then you must assign $DIALOG to a variable and then test the variable. Many dialog boxes that have only a few controls can be processed by using the WHILE/ENDWHILE loop. Remember from the README.WAS example that the first Normal push button returns a 10 and the Cancel button returns a 1. When either button is selected, the WHILE statement group ends and the procedure returns to the calling procedure with the variable stat assigned the value of the button pressed.

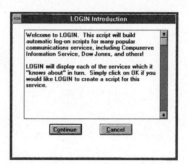

FIG. 12.3

The dialog box displayed by the intro procedure.

The following procedure cserve creates a login script for CompuServe Information Service and creates a dialing directory entry for CompuServe if one doesn't exist. This procedure is representative of those for the other services included in the script.

```
proc cserve
    string   sfile,temp
    scrname = "cserve"
    user = ""
    passw = ""
    cis1 = ""
    cis2 = ""
    msg = ""
    call get_cisphone
    if stat != 1
        phone = cis1
    endif
```

The get_cisphone procedure (described later in this section) returns a phone number in the cis1 variable for CompuServe in the city selected. If stat is not equal to 1, the telephone number is assigned to phone.

```
        call updtdef
```

The updtdef procedure displays the dialog box that allows entry of the user ID, password, and the name of the dialing directory entry that will be added if no CompuServe entry exists.

```
    if stat == 30
```

Here stat is tested for a value of 30, which is the indication that the Skip button was selected. If stat is equal to 30, execution proceeds to the last ENDIF in the procedure.

30 is the value returned by $DIALOG when a PUSHBUTTON with the update option is selected. When a push button has the update option and is selected, the dialog box will not be destroyed as with the other push buttons, Cancel and Normal. Using the update option enables the script to change variables displayed in the dialog box.

```
    strcmpi phone ""
```

This statement tests to see if the phone variable contains a number by comparing it to a null string ("").

```
    if failure
```

The statements following the IF FAILURE command are executed if a phone number is in the variable.

The FAILURE global variable returns a value based on the last testable statement—in this case the STRCMPI. FAILURE returns a 1 (or TRUE) if phone is null and 0 (or FALSE) if phone contains a number.

```
    dialadd service phone scrname entry
```

The DIALADD statement is used to add an entry to the currently loaded Dialing Directory. The entry is added as the last entry in the directory. The entry number added is assigned to the last parameter in the statement, which in this case is entry. The first three arguments of the statement, in order, are the name of the entry, the phone number, and the script name associated with the entry.

```
        dialent = service
        set dialdir access entry
        set port parity even
        set port databits 7
        set port stopbits 1
        set terminal type 25
        set protocol CISB
        set port duplex full
        set dialdir access off
    endif
```

These statements set the new dialing directory entry to the proper settings for CompuServe. The SET DIALDIR ACCESS statement causes all following SET statements to apply to a dialing directory entry rather than the current setup. Be sure to use SET DIALDIR ACCESS OFF in any script that modifies a dialing directory entry.

```
          sfile = scrname
          strcat sfile ".was"
          fopen 0 sfile CREATE TEXT
```

Now the script has the user ID, the password, the telephone number, and script name necessary for the login script. The FOPEN statement creates the file and the following statements "write the script." The 0 in the FOPEN statement is specified as an identifier for the file. The following statements use the 0 identifier to write to the file just created. The text option causes the FPUTS commands to add a carriage return and line feed to each line.

```
          fputs 0 ";Login to Compuserve - created by LOGIN"
          fputs 0 ";************************************************"
          fputs 0 ";* CSERVE.WAS - script file created by LOGIN to  *"
          fputs 0 ";*              dial compuserve with user's ID    *"
          fputs 0 ";************************************************"
          fputs 0 "proc main"
          fputs 0 "    integer ent"
          fputs 0 "    while $TXCOUNT"
          fputs 0 "    endwhile"
          fputs 0 "    if ! $FROMDDIR"
          fputs 0 "       set terminal type 25"
          fputs 0 "       set port parity even"
          fputs 0 "       set port databits 7"
          fputs 0 "       set port stopbits 1"
          fputs 0 "       set protocol CISB"
          strfmt temp "       dialfind `"%s`" ent" dialent
          fputs 0 temp
          fputs 0 "       if found"
          fputs 0 "          dial ent"
          fputs 0 "       else"
          strfmt temp "       usermsg `"%s not found in this
                          dialing directory'"" dialent
          fputs 0 temp
          fputs 0 "       endif"
          fputs 0 "    endif"
          fputs 0 "    while $DIALING"
          fputs 0 "    endwhile"
          fputs 0 "    pause 1"
          fputs 0 "    if $CARRIER                      "
          fputs 0 "       transmit `"^C`"               "
          fputs 0 "       waitfor `"User ID:`" 15"
          strfmt temp "       transmit `"%s`"" user
          fputs 0 temp
          fputs 0 "       transmit `"^M`"              "
          fputs 0 "       waitfor `"Password:`" 15"
```

```
strfmt temp "           transmit `"%s`"" passw
fputs 0 temp
fputs 0 "        transmit `"^M`"              "
fputs 0 "        waitfor `"!`" 60             "
fputs 0 "        set terminal enquiry cisb"
fputs 0 "        transmit `"g dstorm^M`" ; Delete this line if you"
fputs 0 "                                 ; do not wish to go to the"
fputs 0 "                                 ; Datastorm forum"
fputs 0 "   endif                    "
fputs 0 "endproc"
fclose 0
```

This statement closes the file

```
Add_Prgm_Item("cserve.was", "Cserve")
```

Add_Prgm_Item is the procedure to add a CompuServe icon to the Program Manager.

```
endif

phone = ""
```

Sets the phone number to null to prepare for the next service.

```
endproc
```

The next procedure displays a dialog box that includes a list box containing the local CompuServe telephone numbers for cities throughout the United States. The content of this list is found in the file CISPHONE.TXT. The user is prompted to select the local telephone number and select OK.

```
proc get_cisphone
    integer x
    string tmp
    fetch aspect scriptpath cphone
    addfilename cphone "cisphone.txt"
```

These statements assign to the variable cphone the fully qualified path for the file that contains the CompuServe telephone numbers.

```
dialogbox 124 7 222 199 3 "Choose CIS Access Number"
    flistbox 16 48 197 105 cphone tabstr single cis1
    pushbutton 46 176 40 14 "&OK" normal default
    pushbutton 145 177 40 14 "&Cancel" cancel
    text  18 8 194 35 left "Choose a CompuServe access \
    number, or press Cancel to enter a number manually."
    checkbox 86 153 63 11 "Long Distance?" longd
enddialog
```

This dialog box uses the FLISTBOX statement to display the contents of the telephone number file (see fig. 12.4). The FLISTBOX, like the FTEXT statement used in the README.WAS example, displays the contents of a disk file. Unlike the FTEXT, however, the FLISTBOX displays each line in the file as one item in a standard Windows list box.

FIG. 12.4

The dialog box displayed by the get_cisphone procedure.

The FLISTBOX in this procedure also uses the optional variable `tabstr`. This global variable sets tab stops in the box, making the list much easier to read. The tabs are defined in a global string variable. Each tab stop is identified as the number of dialog units measured from the left side of the list box. A dialog unit is defined as 1/4th the width of the average character of the font used in the list box.

The `single` option is used to specify that the list box will allow only one item in the list to be selected. When the item is selected, the variable `cis1` is assigned its value. The `multiple` option can be specified in cases in which the script allows more than one item in the list to be selected. In this case, the selected items are written to a file named in a global string variable.

The CHECKBOX statement displays a standard check box and assigns the variable `longd` equal to 1 if the box is checked; 0 if it is not checked.

```
stat = $DIALOG
while stat != 1 && stat != 10
    stat = $DIALOG
endwhile
```

Stay in the WHILE loop until the OK or Cancel push button is selected. Like the push buttons, the value of $DIALOG also is assigned specific values when an item in the FLISTBOX is selected or the check box changes state. This script ignores these values, but they can be used in cases in which you want to change variables displayed in the dialog box based on the selection.

```
      strlen cis1 x
      tmp = "1-"
      if x > 0
         substr cis1 cis1 0 14
         if longd
            strcat tmp cis1
            cis1 = tmp
         else
            substr cis1 cis1 6 8
         endif
      endif
   endproc
```

The final statements in this procedure test the variable cis1 to see if it contains an entry selected from the list (length greater than 0 from the STRLEN statement). The statement IF longd also checks to see if the long distance box is checked. If nothing is selected in the list, the IF statement group is exited and the procedure returns. Otherwise, the SUBSTR command copies the first 14 characters from the cis1 variable back into cis1, leaving the variable with just the area code and number. This operation removes the city name, state, and baud rate from the cis1 variable. If the long distance box is checked, the STRCAT statement adds the 1- to the telephone number and the procedure returns. If the longd variable is 0 (ELSE), the area code is removed by the second SUBSTR command by beginning the substitute at the 6th character position. This procedure doesn't address a third condition—the 1- without the area code. Later in this chapter, an example shows how to include this condition in the script.

The updtdef procedure displays a dialog box that the script uses to get the information needed to create the login scripts. If the user selected an entry in the get_csiphone procedure, a telephone number will be in the variable phone, and the variable service will contain "CompuServe". The VTEXT statement displays the contents of the service variable and the EDITBOX displays the contents of phone when the dialog box appears.

```
   proc updtdef
      integer ent
      dialent = ""
      if flg
         updatedlg -1
      else
         flg = 1
```

The variable flg (initially defined as a global variable with a value of 0) is used to determine if this is the first time the procedure has been entered. If it is, flg will be set to 1 and the dialog box will be displayed. If this is not the first time the procedure has been entered, then the

UPDATEDLG statement will be executed and the dialog box statements skipped. The UPDATEDLG statement updates variables displayed in the dialog box to reflect changes made to the variables after the initial dialog box display or since the last UPDATEDLG. In the case of this script, this dialog box is used to provide the user input for several services in sequence. Each time the user selects the OK or Skip button, in this dialog, the main procedure and the service-specific procedure change variables. These variables are updated (UPDATEDLG) when the procedure is re-entered.

```
dialogbox 122 8 200 236 3 "LOGIN Script Builder"
    vtext 24 9 161 15 center service
    text   14 52 34 8 left "User ID:"
    text   15 70 34 8 left "Password"
    text   16 88 50 17 left "Dialing Directory Entry"
    editbox 79 49 108 13 user
    editbox 78 68 108 13 passw masked
    editbox 78 91 108 13 dialent
    text   20 115 165 25 left "If you have no dialing \
    directory entry for this service, enter the number below."
    text   16 145 56 11 left "Phone Number"
    editbox 80 144 108 13 phone
    pushbutton   17 169 40 14 "&OK" update default
    pushbutton   85 168 40 14 "&Skip" update
    pushbutton  146 168 40 14 "&Cancel" cancel
    vtext 20 193 169 36 left msg
enddialog
endif
```

The dialog box displayed in figure 12.5 enables the user to enter a user ID, password, telephone number, and a dialing directory entry so that the LOGIN script can create an automatic login script for CompuServe.

The dialog box displayed by the updtdef procedure.

```
stat=$DIALOG
while stat !=30 && stat != 31 && stat != 1
    stat=$DIALOG
endwhile
```

This time the WHILE loop tests for $DIALOG values of 30, 31, and 1. The 30 and 31 indicate that a push button with the update option has been selected in the dialog box. A normal (modal) dialog box is destroyed when a Normal or Cancel push button is selected. If a push button is selected that has the update option, however, the dialog box will not be destroyed when it is selected. $DIALOG will return values beginning with 30. The update option enables the script to change variables and, as is done in this procedure, change the information shown in the dialog using UPDATEDLG. Windows ASPECT also supports "modeless" dialog boxes that allow the rest of PROCOMM PLUS for Windows to be active (for example, select menus, the Action Bar, and so on) while the dialog box is displayed.

```
strcmpi phone ""

if success
    atoi dialent ent
    set dialdir access ent
    dialent = $D_NAME
endif
```

If no phone number was entered (indicating that the dialing directory entry already exists), the dialing directory entry name is assigned to the variable dialent and is used when the login script is generated.

```
endproc
```

This procedure uses Dynamic Data Exchange (DDE) commands to add a program item to the PROCOMM PLUS for Windows group for each login script generated.

```
proc Add_prgm_item
strparm cmd
strparm title

long ddechan = 0
string buffer,pathname

    ddeinit ddechan "progman" "progman"    ;test to see if
                                           ;progman is there
```

To begin a DDE session with another program, the conversation must be initiated using the DDEINIT command. If the command is successful, a "channel" number is returned in the long variable ddechan that must be referenced in all DDE conversations with the server program.

```
if ddechan == 0                    ;guess not...
    usermsg "Progman is not present, program items \
    will not be added"
    return
endif
```

If the initiate was not successful, a 0 will be returned in the `ddechan` variable. This IF tests for this condition and will display a message box with that information. The procedure will return to the calling procedure when the user selects the OK button in the message box. The DDEINIT may fail if Windows is installed using a different shell such as Norton Desktop for Windows.

```
ddeexecute ddechan "[CreateGroup(PCPLUS/Win)]"
```

The DDEEXECUTE command is used to execute a function that the server program supports through DDE. The execute command is usually a string contained in square brackets ([]) but may vary from program to program. You need to check the documentation of the program to find the execute commands it supports and the proper syntax to use with the commands. The DDEEXECUTE command creates a Program Group in the Program Manager, and will have the title PCPLUS/Win. If a group with the same title already exists, the Program Manager ignores the command.

```
strcpy pathname $pwtaskpath
addfilename pathname "pw.exe"
```

Assign the fully qualified path of the PROCOMM PLUS for Windows executable file to the variable `pathname`.

```
strfmt buffer "[AddItem(%s %s,%s,%s,1)]" pathname cmd
    title pathname
```

The STRFMT command, as used in this statement, is very useful for formatting strings. The first parameter in the statement is the string variable that will receive the formatted information. The next is a quoted string containing text and format specifiers. The format specifiers begin with a % sign and are followed by one or more characters indicating how the variable is formatted. In this STRFMT statement, only the `%s` specifier is used, which causes the contents of the string variables that follow to be included in the formatted result. See the on-line help topic "Formatting Text and Strings" for more information on this subject.

When the STRFMT statement is executed, the variable `buffer` would contain something like this: [AddItem(d:\prowin\pw.exe cserve.was,Cserve,d:\prowin\pw.exe,1)].

```
ddeexecute ddechan buffer
```

This DDEEXECUTE sends the AddItem command created in the statement above to the Program Manager. When the Program Manager receives this command, an icon, with the command to run the script just created, appears in the PCPLUS/Win group.

```
ddeterminate ddechan
```

Any DDE conversation should be terminated by using the DDETERMINATE command to release memory set aside while the channel is open.

```
endproc

proc cleanup
    usermsg "Thank you for using LOGIN"
    exit
endproc
```

This cleanup procedure is called whenever the user wants to exit the script. You also will recall that this is the same procedure called when the WHEN USEREXIT command triggers.

CSERVE.WAS

This script automatically logs the user into CompuServe using the information provided in the LOGIN.WAS script. It is very typical of login scripts for any service. It tests for a given prompt sent by the host and sends the proper response.

The following Windows ASPECT statements are introduced in this script:

```
$TXCOUNT
$FROMDDIR
DIALFIND
DIAL
$DIALING
$CARRIER
WAITFOR
TRANSMIT
SET TERMINAL ENQUIRY
```

This script was created by LOGIN.WAS. Compare the FPUTS statements from the LOGIN.WAS example to see how they compare to the actual file created. This script can be run when the CompuServe entry is dialed from the Dialing Directory or run alone by double-clicking on the CServe icon in the Program Manager.

```
;Login to Compuserve - created by LOGIN
;****************************************************
;
;* CSERVE.WAS - script file created by LOGIN to  *
;*              dial compuserve with user's ID   *
;****************************************************
;
proc main
    integer ent
    while $TXCOUNT
    endwhile
```

This WHILE loop waits until no more characters are in the transmit buffer. If the script was started from the Dialing Directory, PROCOMM PLUS for Windows may still be sending commands to the modem and the script should not try to login during this time.

```
    if ! $FROMDDIR
```

The system variable $FROMDDIR returns a TRUE if the script was started from the Dialing Directory. If it was not, then the following SET statements will configure PROCOMM PLUS for Windows with the proper settings for CompuServe.

```
    set terminal type 25
```

Terminal type 25 specifies the VIDTEX emulation. The SET TERMINAL TYPE statement will accept either an index, as used here, or the key word VIDTEX. The index value for all emulations can be found in the on-line help topic "Named Tables and Index values."

```
    set port parity even
    set port databits 7
    set port stopbits 1
    set protocol CISB
    dialfind "CompuServe" ent
```

The DIALFIND command searches all Name fields in the currently loaded Dialing Directory and returns the number of the entry where the name is found.

```
    if found
        dial ent
```

Because the script was not started from the Dialing Directory, the script needs to dial the CompuServe access number. The DIAL command dials CompuServe, using the number found in the CompuServe entry.

```
    else
        usermsg "CompuServe not found in this dialing directory"
    endif
endif
```

If the script was started from the Dialing Directory (determined by the IF ! $FROMDDIR statement listed earlier in this section), script execution will proceed to the statement following the second ENDIF in the preceding statement. The Set statements in this section of code can be skipped because the Dialing Directory sets the parameters and dials the number.

```
      while $DIALING
      endwhile
```

The system variable $DIALING is TRUE while PROCOMM PLUS for Windows is dialing a number.

```
      pause 1
      if $CARRIER
```

The system variable $CARRIER is TRUE when the modems Carrier Detect signal is active.

```
          transmit "^C"
          waitfor "User ID:" 15
          transmit "77700,770"
          transmit "^M"
          waitfor "Password:" 15
          transmit "sammy spade"
          transmit "^M"
          waitfor "!" 60
          set terminal enquiry cisb
          transmit "g dstorm^M" ; Delete this line if you do not
                              ; wish to go to the Datastorm forum
      endif
   endproc
```

The remainder of the procedure uses the WAITFOR commands to look for a matching string received on the COM port and uses the TRANSMIT command to send the text in the quoted strings at the proper time. The SET TERMINAL ENQUIRY CISB command causes PROCOMM PLUS for Windows to monitor and respond to the CompuServe micro enquiry sequence. This response tells CompuServe that PROCOMM PLUS for Windows software is being used and that it supports on-line GIF viewing and uses the B Plus protocol.

MENU.WAS

This example demonstrates the creation of Windows ASPECT menus. Windows ASPECT uses three statements to modify the menu selections available while PROCOMM PLUS for Windows is running.

The MENUBAR command returns an identifier for a new menu bar that you can use to replace the normal menu bar. You can create up to 16 menu bars in addition to PROCOMM PLUS for Windows' normal menu bar.

The MENUPOPUP command is used to attach a top-level selection to a menu bar or to another popup menu. A popup menu does not allow selection of an item but displays a list of items. For example, the File selection on the normal menu bar is a popup menu; the Kermit Command is an example of a popup attached to a popup.

The MENUITEM command then is used to actually create an item that notifies the script when it has been selected. Menu items can be attached to a menu bar or a popup menu.

Windows ASPECT menus and popups can be added to the PROCOMM PLUS for Windows popup menus: File, Edit, Scripts, Communication, Window, Help, or to the normal menu bar. If popups or menus are added to the normal menu bar, they will appear to the right of the Help selection. Menus and popups can be added in many combinations to the menu bars created by using the MENUBAR command. The following example script shows how to add two menu items to the normal menu bar, a menu item to the Window popup, and create and display a new menu bar. The sample also shows how to enable and disable menu items.

Enter the following main procedure in your text editor and save it as MENU.WAS. Compile and run it to see how Windows ASPECT menu statements appear and operate.

The following Windows ASPECT statements are introduced in this script:

```
$PWMENUBAR
MENUITEM
SHOWMENU
MENUBAR
MENUPOPUP
WHEN MENU
$MENU

;My first Windows ASPECT custom menu.

integer oldmenubar, newmenubar, menupopup2, enabled = 0
```

Define global variables that will contain the IDs of the old menu bar, the new menu bar, a popup menu, and a flag to contain the enabled status of the popup.

```
proc main
integer menupopup1, menupopupopup
   oldmenubar = $pwmenubar
```

In order to add menus to PROCOMM PLUS for Windows normal menu bar, and return to it, the ID of the current PROCOMM PLUS for Windows normal menu bar is assigned to the variable oldmenubar.

```
menuitem oldmenubar 10 "New Menubar!"
menuitem oldmenubar 99 "Exit Script!"
```

These statements add two new menu items to the current menu bar (oldmenubar). The first menu is used to change to the new menu bar (ID of 10) and the other menu is used to exit the script (ID of 99). These menu items will appear (in the order that they occur in the script) to the right of the Help popup.

```
menuitem 4 separator
menuitem 4 20 "Script Window"
```

These commands will add a separator (horizontal line) and a menu called Script Window to the normal Window popup selection. Windows ASPECT reserves the values 0 through 5 to identify the normal menu bar popups from left to right. 5 is the ID of the Window popup.

```
showmenu oldmenubar
```

The SHOWMENU command causes the changes made to the normal menu bar to be shown.

```
menubar newmenubar
```

Obtain an ID for a new menu bar and store the value in newmenubar.

```
menuitem newmenubar 11 "Normal Menu!"
```

Put a menu item on the new menu bar called Normal Menu. When Normal Menu is selected, it will return 11 in the $MENU system variable.

```
menupopup newmenubar "First Menu" menupopup1
```

Put a popup selection called First Menu on the new menu bar. The integer variable menupopup1 will contain the identifier used by the statements immediately following to attach menu items to the First Menu popup.

```
menuitem menupopup1 12 "First Menu Item"
menuitem menupopup1 13 "Second Menu Item"
menuitem menupopup1 separator
menuitem menupopup1 14 "Third Menu Item"
menuitem menupopup1 15 "Enable/Disable Second Menu Items"
menupopup newmenubar "Second Menu" menupopup2
```

Add a second popup called Second Menu to the new menu bar identified by menupopup2.

```
menupopup menupopup2 "Popup" menupopupopup
menuitem menupopupopup 16 "First Popup"
menuitem menupopupopup 17 "Second Popup"
```

The preceding three statements add a popup to the Second Menu popup. This demonstrates the creation of a menu item list attached to another popup.

```
menuitem menupopup2 18 "After Popup"

when menu call process
while 1
endwhile
endproc
```

The WHEN MENU event command is used to call a procedure when the operator selects a Windows ASPECT menu. The procedure process then can use the system variable $MENU to determine which menu was selected.

```
proc process

switch $menu
    case 10
        showmenu newmenubar
    endcase
    case 11
        showmenu oldmenubar
    endcase
    case 12
        usermsg "First Menu, First Menu Item selected."
    endcase
    case 13
        usermsg "First Menu, Second Menu Item selected."
    endcase
    case 14
        usermsg "First Menu, Third Menu Item selected."
    endcase
    case 15
        if enabled == 0
            disable menu 16 18
            enabled = 1
        else
            enable menu 16 18
            enabled = 0
        endif
    endcase
    case 16
```

```
        usermsg "Second Menu, First Popup selected."
    endcase
    case 17
        usermsg "Second Menu, Second Popup selected."
    endcase
    case 18
        usermsg "Second Menu, After Popup selected."
    endcase
    case 20
        usermsg "Script Window Item selected."
    endcase
    case 99
        exit
    endcase
endswitch

endproc
```

The process procedure is simply a skeleton SWITCH statement group with CASEs based on the $MENU system variable. Message boxes are displayed for each of the menu items selected, except for case 15, which is processed when the Enable/Disable Second Menu Items option is selected from the First Menu popup. The Enable/Disable code segment uses the DISABLE and ENABLE commands to alternately gray and ungray the menu items under the Second Menu popup. Menu items on the PROCOMM PLUS for Windows Normal menu bar also can be controlled using the DISABLE and ENABLE commands. See the table listing PROCOMM PLUS for Windows menu item ID values in the on-line help topic DISABLE.

PKSEND.WAS and PKRECV.WAS

The packet send and receive Windows ASPECT commands are an interesting and useful set of statements for script writers interested in developing client server types of communications programs. These statements enable scripts to easily send error-free strings (including binary data) to each other through the communication port. When a script wants to send data using the PKSEND command, PROCOMM PLUS for Windows puts the data, including a script-specified integer identifier, into a packet. PROCOMM PLUS for Windows also inserts into the packet an internal identifier and checks characters based on the contents of the packet. This complete packet then is sent through the communication port and PROCOMM PLUS for Windows waits for an acknowledgment from the receiver. If the acknowledgment is received, PROCOMM PLUS for Windows notifies the script through the $PKSEND global variable or with a WHEN PKSEND event call. PROCOMM PLUS will automatically attempt to resend the packet several times during the time-out period specified in the PKMODE statement or the PKSEND statement. If acknowledgment is not received successfully during the time-out period, the script is notified.

The receiving side operates in a similar manner. PROCOMM PLUS for Windows is put in packet mode with the PKMODE ON statement, and the script executes the PKRECV command. When a packet is received successfully, the script is notified with the $PKRECV system variable or through a WHEN PKRECV event call. The script then can use a SWITCH statement group, based on the contents of the integer identifier contained in the packet, to determine its contents.

These statements will be useful for scripts transmitting environmental or process data as well as on-line games. The following examples titled PKRECV.WAS and PKSEND.WAS can be found as Sample Code in the on-line help under their respective command names. In early releases of the help database, the sample code for the PKSEND command was an incorrectly labeled copy of the PKSEND script. If you have the early help file, get the new file from the DATASTORM BBS or use the sample described here to experiment with these scripts. They use the PKSEND and PKRECV commands to transmit a disk file. The scripts will need to be run in coordination and the file transfer process started within the initial one-minute time out period.

The following Windows ASPECT statements are introduced in this script:

```
PKMODE
WHEN PKSEND
DIR
SUCCESS
GETFSIZE
PKSEND
$PKSEND
FUNC ENDFUNC
```

```
;pksend


;*****************************************************************************
;
;* This script must be used with the script example shown for pksend.   *
;* You must run PROCOMM PLUS for Windows on two machines one running     *
;* this script and the other running the pksend script.  The two        *
;* machines should be connected with modem or a null modem cable.        *
;*****************************************************************************
;
```

```
string filename, packet, eofpacket
string fname
integer blocknum, bytesread
integer packetactive, eofsent
long filesize

proc main
   pkmode on 60 60      ; turn packet mode on with timeouts
```

The PKMODE ON statement puts PROCOMM PLUS for Windows in packet mode. When in packet mode, no characters will be transmitted when keys are typed and no characters will be displayed if they are received.

```
   when pksend call send_packet     ; when a packet is
                                     ; xmitted call
   send_packet
```

The WHEN PKSEND statement calls the send_packet procedure when the status of the PKSEND command changes.

```
   when userexit call _exit    ; if user closes script call _exit

   dir "*.*" filename          ; display a file open dialog
```

DIR displays a standard file open dialog box allowing selection of the file to send. The DIR command sets the SUCCESS flag TRUE if a file is selected and the OK button is pressed.

```
   if not success             ; if the user closes the box
      exit                    ; or presses ESC then exit
   endif
   fopen 0 filename read     ; open the file selected

   if not success            ; if file open error the exit
      errormsg "Can't open %s!" filename
      exit
   endif
   getfsize filename filesize   ; get the filesize
```

GETFSIZE returns the size in bytes of the file selected in the DIR command.

```
      blocknum = 1      ; packet number 1 will contain the filename
      fname=name_extract(filename)   ; strip the path from the
                                     ; beginning of the filename
      strlen fname i1             ; get the length of the filename
      pksend blocknum fname i1    ; send packet 1
```

This command sends a packet containing the name of the file to be sent. The value of the blocknum variable, which is assigned to 1, is sent with the packet to identify it as the file name packet.

```
        blocknum++                 ; inc packet number
        packetactive = 1           ; set flag for while loop
        eofsent = 0                ; set flag for EOF

        while packetactive         ; loop while flag is set
        endwhile
    endproc
```

The script will now "spin" in the WHILE loop until the WHEN PKSEND event statement calls send_packet or the WHEN USER event statement calls the _exit procedure. When the file has been sent, the send_packet procedure will make the packetactive variable false. The script then will terminate.

```
proc send_packet
    integer stats = $PKSEND     ; check the status of $PKRECV
```

The $PKSEND system variable returns the status of the PKSEND command. This procedure tests the value of the $PKSEND (which has been assigned to the variable stats) and takes appropriate action.

```
        switch stats
          case 1                     ; packet sent OK
            if eofsent
                packetactive = 0   ; set flags
                eofsent = 0
                exitswitch
```

If the last packet sent (indicated by eofsent being TRUE) contained the last bytes in the file, the global variables packetactive and eofsent are set to 0 and the switch statement group is exited.

```
endif
fread 0 packet 255 bytesread    ; read in a block from the file
```

Attempt to read 255 bytes from the file.

```
        if bytesread==0      ; if no more bytes to read
            fclose 0         ; close the file
            eofsent = 1      ; set EOF flag
            strset eofpacket 24 128     ; set setting to ASCII 24
            pksend 200 eofpacket 128    ; end of xfer set packet
                                        ; number to 200
            statmsg "Last Block sent!"
            exitswitch
        endif
```

The IF statement now is used to test to see if any bytes were read from the file. If no more bytes were read, then the last packet contained all the bytes in the file. The file is closed. The eof flag is set and a packet with the special identifier 200 containing 128 EOF characters is sent.

```
pksend blocknum packet bytesread   ; otherwise send a block of data
blocknum++             ; increment the packet number
if blocknum==100    ; if packet number is 100 start
    blocknum=2         ; reset packet number to 2
endif
```

If characters were read from the file, they are sent with the PKSEND command. The variable blocknum is incremented until it reaches 100, in which case it is reset to 2. blocknum is the identifier sent with each packet. This script uses 1 in blocknum as the identifier for the packet containing the file name being sent. 2 through 99 in blocknum identify packets containing the data in the file and 200 identifies the end of file packet.

```
endcase

case 2                   ; timeout error
    packetactive = 0
    eofsent = 0
    fclose 0
    termwrites "Timeout!"
    beep
endcase
```

When $PKSEND returns a 2, it is an indication that PROCOMM PLUS for Windows has exceeded the timeout period (caused by not receiving a valid packet) specified in the PKMODE or the PKSEND command. This case simply sets global variables indicating the problem, and then returns. Your script may want to handle this error in a different way.

```
case 3                         ; error
    packetactive = 0
    eofsent = 0
    fclose 0
    termwrites "Error! Packet resent"
endcase
```

When $PKSEND returns a 3, it indicates that PROCOMM PLUS for Windows has attempted to send the packet but has received errors on the COM port. These errors may include parity or overruns caused by noisy telephone lines. PROCOMM PLUS for Windows will still attempt to send the packet during the timeout period, but this error condition usually means that the communication circuit is not reliable. This case simply sets global variables indicating the problem, and then returns.

```
        case 4                              ; abort
           packetactive = 0
           eofsent = 0
           fclose 0
           termwrites "Transfer canceled by Receiver!"
        endcase
     endswitch
  endproc
```

Case 4 indicates that PROCOMM PLUS for Windows has received a
packet abort sequence. When the characters 18 Hex and E7 Hex (the
packet abort sequence) are received, $PKSEND returns a 4 and
PROCOMM PLUS for Windows switches from packet send mode to
packet receive mode.

```
  proc _exit                 ; user stopped the script so exit
     statmsg "Script aborted!"
     exit
  endproc
```

This procedure is executed when the user wants to stop the script. Any
temporary files that your script has created should be deleted in an exit
script similar to this.

```
  ;************************************************************
  ;* This function extracts just the filename from a fully  *
  ;* qualified path                                          *
  ;************************************************************
  func name_extract: string
  string newname          ; filename to return integer index,
                          ; position, len
  strparm fn              ; fully qualified path and filename
```

Define the string parameter that will receive the full path name when this
function is called, and then define local variables.

```
     while 1                     ; loop forever
        strfind fn "\" index     ; find a backslash
        if not found             ; if not found exit loop
           exitwhile
        endif
        position=index+1    ; set position 1 char past
                            ; where "\" was found
        strlen fn len       ; get the length
        len=len-position    ; subtract position
        substr newname fn position len   ; substring out LEN
                                         ; number of characters
        fn=newname          ; assign new name
     endwhile
```

```
      return newname             ; return new filename
   endfunc
```

The statements in the WHILE loop search for a backslash and then remove any characters up to and including the backslash. The process is
repeated until no more backslashes occur, leaving only the file name in
newname, which is returned by the function.

PKRECV.WAS

The following Windows ASPECT statements are introduced in this script:

WHEN PKRECV
$PKRECV
PKRECV

```
integer blocknum, length ,stats, packetactive
string filename, databuff

proc main
   fetch dnldpath filename
   pkmode on 60 60                  ; turn packet mode on with timeouts
   when pkrecv call get_packet      ; when a packet comes in call get_packet
   when userexit call _exit         ; if user closes script call _exit
   packetactive = 1                 ; flag for while loop

  while packetactive                ; loop while flag is set
  endwhile
endproc
```

The main procedure of PKRECV.WAS is identical to the PKSEND.WAS
script, except that the WHEN PKRECV command replaces the WHEN
PKSEND.

```
proc get_packet
   stats = $pkrecv                  ; check the status of $PKRECV
   switch stats
      case 0                        ; nothing
         statmsg "Waiting for packet"
      endcase
```

$PKRECV returns a 0 (the default state) while PROCOMM PLUS for Win-
dows is waiting for a packet.

```
      case 1                        ; packet successfully received
         statmsg "Packet Received"
```

```
              pkrecv blocknum databuff length
              save_packet()
          endcase
```

This case is processed when the packet has been received successfully. Next, the save_packet procedure is called to write the packet to the disk file.

```
          case 2                          ; timeout
              statmsg "Timeout"
              packetactive = 0
              beep
          endcase
```

PROCOMM PLUS for Windows has not received a valid packet during the timeout period specified in the PKMODE ON command.

```
          case 3                          ; error
              statmsg "Error! ...Packet resent"
              packetactive = 0            ; reset flag to exit while loop
                                          ; in MAIN
          endcase
```

When $PKRECV returns a 3, it indicates that PROCOMM PLUS for Windows has received errors on the communication port. These errors are due to over-runs or parity errors and usually indicate that the communication link is bad. Generally when this type of error occurs, a reconnection to the host should be attempted to get a better line.

```
      endswitch
  endproc

  proc save_packet
      statmsg "[%d] [%s]" blocknum databuff
      if blocknum==1                 ; packet number 1 contains a filename
          addfilename filename databuff  ; add filename to download path
          fopen 0 filename create        ; open file
          if not success                 ; if file open error exit script
              usermsg "[%s]" filename
              errormsg "Can't open file!"
              exit
          endif
      else
          if blocknum==200               ; packet number 200 is EOF packet
              fclose 0                   ; close the file
              usermsg "Transfer Complete!"
              packetactive = 0           ; reset flag to exit while loop
```

```
                              ; in MAIN
    else
        fwrite 0 databuff length    ; otherwise the packet is file data
    endif                           ; to be written
  endif
endproc
```

The save_packet procedure uses the ID sent with each packet to determine the contents of the packet. If the packet has an ID of 1, it contains
the file name. The procedure then assigns the fully qualified file name to
the filename variable and attempts to create the file by using the FOPEN
command. If the file cannot be opened, the script exits.

If the packet has an ID of 200, it is the end of file packet and has no data.
The file is closed and the packetactive variable is set to 0, indicating
that the transfer is complete. If the packet doesn't meet either of these
conditions (meaning it contains data from the file), it is written to the
disk file.

```
proc _exit              ;  user stopped the script so exit
    statmsg "Script aborted!"
    exit
endproc
```

Using the Dialog Editor To Modify LOGIN.WAS

Two of the additional programs supplied with PROCOMM PLUS for Windows are used to help with the generation of Windows ASPECT scripts:
the Dialog Editor and the User Window Builder. Most all Windows
ASPECT scripts at one time or another need to prompt or obtain information from the user. Dialog boxes are the most useful way of doing this.
The Dialog Editor enables you to graphically design a dialog box by using drawing-type tools. The Dialog Editor then creates the Windows
ASPECT commands that can be used in a Windows ASPECT script to
produce the dialog box. The Windows ASPECT dialog box commands
can be saved to disk or pasted directly into the script. In addition, the
dialog box commands in a script can be copied from the text editor and
pasted into the dialog box editor. This enables changes to be made easily during the script development process. This section of the chapter
discusses operation of the PROCOMM PLUS for Windows Dialog Editor
and how the Windows ASPECT commands are used to handle dialog
boxes. The next section in this chapter discusses the User Window
Builder.

In this example, you modify a dialog box in an existing script, LOGIN.WAS. The procedure `get_cisphone` displays a dialog box with a list of CompuServe access numbers with a long distance option. The way the script is currently written, a 1- is added to the area code and telephone number when the long distance option is checked. In some cases the user may want the 1- without the area code. This example will modify the dialog box to include this option and the associated commands.

To modify the dialog box, follow these steps:

1. Open LOGIN.WAS in the text editor you use to edit Windows ASPECT scripts.

2. Locate the `get_cisphone` procedure and copy into the Windows Clipboard all Windows ASPECT commands beginning with the DIALOGBOX statement, up to and including the ENDDIALOG statement.

3. Run the PROCOMM PLUS for Windows Dialog Editor and select the Edit, Paste Dialog menu item.

   You should see the Choose CIS Access Number dialog box displayed in the Dialog Editor.

4. Click on the Long Distance? check box. You should see 8 handles appear on the check box control. The term *control* is used here to refer to any object that can be displayed in a dialog box.

5. Click anywhere within the control and drag it to the left side of the list box. You can do fine positioning of any control by using the keyboard cursor-movement keys.

6. Select the CheckBox item under the Controls menu.

7. Move the + cursor to the right side, just under the list box, and click the left mouse button.

   You should see a check box.

8. Double-click within the check box to display the Check Box Options dialog box and type *Include Area Code?* in the Text: edit field.

9. Type *areacode* in the Variable Name edit field, and then choose OK.

   The check box now should show part of the `Include Area Code?` text.

10. Click anywhere within the newly created check box. Click the middle handle on the right side of the control and drag it to the right until the control is wide enough to display all the `Include Area Code?` text (see fig. 12.6).

11. When you have moved the check box controls to their correct positions, select the Edit, Copy Dialog menu item.

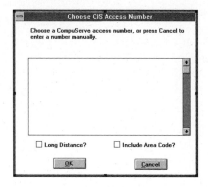

FIG. 12.6

The modified dialog box from LOGIN.WAS.

12. In the text editor, paste the modified dialog box code back into the script. Be sure to replace the old dialog box script statements with the modified dialog box statements.

The new get_cisphone procedure shows changes made to the dialog box and additional statements to process the Include Area Code? check box.

```
integer areacode      ;Create a new global variable area code.
proc get_cisphone
   integer x
   string tmp

   fetch aspect scriptpath cphone
   addfilename cphone "cisphone.txt"


   dialogbox 124 8 222 199 3 "Choose CIS Access Number"
      flistbox 16 48 197 105 cphone tabstr single cis1
      pushbutton 46 176 40 14 "&OK" normal default
      pushbutton 145 177 40 14 "&Cancel" cancel
      text  18 8 194 35 left "Choose a CompuServe access \
      number, or press Cancel to enter a number manually."
      checkbox 25 153 63 11 "Long Distance?" longd
      checkbox 120 153 81 11 "Include Area Code?" areacode
   enddialog
```

The new dialog box now has the Include Area Code? check box.

```
      disable ctrl 71
```

The DISABLE command "greys out" the Include Area Code? check box. The number 71 in the DISABLE command identifies the second check box in the dialog box statement group. The DISABLE control also can be used to gray out menu items.

```
      stat = $DIALOG
      while stat != 1 && stat != 10
         stat = $DIALOG
         if stat == 70 && longd != 1
            disable ctrl 71
            areacode = 0
            updatedlg 1
         elseif stat == 70 && longd == 1
            enable ctrl 71
         endif
      endwhile
```

The statements added to the WHILE loop enable and disable the Include Area Code? check box. When the user checks the Long Distance? check box, the variable stat ($DIALOG) will be assigned a value of 70 (the ID value of the first check box in the dialog box statement group). The statements immediately following the IF will execute when the Long Distance? box is unchecked. These commands disable the Include Area Code? control, set the variable associated with the Include Area Code? (areacode) to 0, and uncheck the Include Area Code? check box. When the Long Distance? box is checked (ELSEIF), the Include Area Code? box will be made active.

```
      strlen cis1 x
      tmp = "1-"
      if x > 0
         substr cis1 cis1 0 14
         if areacode != 1
            substr cis1 cis1 6 8
         endif
```

These statements remove the area code from cis1.

```
         if longd == 1
            strcat tmp cis1
            cis1 = tmp
         endif
      endif
   endproc
```

These statements add 1- to the telephone number.

USERWIN.WAS and the Windows User Window Builder

The other utility program provided with PROCOMM PLUS for Windows, used to aid in the development of Windows ASPECT scripts, is the User Window Builder. The User Window is a rectangle that can be defined to occupy all or part of the PROCOMM PLUS window. This window then can be used to display Windows metafiles, bit maps, and other objects such as push buttons and icons. The User Window allows the creation of a graphical menuing system. Like the Dialog Editor, which is used to graphically create dialog boxes, the User Window Builder is used to graphically design the User Window. Both programs create the Windows ASPECT commands to be used in your script.

In this example, you create a User Window displaying a map of the United States. Each region has a push button, which can be selected to execute a segment of code. This example shows how to process the $OBJECT system variable by using a skeleton SWITCH statement group. You can modify this SWITCH procedure to suit your own needs.

To create a User Window, follow these steps:

1. Run the User Window Builder by double-clicking the User Window Builder icon in the Program Manager, or by selecting the PW User Window Builder menu item from the PROCOMM PLUS for Windows command menu. (Fig. 12.7 shows the User Window Builder.)

   Notice that the window imitates the PROCOMM PLUS window. The Term Window menu item can be used to add or remove the action bar and meta keys for User Window scripts that need the additional display area.

2. Select the User Window, Background menu item.

3. Type 0 128 128 in the Red, Green, and Blue edit boxes, respectively. This sets the background color of the User Window to a soft blue-green.

4. Select the Background Metafile Graphics radio button.

5. Select the Options push button. In the Metafile Background Options dialog, select the Maintain Aspect Ratio radio button, and then choose OK.

6. Select the New push button. In the Background Metafile Open dialog, select the US_COLOR.WMF metafile, and then choose OK. The metafile can be found in the \ASPECT\DEMO directory.

7. Select OK to remove the User Window Background dialog box.

8. Select the Objects, PushButton menu item and place the buttons over each region on the map, as shown in figure 12.7.

9. Double-click each button and enter the region name in the Text edit box, and then type an exclusive ID number for each button. This example uses the following ID numbers:

Region	ID
West	1
Mountain	2
Plains	3
Midwest	4
Northeast	5
South	6
Texas	7
Alaska & Hawaii	8

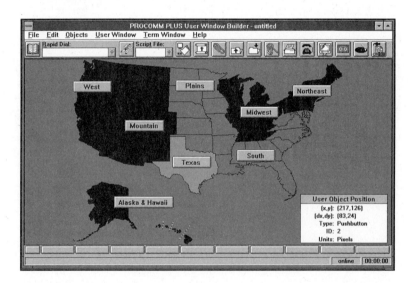

FIG. 12.7

User Window Builder with U.S. Map and Buttons.

10. When you have positioned, named, and given each button an ID, select the Edit, Copy Window menu item.

11. Run the text editor you use for editing Windows ASPECT scripts and paste the User Window commands into the main procedure of a new script, and then add the additional statements as shown next.

The position and size values for each push button may appear differently in your file depending on the order, position, and size of the buttons as you place them.

```
;My first User Window script.
proc main

    defuserwin full window 100 0 128 128 metafile
    metafilebkg center center exact "d:\prowin\aspect\demo\us_color.wmf"
    pushbutton 1 0 1169 1438 623 "West" background
    pushbutton 2 1941 3273 1439 623 "Mountain" background
    pushbutton 3 3813 1117 1438 623 "Plains" background
    pushbutton 4 6205 2545 1438 624 "Midwest" background
    pushbutton 5 8163 1377 1438 649 "Northeast" background
    pushbutton 6 6083 4857 1439 649 "South" background
    pushbutton 7 3692 5221 1438 649 "Texas" background
    pushbutton 8 1542 7377 2202 649 "Alaska && Hawaii" background
    paint
    when object call process
    while 1
    endwhile
endproc
```

The DEFUSERWIN statement creates the user window that occupies the "FULL" PROCOMM PLUS for Windows "WINDOW." The 100 that follows is a place holder in this case because FULL implies 100%. The next three numbers, 0 128 128, represent the background color; METAFILE indicates that objects placed on the User Window will respond as if a metafile were displayed, even without a background.

The METAFILEBKG statement specifies that the metafile will be centered both horizontally and vertically. The EXACT option indicates that the metafile will be displayed with the same height-to-width ratio as the metafile that was created.

The PUSHBUTTON parameters include the ID number, four numbers representing their placement and size, the text to appear in the button, and BACKGROUND. The BACKGROUND option indicates that the button will stay positioned over the same relative spot in the User Window. For objects that can be resized (push buttons, hotspots, and metafiles), the BACKGROUND option also means that the object will be resized in proportion to the resizing of the User Window.

As you can see, the User Window Builder is almost indispensable for creating these displays. Experiment with the different options for the background and objects. Notice the effect they have on the display and their action when the user window is resized.

The PAINT command causes the background and objects to actually be displayed on-screen.

Objects can be added, moved, or removed at any time by the script. The PAINT command is used to update on-screen the objects that have been added, moved, or removed.

The WHEN OBJECT command calls the process procedure when an object on the User Window has been selected. The following is a skeleton procedure that will display a message box with information about the selected button. You can add your own statements to perform the functions you want when the buttons are selected.

```
proc process
string which
integer button
   switch $object
      case 1
         which = "West Region selected."
         sdlgmsgbox "User Window Demo" which information okcancel button
         if button == 1
            return
         endif
         exit
      endcase
      case 2
         which = "Mountain Region selected."
         sdlgmsgbox "User Window Demo" which information okcancel button
         if button == 1
            return
         endif
         exit
      endcase
      case 3
         which = "Plains Region selected."
         sdlgmsgbox "User Window Demo" which information okcancel button
         if button == 1
            return
         endif
         exit
      endcase
      case 4
         which = "Midwest Region selected."
         sdlgmsgbox "User Window Demo" which information okcancel button
         if button == 1
            return
```

```
         endif
         exit
      endcase
      case 5
         which = "Northeast Region selected."
         sdlgmsgbox "User Window Demo" which information okcancel button
         if button == 1
            return
         endif
         exit
      endcase
      case 6
         which = "South Region selected."
         sdlgmsgbox "User Window Demo" which information okcancel button
         if button == 1
            return
         endif
         exit
      endcase
      case 7
         which = "Texas selected."
         sdlgmsgbox "User Window Demo" which information okcancel button
         if button == 1
            return
         endif
         exit
      endcase
      case 8
         which = "Alaska Hawaii selected."
         sdlgmsgbox "User Window Demo" which information okcancel button
         if button == 1
            return
         endif
         exit
      endcase
   endswitch
endproc
```

This procedure is simply a SWITCH statement group that uses the system variable $OBJECT as the tested parameter. $OBJECT returns the ID value of the selected object.

SDLGMSGBOX displays a message with different icons and 1, 2, or 3 buttons, depending on the key word parameters. INFORMATION displays an icon and OKCANCEL displays 2 buttons labeled OK and Cancel. The last parameter returns the value (1 for OK, 2 for Cancel) of the button selected. The variable button is tested by the IF statement, returning to PROC MAIN if the OK button is pressed, and exiting if the Cancel button is selected. See the on-line help topic for more information on the use of the SDLGMSGBOX command.

Enter the process procedure following the main procedure created using the User Window Builder in your editor and save it as USERWIN.WAS. Compile and run the script to display your first User Window Graphic menu.

You can modify this script to display another User Window screen by creating another procedure with the plains map. PLAINS.WMF also can be found in the \ASPECT\DEMO directory.

Change USERWIN.WAS as shown below so that case 3 of the SWITCH $DIALOG statement group calls the plains procedure:

```
case 3
   which = "Plains Region selected."
   sdlgmsgbox "User Window Demo" which information okcancel button
   if button == 1
      plains()
      return
   endif
   exit
endcase
```

Using the User Window Builder and figure 12.8 as a guide, create the following procedure:

```
proc plains
   remove userwin
   paint
   defuserwin full window 100 0 0 255 metafile
   metafilebkg center center exact "plains.wmf"
   pushbutton 100 813   1003 1730 613 "North Dakota" background
   pushbutton 101 2976 1476 1500 613 "Minnesota" background
   pushbutton 112 1021 2730 1730 613 "South Dakota" background
   pushbutton 113 1211 4373 1471 613 "Nebraska" background
   pushbutton 114 1765 5989 1366 613 "Kansas" background
   pushbutton 115 1920 7799 1384 613 "Oklahoma" background
   pushbutton 116 3824 7994 1470 613 "Arkansas" background
   pushbutton 117 3668 5989 1453 613 "Missouri" background
   pushbutton 118 3318 3899 1175 613 "Iowa" background
   paint
endproc
```

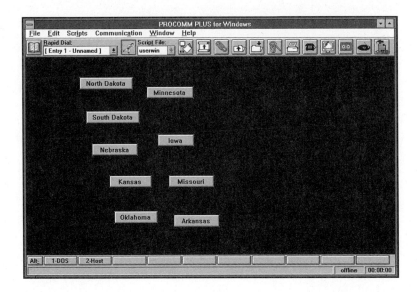

FIG. 12.8

Plains Region
displayed from
USERWIN.WAS.

The REMOVE USERWIN command removes the USA map metafile background, the User Window, and all push button objects placed on the window. Using the REMOVE command, you can remove just the BACK-GROUND. You also can remove OBJECTs by using their IDs. The PAINT command then must be issued to display the change. You can expand the PROCESS procedure to include the push button IDs in the `plains` procedure.

Summary

This chapter introduced the general script writing process by discussing the structure of a Windows ASPECT program and the relationships between the major sections. This chapter has taken you through the steps of script design, writing, and testing in order to provide you with the information needed to develop your own communications utility program. Several scripts have been described as examples of real life ideas for using the concepts taught. Use these scripts, and the others provided by DATASTORM TECHNOLOGIES, as guidance to help you put the power of Windows ASPECT to work for you.

Installing and Starting PROCOMM PLUS for Windows

This appendix explains how to install PROCOMM PLUS for Windows on a hard disk and begin using the program. During installation, you can set several PROCOMM PLUS for Windows parameters so that the program runs properly on your computer the first time.

Understanding System Requirements

Before installing PROCOMM PLUS for Windows, make sure that your system meets the program's minimum requirements. To run PROCOMM PLUS for Windows, you must be using the following:

- An IBM PC/AT 286,386,486 compatible computer

- An installed copy of Microsoft Windows 3.0 or higher

- A mouse or other pointing device

■ A modem hooked into a telephone line or a null modem hookup to another computer

■ A serial connection to the modem or null modem hookup

If you have a choice of modems, the modem should recognize the Hayes AT command set (usually referred to as a Hayes-compatible modem), but you can use virtually any modem with PROCOMM PLUS for Windows.

Before you install PROCOMM PLUS for Windows, you need to know the answers to several questions:

■ Will your computer be connected to other computers through a modem (via telephone lines), by direct connection (null modem), or both?

■ Which COM port will your computer be using? If you are not sure, refer to Appendix B, "Installing a Modem," for more information on communications ports. If your computer has only one serial port and your modem is attached to that port, it is probably the COM1 port.

■ What is the serial number for your copy of PROCOMM PLUS for Windows? Check your reference card. You need to enter this number during the installation process.

■ In what directory do you want to store PROCOMM PLUS for Windows? (The usual directory is C:\PROWIN.)

■ What type of modem are you using? The installation procedure provides a list of modems from which you can choose the appropriate model. If your model is not listed but is compatible with a Hayes 1200- or 2400-baud modem, choose the appropriate Hayes-compatible option.

■ Does your telephone system support tone or pulse dialing? What dialout prefix, if any, do you normally need to dial before getting an outside line? (Often this is 9.)

Installing PROCOMM PLUS for Windows

The PROCOMM PLUS for Windows Distribution Disk 1 contains a special installation program, INSTALL.EXE, that enables you to install the PROCOMM PLUS for Windows program and set several PROCOMM PLUS for Windows parameters so that the program runs properly on your computer the first time.

WARNING: Do not use the DOS COPY command to copy PROCOMM PLUS for Windows files from the distribution disk to your hard disk or a floppy disk. You must use the INSTALL program to install the program properly.

To use the PROCOMM PLUS for Windows installation utility, insert the PROCOMM PLUS for Windows Disk 1 into drive A of your computer.

Begin the Windows program on your computer, if it is not already running. From the File menu on the Windows Program manager, choose the Run option (Alt-F,R). A screen similar to the one shown in figure A.1 appears. In the Command Line field, type the command *a:install* and press Enter to begin the installation process. If your PROCOMM PLUS for Windows installation disk is in another drive (such as B:), use the proper drive name in place of a:.

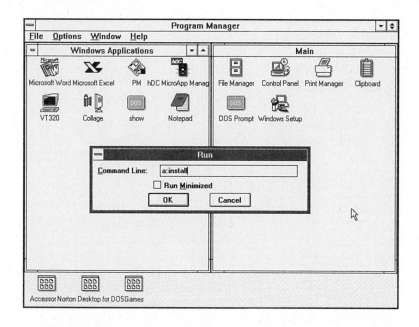

The following discussion leads you through the PROCOMM PLUS for Windows installation process. After typing the Install command and pressing Enter, you are greeted by a welcome screen. Whenever a screen appears, you can usually continue to the next screen by pressing Enter. After the greeting and copyright screen, you see the initial installation screen, shown in figure A.2. This screen contains a brief description of the installation process.

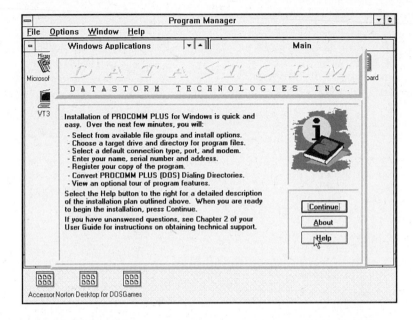

FIG. A.2

Initial installation
screen.

Notice the three buttons at the bottom right of the screen: Continue, About, and Help. These or similar buttons appear on most screens during the installation process. To choose one of these options, point to the option with the mouse pointer and click, or press the Alt key and press the underlined character of the option you want. To choose About, for example, you press Alt-A. If the button currently contains the *highlighter* (you can see it on this screen as a box around Continue), you can press Enter to choose that option.

If you choose the About option, copyright information about the program is displayed. If you choose Help, a help screen containing information about performing the installation appears.

After you have read the information on the initial installation screen, choose Continue to move to the next screen, Installation Options (see fig. A.3). This screen enables you to choose what part of the PROCOMM PLUS for Windows program to load onto your computer. You can simply choose the Begin option to continue with a normal installation. If you have special needs, however, you may want to customize the installation.

To customize the installation, you can choose specific parts of the program to load. If you do not have enough space on your hard disk to hold the entire program, for example, you can choose not to copy parts that you do not need. The Available option contains available options not currently scheduled to be loaded. The Selected box contains the features of the program to be loaded.

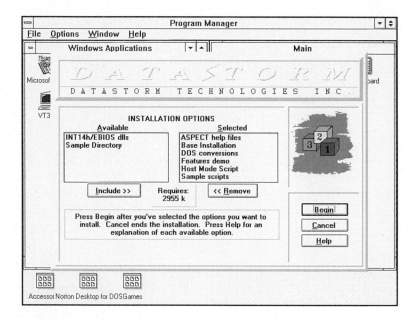

Installation options.

To move an item from the Available box to the Selected box, click the item, or press Alt-A and then press the up- or down-arrow key until the item is selected. Next, click Include or press Alt-I. The chosen item is moved to the Selected box. To move an item from the Selected box to the Available box, click the item to highlight it, or press Alt-S and then the arrow keys to highlight an item. Next, click Remove or press Alt-R. If you do not understand the terms used for the installation options, you can choose Help (Alt-H) to display additional information about these terms.

Most users should choose to install the program using all of the default options. The INT14h/EBIOS DLLS option should be chosen only if you are using a communication device other than a standard modem or serial port—for example, if you are redirecting data to an asynchronous communications server. The Sample Directory option contains a collection of top BBSs around the country. Choose this option if you want this directory.

After you have included all the features you want to install in the Selected box, choose Begin to continue with the installation. The next dialog box in which you need to make a choice is Target Directories, shown in figure A.4.

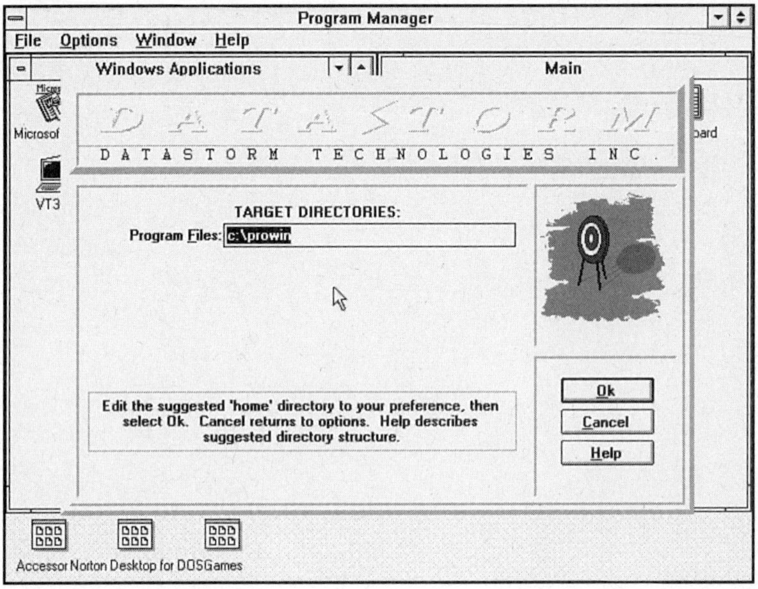

FIG. A.4

Defining the Program
Files directory in the
Target Directories box.

The target directory is the Program Files directory, where the
PROCOMM PLUS for Windows main file is stored. This directory is generally named \PROWIN. Unless you have a specific reason to change the
name, choose Ok (Alt-O) to continue the installation. Other directories
used to store files are defined by default as subdirectories of the Program Files (\PROWIN) directory. As figure A.5 shows, you can define up
to six target directories (including the Program Files directory). The
directories are as follows:

- *Program Files*. Contains the main files for the program plus supporting files.

- *Capture Files*. Contains files created when you capture information
  from the Terminal Display screen.

- *Dialing Directories*. Contains phone numbers and other information
  about the computer systems that you will access.

- *ASPECT Scripts*. Contains Windows ASPECT scripts.

- *Download Files*. Stores files that can be downloaded.

- *Upload Files*. Stores uploaded files.

If you want to change a directory name, point to the directory field and
enter a new name; alternatively, press Alt plus the underlined character
of the field name and enter the new directory name. If all these directories are acceptable, choose Ok (Alt-O) to continue.

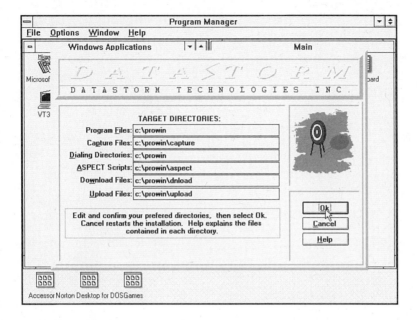

Defining the target
directories.

After you have defined the target directories, the install program begins
to copy files from the installation disks to your hard disk. A *progress bar*
informs you of the progress being made (see fig. A.6).

FIG. A.6

The installation
progress screen.

During the copying process, you are prompted to insert Disk 2, Disk 3, and so on until all the information is copied to your hard disk.

After all files are copied to the disk, several dialog boxes appear that enable you to set up the program for your particular computer configuration. The first such screen is the Default Connection screen (see fig. A.7).

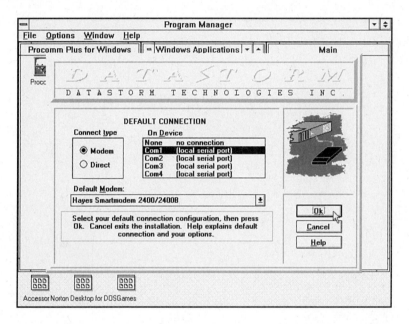

FIG. A.7

The Default
Connection screen.

This screen enables you to specify your connection type, communication device, and modem. You can change this information later in the Current Setup menu, as discussed in Chapter 8, "Tailoring PROCOMM PLUS for Windows." Please reference this chapter if you need more information about the choices in this dialog box.

The Connect Type option enables you to specify whether your computer is primarily using a modem or a direct connection. A *modem connection* connects your computer to other computers through a modem (see Appendix B). A *direct connection* is a setup in which two computers are attached with a null modem cable. To choose a connect type, point to the option you want and click; alternatively, you can press Alt-T, use the arrow keys to place the highlighter on your choice, and then press the space bar.

The On Device box contains information about the connection you will be using. On most computers, you choose COM1 or COM2, depending on the hardware setup. This setting is critical. Make sure that you indicate the correct COM port, or PROCOMM PLUS for Windows will not communicate with your modem, and your modem will not be able to dial or connect to another computer. To make a selection, point to the device you want and click; alternatively, press Alt-D, and then use the arrow keys to highlight your choice.

The Default Modem option enables you to select the modem you are using. This modem list contains more than 200 different modem types. To select a modem, click the modem field or press Alt-M. Then press the arrow keys to scroll through the list of available modems. Alternatively, click the down-arrow key to the right of the field to pull down a *drop box*. Then you can point to the up- or down-arrow keys on the drop box to scroll through the list of modems.

The complete list of modems in the PROCOMM PLUS for Windows installation program follows:

>direct connect
>Amiga 1200RS
>Anchor Volksmodem 1200
>Anchor 2400E
>AT&T 224 CEO
>AT&T Model 4000
>ATI 2400etc
>ATI 2400etc V.42
>ATI 9600etc
>Avatech 2400E
>BSM Quik Com MNP
>Cardinal 2400 MNP
>Cardinal 9650 V.32
>Cermetek 1200 Modem/1200 SPC/Security Modem
>Cermetek 2400 R/2400 SPC
>Compaq Enhanced Internal Modem (V.42bis)
>Companion CTS212AH
>CompuCom Speedmodem
>Concord Data CDS 224 Autodial
>DataTrek 624 (UK)
>DataTrek 624 (US)
>DataTrek 2424(MNP)
>DataTrek V.32
>Delta Gold DM 1200 Dell Data/Fax Modem
>Digicom DSI 9624
>Digicom DSI 9624 Plus
>E-Tech Bullet PC 2400MH
>E-Tech E2400M
>E-Tech E9696M
>E-Tech PC9696M
>Everex Evercom 12e

Everex Evercom 24e
Everex 11-24e
Everex EV941
Everex Evercom 24e+ (MNP 5)
Everex Carrier 24
Everex Carrier 24/96
Everex Carrier 24/96E
EverFax 24/96E
EverFax 96E+
Fastcomm 2496/Turbo
Fastcomm 9696
Forval 1M1440
General DataComm Desktop 596
GVC Super Modem 2400 MNP-5
GVC Super Modem 9600
GVC Ultra 14400
Hayes-Compatible 1200-Baud Modem
Hayes-Compatible 2400-Baud Modem
Hayes Personal Modem 1200
Hayes Personal Modem 2400
Hayes Smartmodem 1200/1200B
Hayes Smartmodem 2400/2400B
Hayes Smartmodem V Series 2400/2400B
Hayes Smartmodem V Series 9600/9600B V.32
Hayes Optima 9600
Hayes Ultra 9600
Hayes Ultra 14400
Hayes V Series 2400/2400B V.42
Hayes V Series 9600/9600B V.42
Hayes ISDN Terminal Adapter
IBM Modem 1200 (5841)
IBM PC 2400 bps Modem
IBM PS/2 Data/Fax Modem
IBM 7855 Model 10
Image Twincom 96/42i
InfoMate 212A/PC
InfoMate 212X/PC
Intel 2400B
Intel 2400B MNP
Intel 2400EX MNP
Intel 9600EX
Intel SatisFAXtion Board
Intel 14400EX
Maxwell Modem 300PC/300V Maxwell Modem 1200PC/1200V
The Maxwell Modem 1200VP
The Maxwell Modem 2400PC

MegaHertz EasyTalk 1200
MegaHertz EasyTalk 2400
MicroCom AX/2400 MNP4
MicroCom AX/2400c MNP5
MicroCom AX/9612c
MicroCom AX/9624c
MicroCom QX V.32c
MicroCom QX 2400t
MicroCom Qx
MicroCom 4232hs
MicroCom Keycard 2400
Miracom Keycard 3000
Miracard WS4000/PC
Motorola-Codex 2264
Motorola-Codex 3220
Motorola-Codex 3260 Series
MultiTech MultiModem 224/224PC
MultiTech MultiModem 224E/224EC/PC3
MultiTech MultiModem 224E7 V.42bis
MultiTech MultiModem V.32 EAB V.42bis
MultiTech Multimodem 696E
MultiTech MultiModem V.32
NEC N2431/2431C
Novation Professional 2400
Novation Smart-Cat 103/212
Okidata CLP 296
Okidata Okitel 2400 Plus/2400B Plus
Okidata Okitel 2400/2400B
Okidata Okitel 1200/1200B
Okidata Okitel 9600
Pace Linnet 1200
Pace Linnet PC Card (300 baud)
Pace Linnet Series 4
Pace Linnet Ultralink Quad
Pace Linnet Ultralink 32
Penril Datalink 1200
Penril Datalink 2400
Practical Peripherals Practical 1200
Practical Peripherals Practical 2400
Practical Peripherals 2400SA
Practical Peripherals Pocketmodem
Practical Peripherals 2400SA MNP
Practical Peripherals 2400SA V.42bis
Practical Peripherals PM9600SA V.32
Premier Innovations P2400/2400E
Prometheus Pro Modem 1200

Prometheus 2400 MCT-24I Half-card
Prometheus 9600 MNP
Prometheus Promodem Ultima Racal-Milgo RMD 3221
Racal-Vadic 1200PA
Racal-Vadic 2400/PS
Racal-Vadic 2400LC
Racal-Vadic LC2400PC
Racal-Vadic 2400PA
Racal-Vadic 2400PA Model 2
Racal-Vadic 2400VP
Racal-Vadic 9600VP
Racal-Vadic 9632PA
Racal-Vadic VA212
Racal-Vadic VA3451
Supra Modem 2400
Supra 2400 MNP
Supra 2400 Plus (V.42bis)
Supra 9600
Sysdyne MDM 24H
Tandy 1200-bps Half Card
Telebit Internal PC Card W/MNP
Telebit T1000
Telebit T1500-V.42 mode
Telebit T2500 V.42 mode
Telebit T1500-MNP mode
Telebit T2500-MNP mode
Telebit T2000
Telebit T3000 (57.6K baud)
Telebit Trailblazer/Trailblazer Plus
Telebit Q-Blazer
Universal Data Systems Fastalk 2400
UDS V.32/v.42
USD V.3224/V.3225
USD V.3227
US Robotics Sportster 1200/1200 PC
US Robotics Sportster 2400/2400 PC
US Robotics 2400PC
US Robotics 2400 MNP
US Robotics Courier 2400
US Robotics Courier 2400e/ 2400e/ps
US Robotics Courier 2400PC
US Robotics Courier HST
US Robotics Courier HST V.42
US Robotics Courier HST-ASL
US Robotics V.32
US Robotics V.32bis-ASL

US Robotics Dual Standard
US Robotics Dual Standard V.32bis-ASL
Ven-Tel 212Plus
Ven-Tel Halfcard
Ven-Tel Halfcard 24
Ven-Tel 2400 Plus II
Ven-Tel 9600 Plus/Plus II
Ven-Tel PCM2400E Ven-Tel Pathfinder
ViVa 24&2496if
ViVa 24fx & 24i/fx
ViVa 24m
ViVa 24im
ViVa 2442i
ViVa 9642e
Zeos Notebook Modem
Zoom Modem PC 1200
Zoom Modem PC 2400
Zoom Modem V.42bis
Zoom Modem V.32 Turbo

If your modem is not listed, select the one closest to your modem. The USRobotics Microlink 2400, for example, uses the same commands as the USRobotics Courier 2400. When in doubt, select the Hayes modem with the same maximum speed. Refer to your modem's manual and to Chapter 8, "Tailoring PROCOMM PLUS for Windows," to determine whether you need to modify the modem commands inserted by the installation program.

When you finish making your selections on the Default Connection dialog box, choose Ok (Alt-O) to continue the installation. If you do not understand the terms used for the installation options, you can choose Help (Alt-H) to display additional information about these options.

After you choose Ok, the installation program displays the Program Defaults dialog box (see fig. A.8). This dialog box enables you to choose several options, all of which you can change later in the Setup procedure described in Chapter 8. If you do not yet know enough about these options to make changes, just accept the defaults. You can change them later if necessary.

The Phone option enables you to specify whether your telephone uses the tone or pulse method for dialing. (Most modern phone systems use the tone method.) If your phone system uses only rotary dial phones, you must choose the pulse option to have dial-out capability. To choose Tone or Pulse, click the option or press Alt-T or Alt-U.

The Protocol option enables you to choose a default file transfer protocol. If you will be connecting computers using PROCOMM products, the

Zmodem method is recommended. If you will be accessing another computer system that uses a different protocol, choose that option as the default. See Chapter 5, "Transferring Files," for more information on transfer protocols.

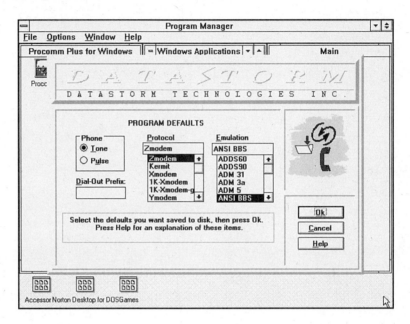

FIG. A.8

The Program Defaults dialog box.

The Emulation option enables you to choose the default terminal emulation. The most common choices are ANSI BBS for connection to bulletin board systems and VT102 for connection to a wide variety of mainframes and PC-based systems. You need to determine the emulation the system you will be connected to requires. See Chapter 10, "Terminal Emulation," for more information on these options.

When you have finished making your selections on the Program Defaults dialog box, choose Ok (Alt-O) to continue the installation. If you do not understand the terms used for the installation options, you can choose Help (Alt-H) to display additional information about these options.

The User Information dialog box captures information about you so that you can automatically register your copy of PROCOMM PLUS for Windows (see fig. A.9). Enter your name and product serial number in this dialog box. (The serial number is on the card just inside the user's manual.) You can move from field to field by clicking the field or by pressing Tab or Shift-Tab.

When you finish entering information in the User Information dialog box, choose Ok (Alt-O) to continue the installation. If you need more information about entering information in the box, you can choose Help (Alt-H).

After you enter the information, the Registration Information dialog box appears (see fig. A.10).

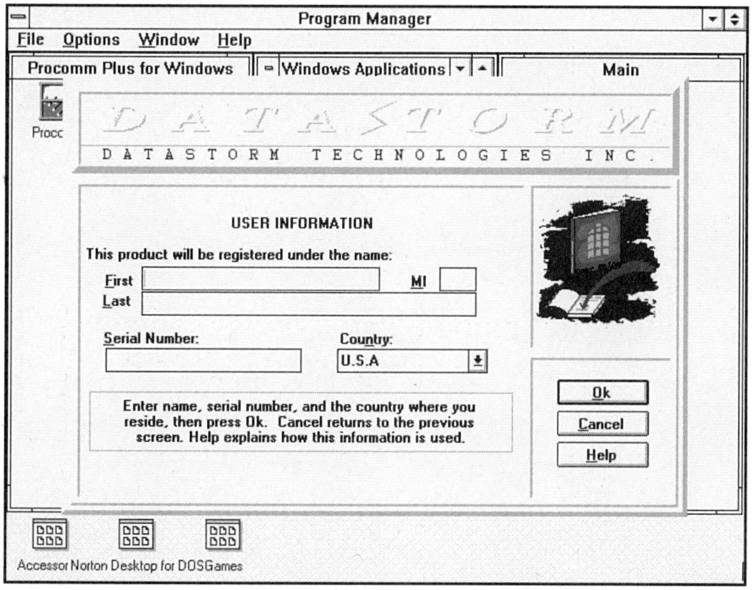

FIG. A.9

The User Information dialog box.

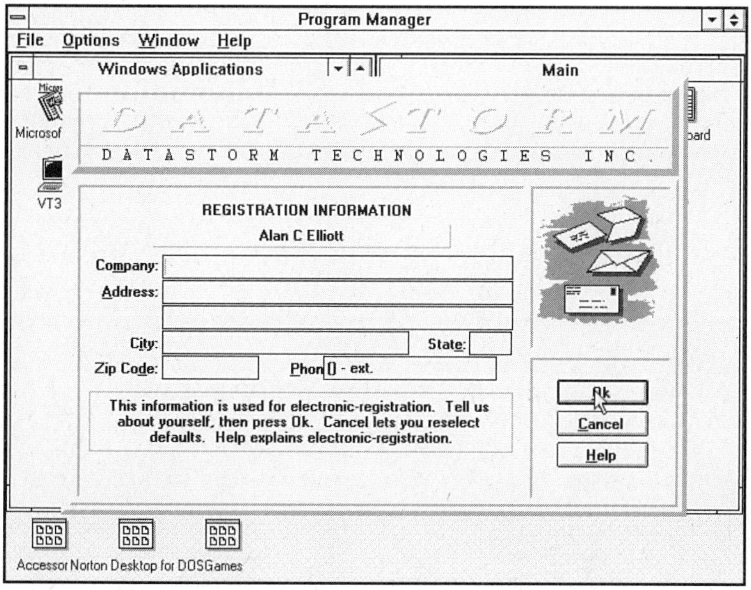

FIG. A.10

The Registration Information dialog box.

The Registration Information screen captures information that enables you to register your copy of PROCOMM PLUS for Windows electronically.

Following the Registration screen, you are given the opportunity to convert directory files from an old PROCOMM PLUS format to the Windows version. Figure A.11 shows the Select Dialing Directories to Convert dialog box. If you do not have files to convert, select Quit (Alt-Q). If you have old Procomm directories to convert, specify which files to convert; then choose Convert (Alt-C).

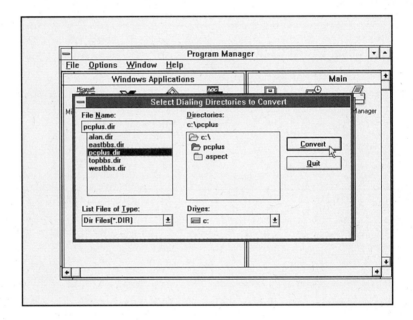

To specify the files to convert, first double-click the root directory (C:\) in the Directories box to display the directory containing your old files. A directory tree appears in the box. Point to the directory containing the old directories (PCPLUS, for example) and double-click. The PROCOMM PLUS directory files in that DOS directory appear in the File Name list box. Highlight the file to convert by clicking the file, or press the up- and down-arrow keys until the file is highlighted. To highlight multiple files to convert, point to a file name; then click and drag across several files. When you have highlighted the files to convert, choose Convert.

When you choose to convert, a Verify dialog box appears (see fig. A.12). In this box, you specify the version of PROCOMM you are converting from and the name of the converted file. Choose Convert to convert the file (Alt-C), Skip File (Alt-S) to skip the conversion of this file, or Quit (Alt-Q) to quit the conversion process.

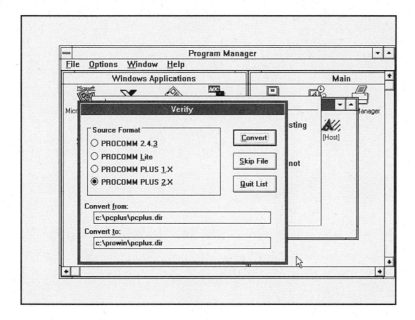

The Verify dialog box.

When you finish converting, or if you skip the conversion process, the install program builds a PCPLUS/Win window and begins the PROCOMM PLUS for Windows program. The first time you run the program, you are given the option of using Electronic Registration. Figure A.13 shows the initial registration notice.

The Electronic Registration screen.

To continue with registration, choose Yes. Choose No if you do not want to register, or choose Later to register at a later time. If you choose to register now, make sure that your modem is turned on. The registration calls the DATASTORM registration line (toll free) and sends your registration information automatically.

Installation of PROCOMM PLUS for Windows is not yet complete, however. When the registration ends, the PROCOMM PLUS for Windows Terminal Display screen appears. You can end PROCOMM PLUS for Windows by choosing Exit from the File menu (Alt-F, X). When you return to the Microsoft Windows Program Manager, you see that a PCPLUS/Win window has been created, containing several PROCOMM PLUS for Windows programs (see fig. A.14).

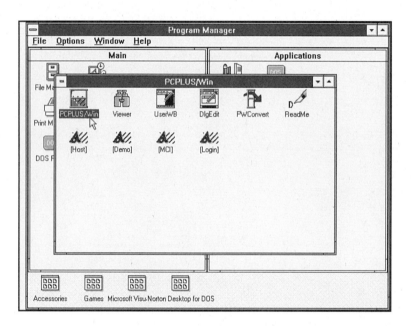

FIG. A.14

The PCPLUS/Win window in the Program Manager.

This window enables you to begin the main program or to choose from several other programs. To begin PROCOMM PLUS for Windows from this menu, point to the PCPLUS/Win icon and double-click. The icons in the PCPLUS/Win window initiate the following programs:

Program	Description
PCPLUS/Win	The main PROCOMM PLUS for Windows program
Viewer	The GIF graphics file viewer
UserWB	The Window Builder for Aspect program development

Program	Description
DlgEdit	The Windows Aspect Dialog editor
PWConvert	Converts old ProComm directories to Windows version
ReadMe	Contains additional information not in the manual
Host	Begins the Host mode script
Demo	Begins the Demo program
MCI	Begins the MCI electronic mail program
Login	Begins the Login program that sets up login procedures for several popular dial-in systems

Following installation of PROCOMM PLUS for Windows using the installation defaults, your disk directory C:\PROWIN contains the files listed in table A.1.

Table A.1. Files Copied to Hard Disk by the Installation Utility

File Name		Description
TOUR		<DIR> Tour directory
CAPTURE		<DIR> Capture directory
ASPECT		<DIR> Aspect Scripts directory
UPLOAD		<DIR> Upload directory
DNLOAD		<DIR> Download directory
README	WRI	Supplemental information not in manual
WMODEMS	DAT	Install information about modems
CONVERT	EXE	Converts PCPLUS directories to Windows
PWUSERWB	EXE	Window Builder Program for Aspect program development
PWDLGED	EXE	Dialog Editor for Aspect program development
ASPCOMPW	EXE	Windows Aspect compiler
PWVIEWER	EXE	Program to view GIF files
PW	EXE	Main PROCOMM PLUS for Windows Program

continues

Table A.1. Continued

File Name		Description
PWASPHLP	HLP	Main Aspect Help file
PWHELP	HLP	Main Help file
PWUSERWB	HLP	Help file for Window Builder program
PWVIEWER	HLP	Help file for viewer
PWDLGED	HLP	Help file for the Dialog Editor
PWKEYMAP	FON	Font file for key mapping
PWTRMNL	FON	Font file for terminal fonts
DEFAULT	KEY	Default key mapping file
DEFAULT	KBD	Default keyboard file
PW	PRM	Information about terminal emulations
PW	DIR	Default Dialing Directory file
DEFAULT	XLT	Default Translate file
REGISTER	DAT	Registration data

Starting PROCOMM PLUS for Windows

Now that your program is installed, you are ready to start PROCOMM PLUS for Windows. To begin the program, you must be in the Windows operating environment. If the PCPLUS/Win window is not currently in view on the Program Manager screen, it should be a minimized icon, usually at the bottom of the Program Manager window. Double-click the PW icon to open that window. From the PW window, double-click the PCPLUS/Win icon to begin the PROCOMM PLUS for Windows program.

Now you are ready to use PROCOMM PLUS for Windows. Happy communicating!

Installing a Modem

One of the basic requirements of computer communications is a modem—the piece of hardware that accomplishes modulation and demodulation so that a digital computer can communicate over analog phone lines. Without a modem at each end of the phone line, the two computers cannot communicate. Refer to Chapter 1 for a general discussion of modems.

Modem manufacturers often produce modems in internal and external versions. The procedure for installation varies, depending on the type of modem you are installing.

Connecting an External Modem

An external modem is usually a metal or plastic box about 10 inches by 6 inches by 2 inches, with a panel of LED (light-emitting diodes) on the front. The modem is connected to your PC by a serial cable and powered by an AC adapter. The modem has at least one telephone jack for connecting the modem to the telephone line and often a second jack for connecting a telephone.

To connect your external modem to your computer and prepare it for communication, you need a few other parts: a serial port and a serial cable to connect the modem to the serial port.

A relatively new type of external modem is small enough to fit in your pocket and can run on batteries. These mini-modems typically plug directly into a serial port on your computer and are particularly handy for laptop-computer users. This type of external modem requires a serial cable only if the serial port on your computer has a different number of pins than the connector on the modem.

Choosing a Serial Port

Your computer must have an available *serial port* (COM port) to which you can connect your external modem. If all the serial ports on your computer are in use (for example, by a mouse, printer, and plotter), you need to add another serial port to your computer. You can find serial ports on many types of integrated circuit boards (referred to generically in this discussion as *serial cards*), many of which may contain other types of input/output devices, such as parallel ports and game ports. Make sure that any board you obtain will fit into an available slot on the expansion bus of your computer.

The expansion bus is located inside your computer box, on the system board. The expansion bus contains the slots where you plug in expansion boards, such as a serial port board or a modem board. The common types of bus are ISA (Industry Standard Architecture), EISA (ISA enhanced), and MCA (microchannel architecture).

Serial ports are numbered COM1, COM2, COM3, and COM4. Versions of DOS prior to DOS 3.3 support only COM1 and COM2. Nearly all serial cards can be configured as COM1 or COM2 by flipping a DIP (dual in-line package) switch or by moving a jumper; not all serial cards can be configured as COM3 or higher, however. Before you buy a card, make sure that it will meet your needs.

When you are using more than one serial port, use COM1 or COM2 for communications if possible. The most typical configuration is to connect your mouse to COM1 and modem to COM2. Although PROCOMM PLUS for Windows enables you to address serial ports numbered through COM8, you may experience conflicts between your modem and other peripheral devices attached to your computer through other serial ports. COM1 and COM3, for example, typically use the same IRQ line. With a mouse connected to COM1 and a modem connected to COM3, you may have problems running PROCOMM PLUS for Windows or other programs.

Choosing a Serial Cable

A *serial cable* is one of the simplest pieces of hardware used in your system, but it is crucial to successful PC communications. The serial cable connects a serial device to a serial port—in this case, a modem to the serial port on your PC. A serial cable is therefore quite often referred to as a *modem cable*. Not all serial cables have the same number of pins on each end. Make sure that the cable you buy matches your computer and your modem.

Users sometimes confuse modem cables with null-modem cables, which serve a different function. To minimize confusion, the discussion that follows refers to the cable that connects a modem to a serial port simply as a serial cable. Refer to "Connecting Computers with a Null-Modem Cable" later in this appendix for information about null-modem cables.

On the IBM PC, PC/XT, and PS/2 computers as well as on most compatibles, each serial port is a D-shaped connector with 25 protruding metal pins located on the back of the computer. This type of connector is called a DB-25 M (male) connector. The connector on the serial cable that attaches the modem to this serial port therefore must have 25 holes to match the male connector's 25 pins. The connector is called a DB-25 F (female) connector. Most external modems have a DB-25 F serial connector, so the typical serial cable must have a DB-25 M connector on one end and a DB-25 F connector on the other end.

The 25 pins on a DB-25 serial port connector correspond to the 25 circuits defined by the Electronic Industries Association Recommended Standard 232, revision C, referred to as the RS-232C standard or just RS-232. When used for asynchronous communications, however, only 9 of the 25 pins normally are used: pins 2, 3, 4, 5, 6, 7, 8, 20, and sometimes 22. The IBM PC AT and many compatibles therefore use a 9-pin DB-9 connector instead of the DB-25. (Some 25-pin serial cables also use pin 1, the Frame Ground (FG) circuit; this circuit usually is not necessary, however, so 9-pin cables do not use the FG circuit.) When connecting a modem to an IBM PC AT or AT-compatible, you usually need a serial cable with a DB-9 F on one end (to connect to the computer) and a DB-25 M on the other end (to connect to the modem).

The RS-232 standard defines two types of serial devices: data terminal equipment (DTE) and data communications equipment (DCE). The standard is designed so that DTE devices connect directly to DCE devices. The serial port on your computer is configured as a DTE device, and your modem is configured as DCE device.

Table B.1 lists the names given by the RS-232 standard to the nine circuits commonly used in asynchronous communications, from the point of view of a DTE device. The table indicates the pin to which each circuit is assigned on a DB-25 and a DB-9 connector. This table also tells how circuits should be configured in a serial cable that has a DB-25 pin connector on one end and a DB-9 pin connector on the other end.

Table B.1 RS-232 DTE Circuits in DB-25 and DB-9 Connectors

Circuit name	Abbreviation	DB-25 pin	DB-9 pin
Transmit Data	TD	2	3
Receive Data	RD	3	2
Request To Send	RTS	4	7
Clear To Send	CTS	5	8
Data Set Ready	DSR	6	6
Signal Ground	SG	7	5
Data Carrier Detect	DCD	8	1
Data Terminal Ready	DTR	20	4
Ring Indicator	RI	22	9

The pin assignments for a DCE device are the same as those shown in table B.1 except that pins 2 and 3 are reversed. When you connect a DTE device to a DCE device, the Transmit Data (TD) circuit on one end is connected to the Receive Data (RD) circuit on the other end.

After you obtain the proper serial cable, fasten the cable securely to your computer and to the modem using the screws provided. Many communication problems can be traced to loose cable connections.

Installing an Internal Modem

Each internal modem is built on a circuit board that plugs into an empty expansion slot inside your PC. Some internal modems are long enough to fill up a long expansion slot, but others need only a half-size slot.

The steps for installing an internal modem depend on the brand and the model of PC you have. This section is intended only as a general guide. Read your PC owner's manual and the modem's documentation for the proper procedure.

> **CAUTION:** Before you open or do anything inside your computer, TURN OFF ALL POWER AND UNPLUG your computer.

Avoid discharging static electricity into an internal modem. Before touching the modem, touch a large metal object, such as your computer's chassis. This action discharges into the metal object any static electricity that has built up on your body.

Before you install the modem, read the following section to determine whether you need to change the modem's configuration settings. If your modem is configured by DIP switches, you may not be able to reach the switches after the board is installed.

Unlike an external modem, an internal modem is not connected to a serial port. The modem board, however, contains a special chip called the UART (universal asynchronous receiver/transmitter), which is actually a built-in serial port. The modem therefore counts as one of the computer's serial ports. Determine which serial ports are installed and configure your modem as a different port. If your computer has only one serial port installed—COM1, for example—configure the modem as COM2. If your computer has two serial ports, however, you need to be able to configure the modem as COM3. Nearly all internal modem cards can be configured as COM1 or COM2 by flipping a DIP switch or moving a jumper, but not all can be configured as COM3 or higher. Make sure before you purchase a card that it will meet your needs.

After configuring the modem, turn off the power to your computer and unplug it. Open the computer's case and locate an empty expansion slot. Remove the retaining screw of the metal slot cover on the back of the computer; then take off the cover. Slide the card into the slot. Carefully, but firmly, press the card down until it is seated securely. Replace the retaining screw and the cover.

Configuring the Modem

You must configure a modem to take advantage of its features. Some modems, internal or external, are configured by using DIP (dual in-line package) switches. Other modems are configured with software commands. Refer to your modem's manual to determine the proper method (by DIP switch or by software) and configure the modem as specified in the following list. Configured to these settings, your modem will work properly with PROCOMM PLUS for Windows. If you purchase a modem that is unable to function as described here, you will not be able to take full advantage of PROCOMM PLUS for Windows.

Be sure to configure your modem so that it does the following:

- The computer controls the Data Terminal Ready (DTR) signal, and the modem follows the actual state of the DTR signal.

- The modem generates verbal result codes.

- Result codes are displayed.

- Keyboard commands are displayed in Command mode.

- Auto Answer is off.

- The modem controls the Data Carrier Detect signal (DCD or CD), asserting the DCD signal only when the modem detects a carrier signal from a remote modem.

- The AT command set is enabled.

- The Escape code (+++) does not hang up the modem.

If your modem is configured using software commands, you may be able to use the Initialization Command option on the Modem Setup screen to send the proper commands to your modem each time PROCOMM PLUS for Windows starts. The initialization command inserted by the PROCOMM PLUS for Windows installation utility for a Hayes 2400 modem, for example, includes the software command to control the DTR signal with the computer and the DCD signal (AT&C1&D2) with the modem. (See Chapter 8, "Tailoring PROCOMM PLUS for Windows" for more information.)

Setting Up an Error-Control or Data-Compression Modem

Several manufacturers now produce modems that perform error control instead of requiring that the communications software perform this chore. When a modem performs error control, error detection and the overall speed of transmission are superior to software error-checking. Many modems that provide built-in error control also compress the data as it is sent. A compatible modem on the other end decompresses the data.

For error control to work, however, the modems on both ends of the connection must use the same error-control protocol. Two types of error-control protocols have developed a significant following: Hayes and MNP Classes 1 through 4. Fortunately, an industry standard has emerged that incorporates the two competing error-control schemes: CCITT V.42. Similarly, two popular data compression algorithms are used by competing manufacturers: Hayes and MNP Class 5. A new international standard has emerged to replace the two types of error-control protocols and schemes: CCITT V.42bis. See Chapter 1 for more information about these error-control and data-compression standards.

Regardless of the type of error-control or data-compression modem you use, the modem at the other end must be compatible for you to recognize any benefit. Even with compatible modems, you also have to set up the modem and PROCOMM PLUS for Windows properly, or your modem will not give you the added transmission speed you are looking for. Keep in mind that the modems connect at their nominal speed (2400 bps for a 2400-bps modem, for example); through data-compression algorithms, however, data throughput can be much faster. The data must therefore flow between your computer and your modem at a rate higher than the connection speed between the two modems. If you set PROCOMM PLUS for Windows at the same rate as the connect rate, you defeat the purpose of the modem.

The software commands for setting up the modem vary among manufacturers; check your modem manual for the appropriate commands. (Some modems use DIP switches instead of software commands.) In order to achieve maximum throughput, set up PROCOMM PLUS for Windows and your modem as follows:

1. Set PROCOMM PLUS for Windows' baud rate to the highest rate allowed by the modem. This rate is often 9600 for a 2400-bps modem, or 19200 for a 9600-bps modem. Change all your dialing directory entries to this higher rate as well.

2. Use the Modem Setup screen to deselect the Auto Baud Detect option. (See Chapter 8, "Tailoring PROCOMM PLUS for Windows.") If you are using a 2400-bps error-control/data-compression modem, for example, the modems connect at 2400 bps. You have set PROCOMM PLUS for Windows's baud rate to 9600 bps, however, and you don't want PROCOMM PLUS for Windows to adjust the rate down to 2400.

3. Use the Modem Setup screen to select the Hardware Flow Control (RTS/CTS) option. (See Chapter 8, "Tailoring PROCOMM PLUS for Windows.") Also send a software command to your modem to enable RTS/CTS handshaking.

4. Issue the software command to your modem to activate the error-control and data-compression features.

5. Set the modem so that it follows the actual state of the Data Terminal Ready (DTR) signal (AT&D2 is the usual command) and the modem controls Data Carrier Detect (DCD or CD) signal (AT&C1 is the usual command).

6. Save the modem's configuration to nonvolatile memory (AT&W0 is the usual command). Even when you turn off the modem, the new settings are stored in nonvolatile memory.

7. Use the Modem Setup screen to set the Initialization Command option in the Modem Commands Options screen to ATZ^M (see Chapter 8). This command is the standard AT command to reset nonvolatile memory to the currently stored settings. In other words, when PROCOMM PLUS for Windows starts, it sends this command to the modem, and the modem retrieves the setup values you stored in nonvolatile memory.

8. Use the Modem Setup screen to change all the connect messages in the Modem Result Messages screen to CONNECT. (See Chapter 8.)

Connecting to the Telephone Line

Your modem has at least one phone jack—usually on the back or side of the modem. If you have only one jack, connect it using a phone cable with a modular (RJ-11) phone plug to the telephone outlet on the wall. If your modem has two phone jacks, connect the one marked Line to the jack in the wall. The other jack on your modem, usually marked Phone, is for connecting a telephone. Sometimes the jacks have no markings. In that case, attach either jack to the wall telephone outlet and plug your phone into the other.

Usually your modem comes with the necessary cable for connecting your modem to the telephone line. If not, you can find cables in electronics, hardware, department, drug, and sometimes even grocery stores. If the telephone jack on the wall is the older square type with four holes, you need an adapter. Many stores carry adapters of this sort.

In many business applications, you may want to attach your modem to a multiple telephone circuit. Multiple handsets are attached to the circuit. Each phone can use any line on the circuit when the user presses one of the buttons on the base of the handset. When someone uses a line on the multiple telephone circuit, a light on every attached handset shows that the line is in use. A person who wants to place a call looks for a button that is not lighted, presses the button, and uses the line. You can use a modem on such a system, but do so only if your modem supports the system.

If you plan to attach your phone to a line available on a multiple telephone circuit, check your modem manual to see whether your modem has a way to support multiple telephone installations (DIP switch 7 on many popular modems). This type of phone connection may be referred to in your modem documentation as RJ-12 or RJ-13. These names are the designations for the two types of modular jacks usually used to connect a single phone line to a multiple telephone system. If your modem does not have such a setting, or if you fail to set it correctly, the lights on the handsets attached to the system will not illuminate for your modem's line even when the modem is in use and connected to another computer. In this case, someone is likely to pick up the line to make a call while your PC is connected, interrupting and possibly disconnecting your transmission.

When you connect your modem to an RJ-12 or RJ-13 jack, make sure that the phone cable contains four wires. You can look at the plug at the end of the cable and count the copper wires. Only two wires are needed for a single phone system (or a multiple phone system with no lighted buttons). One of the other two wires, however, is used to light the buttons on multiple telephone system handsets when your modem is in use. Of course, before you place a call with your modem on such a system, check to see whether the line you intend to use is free.

Connecting Computers with a Null-Modem Cable

An increasingly common situation in offices that use PCs is the need to connect one computer directly to another without going through a modem or telephone line. You may have a laptop computer that has 3 1/2-inch disk drives, for example, and a desktop PC with only a 5 1/4-inch disk drive. You want to transfer data from the laptop PC to the desktop PC using PROCOMM PLUS for Windows.

To transfer data between two computers without a modem, you can use a *null-modem cable* (sometimes referred to simply as a *null modem*). The easiest way to think of this device is to focus only on pins 2 and 3 of the cable and compare this type of cable to a normal serial cable. Because both PCs' serial ports comply with the DTE configuration, a normal serial cable cannot enable the PCs to communicate because the TDs would be connected and the RDs would be connected. Instead, a null-modem cable (among other things) switches pins 2 and 3 on one end of the cable. The result is that TD on one end now is connected to RD on the other, and vice versa. This connection allows communication between the computers attached by the null-modem cable without the need for a modem or telephone line.

Null-modem cables usually are available in computer stores and by mail order. Sometimes a null modem is sold as an adapter that connects to a normal serial port, converting it to a null-modem cable. You also can rewire a normal serial cable to convert it to a null-modem cable, as depicted in figures B.1 and B.2. The cable must have a female connector on both ends, however, so that it can be connected to the two serial ports.

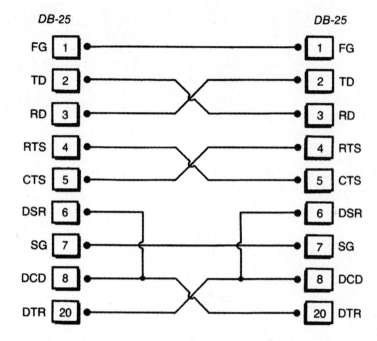

FIG. B.1

Circuit connections for a null-modem cable with DB-25 connectors.

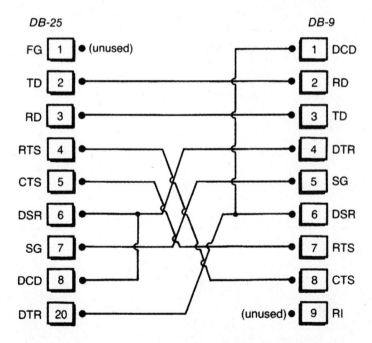

FIG. B.2

Circuit connections for a null-modem cable with a DB-25 connector on one end and DB-9 connector on the other.

The Host mode is the easiest way to use PROCOMM PLUS for Windows to transfer files between computers connected by a null-modem cable. Activate Host mode on one of the computers and then log on and control the file transfer from the other computer. For this method to work properly, however, you must modify a Host mode setting on the computer in Host mode. Use the setup utility to set the Connection Type option on the Host Mode Utility screen to Direct. Refer to Chapter 9, "Using Host Mode," for more information.

ASCII Codes

This appendix presents the IBM ASCII character set with their corresponding decimal and hexadecimal values. These ASCII codes may be useful in developing meta commands and in creating Windows ASPECT scripts. The Decimal column gives the Decimal ASCII code for the characters 0 to 255. The Hexadecimal column gives the hexadecimal equivalent to the decimal number. The Meaning or Character column gives the control code ^ plus a character, the meaning of the code, or the actual ASCII character.

Decimal	Hexadecimal	Meaning or Character
0	0	^@ NUL (null)
1	1	^A SOH (start-of-header)
2	2	^B STX (start-of-transmission)
3	3	^C ETX (end-of-transmission)
4	4	^D EOT (end-of-text)
5	5	^E ENQ (enquiry)
6	6	^F ACK (acknowledge)
7	7	^G BEL (bell)
8	8	^H BS (backspace)
9	9	^I HT (horizontal tab)
10	A	^J LF (line feed - also ^Enter)
11	B	^K VT (vertical tab)
12	C	^L FF (form feed)
13	D	^M CR (carriage return)
14	E	^N SO

Decimal	Hexadecimal	Meaning or Character
15	F	^O SI
16	10	^P DLE
17	11	^Q DC1
18	12	^R DC2
19	13	^S DC3
20	14	^T DC4
21	15	^U NAK
22	16	^V SYN
23	17	^W ETB
24	18	^X CAN (cancel)
25	19	^Y EM
26	1A	^Z SUB (also end-of-file)
27	1B	^[ESC (Escape)
28	1C	^\ FS (field separator)
29	1D	^] GS
30	1E	^^ RS (record separator)
31	1F	^_ US
32	20	Space
33	21	!
34	22	"
35	23	#
36	24	$
37	25	%
38	26	&
39	27	'
40	28	(
41	29	)
42	2A	*
43	2B	+
44	2C	,
45	2D	-
46	2E	.
47	2F	/
48	30	0
49	31	1
50	32	2
51	33	3
52	34	4
53	35	5
54	36	6
55	37	7
56	38	8
57	39	9
58	3A	:
59	3B	;
60	3C	<
61	3D	=
62	3E	>
63	3F	?
64	40	@
65	41	A
66	42	B

Decimal	Hexadecimal	Meaning or Character
67	43	C
68	44	D
69	45	E
70	46	F
71	47	G
72	48	H
73	49	I
74	4A	J
75	4B	K
76	4C	L
77	4D	M
78	4E	N
79	4F	O
80	50	P
81	51	Q
82	52	R
83	53	S
84	54	T
85	55	U
86	56	V
87	57	W
88	58	X
89	59	Y
90	5A	Z
91	5B	[
92	5C	\
93	5D	]
94	5E	^
95	5F	_
96	60	`
97	61	a
98	62	b
99	63	c
100	64	d
101	65	e
102	66	f
103	67	g
104	68	h
105	69	i
106	6A	j
107	6B	k
108	6C	l
109	6D	m
110	6E	n
111	6F	o
112	70	p
113	71	q
114	72	r
115	73	s
116	74	t
117	75	u
118	76	v

Decimal	Hexadecimal	Meaning or Character
119	77	w
120	78	x
121	79	y
122	7A	z
123	7B	{
124	7C	|
125	7D	}
126	7E	~
127	7F	Del
128	80	Ç
129	81	ü
130	82	é
131	83	â
132	84	ä
133	85	à
134	86	å
135	87	ç
136	88	ê
137	89	ë
138	8A	è
139	8B	ï
140	8C	î
141	8D	ì
142	8E	Ä
143	8F	Å
144	90	É
145	91	æ
146	92	Æ
147	93	ô
148	94	ö
149	95	ò
150	96	û
151	97	ù
152	98	ÿ
153	99	Ö
154	9A	Ü
155	9B	¢
156	9C	£
157	9D	¥
158	9E	₧
159	9F	ƒ
160	A0	á
161	A1	í
162	A2	ó
163	A3	ú
164	A4	ñ
165	A5	Ñ
166	A6	ª
167	A7	º
168	A8	¿
169	A9	⌐

Decimal	Hexadecimal	Meaning or Character
170	AA	¬
171	AB	½
172	AC	¼
173	AD	¡
174	AE	«
175	AF	»
176	B0	░
177	B1	▒
178	B2	▓
179	B3	│
180	B4	┤
181	B5	╡
182	B6	╢
183	B7	╖
184	B8	╕
185	B9	╣
186	BA	║
187	BB	╗
188	BC	╝
189	BD	╜
190	BE	╛
191	BF	┐
192	C0	└
193	C1	┴
194	C2	┬
195	C3	├
196	C4	─
197	C5	┼
198	C6	╞
199	C7	╟
200	C8	╚
201	C9	╔
202	CA	╩
203	CB	╦
204	CC	╠
205	CD	═
206	CE	╬
207	CF	╧
208	D0	╨
209	D1	╤
210	D2	╥
211	D3	╙
212	D4	╘
213	D5	╒
214	D6	╓
215	D7	╫
216	D8	╪
217	D9	┘
218	DA	┌
219	DB	█

Decimal	Hexadecimal	Meaning or Character
220	DC	▄
221	DD	▌
222	DE	▐
223	DF	▀
224	E0	∝
225	E1	β
226	E2	Γ
227	E3	π
228	E4	Σ
229	E5	σ
230	E6	µ
231	E7	τ
232	E8	Φ
233	E9	θ
234	EA	Ω
235	EB	δ
236	EC	∞
237	ED	φ
238	EE	∈
239	EF	∩
240	F0	≡
241	F1	±
242	F2	≥
243	F3	≤
244	F4	⌠
245	F5	⌡
246	F6	÷
247	F7	≈
248	F8	°
249	F9	·
250	FA	·
251	FB	√
252	FC	ⁿ
253	FD	²
254	FE	■
255	FF	

Symbols

^ caret, 180-181
+++ (escape code), 229
^[(Esc) meta key control code, 181
[] (square brackets), 339, 410
\ (backslash), 326
{} (curly brackets), 339
| (vertical bar), 339
~ (tilde), 209
↓ (move down one line) Notepad keyboard shortcut, 162
← (move one space to left) Notepad keyboard shortcut, 162
→ (move one space to right) Notepad keyboard shortcut, 162
↑ (move up one line) Notepad keyboard shortcut, 162
1200-baud Hayes modem, 438
1K-XMODEM file-transfer protocol, 134, 145-146
1K-XMODEM-G file-transfer protocol, 134, 145-146
2400-baud Hayes modem, 438
9-pin DB-9 connector, 459

A

Abort option, 276, 280
ABORTDKERMIT PADCHARNLD command, 358-382
ABORTDNLD command, 357-382

aborting
    Host mode, 281
    messages, 276
About option, 163, 440
About PROCOMM PLUS command, 57
AC adapter, 457
accessing
    communications programs, 12-14
    DOS commands, 152
    Help menu, 50-57, 87, 163-164
    Host Mode, 271-272
    text files, 94
Action Bar, 34
    activating, 49
    deactivating, 49
    menu commands, 49
        Capture Action, 39
        Clear Screen Action, 40
        Compile/Edit Action, 41
        Dialing Directory Action, 37
        File Clipboard Action, 39
        Hangup Action, 40
        Playback File Action, 40
        Printer Action, 40
        Rapid Dial, 37
        Receive File Action, 39
        Script File, 38
        Scrollback/Pause Action, 38
        Send File Action, 39
        Setup Action, 38
        Start Record Action, 40
        Start Script Action, 38
    option, 213

J-K

X-Z

Free Catalog!

Mail us this registration form today, and we'll send you a free catalog featuring Que's complete line of best-selling books.

Name of Book _____

Name _____

Title _____

Phone (___) _____

Company _____

Address _____

City _____

State _____ ZIP _____

Please check the appropriate answers:

1. Where did you buy your Que book?
   - ☐ Bookstore (name: _____)
   - ☐ Computer store (name: _____)
   - ☐ Catalog (name: _____)
   - ☐ Direct from Que
   - ☐ Other: _____

2. How many computer books do you buy a year?
   - ☐ 1 or less
   - ☐ 2-5
   - ☐ 6-10
   - ☐ More than 10

3. How many Que books do you own?
   - ☐ 1
   - ☐ 2-5
   - ☐ 6-10
   - ☐ More than 10

4. How long have you been using this software?
   - ☐ Less than 6 months
   - ☐ 6 months to 1 year
   - ☐ 1-3 years
   - ☐ More than 3 years

5. What influenced your purchase of this Que book?
   - ☐ Personal recommendation
   - ☐ Advertisement
   - ☐ In-store display
   - ☐ Price
   - ☐ Que catalog
   - ☐ Que mailing
   - ☐ Que's reputation
   - ☐ Other: _____

6. How would you rate the overall content of the book?
   - ☐ Very good
   - ☐ Good
   - ☐ Satisfactory
   - ☐ Poor

7. What do you like *best* about this Que book?
   _____
   _____

8. What do you like *least* about this Que book?
   _____
   _____

9. Did you buy this book with your personal funds?
   - ☐ Yes   ☐ No

10. Please feel free to list any other comments you may have about this Que book.
   _____
   _____
   _____

que

Order Your Que Books Today!

Name _____

Title _____

Company _____

City _____

State _____ ZIP _____

Phone No. (___) _____

Method of Payment:

Check ☐ (Please enclose in envelope.)

Charge My: VISA ☐   MasterCard ☐

American Express ☐

Charge # _____

Expiration Date _____

Order No.	Title	Qty.	Price	Total

You can **FAX** your order to **1-317-573-2583**. Or call **1-800-428-5331, ext. ORDR** to order direct.
Please add $2.50 per title for shipping and handling.

Subtotal _____

Shipping & Handling _____

Total _____

que

BUSINESS REPLY MAIL

First Class Permit No. 9918   Indianapolis, IN

Postage will be paid by addressee

11711 N. College
Carmel, IN 46032

BUSINESS REPLY MAIL

First Class Permit No. 9918   Indianapolis, IN

Postage will be paid by addressee

11711 N. College
Carmel, IN 46032